Ivan Maistrenko

BOROT'BISM

A Chapter in the History of the Ukrainian Revolution

Edited by Christopher Ford

With a foreword by Marko Bojcun

Translated by George S.N. Luckyj
with the assistance of Ivan L. Rudnytsky

Revised and Expanded Edition

ibidem-Verlag
Stuttgart

Bibliografische Information der Deutschen Nationalbibliothek
Die Deutsche Nationalbibliothek verzeichnet diese Publikation in der Deutschen Nationalbibliografie; detaillierte bibliografische Daten sind im Internet über http://dnb.d-nb.de abrufbar.

Bibliographic information published by the Deutsche Nationalbibliothek
Die Deutsche Nationalbibliothek lists this publication in the Deutsche Nationalbibliografie; detailed bibliographic data are available in the Internet at http://dnb.d-nb.de.

Revised and Expanded Edition

First published in 1954 by the Research Program on the USSR, New York

∞

Gedruckt auf alterungsbeständigem, säurefreien Papier
Printed on acid-free paper

ISSN: 1614-3515

ISBN-13: 978-3-8382-1107-7

© *ibidem*-Verlag
Stuttgart 2019

Alle Rechte vorbehalten

Das Werk einschließlich aller seiner Teile ist urheberrechtlich geschützt. Jede Verwertung außerhalb der engen Grenzen des Urheberrechtsgesetzes ist ohne Zustimmung des Verlages unzulässig und strafbar. Dies gilt insbesondere für Vervielfältigungen, Übersetzungen, Mikroverfilmungen und elektronische Speicherformen sowie die Einspeicherung und Verarbeitung in elektronischen Systemen.

All rights part of this publication may be reproduced, stored in or introduced into a retrieval system, or transmitted, in any form, or by any means (electronical, mechanical, photocopying, recording or otherwise) without the prior written permission of the publisher. Any person who does any unauthorized act in relation to this publication may be liable to criminal prosecution and civil claims for damages.

Printed in the EU

Soviet and Post-Soviet Politics and Society (SPPS) Vol. 61
ISSN 1614-3515

General Editor: Andreas Umland,
Institute for Euro-Atlantic Cooperation, Kyiv, umland@stanfordalumni.org

Commissioning Editor: Max Jakob Horstmann,
London, mjh@ibidem.eu

EDITORIAL COMMITTEE*

DOMESTIC & COMPARATIVE POLITICS
Prof. Ellen Bos, *Andrássy University of Budapest*
Dr. Gergana Dimova, *University of Winchester*
Dr. Andrey Kazantsev, *MGIMO (U) MID RF, Moscow*
Prof. Heiko Pleines, *University of Bremen*
Prof. Richard Sakwa, *University of Kent at Canterbury*
Dr. Sarah Whitmore, *Oxford Brookes University*
Dr. Harald Wydra, *University of Cambridge*

SOCIETY, CLASS & ETHNICITY
Col. David Glantz, *"Journal of Slavic Military Studies"*
Dr. Marlène Laruelle, *George Washington University*
Dr. Stephen Shulman, *Southern Illinois University*
Prof. Stefan Troebst, *University of Leipzig*

POLITICAL ECONOMY & PUBLIC POLICY
Dr. Andreas Goldthau, *Central European University*
Dr. Robert Kravchuk, *University of North Carolina*
Dr. David Lane, *University of Cambridge*
Dr. Carol Leonard, *Higher School of Economics, Moscow*
Dr. Maria Popova, *McGill University, Montreal*

FOREIGN POLICY & INTERNATIONAL AFFAIRS
Dr. Peter Duncan, *University College London*
Prof. Andreas Heinemann-Grüder, *University of Bonn*
Prof. Gerhard Mangott, *University of Innsbruck*
Dr. Diana Schmidt-Pfister, *University of Konstanz*
Dr. Lisbeth Tarlow, *Harvard University, Cambridge*
Dr. Christian Wipperfürth, *N-Ost Network, Berlin*
Dr. William Zimmerman, *University of Michigan*

HISTORY, CULTURE & THOUGHT
Dr. Catherine Andreyev, *University of Oxford*
Prof. Mark Bassin, *Södertörn University*
Prof. Karsten Brüggemann, *Tallinn University*
Dr. Alexander Etkind, *University of Cambridge*
Dr. Gasan Gusejnov, *Moscow State University*
Prof. Leonid Luks, *Catholic University of Eichstaett*
Dr. Olga Malinova, *Russian Academy of Sciences*
Dr. Richard Mole, *University College London*
Prof. Andrei Rogatchevski, *University of Tromsø*
Dr. Mark Tauger, *West Virginia University*

ADVISORY BOARD*

Prof. Dominique Arel, *University of Ottawa*
Prof. Jörg Baberowski, *Humboldt University of Berlin*
Prof. Margarita Balmaceda, *Seton Hall University*
Dr. John Barber, *University of Cambridge*
Prof. Timm Beichelt, *European University Viadrina*
Dr. Katrin Boeckh, *University of Munich*
Prof. em. Archie Brown, *University of Oxford*
Dr. Vyacheslav Bryukhovetsky, *Kyiv-Mohyla Academy*
Prof. Timothy Colton, *Harvard University, Cambridge*
Prof. Paul D'Anieri, *University of Florida*
Dr. Heike Dörrenbächer, *Friedrich Naumann Foundation*
Dr. John Dunlop, *Hoover Institution, Stanford, California*
Dr. Sabine Fischer, *SWP, Berlin*
Dr. Geir Flikke, *NUPI, Oslo*
Prof. David Galbreath, *University of Aberdeen*
Prof. Alexander Galkin, *Russian Academy of Sciences*
Prof. Frank Golczewski, *University of Hamburg*
Dr. Nikolas Gvosdev, *Naval War College, Newport, RI*
Prof. Mark von Hagen, *Arizona State University*
Dr. Guido Hausmann, *University of Munich*
Prof. Dale Herspring, *Kansas State University*
Dr. Stefani Hoffman, *Hebrew University of Jerusalem*
Prof. Mikhail Ilyin, *MGIMO (U) MID RF, Moscow*
Prof. Vladimir Kantor, *Higher School of Economics*
Dr. Ivan Katchanovski, *University of Ottawa*
Prof. em. Andrzej Korbonski, *University of California*
Dr. Iris Kempe, *"Caucasus Analytical Digest"*
Prof. Herbert Küpper, *Institut für Ostrecht Regensburg*
Dr. Rainer Lindner, *CEEER, Berlin*
Dr. Vladimir Malakhov, *Russian Academy of Sciences*

Dr. Luke March, *University of Edinburgh*
Prof. Michael McFaul, *Stanford University, Palo Alto*
Prof. Birgit Menzel, *University of Mainz-Germersheim*
Prof. Valery Mikhailenko, *The Urals State University*
Prof. Emil Pain, *Higher School of Economics, Moscow*
Dr. Oleg Podvintsev, *Russian Academy of Sciences*
Prof. Olga Popova, *St. Petersburg State University*
Dr. Alex Pravda, *University of Oxford*
Dr. Erik van Ree, *University of Amsterdam*
Dr. Joachim Rogall, *Robert Bosch Foundation Stuttgart*
Prof. Peter Rutland, *Wesleyan University, Middletown*
Prof. Marat Salikov, *The Urals State Law Academy*
Dr. Gwendolyn Sasse, *University of Oxford*
Prof. Jutta Scherrer, *EHESS, Paris*
Prof. Robert Service, *University of Oxford*
Mr. James Sherr, *RIIA Chatham House London*
Dr. Oxana Shevel, *Tufts University, Medford*
Prof. Eberhard Schneider, *University of Siegen*
Prof. Olexander Shnyrkov, *Shevchenko University, Kyiv*
Prof. Hans-Henning Schröder, *SWP, Berlin*
Prof. Yuri Shapoval, *Ukrainian Academy of Sciences*
Prof. Viktor Shnirelman, *Russian Academy of Sciences*
Dr. Lisa Sundstrom, *University of British Columbia*
Dr. Philip Walters, *"Religion, State and Society", Oxford*
Prof. Zenon Wasyliw, *Ithaca College, New York State*
Dr. Lucan Way, *University of Toronto*
Dr. Markus Wehner, *"Frankfurter Allgemeine Zeitung"*
Dr. Andrew Wilson, *University College London*
Prof. Jan Zielonka, *University of Oxford*
Prof. Andrei Zorin, *University of Oxford*

While the Editorial Committee and Advisory Board support the General Editor in the choice and improvement of manuscripts for publication, responsibility for remaining errors and misinterpretations in the series' volumes lies with the books' authors.

Soviet and Post-Soviet Politics and Society (SPPS)
ISSN 1614-3515

Founded in 2004 and refereed since 2007, SPPS makes available affordable English-, German-, and Russian-language studies on the history of the countries of the former Soviet bloc from the late Tsarist period to today. It publishes between 5 and 20 volumes per year and focuses on issues in transitions to and from democracy such as economic crisis, identity formation, civil society development, and constitutional reform in CEE and the NIS. SPPS also aims to highlight so far understudied themes in East European studies such as right-wing radicalism, religious life, higher education, or human rights protection. The authors and titles of all previously published volumes are listed at the end of this book. For a full description of the series and reviews of its books, see www.ibidem-verlag.de/red/spps.

Editorial correspondence & manuscripts should be sent to: Dr. Andreas Umland, Institute for Euro-Atlantic Cooperation, vul. Volodymyrska 42, off. 21, UA-01030 Kyiv, Ukraine

Business correspondence & review copy requests should be sent to: *ibidem* Press, Leuschnerstr. 40, 30457 Hannover, Germany; tel.: +49 511 2622200; fax: +49 511 2622201; spps@ibidem.eu.

Authors, reviewers, referees, and editors for (as well as all other persons sympathetic to) SPPS are invited to join its networks at
www.facebook.com/group.php?gid=52638198614
www.linkedin.com/groups?about=&gid=103012
www.xing.com/net/spps-ibidem-verlag/

Recent Volumes

190   A. Salem, G. Hazeldine, D. Morgan (eds.)
Higher Education in Post-Communist States
Comparative and Sociological Perspectives
ISBN 978-3-8382-1183-1

191   Igor Torbakov
After Empire
Nationalist Imagination and Symbolic Politics in Russia and Eurasia in the Twentieth and Twenty-First Century
With a foreword by Serhii Plokhy
ISBN 978-3-8382-1217-3

192   Aleksandr Burakovskiy
Jewish-Ukrainian Relations in Late and Post-Soviet Ukraine
Articles, Lectures and Essays from 1986 to 2016
ISBN 978-3-8382-1210-4

193   Olga Burlyuk, Natalia Shapovalova (eds.)
Civil Society in Post-Euromaidan Ukraine
From Revolution to Consolidation
With a foreword by Richard Youngs
ISBN 978-3-8382-1216-6

194   Franz Preissler
Positionsverteidigung, Imperialismus oder Irredentismus?
Russland und die „Russischsprachigen", 1991–2015
ISBN 978-3-8382-1262-3

195   Marian Madela
Der Reformprozess in der Ukraine 2014-2017
Eine Fallstudie zur Reform der öffentlichen Verwaltung
Mit einem Vorwort von Martin Malek
ISBN 978-3-8382-1266-1

196   Anke Giesen
„Wie kann denn der Sieger ein Verbrecher sein?"
Eine diskursanalytische Untersuchung der russlandweiten Debatte über Konzept und Verstaatlichungsprozess der Lagergedenkstätte „Perm'-36" im Ural
ISBN 978-3-8382-1284-5

197   Alla Leukavets
The Integration Policies of Belarus and Ukraine vis-à-vis the EU and Russia
A Comparative Case Study Through the Lenses of a Two-Level Games Approach
ISBN 978-3-8382-1247-0

198   Oksana Kim
The Development and Challenges of Russian Corporate Governance I
The Roles and Functions of Boards of Directors
With a foreword by Sheila M. Puffer
ISBN 978-3-8382-1287-6

Levko Maystrenko
15 December 1925–20 June 2010

Dedicated to the memory of Levko without his support and solidarity the republication of his father's book would not have been possible.

Ivan Maistrenko
28 August 1899–18 November 1984

Contents

Acknowledgements 13
Foreword by *Marko Bojcun* 15
Editors Note 17
Introduction by *Christopher Ford* 19
    1.   The Ukrainian Revolution from today's vantage point... 20
    2.   The Colonial Terrain and Social Forces
        of the Revolution 26
    3.   Problems of the Ukrainian Revolution 35
    4.   The Tragedy of the Russo-Ukrainian War 47
    5.   The War within the Ukrainian Peoples Republic 50
    6.   What might have been and legacy of the Borotbisty 67
    Illustrations 71
    Biographical Sketch of Ivan Maistrenko 74

Introduction to the 1954 edition by *Ivan Maistrenko* 97
1   Historical Antecedents 101
    A.   Components of Ukrainian Political Thought 101
        1.   The Russian Influence 101
        2.   The Cult of the Peasant 104
        3.   Romantic Nationalism: The Search for Self-Existence 107
    B.   Ideological Precursors of *Borotbism* 108
        1.   Drahomanov: The Father of Ukrainian Political Parties. 108
        2.   Marxism Enters Ukraine 109
    C.   The Experience of the
        Revolutionary Ukrainian Party (RUP) 111
        1.   The Problem of National Liberation 111
        2.   Formulation of the National Program 112
        3.   Nationalism Splits the RUP 113
        4.   The Lesson of the Spilka 114

2 **Origins of the Ukrainian Party of Socialist Revolutionaries (UPSR), Predecessor of Borotbism**............ 117
    A. Ideological Background of the UPSR 117
    B. The First Attempts at Formation of Ukrainian SR Groups Before 1917 118
    C. The First SR Groups and Party Program 120

3 **Ukrainian Party of Socialist Revolutionaries in 1917** 123
    A. From the First to the Second Congress of the UPSR 123
        1. The First Congress of the UPSR 123
        2. The Growth and Influence of the UPSR............................. 125
    B. From the Second to the Third Congress of the UPSR .. 128
        1. The Second Congress of the UPSR and its Turn to the Left.. 128
        2. Influence of Bolshevik Ideas on the Ukrainian Revolution and on the UPSR 130
    C. From the Third Congress of the UPSR to the Liquidation of Ukrainian Revolutionary Democracy ... 134
        1. The Third Congress of the UPSR and the Party's movement toward the Soviet position 134
        2. The Impact of the Russo-Ukrainian War 136
        3. Failure of a Left SR Coup and of a Right SR Government 139

4 **The Borotbisty Under the Hetmanate** 143
    A. Worker and Peasant Opposition to the Hetman Coup.. 143
        1. The Second All-Ukrainian Peasants' Congress 143
        2. The Second All-Ukrainian Workers' Congress 144
    B. The Fourth Congress of the UPSR and the Split............ 145
        1. The Fourth Congress 145
        2. Aftermath of the Congress.. 149
    C. The Program of the Borotbisty 153
        1. The Platform of the New Central Committee 153
        2. The Weapon of Terror 155
        3. The National Question 156

	D.	Movement of the Borotbisty Toward a Non-Bolshevik Soviet Platform 160
		1. The Kharkiv Province Party Conference............................ 160
		2. The August Conference of Party Emissaries 161
5	**The Borotbisty in Revolt Against the Hetmanate and the Directory** **167**	
	A.	The General Uprising Against the Hetmanate 167
	B.	Disaffection with the Directory.. 170
		1. Failure of the Directory's Military and Foreign Policy ... 170
		2. Peasants' Congresses Under Borotbist Influence............. 172
	C.	Final Attempts to Reunite the UPSR 173
	D.	Borotbist Ties with Pro-Soviet Parties............................ 176
	E.	Inherent Weakness of the Borotbisty 179
6	**The Second Period of Bolshevik Rule in Ukraine**............ **181**	
	A.	The Bolshevik Approach to the Ukrainian Problem.... 181
	B.	Borotbist Efforts to Form a Government 183
		1. The Borotbist Central Revolutionary Committee 183
		2 Attempted Use of Hryhoryiv's Army 185
	C.	Implementation of Bolshevik Occupation Policy 191
	D.	Borotbism in Crisis 195
		1. Internal Party Differences 195
		2. Rejection by the CP(b)U 196
	E.	Joint Action Against Hryhoryiv....................................... 197
		1. Bolshevik Detente with the Borotbisty............................. 197
		2. Hryhoryiv's revolt against the Bolsheviks...................... 198
7	**Borotbisty in the Denikin Underground**.............................. **205**	
	A.	Formation of the Ukrainian Communist Party (Borotbisty): UCP(B) 205
	B.	Two Views on the Formation of the UCP(B).................. 209
		1. The "Dual Roots" Theory... 209
		2. The Bolshevik Argument 210
	C.	Borotbist Opposition to the Denikin Regime................. 214
		1 The Borotbist Underground in Kyiv 215

		2.	Borotbist Activity Among the Partisans 219

8 The third Period of Bolshevik Rule in Ukraine 225
- A. Bolshevik Re-Examination of the Ukrainian Problem ... 225
  - 1. Bolsheviks Face to Face with the Ukrainian Problem 225
  - 2. The Guiding Hand of Lenin 226
- B. Bolshevik Resolutions 229
  - 1. The Russian Bolsheviks 229
  - 2. The Ukrainian Bolsheviks 231
  - 3. The Borotbist-Ukrainian Bolshevik Agreement 234
- C. Final Borotbist Attempt To Organize
   A Ukrainian Red Army 235
  - 1. Interlude with Makhno 236
  - 2. Alliance with Ataman Volokh 236
  - 3. The Trotsky Order 241
- D. The Growth and Dissolution of the UCP(B) 242
  - 1. The Spread of Borot'bism Among the Masses 242
  - 2. The Bolshevik Ring Around the Borotbisty 244
  - 3. Dissolution of the UCP(B) 247
- E. Divers Views on the Dissolution Of The Borotbisty 250

9 The Borotbisty in the CP(b)U 257
- A. The CP(b)U and the UCP(b) Compared 257
  - 1 Composition of the CP(b)U 257
  - 2. Composition of the UCP(b) 259
- B. A Letter From a Ukrainian SR Emigre 262
- C. Borotbism Versus Philistinism in the CP(b)U 265
- D Shumskism 269

Appendix 1 Reminiscences of the Borotbist Organization
in the District of Kobeliaky 277

Appendix 2 Biographical Sketches of Individual Borotbisty 295

Appendix 3 Platform of the Central Committee of the
Ukrainian Party of Socialist Revolutionaries: The Present State
of Affairs and Party Tactics (approved by Central Committee
on June 3, 1918) 313

Appendix 4 Draft Decree on Encouraging the Development of Culture of the Ukrainian People 321
    Explanatory Note to the Decree 321
    Text of the Decree 323

Appendix 5 Memorandum of the Ukrainian Communist Party (Borotbisty) to the Executive Committee of the Third Communist International 329
    I   330
    II   333
    IV [sic] 336

SPECIAL SUPPLEMENT
Soviet Responses to Maistrenko's Borotbism 341
Bibliography 349
    A. General Works 349
    B. Congresses and Conferences 352
        1. Communist International 352
        2. CP(b)U 352
        3. RSDRP(b) and RCP(b) 352
    C. Articles 353
    D. Letters, Speeches, Draft Projects, Resolutions 354
Index of Names 357
Index of Subjects 363
Notes 371

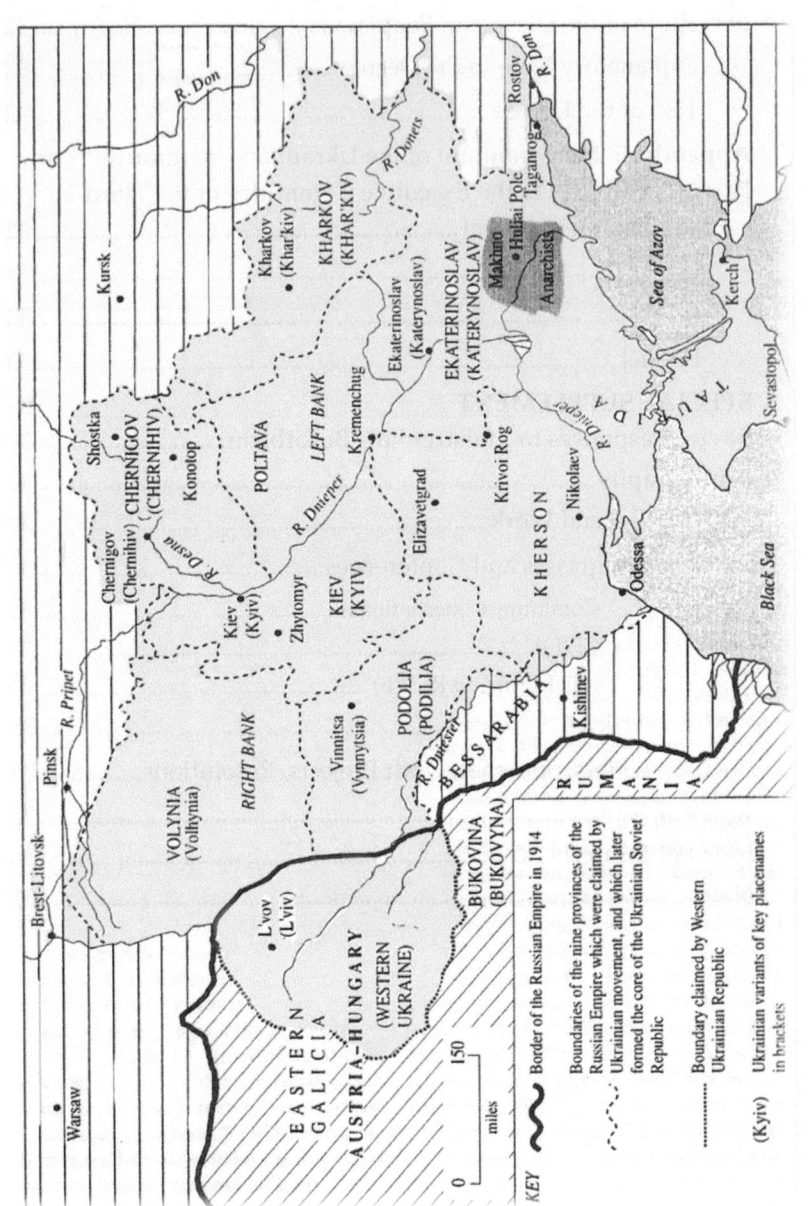

Acknowledgements

The author records his affectionate gratitude to his friend Edward Dune, a noble fighter for freedom in Soviet Russia, who died in Paris on January 21, 1953. Mr. Dune assisted the author in locating rare source materials in the Bibliotheque de Documentation Internationale Contemporaine and the Bibliotheque Nationale in Paris.

The author wishes to thank the Research Program on the U.S.S.R., through whose assistance this study was made possible. Special thanks go to Dr. Alexander Dallin, former Associate Director of the Research Program, for suggesting the theme of the present study. The author thanks Dr. John S. Reshetar, Jr. of Princeton University for reading the manuscript, Dr. George S.N. Luckyj of the University of Toronto, who made the original translation, and Mr. Ivan L. Rudnytsky for his assistance in the translation and editing. Mr. Peter Dornan of the Research Program edited the text; the author is particularly grateful to him for this work. He also thanks Mr. Nelson Glover, who prepared the map.

The author's thanks are extended to the Ukrainian Academy of Arts and Sciences in the United States and in particular Mr. Volodymyr Mijakowskij for his and their cooperation in providing photostatic copies of source materials, and to Mr. Hryhory Kostiuk and Mr. Jurij Lawrynenko for reading the biographical material and supplying additional data.

Grateful acknowledgment is made to the Columbia University Press and Mr. Bertram D. Wolfe for permission to reprint excerpts from copyrighted material in Mr. Wolfe's article "The Influence of Early Military Decisions upon the National Structure of the Soviet Union," which appears in *The American Slavic and East European Review*, New York, Vol. IX, No. 3, October 1950, pp. 169–179.

Foreword

MARKO BOJCUN

This new edition of Ivan Maistrenko's 1954 study of the Ukrainian Revolution is a welcome and timely contribution to the English language literature. Appearing on the centenary of that epochal event that has come to be known as "the Russian Revolution" it provides valuable insights into its multinational and regional complexities and the diversity of the communist movement itself. Christopher Ford has also given us a new introduction here that will help the reader situate Maiestenko's work in the broader context of a modern Ukraine emerging from an era of declining European imperialisms and ascendant movements for universal emancipation.

Maistrenko was not just a witness, but an active participant in the revolution and civil war of those years in Ukraine. He challenges several misleading generalisations and stereotypes that have come to dominate the historiography of 1917 and its aftermath. First, he shows on the basis of the Ukrainian case that this revolution was not Russian alone, nor just a working class achievement, but a richly diverse "festival of the oppressed" that broke out all over the Empire and drew into action millions of peasants and workers, nations and national minorities subjugated by Tsarism and Russian imperialism. It was not merely the arena of professional revolutionaries pursuing state power in Petrograd and Moscow, but the efforts of workers, soldiers and peasants in cities, towns and villages alike trying to overcome the major obstacles to their self-emancipation: the War, land hunger, the collapse of industry brought on by the War and national oppression.

Maistrenko illuminates this tumultuous process in Ukraine, focussing in particular on the rural population, the landless peasantry and the agricultural proletariat. He traces the evolution of the Ukrainian Party of Socialist Revolutionaries, which became the largest political party by far in Ukraine at the head of repeated mobilisations of the peasantry in 1917 and during the civil war. He shows how and why the UPSR, a party with roots in the populist and anarcho-socialist traditions, was shaken and split by the events of that period and eventually yielded the *Borot'bisty*, an indigenous Ukrainian communist movement.

Maistrenko's work helps us to understand how the Ukrainian Revolution differed from the Russian as well as how they intersected, and how the Bolsheviks could come to hold state power in Ukraine at the end of the Civil War only by occupying it militarily and subordinating all three communist parties then operating in it to the Russian Communist Party headquartered in Moscow.

The Ukrainian Communist Party (Borot'bisty), as opposed to the Communist Party (Bolsheviks) of Ukraine, fought for an independent Ukrainian soviet republic allied through federation with the Russian soviet republic. It sought membership as an independent party in the Third (Communist) International. The Borot'bisty subsequently played a critical role in the life of their country after their own party was dissolved and they joined the official CP(B)U. They championed Ukraine's cultural revival and its quest for greater political autonomy within the Soviet Union. Practically all of them perished in Stalin's purges in the 1930s.

Ivan Maistrenko was one Borot'bist who survived to tell their story, a chapter in the history of the Revolution that might otherwise been buried in Stalin's mass graves. Moreover, he has left us with more than a political history, but also a personal one with recollections of events he witnessed on the ground and of comrades with whom he worked in the underground, the peasant brigades and the insurgent republic of his own locality. Maistrenko was fluent in Ukrainian and Russian, as well as German by the time he wrote this history. That gave his access to the original documentary sources when he came to compose this study in the early 1950s.

We can now look back on the epoch-changing upheaval of the Revolution a hundred years ago through Maistrenko's unique examination of its eruption in Ukraine.

Editors Note

This new edition of Ivan Maistrenko's *Borotbism* has been reformatted and slightly re-edited from the original 1954 edition. Which was republished in the original format in 2007. A number of aspects of the original text have been updated such as the transliteration of Kiev which is published here as Kyiv. This edition includes not only a new introduction and foreword but also a biographical essay of Ivan Maistrenko and in supplement a review of Soviet responses to *Borotbism*. A number of illustrations have been added including rare pictures provided by Ivan's son Levko Maystrenko and his granddaughter Ulyana. The title of the book has been slightly changed from it original *Borotbism a Chapter in the History of Ukrainian Communism* to *Borotbism a Chapter in the History of the Ukrainian Revolution*.

NOTE TO 1954 EDITION

1. Events occuring between February (March) 1917 and February 1 (14), 1918 are dated in both old style and new style.
2. The boundaries of geographical regions referred to in the text in the pre-revolutionary period are not necessarily coextensive with boundaries established by the Soviet regime.
3. The Ukrainian word *"rada"* has been rendered English by the word council whenever councils in Ukraine are under discussion, except in the case of the Ukrainian Central Rada; the Russian word *"sovet"* also meaning council had been rendered in its English form soviet whenever councils in Russia are under discussion, except in the case of the Russian Council of Peoples Commissars. Soviet has also been used in the phrase Soviet platform, whether this applies to Russia or Ukraine.

Introduction

CHRISTOPHER FORD

Volodymyr Vynnychenko, one of the most well-known Ukrainian leaders in the 20th century, coined the phrase *vsebichne vyzvolennia* — "*Universal* liberation".[1] By this he meant the "*Universal* (social, national, political, moral, cultural, etc.) liberation" of the worker and peasant masses. This striving for "such a total and radical liberation" represented the "Ukrainian Revolution" in the broad historical sense. However the expression the "Ukrainian Revolution" may also be used in the narrower sense, of the great upheavals aimed at this object, the most noteworthy of which marked the years 1917–1920.

According to Vynnychenko, the "*Universal* current" which strove to realize this historical tendency of the revolution comprised the most radical of the socialist parties, the Ukrainian Social Democratic Workers' party (Independentists), or Nezalezhnyky, the Ukrainian Party of Socialist Revolutionaries-Borotbisty and the oppositional currents amongst the Bolsheviks in Ukraine.

The Ukrainian Revolution cannot be understood without sharing the hopes, disappointments and aspirations of its participants. One such participant in those dramatic events that form the subject of this book is its author Ivan Maistrenko. His book tells the story of the revolution through the history of one element of that "*Universal* current" — the Borotbisty.[2] One of the first significant accounts of the revolution in English, *Borotbism* is a unique work whose republication comes at a time of increased interest in Ukraine. Yet amidst the array of materials now available to the reader, there remains a deficiency with regard to the pivotal role of Ukrainian Revolutionary socialism in those years.

This problem of the revolution's historiography is not new and its continuation makes this book as important today as when it first appeared in 1954. Maistrenko's work remains the principal study of the Borotbisty, the majority left wing of the Ukrainian

Party of Socialist-Revolutionaries – the largest party of the revolution.[3]

1. The Ukrainian Revolution from today's vantage point.

Ivan Maistrenko's *Borotbism* compels us to return to this 'rebirth of a nation' not merely to mark the 100th anniversary of the Ukrainian Revolution but also in recognition that a review of the past is essential to grasp the challenges of the present. This can be seen in the changed circumstances in which Maistrenko's book is presented in contrast to when it first appeared in 1954.[4] Since the Euromaidan in 2014 and the Russo-Ukraine war there has been a surge of interest in Ukraine; this is a progressive development it is however coupled with new depths of retrogression as regards attitudes to the Ukrainian question.

Recent years have demonstrated how Russia's imperial past continues to echo into what was presumed to be the "post-imperial" present; we have witnessed a revival of a narrative advanced by the White movement during the Civil War. Its advocates base their interpretation of the Ukrainian question on a set of key principles:

1. "Great Russia, "Little Russia" and "Belarus" are three branches of the one Russian people,
2. Russian language and culture is the common achievement of one, leading Russian people;
3. "Little Russia", i.e. Ukraine, is an inseparable part of a unitary Russia;
4. ; the idea of a separate Ukrainian nation is manufactured by foreign powers for the dismemberment and weakening of Russia.[5]

Interpretations of the Ukrainian question by contemporary Russian leaders are essentially the same; they have equipped the current form of the Russian state power with ideas inherited from their Tsarist ancestors. The reburial of General Denikin in 2005 with full military honors at Moscow's Donskoi monastery was an apt symbol of this reconnection with Empire.

That Denikin secured Western sponsors for the Russian nationalist cause is understandable; that Vladimir Putin can harness support of the contemporary European far-right is no surprise.[6] What is significant, and perhaps surprising to some, is the support by sections of the left for restoring the Tsarist colony in Ukraine of *Novorossiya* (New Russia).[7] Stalinism was imbued with the Russian nationalist tradition, and whilst current neo-Stalinism assists Kremlin foreign policy with its veneer of an "anti-fascist struggle in Ukraine", the Russian oligarchic elite make no pretense of a communist camouflage in acting as heir and guardian of the imperialist policies of the Tsars.[8]

Maistrenko's *Borotbism* challenges this retrogression; it repudiates the falsification and revision of the array of self-appointed experts on Ukraine that have surfaced, and who reduce the Ukrainian Revolution of 1917–21 to a series of failed states sponsored by foreign powers.[9] It reasserts the history of the revolution as a struggle for social and national emancipation by the Ukrainian people themselves.

Such conflicts over the history of Ukraine are not new and often become focal points for the greater conflict between Ukrainian nationalism and Russian chauvinism; the contemporary controversies are themselves intimately linked to the recurrence of the Ukrainian question with it domestic and international considerations. The current context in which the Ukrainian question is posed is one that Maistrenko foresaw with remarkable accuracy in the 1950's.[10] That imperialist expansion was generating a future challenge to Moscow's hegemony, where each national bureaucracy would one day come into conflict with the Russian bureaucracy. In addition he foresaw that the Soviet bureaucracy would welcome the restoration of private-capitalism, provided it ensured their continued privilege. It was this re-composition of a *nouveau nomenklatura* that emerged after the Ukrainian resurgence of 1989–1991 attained formal independence.[11]

This is the root of the current complexities in which the big business power of the oligarchs has been the dominant influence on the politics and economy of Ukraine. Whilst in the face of western rivalry, Russia has continued to seek to protect its business interests and influence in Ukraine, which is viewed from the strategic perspective as part of the "greater Russian world" within the "near abroad" of post-USSR space.[12] Maistrenko considered "Stalinism, the Modern Form of Russian Imperialism"; under Putin this has taken on a new form of appearance.[13] Motivated by what it views as its national security interests Russia's rulers continue to adopt methods of encroachment to protect their regime from destabilizing influences and have revived the old *"gendarme* of European reaction".[14] This role of policing of the territory of empire was deployed following the Euromaidan in 2014.

Euromaidan saw the mobilization of wide sections of society aspiring to greater democracy, equality and human rights. This *political* revolution toppled President Yanukovych, driving a wedge into the neo-colonial power relations Russia exercised in Ukraine. In response, the deposed Donetsk clan of oligarchs and those connected to them; concerned for their vested interests instigated the separatist movement. This revanchist movement converged with the interests of Russia's elite, the Kremlin organizing, arming and directly reinforcing its proxy forces.[15] The ensuing war in Donbas in 2014 has echoes of the 1914 occupation of eastern Galicia by the Russian Imperial Army. Viewed as the *piedmont* of the Ukrainian movement, the Tsar declared it "a Russian land from time immemorial". With support of the small groups of local Russian nationalists they set about forcibly Russifying the populace and persecuting Jews. Putin has proved no more attractive to Ukrainians than the Tsar, and the reach of Russian ultra-nationalists has suffered a long historical retreat from Lviv to Luhansk.

The Russian intervention in 2014 posed an existential threat to Ukraine. It generated a surge in national consciousness with the mass self-activity flowing from Euromaidan into a resistance that checked and isolated the aggression. But whilst the occupants of 1914 contributed to the fermenting of the 1917 revolution, the 2014 aggression assisted in the subverting of the original ideals of the Euromaidan revolution. Hopes for social and democratic change have been inhibited by the failure to dislodge the oligarchic elite, who have used the cover of the necessities of war to safeguard their own position and mold policies that serve their needs.

This situation has also flowed into the history of the Ukrainian Revolution, which is refracted through the prism of current politics. In this context Maistrenko's *Borotbism* is more than just an historical document. The debates during and after the revolution of 1917–1921 about the relative importance of national and/or social emancipation are of great importance in contemporary Ukraine. As a consequence of recent events Ukraine has veered further from Moscow's orbit, naturally posing new considerations of how the nation defines itself, which in turn have become enmeshed with how history is understood.

A new turn in the approach to history has taken place since 2014, which poses such choices as between "two models of historical memory — the patriotic nation-building and the communist-imperialist".[16] After many years in which the history of Ukraine has faced severe constraints, during which Stalinist and Russophile political forces have fiercely resisted a Ukrainian alternative. In this context the recognition now afforded the Ukrainian Revolution can be considered a progressive development. Nevertheless this decolonization of history whilst seeking to escape past constraints is simultaneously fostering new ones set out in an official state historical narrative overseen by the group of publicists who run the Ukrainian Institute for National Remembrance (UINR).[17]

In the new state narrative the revolution of 1917–1921 is placed within a unilineal historical development towards statehood. Instead of a fetishized Lenin and Stalin we are presented with Petlyura, Skoropadsky and above all Bandera, as if they alone represent the Ukrainian movement and almost Ukraine itself.[18]

In this new narrative, movements such as the Borotbisty are outsiders from a revolution of which they were a vital element. The continuity and similarity of approach by the current nationalist and former Stalinist narratives is striking. This is illustrated by their treatment of the national cultural revival of the 1920s, driven forward by former Borotbisty and other Ukrainian left-wing socialists. In the USSR the Borotbisty were concealed for decades and only ever cited in the pejorative. Today their role is demeaned again with

Volodymyr Viatrovych Director of UINR crassly comparing the 1920s "blossoming of Ukrainian culture" to the "successes in Hitler's economic policies" asking "should this blossoming, which eventually grew into an executed renaissance in the subsequent decade, serve to justify a regime guilty in the intentional murder of millions of Ukrainians?".[19] (One can only speculate how long the memorial to Oleksander Shumsky, the Borotbist leader, will stand in Zhytomyr.)

The current official history seeks to sanitize the revolution of radical socialist content, and places conservatives centre stage. None more so than the wartime era integral nationalists notably the Stepan Bandera led Organization of Ukrainian Nationalists.[20] The latter are presented as heirs to 1917–1921 revolution. The glorification and paradoxes of Bandera in contemporary Ukraine deserve a study in its own right. But in relation to approaches to the revolution of 1917–1921 it brings to the fore a clash of conceptions of Ukraine which are not new, and were already posed when Bandera re-emerged after the war seeking to influence the Ukrainian emigrants in displaced persons camps in Europe.

Maistrenko, the former Borotbist, castigated the *Banderivsti* in an article in the left-wing paper *Vpered*, "Considering the Ukrainian National Revolution and Nationalist Reaction", branding Bandera as "the ideological mummy from Galicia in the 1930s" and "a nationalist, but of an old, reactionary school".[21] The revolution envisaged by the Banderivsti tradition diverges from the revolution of 1917, whose leadership belonged to the Ukrainian socialist parties.[22]

This retrogression we see today was already being challenged by no less a figure than Volodymyr Vynnychenko, one of the most popular figures of the revolution and leader of the first independent Ukrainian State. After meeting with him in France Maistrenko and his comrades of the Ukrainian Revolutionary Democratic Party, published a pamphlet by Vynnychenko which speaks to our current controversies.[23] Recalling that their "Ukrainian spring" had faced numerous enemies, Vynnychenko argued their defeat was not only due to physical power but their political disorder. The Bolsheviks had an "intense fear of losing the colony" but also "raised the banner of the most decisive social and economic revolution which was the cry of the Ukrainian worker-peasant masses."[24] The question was posed as: "either national liberation, or social, or 'Ukraine', or 'land and factories". The central body of the revolution, the "Central Rada did not try to combine these two slogans", believing "the enthusiasm of the national rebirth would be above all other interests." And in the Central Rada, there was a lack of sufficient understanding of the moment, unanimity, and the determination to become the vanguard of the masses, to act as an expression not only of their national but also their social and economic interests.[25]

Vynnychenko saw this as a recurrent problem, the followers of Bandera taking an even more dogmatic approach and refusal to learn from history:

> The Bandero-UHVRist youth, teaching me how to fight for Ukraine, categorically told me that only idiots and traitors raise the question of what Ukraine should be. For them, this question has no weight, only Ukraine.[26]

Vynnychenko saw a different historical tendency of the revolution than the uniform one set forth in today's official historical narrative in Ukraine. In contrast Vynnychenko emphasized they did not all think the same way, the revolution created a current of "one-sided liberation" (*odnobichnoho vyzvolennya*) focused on national-statehood—and the "*Universal* current" that sought a "comprehensive liberation" (*vsebichnoho vyzvolennya*) both social and national.[27] The members of the "*Universal* current" comprised the left-wing Ukrainian Socialist-Revolutionaries (Borotbisty) and left-wing Ukrainian Social Democrats (Ukapisty).[28] Maistrenko was active is both parties. One reviewer of *Borotbism* wrote: "It is almost impossible to speak accurately of Ukrainian nationalism; rather there are many factions of Ukrainian nationalists".[29]

Maistrenko's *Borotbism* presents a different view of the revolution than those which see to shroud it as a fight between an undifferentiated mass of Ukrainian people in struggle with the Russian Empire. It is a valuable record of events that were pivotal to the development, if not a foundation event of modern Ukraine.

2. The Colonial Terrain and Social Forces of the Revolution

The events presented in *Borotbism* took place in a setting very different from our own time; on the eve of the revolution the world generally knew little of Ukraine. The territory inhabited by Ukrainians was partitioned between the Austro-Hungarian and Russian Empires, the majority having been held in a colonial position by Tsarist Russia for over two and a half centuries. But contrary to the prognosis of some the development of capitalism did not render permanent its status as a so-called "non-historic" nation.[30] Though this was not for the want of trying; in the mind of Moscow there was no Ukraine; only the southern province known derogatorily as Malorossia—'Little Russia'.

Pursuing the policy of Russification and consolidation of its power in Ukraine, the Tsarist government deprived the Ukrainian people of the right to develop their culture, including the language. In 1720 a decree prohibited publishing (except religious books), in 1863 the 'Valuev Circular' declared "no separate Ukrainian language has ever existed, exists or can exist". In 1876 the Ems Ukaz banned not only printing but bringing Ukrainian books from abroad. The ban lasted until 1905, by 1908 harassment saw publishing plummet again.

In the provinces of Galicia and Bukovyna, under the rule of the Habsburgs the legal Ukrainian movement developed apace. From this "Ukrainian piedmont" it exerted influence and provided a base for the movement in the Russian Empire. In contrast under Tsarist absolutism the Ukrainian movement faced a protracted struggle, Tsarism responding with hostility qualitatively different from its attitude towards a number of other nationalities. This can be explained by the role Ukraine played in the foundation of the Empire.

Ukraine's subordination to Moscow can be traced to the mid-17th century, after the Cossack-led revolution against the Polish-Lithuanian rule, the new Ukrainian state entered into the Treaty of Pereyalsav with the Tsardom of Muscovy. It is matter of controversy to this day; in Russian history it was a 'reunion' which gradually saw Russia gradually supplanting Polish influence. The subsequent ingestion of the 'republic of the Cossacks' by the Tsardom of Muscovy, brought with it the acquisition of the black earth belt, the coasts of the Black Sea and rich natural resources. This metamorphosed Muscovy into the Russian Empire, a factor of no small importance in the mind of Russian nationalism to this day.[31]

The social and economic geography of Ukraine was changed drastically under Russian rule. Previously autonomous Ukraine had boasted for the time a relatively representative form of government, a free peasantry, an industry and agriculture more advanced than in Russia. It was transformed into what the 1920s Soviet economist Mykhaylo Volobuyev characterized, as a colonial dependence of a "European type".[32] A combined drive of the Russian state and western European capital saw huge strides in the development of capitalism at the turn of the century. French, Belgian, British and German capitalists owned much of coal, ore, iron and steel in Ukraine. This growth generated contradictory tendencies for the economic terrain, as Volobuyev observed:

> Those who speak of unity of the pre-revolutionary Russian and Ukrainian economies, have only in mind the first tendency and forget about the second — the centrifugal, or rather — of the desire to join the world economic system directly, and not through the intermediary of the Russian economy. The process of concentration on a capitalist basis is reflected in the contradictory forms of autarchic tendencies. Therefore we should not deceive ourselves by the fact of concentrating tendencies in the Russian pre-revolutionary economy. Alongside these tendencies it is necessary to also see the separatist forces of the Ukrainian economy. Therefore, the question, of whether there was a single Russian pre-revolutionary economy, should be answered as follows: it was a single economy on an antagonistic, imperialist basis, but from the viewpoint of centrifugal forces of the colonies oppressed by her, it was a complex of national economies. In this way, we provide the answer to the first question that was posed at the beginning of this article. The Ukrainian economy was not an ordinary province of Tsarist Russia, but a country that was placed in a colonial position.[33]

Stifling key sectors of indigenous industry, the policies of Tsarism were designed to transform Ukraine into a supplier of raw materials for Russia, a market for Russian manufactured goods, and protect Russian industry from Ukrainian competition.[34] Symptomatic was the transport system; as opposed to railways which ran from Ukrainian centers to Black Sea ports and west, they were instead constructed on a north-south axis reflecting the needs of Russian business interests.

The colonial position of Ukraine impacted on the state, capital, labor relations and composition of the social classes. The capitalist class was non-Ukrainian, prompting Ukrainian socialists to consider their nation as bourgeoisless (*bezburzhaunist*).[35] The small capitalist class considered itself the regional section of the all-Russian bourgeoisie; politically it was an outpost of Russian conservatism.

In 1897 there were a total of 1.5 million workers, of whom 44 per cent were Ukrainian; seasonal agricultural workers comprised an estimated 2 million.[36] By 1917 the working class numbered 3.6 million, employed in industry, railways, urban and village artisan workplaces, construction, servants, transit and over one million were agricultural laborers.[37] In 1917, inclusive of their dependents the working class accounted for 6.5 million people, 20.8 per cent of the population of Russian-ruled Ukraine. The largest contingent of the working class was formed by agricultural laborers -1.2 million.[38]

Alongside the high levels of industrial development, European investment and enterprises with the latest western machinery was dreadful social conditions. In 1910 wages in Ukraine were one-quarter that of Western Europe, housing and working conditions were amongst the worst in Europe. In the Left-Bank and Right-Bank of Ukraine where the majority of Ukrainian workers were located, wages were amongst the lowest in the Empire. In 1897, 52 per cent of Ukraine's industrial working class was illiterate, exacerbated by an absence of schools in the native language.

The working class bore the stigmata of colonialism; it was not formed by a transfer of the Ukrainian peasants to the proletariat. In 1917, 40 per cent of workers were Ukrainian (largely in rural areas), Russians formed 40 per cent, Jews 10 per cent, and the remainder other nationalities. In industrial centers, a pattern of Russian hegemony could be found in factory labor and plant management, a Russian and Russified upper strata developed in the higher paid skilled posts.[39] Ukrainian new entrants found Russian not only the language of the state but of the labor regime, the factory owner and foreman.⁴⁰

These developments posited the national question at the point of production through a division of labor which relegated Ukrainians to the lower strata, under-represented in heavy industry and over-represented in service and agricultural sectors. Flexible labor was widespread, there were a high proportion of temporary workers in factories — in the Donbas almost all temporary workers were Ukrainian.⁴¹

It was not coincidental that Russian nationalism expressed itself in extreme forms in Ukraine where the notorious Black Hundreds were well organized. The working class was not immune to chauvinism; the observations of a blacksmith in Yuzovka (Donetsk) of a demonstration during 1905 provide a flavor: 'who's running this?.... A bunch of Khokholy and Zhidy', derogatory terms for Ukrainians and Jews.⁴²

Anti-Semitism was deliberately fostered, previously Russia forbade Jews on its territory, when the Tsar acquired Right Bank Ukraine (lands west of the Dnipro River) it contained a considerable Jewish populace. The Tsar Catherine created the notorious "Pale of Settlement" in much of Ukraine, Belarus and parts of western Russia. An area Jews could settle but not own land with proscriptions on movement. The five million Jews were subjected to institutional discrimination; recurrent violence and poverty that saw two million emigrate between 1881–1914.

Colonial dependency characterized the process of urbanization; this relationship reshaped old cities and established new ones. The stimulus to urban growth was both strategic and economic, the need to establish a strong Russian presence and the extraction of raw materials. The imposition of serfdom in Ukraine after the Russian conquest tied the peasant to the land and curtailed social mobility, obstructing their movement to cities. The cities and large towns evolved into enclaves of Russians and Russified colonizers. As industrialization accelerated, the landscape became a scene of social and national disparities. According to the Imperial census of 1897, Ukraine had a population of 23,430,000; Ukrainians predominated on the Left-Bank and Right-Bank but by a narrower majority in the southern steppe region. This overall demography is presented in Tables 1 and 2.

Table 1. National composition of Russian-ruled Ukraine – 1897[43]

Nationality	Number	% of the total
Ukrainians	17,040,000	71.5
Russians	2.970,000	12.4
Jews	2,030,000	8.5
Germans	502,000	2.1
Poles	406,000	1.7
Romanian/Moldovans	187,000	0.8
Belarusians	222,000	0.9
Tatars	220,000	0.9
Greeks	80,000	0.3
Bulgarians	68,000	0.3
Czechs	37,000	0.2
Others	71,000	0.3
Total	23,833,000	99.9

Table 2. Nationalities in Provinces of Russian-ruled Ukraine – 1897[44]

Province	Ukrainians	Russians	Jews	Total
Katerynoslav	1,456,000	365,000	99,000	2,113,000
Kharkiv	2,009,000	441,000	13,000	2,492,000
Kherson	1,462,000	575,000	322,000	2,733,000
Kyiv	2,819,000	209,000	430,000	3,559,000
Podillia	2,442,000	99,000	369,000	3,018,000
Poltava	2,583,000	73,000	110,000	2,778,000
Volhynia	2,096,000	105,000	395,000	2,989,000
Total	14,867,000	1,867,000	1,738,000	19,682,000
%	75.5	9.5	8.8	

The contrast between the overall population and that of the cities can be seen when compared to the gubernia in which they were situated. As illustrated in Table 3. The colonial pattern of urbanization ensured the primacy of Russians and other non-Ukrainian minorities in the urban power centers, illustrated in the composition of the Civil Service in Ukraine of which 47 per cent were Russians and 31 per cent Ukrainians.[45] Whilst Ukrainian speakers constituted 80 per cent of the rural population, they constituted one-third of the urban population.[46] Ukrainians who migrated to cities were subject to pressures of assimilation in a Russified environment. This was not accidental but corresponded with the colonial policy of the Imperial government.[47]

Table 3. Nationalities by language in cities of Russian-ruled Ukraine — 1897[48]

City	Total Population	Ukrainians (%	Russians of Total)	Jews
Odessa	403,815	9.4	49.0	30.8
Kyiv	247,723	22.2	54.2	2.1
Kharkiv	173,989	25.9	63.2	5.7
Katerynoslav	112,839	15.8	41.8	35.4
Mykolaiv	92,012	8.5	66.3	19.5
Zhytomyr	65,895	13.9	25.7	46.4
Kremenchuk	63,007	30.1	19.3	46.9
Yelisavetgrad	61,488	23.6	34.6	37.8
Kherson	59,076	19.6	47.2	29.1
Poltava	53,703	56.0	20.6	19.9
Berdychiv	53.351	8.2	8.6	77.1

Remarkably, despite mass migration of a million peasants, and the loss of 1.2 million inhabitants in the First World War, the population of Ukraine saw a 33 per cent increase to 31,214,000 between 1897 and 1917.[49] The urban population doubled from the three million inhabitants of 1897, increasing from 13.2 per cent of its total population to 20 per cent in 1917. These demographic shifts however did not change the social-class structure, and Ukrainians remained marginalized.

Analysis of the population of the strategically vital urban centers illustrates the predicament of the Ukrainian movement. In 1917 the intelligentsia and white-collar staff formed 26 per cent of the total urban population, and the petty-bourgeoisie and bourgeoisie another 29 per cent. These middle-class strata represented some 55 per cent of the urban population, with the proletariat, at 23 per cent, and the semi-proletariat, at 21 per cent. Ukrainians were poorly represented in the first two groups, and formed a majority of the latter.[50] In Kyiv two thirds of Ukrainians were classed as workers, servants or unemployed.[51] The resulting alienation was captured by the Ukrainian Marxist Vasyl Shakhray considered this demography:

> reflected the centuries-old government of the Tsarist bureaucracy and the Russian bourgeoisie, landowners and capitalists. As in a "drop of water the sun is reflected in all the colors of the rainbow, so these figures reflect the result of the national, social, political and cultural oppression that Ukraine had experienced for centuries.[52]

In considering the awakening Ukrainian masses, Shakhray asked how it can be a surprise that the Ukrainian peasant was so suspicious of their foreign overlords, of 'the Jewish-merchant, the Great Russian-official, an assistant to the Polish-landowner, the clerk.' Writing through the eyes of a peasant Shakhray wrote:

> The city rules the village and the city is 'alien'. The city draws to itself all the wealth and gives the village nothing in return. The city extracts taxes, which never return to the village, to Ukraine. During the 14 years from 1900–1914, 8 of the Ukrainian provinces gave 7507 million, and of that only 4099 million (54 per cent) was spent on Ukraine, and 3409 million (45.6 per cent were lost to Ukraine. In the city one must pay bribes to the official, be freed from bullying and red tape. In the city the merchant is lying, selling and buying. In the city the landlord eats good things collected in the village. In the city the lights are burning, there are schools, theatres, and music plays. The city is expensively dressed as for a holiday, it eats and drinks well, many people promenade.
> In the village there is, except for hard work, impenetrable darkness and misery, almost nothing. The city is aristocratic it is alien. It is not ours, not Ukrainian. It is Great-Russian, Jewish, Polish, but not ours, not Ukrainian.[53]

Regarded the breadbasket of Europe, Ukrainian was synonymous with peasant. In 1917 Ukraine remained an agrarian country; 80 per cent of the population lived in the countryside and 68 per cent relied on agriculture for their livelihood.[54] It was here that the social and national questions became enmeshed in an explosive cocktail, setting the scene for the agrarian revolution of 1917 and the base of movements such as the Borotbisty.

In the four years prior to the 'Emancipation' reform of 1861, Ukraine saw an estimated 276 peasant uprisings, but the end of serfdom did not solve the agrarian problem. The reform created new obstacles, the peasantry faced the curtailment of the area of land available for their use, an excessive redemption, preventing buying back the land which was originally theirs, they were burdened by excessive payments, iniquitous income tax, land tax, an array of dues and a series of labor duties leftover from serfdom.

A process of social differentiation of the peasantry occurred in the context of capitalist development though not as presented by certain historians and Soviet literature.[55] The latter placed particular emphasis on the rich peasants the 'kulaks' (kurkul in Ukrainian) — a term of abuse used frequently for any expression of Ukrainian nationalism. The standard categories of Soviet literature of which much historical data has been drawn, divided the peasantry into poor, middle and rich famers, the kulak. These categories are based on landholdings, and on this basis almost half of the peasant population of Ukraine in 1917 was poor, one-third middle strata.[56] A high proportion of poor peasants' worked elsewhere, agricultural laborers, or in trades, over a million left their homes each year to work in seasonal worker.[57]

The national composition of the class of landowners further entwined the national and agrarian question. Of some 25 million rural inhabitants the class of landowners comprised 1.1 per cent yet controlled 30 per cent of the land.[58] Alongside the Russian state, church and monasteries, a third of arable land was held by a class of which three out of four were Russians or Poles.[59] There was further estrangement from the petty traders who bought the grain at the cheapest price and in return sold manufactured goods at the highest price; only one out of seven was Ukrainian.[60] In Right-Bank Ukraine, in Kyiv, Podillia and Volhynia provinces where large latifundia remained since the era of Polish rule; poverty was the most acute in the Empire.[61]

Already in 1902 mass peasant strikes in Poltava and Kharkiv began to fuse social demands with that of an autonomous Ukraine.

Socio-economic inequality of the colonial agrarian system was a major factor in the developing revolutionary ferment in the

Ukrainian provinces, but as Holubnychy points out there were several factors to take into account. It is also necessary to appreciate that the agrarian revolution that unfolded in 1917 was not in isolation but was part of a wider revolutionary situation. The experience of the 1902 strikes and the 1905 revolution was alive, education was spreading literacy in the countryside and assisted the extensive socialist and cooperative agitation, youth had gained experience in the Army, and the overall acute situation was exacerbated by the war.[62] Karl Kautsky the foremost figure of international socialism before 1917 had observed of Ukraine:

> Capitalism develops in only one dimension for the Ukrainian people — it proletarianizes them, while the other dimension — the flowering of the productive forces, the accumulation of surplus and wealth — is mainly for the benefit of other countries. Because of this, capitalism reveals to Ukrainians only its negative, revolutionizing dimension...it does not lead to an increase in their wealth.[63]

The development of capitalism in Ukraine was not an isolated process, it occurred in the context of an expanding capitalist system which integrated the Russian Empire into the world economy through social, economic, military and political connections. Divided between rival empires that were part of two opposed camps, the Ukrainian question was situated in a vital strategic vector of European capitalism. It was in the strategic interests' of European capital to prevent a Ukrainian republic emerge, especially one constituted by the labor and socialist movement.

In Ukraine a nation of workers and peasants with no nationally conscious capitalist class it logically followed that the driving forces of the revolution should correspond to the nation's character. This had already been illustrated in the influential work of the leading theorist of the Ukrainian Social Democrats, Mykola Porsh that the:

> Thus only the proletariat can assume the leadership in the struggle for autonomy.... the Ukrainian national movement will not be a bourgeois movement of triumphant capitalism as in the case of the Czechs. It will be more like the Irish case, a proletarian and semi-proletarianized peasant movement.[64]

These contours of the Ukrainian movement were already apparent in 1905, having produced its own organic intellectuals and organized in political parties, unions, co-operatives, cultural and Prosvita educational associations. The movement which emerged at the start of the 20th century contained an energetic current which was strongly influenced by socialist thought and the struggles of the worker-peasant masses. It was the starting point of a new period for the Ukrainian movement. The scale and power of the revolution in Ukraine would come as a surprise even to those who had expected it and worked for it.

3. Problems of the Ukrainian Revolution

With the overthrow of the autocracy in 1917 the Ukrainian Revolution soon differentiated itself from the wider Russian Revolution, setting as its task the achievement of national emancipation through the creation of a Ukrainian Republic. This national and democratic revolution also awoke the social revolution; the unfolding of this threefold revolutionary process constitutes the history of the Ukrainian revolution in its first year.

The first phase spanned from the February Revolution to the October seizure of power by the Central Rada and proclamation of the Ukrainian Peoples Republic (UNR) in 1917, the upsurge of the workers-peasants revolution and the dislocation of the revolutionary movement, followed by defeat by the Austro-German and conservative forces in 1918. It is at this point in the revolutionary process that we witness the emergence of the Borotbisty.

This period was one of unprecedented self-organization and mobilization of the masses, the Ukrainian movement comprised a bloc of the middle class, peasantry, workers and the revolutionary-democratic intellectuals, centered in the Ukrainian Central Rada [Council].

The Central Rada was a mass assembly consisting of councils of peasants', soldiers' and workers' deputies, it expanded its constituency, drawing in the national minorities, included the pioneering organization of Jewish national autonomy.[65]

Table 4

Ukrainian Central Rada	Number of delegates
All-Ukrainian Council of Peasant Deputies	212
All-Ukrainian Council of Military Deputies	158
All-Ukrainian Council of Workers' Deputies	100
Representatives of the general (non-Ukrainian) Councils of Workers' and Soldiers Deputies	50
Ukrainian socialist parties	20
Russian socialist parties	40
Jewish socialist parties,	35
Polish socialist parties	15
Representatives of towns and provinces (elected mainly at peasant, worker and all-national congresses)	84
Representatives of trade, educational, economic and civic organizations and national parties (Moldavians, Germans, Belarusians, Tatars and others).	108

By the end of July 1917 the Central Rada consisted of 822 deputies including the representatives of the national minorities. It elected an executive body the Mala (Little) Rada, and after proclaiming autonomy a General Secretariat, the embryonic autonomous government of Ukraine.

The very existence of the Central Rada, the revolutionary parliament of Ukraine was an historic achievement; this movement transformed the situation from one where officially Ukraine did not even exist, to one in which by July 1917 the duplicitous and hostile Russian Provisional Government was forced to recognize it as a 'higher organ for conducting Ukrainian national affairs'.[66] In historical terms the Central Rada represented for Ukraine what the Easter Rising and First Dáil did for the Irish Republic.

The leaders and parties at the forefront of the Ukrainian movement were exclusively socialists, ranging from the moderate Ukrainian Party of Socialist-Federalists to the Marxist Ukrainian Social-Democratic Workers Party (USDRP), to the mass Ukrainian Party of Socialist Revolutionaries (UPSR). The chairman of the Central Rada was the historian Mykhailo Hrushevsky a socialist aligned with the UPSR, and the President of the General Secretariat, was the Volodymyr Vynnychenko of the USDRP.

The revolution in Ukraine did not mirror the situation in Russia of 'dual power' between the state and the councils of workers and soldiers deputies — soviets. This period of the struggle for national emancipation was characterized by profound social and political contradictions. Following the February revolution, the administrative organs of Imperial Russia such as the Military District Commissars, town and city dumas, remained intact. Like the Provisional Government they viewed the Central Rada with antagonism. Separate workers, peasants and soldiers' soviets arose throughout Ukraine, in industrial Kryvyi Rih-Donets region alone there were 140 soviets.

In the first phase of the revolution the Russian Social Democratic Workers Party (Mensheviks) and the Russian Party of Socialist Revolutionaries leaders in a number of soviets refrained from addressing the Ukrainian question.[67] Nezbolin the Russian SR chairman of the Kyiv Soviet denounced the demand for autonomy "as a stab in the back for the Russian revolution".[68]

In the Kyiv a regional meeting of Mensheviks in April opposed the Ukrainian movement, and favored limited cultural-national autonomy for the Ukrainian people proclaiming "political autonomy, especially a federation, is harmful".[69] The tendency to block with the Russian middle class and Provisional Government against the Ukrainian movement was recorded by Leon Trotsky:

> The difference in nationality between the cities and the villages was painfully felt also in the soviets, they being predominantly city organizations. Under the leadership of the compromise parties the soviets would frequently ignore the national interests of the basic population. This was one cause of the weakness of the soviets in the Ukraine...... Under a false banner of internationalism the soviets would frequently wage a struggle against the defensive nationalism of the Ukrainians or Mussulmans, supplying a screen for the oppressive Russifying movement of the cities.[70]

This was not uniform, the Poltava Councils of Workers and Soldiers welcomed the "revolutionary act of the Central Rada, which declared the autonomy of Ukraine". And urged "all revolutionary organizations and all citizens living in Ukraine to support the revolutionary aspirations of the Ukrainian people...".[71] In May, the First Congress of Peasant Deputies of Kharkiv province demanded that the Provisional Government "immediately and openly recognize the Ukrainian people's right to national-territorial autonomy'.[72]

The Ukrainian word '*rada*' and Russian '*sovet*', meaning council, are direct transliterations, the Bolshevik leader Yuri Lapchynsky, recalled that there always seemed to be a Ukrainian who would claim he supported soviet power and also the Rada because it was a soviet.[73] Vynnychenko considered at that time the revolution appeared to be following a course concurrent with Ukraine's class composition:

> Thus, it seems that it would have been logical to continue establishing only the workers' and peasants' statehood, which would have corresponded to the entire nation's character. And it seemed to have been so planned during the first period, especially during the struggle against the Provisional Government. And our power seemed to have been established in such a way. The Central Rada really consisted of councils of peasants', soldiers' and workers' deputies, who were elected at the respective congresses and sent to the Central Rada. And the General Secretariat seemed to have been consisting only of socialists. And the leading parties, Social Democrats and Socialist-Revolutionaries, seemed to have been standing firmly on the basis of social revolution.[74]

The wide socialist composition of the Central Rada was reflected in the debates that arose in response to the challenges it faced. In some aspects they were a continuation of controversies that gripped the social democratic workers movement in preceding years over perspectives and character of the revolution.

The Central Rada faced burning questions of ending the war, the agrarian revolution and the drive to workers' control, encapsulated in the slogan '*land for the peasants and factories for the workers*'. By late 1917 leaders of the Central Rada at key moments began to lag behind the pace and aspirations of the popular movement from below.[75] Relations strained between those moderate and centrist elements and the radicalizing rank and file of the movement.

The difficulties of the Central Rada were exacerbated by an often overlooked fact that as it expanded its base it drew in parties such as the RSDRP Mensheviks and the Russian Socialist Revolutionaries, who sat in the Provisional Government. The Menshevik/SR 'Revolutionary Defensist' centrist currents who were for continuing the war and supportive of the Provisional Government was particularly dominant in Kyiv committees of their party. Which was where the Rada was located. They opposed 'independent implementation' to secure of Ukraine's autonomy, on land and ending the war before the convening of the All-Russian Constituent Assembly.[76]

Meanwhile the popular movement pushed for robust action to establish autonomy from Russia, the soldiers demanded their own self-organized regiments and unilateral action for peace. On the pivotal land question the right of centre USDRP leader Bory Martos, and Kost Matsiievch of the UPSF undertook development of policy for the Central Rada — but implementation was delayed pending the Constituent Assembly. Regardless, the agrarian revolution advanced from below, millions of peasants many enrolled in the Ukrainian Peasants Union (*Spilka*) organized by the UPSR, and in Councils of Peasants' Deputies, proceeded to seize land themselves.

The majority in the Central Rada saw the need for a socialist government of Ukraine, but there was also a significant current of socialism who were convinced the they were undergoing a 'democratic revolution', who ruled out the assumption of power by the proletariat, considering the requisite material for a socialist transformation existed in the more developed west and the ripening of the revolution there was unclear. They considered they should assume a 'waiting position setting for themselves the task of organizing the Ukrainian republic as a necessary condition for the successful course of the socialist revolution in Ukraine.'[77] Whilst others disagreed with posing the question in such terms as a solely bourgeois democratic or socialist revolution, they considered social democrats should grasp the idea they faced a new situation. Social Democracy could be victorious but this could not be achieved by the workers alone without help of other classes namely the peasantry.

The national question brought an additional dimension, as the urban working class had a large Russian and Russified element; critics considered the slogan of the '*Dictatorship of the Proletariat*' then coupled with '*All power to the Soviets*', would mean transfer of power largely to the hands of the non-Ukrainians, considering the composition of the small urban proletariat being largely non-

Ukrainian or Russified. The national question was at the heart of the differences, there was support for the transfer of power to the hands of the Soviets in Russia but in Ukraine '*All power to the Central Rada*'. There was little inclination for the Ukrainian democracy to give itself up to the tutelage of Russian socialism long hostile to the Ukrainian cause.

The difficulties were as Vynnychenko explained, not about personalities but politics.[78] The prevailing opinion in the Central Rada leadership was that of securing greater autonomy as a precondition of progress.[79] In this endeavor the Central Rada engaged in a protracted struggle with the Russian Provisional government, which adhered to a colonial mindset of the 'One and Indivisible Russia" in its approach.

After the failed Kornilov coup the Provisional Government convened a Democratic Conference in September 1917. The Central Rada now called for 'a homogeneous revolutionary and socialist government.'[80] Kerensky formed yet another coalition with the conservative Constitutional Democratic (Kadet) Party, with each metamorphosis the more of a silhouette of a government it became, and more it resisted the subject nations. In October after securing the agreement of the Mensheviks, the Jewish Bundists and the Russian SR's the Central Rada agreed to convene a Ukrainian Constituent Assembly. Kerensky ordered the Prosecutor to investigate and summoned Vynnychenko and others to Petrograd — with reports they were to be arrested. It was Kerensky not the Central Rada which fell.

On 25th October power passed to the Petrograd Soviet, the next day the Second All-Russia Congress of Soviets proclaimed the Russian Socialist Federated Soviet Republic led by the Council of People's Commissars. The October Revolution removed the barriers, perceived or otherwise, which stood in the way of Ukrainian self-government. The October conjuncture also saw increasing support for a more radical turn in the trajectory of the Ukrainian Revolution.

The USDRP at their congress had called for more robust action and declared the Russian Revolution as "a prologue to and beginning of the *Universal* socialist revolution".[81] The influential USDRP leader Porsh criticized Social Democrats in the Central Rada for "compromising on class interests in deference of general, national ones", and a congress resolution he co-authored stated:

> That the majority of the Ukrainian Central Rada, being composed of representatives of the petty bourgeoisie, is unable, due to its class composition, to follow the consistent and resolute revolutionary-democratic tactics, leaning now and again towards petty bourgeois nationalism..'.[82]

The historical orthodoxies, both nationalist and Stalinist neglect this radical left tendency within the Ukrainian Revolution, portraying such influences in Ukraine as external, alien, and Bolshevik. Maistrenko's history of the Borotbisty confirms how this tendency grew organically.

The difficulty the radical left of the USDRP and UPSR faced was translating their views into practice. In Russia this radicalization saw the different strands of the popular movement coalesce in the Bolshevik-Left SRs leadership in the soviets, which caught up with the changed mood. In Ukraine the chief characteristic of the situation was one of fragmentation.

The peasants' opposition to the established rulers did not automatically find natural allies and leaders in the urban working class. The salient feature of the revolution was of divergences between these subjective forces, notably the estrangement of the peasantry from sections of the urban workers. Across the whole revolutionary process there were divisions over solutions and which of them should take priority of emphasis between the social and national dimensions.[83] This surfaced most clearly in the winter of 1917–1918, following the October Revolution. In the urban arena, as Vasyl Shakhray noted:

> The Soviets in Ukraine devoted little time to the national movement. They were seized with the struggle with the coalition government in Petrograd, and did not sufficiently value those organized processes which were going on before their own eyes; they stood, so to speak, with their face to Petrograd, and their back to Ukraine.

The Russian Social Democratic Workers Party (RSDRP) was weakly represented in Ukraine before the revolution. In the spring of 1917, both wings of the Russian Social Democrats grew; the Mensheviks had a significant advantage in city councils, trade unions, and workers' organizations. The Bolsheviks received less support in Ukraine than in Russia. In Ukraine better educated workers, especially in large firms where, unlike in Russia, collective bargaining existed, supported the Mensheviks.[84] Neither Bolsheviks nor Mensheviks had a Ukrainian wide organization, they were directly subordinate to their respective Central Committees in Russia.

Russian Social Democracy had long demanded the subordination of all Marxists in the Empire into a single party: *their own*. As a corollary their leaders supported the assimilation of workers into the Russian nation as historically progressive and did not challenge the integrity of the Empire.[85] In contrast the Ukrainian, Jewish and Polish social democrats in Ukraine took up the quest for national self-government as an immediate task, considering that the advent of socialism would promote springtime of nations and national culture.

The Mensheviks joined the Central Rada, but only a section of the Bolsheviks did so, they were organizationally and politically unprepared for a *Ukrainian* revolution. The result was that the leadership of sections of the urban workers movement stood apart from the Ukrainian revolution.

A possible resolution of the cleavages on the social and national questions was increasingly revealed in the idea of a Ukrainian Republic based upon the organizations of workers' and peasants' self-government. That a rapprochement was a possibility can be seen from the example of the initiatives in two of Ukraine's major cities after the October revolution.

In Kyiv a National Committee for the Defense of the Revolution was created by the Central Rada, composed of representatives of all revolutionary organizations in Kyiv and socialist parties in Ukraine.[86] It sought to extend its authority and appealed to all revolutionary organizations to join local committees.[87] In Kharkiv the workers', peasants' and soldiers' councils jointly established a 'Kharkiv Province Military Revolutionary Committee' combined with the Free Ukrainian Rada, trade unions, factory committees and socialist parties. It had a "left orientation and a strong Ukrainian component".[88] In Kyiv there was a hint of a new internal policy based on the union of all revolutionary socialist elements. These sentiments expressed what the majority sought; the potential for a united revolutionary socialist government in Ukraine seemed possible.

But those wishing to give an emerging socialist revolution a Ukrainian character and form were unsuccessful in the vortex of the winter of 1917-1918. The forces that could bring this about did not combine and what unfolded proved a historical tragedy.

No sooner had unity been achieved than the right-wing of the Russian SR's and Mensheviks with the Kadets turned on the Central Rada, attacking it and the Bolsheviks. Within the Central Rada's executive (*Mala Rada*) they 'extorted' a resolution condemning the uprising in Petrograd stating power in each country must pass to the hands of 'all the revolutionary democracy' not exclusively to the hands of the soviets. The newly created socialist front in Ukraine was shattered.

The Kyiv Bolsheviks left the Central Rada and the Revolutionary Committee, Yuriy Pyatakov announcing to loud applause, "on that moment when you would be falling beneath the blows of Russian imperialism, we will be with you with our weapons in our hands".[89] And the USDRP's *Robitnycha Hazeta* wrote: "the Ukrainian people will not forget the service which the Bolsheviks gave, standing alongside them weapons in hand, in defense of the rights of Ukrainian democracy."[90]

The complexities of the revolution were soon revealed when a battle broke out in Kyiv the scene of three political centers of power. On one side was the General Staff of the Kyiv Military District and forces loyal to the deposed Russian government, on the other the Ukrainian Central Rada and the three thousand delegates attending the Third All-Ukraine Military Congress, and finally the Kyiv Soviet of Workers and Soldiers Deputies and Red Guards.

The conservatives and supporters of the Provisional Government sought to make Kyiv a center of Russian counter-revolution. They surrounded the Kyiv Soviet and arrested its Bolshevik leaders. In response a city-wide general strike commenced, barricades were erected and fighting ensued. The Ukrainian Military Congress organized units who joined the fight against the General Staff. The

Ukrainian soldiers intervention on the side of the Soviet decided the battle, defeated, the General Staff fled Kyiv.

When the Military Congress reconvened, in contrast to the earlier *Mala Rada* criticism of the October revolution the soldiers decided they "cannot consider the action of the Bolsheviks anti-democratic". Stating they would ensure that Ukrainian troops were not sent to "fight those who represent the interests of the working people." Having subject its leadership to strong criticism, the soldiers' now demanded the Central Rada immediately take power and proclaim a Ukrainian Republic.

With the apparent expulsion of the Russian conservative elements from Kyiv the Central Rada issued its Third *Universal* proclaiming the Ukrainian People's Republic (UNR). The Rada assumed all power until the convening of the Constituent Assembly of Ukraine. The Third *Universal* announced freedom for all political prisoners, abolition of the death penalty and reaffirmed all freedoms won by the All-Russian revolution, freedom of speech, press, worship, assembly, trade union, strikes, and languages. It granted national-personal autonomy of national minorities. The Rada affirmed it would us use resolute means to achieve peace negotiations at once.

In the social sphere the UNR abolished the right of ownership of all landlord and other lands not worked with one's own labor. These lands were declared the property of "all laboring people" and transferred to them without any compensation. In industry the Republic proclaimed an eight-hour working day and charged the Secretariat for Labor together with the workers representatives to establish immediate state control over production. The UNR sought to broaden the rights of the local bodies of self-government in cooperation with the organs of revolutionary democracy.

At this juncture it is recognized, including by Soviet scholars, that the overwhelming majority of the peasantry favored the Central Rada and the proclamation of the Ukrainian Peoples Republic, it gave rise to hope that soon the key questions would be solved in the interests of the masses. But the Republic faced the difficulty that at the very moment when the barriers were removed to its formation, the solutions it presented to the problems plaguing

Ukraine, though radical; may have been satisfactory a month earlier but were now out of step with the increasingly militant mood of the masses.

At first it seemed the Third *Universal* had caught up with the peasants redistributing estates on a mass scale. But immediately there were efforts to undermine it by moderates, landlords, capitalists and banks. Martos, Secretary of Land Affairs issued a circular prohibiting seizure of land and the *Universal* did not apply to farms of 50 *desiatiny*, worked by one's own labor. Though the transfer of land was promised, the question of when and how was postponed until the convening of the constituent assembly.[91]

There was similar lagging behind the revolution in the factories where the authority of capital was crumbling. The self-organization and confidence of the workers had grown steadily; in May the first major conference of Factory Committees was held in Kharkiv demanding they take over production.[92] By October the factory committees and workers councils had made profound encroachments upon the sovereignty of the employers. It was only in Ukraine that the movement for workers control led to the direct takeovers by workers. Donbas mine committees had took control in September arresting some managers, similarly in Kharkiv factory committees had taken over major city plants.[93] By October the committees were either in joint control or direct control of many workplaces. This demanded labor law which corresponded with the actual situation on the ground.

But having bound itself to agreements with the Provisional Government and prioritizing autonomy the Central Rada had neglected labor relations; these issues were dealt with by the local authorities of the Provisional Government — the commissariats of the Ministry of Labor. As a result in the first phase of the revolution the Central Rada had lost ground in terms of influence in the workplaces. On 12 October a Secretariat of Labor was formed relying 'on the support of workers' organizations' and committed to reorganize labor relations in Ukraine. The Secretariat for Labor (under the Marxists Mykhailo Tkachenko and Mykola Porsh) was charged together with the workers representatives to establish immediate state control over production. But whilst it was to draw up numerous labor laws and projects aimed at improving the lives and strengthening of workers power, it failed to address the immediate implementing of workers control. This indecisiveness of the Central Rada in implementing land and labor policy could only worsen its efforts to consolidate the new Republic.

The Poltava Bolshevik Shakhray writes that the 'Proclamation of the Ukrainian Republic was met with huge demonstrations over all Ukraine. A significant part of the soviets also welcomed it.'[94] The advent of the Ukrainian Peoples Republic also coincided with a surge of support for the radical left, with increased influence of the ideas of the Bolsheviks and left of the Ukrainian socialist parties. In the workers councils of at least seven of the ten largest cities of Ukraine there was support for the UNR.[95] These soviets were already the governing body in key areas of Ukraine, some were Bolshevik led others coalitions, they brought to the fore one side of an unresolved debate over forms of democracy in the republic. Typical of the debates at the time was in the Katerynoslav soviet, where the USDRP and RSDRP(b) united in supporting the uprising in Petrograd, recognition of the Ukrainian Peoples Republic, for soviet power in the city and for the Central Rada to be re-organized 'along the same lines as the soviets are based.'[96]

Overall this conjuncture demonstrated a radical evolution in working class opinion on the national question.[97] But neither the fractious Bolsheviks nor their leadership in Russia were unified around such a reform perspective from within the Ukrainian Peoples Republic.[98] Their approach failed to take account of Ukrainian peculiarities, Pavlo Khrystiuk a leader of the UPSR considered the organic development of the revolution in Ukraine was incomprehensible to the Russian Bolsheviks, once something was done in Russia it had to be transferred in that same form to Ukraine:

> Such a complete negation of the Ukrainian people as such, a negation of the national revolutionary gains of Ukrainian workers, peasants and soldiers and of the unique forms of revolutionary organization forged by them and intended not only for the national-political, but also for the socio-economic struggle, forms that flowed out of the peculiarities of Ukraine's socio-eco-

nomic structure--this negation was simply repugnant and endlessly exasperating for all Ukrainian revolutionary democrats, including the most left-wing elements among them, who already advocated a socialist revolution.[99]

The war that unfolded between the Central Rada and the Council of Peoples Commissars is portrayed particularly by contemporary Ukrainian state/nationalist historiography in binary terms as one of Bolshevik aggression on the part of Russia. However the Russo-Ukrainian war is one aspect of a multifaceted conflict, this saw an external conflict between the governments in Petrograd and Kyiv, and also an internal conflict resulting in a tendency to fragmentation within the revolutionary process in Ukraine itself.

4. The Tragedy of the Russo-Ukrainian War

The ousted rulers of Russia did not resign themselves to the October Revolution, resistance to the efforts of the Council of Peoples Commissars, the government headed by Lenin; began almost immediately. The scope, character and forms of this resistance varied as the Civil War unfolded, it was in this context that the relations between the Central Rada and the Council of Peoples Commissars is set.

In September 1917 the Rada had hosted a Congress of Oppressed Peoples from across the Russian Empire, this anti-colonial assembly called for a new federal republic.[100] This was in continuity with the approach of the Ukrainian movement and the socialists of the subject nations of the Empire since they first emerged in the 19th century. Adhering to this view the Rada had not recognized the new government in Petrograd considering it could not claim authority across the entire Empire, whose peoples were in the process of realizing their self-determination. They advocated a coalition socialist government, federal in character, composed of representatives of the national republics. Set in the context of unfolding conflict within Russia itself it was an unrealizable project which imagined such potentially irreconcilable forces could be combined. Inevitably it drew the Ukrainian Republic into a collision with one or the other of them.

The Rada and its General Secretariat were beset with further difficulties with Petrograd. The local branches of the state bank were exhausting their currency as result of the withholding of shipments of currency by Petrograd. The entire salaried workforce in Ukraine faced total loss of pay. In turn the General Secretariat was restricting export of much needed grain and fuel north until the Bolsheviks agreed the shipment of the gold-backed currency for the banks.

The General Secretariat was also facing tensions with regard to the Ukrainian soldiers stationed in Russia who were demanding the Rada negotiate with the Bolsheviks for their return to Ukraine. This was a continuation of the movement for self-organized Ukrainian units, which even some Soviet historians recognize as a manifestation of the liberation movement of the Ukrainian people. The attitude of the Council of People's Commissars to the Ukrainian People's Republic over this was initially conciliatory. In particular, Ukrainian soldiers from the Guards regiments in Petrograd — Volyn, Pavlovsky, Izmaylovsky, Semenovsky who had participated in the revolutionary events — were formed into the Taras Shevchenko regiment and sent to Kyiv in November. Another part of the Petrograd garrison, the Serdyuk Regiment was formed, and sent to Katerynoslav in early December. If this and other steps indicated efforts at rapprochement they were contradicted by other steps on the frontline.

The Decree on Peace was a central pledge of the Bolshevik government; a full ceasefire was secured on 22 November. However, On 1 December Symon Petlyura UNR Secretary for Military Affairs issued an order forbidding Ukrainian troops on all fronts to carry out the orders of the People's Commissars of Petrograd and to not adhere to the truce.[101] Considering the cry for peace by the Ukrainian soldiers' movement this seems an astounding command, whose execution, if it had been executed, would have undermined the ceasefire across the Eastern front. Petlyura himself was subsequently dismissed from his post by the Mala Rada.

The position of the Peoples Commissar for Foreign Affairs Trotsky published in November 23 in *Izvestia* proposed to accept a representative of the UNR in the delegation to the peace negotiations with Central Powers, approving of the transfer of Ukrainian soldiers from Russia, emphasizing:

> The Ukrainian working masses must in fact understand, that the All-Russian Soviet government will not create any difficulties for the self-determination of Ukraine, whatever forms it may take, and that the Russian government recognizes the Ukrainian Peoples Republic completely and most sincerely.[102]

Discussions continued between Petrograd and Kyiv but by early December relations between them approached an open breach. The Rada finally decided to enter into direct armistice negotiations with the Central Powers. The Russians agreed to recognize the UNR in the talks and the Central Rada as the government, the Russian then disagreed with the Rada over goals. The UNR considered the war lost, sought peace and recognition of unified Ukraine. Trotsky sought to buy time for a revolution in the west to erupt whilst preserving the Soviet government.

Another source of division was the still born effort to create a new central federal government. Practically the only response to the General Secretariat came from the Don Cossack government under General Kaledin. The futility of this endeavor was plain; these Cossack forces were part of a privileged military caste developed as a pillar of the Romanov Empire. The All-Russian Cossack Congress had already opposed the Rada's First *Universal* declaring autonomy. The USDRP had published an appeal by workers to the Central Rada over repression in Rostov and Ukraine's Donbas by Kaledin's forces.[103]

Nonetheless, the General Secretariat did not seek to halt the passage of Cossack divisions through Ukraine to the Don. An appeal by the head of the General Secretariat Vynnychenko refuted criticism declaring it was "recognizing the right of the People's Commissars in Great Russia, as well as that of the Cossacks in the Don region, in Kuban, and in all other lands to manage their own life". It would not be just to hold back either Cossacks, Russian or Ukrainian units who wished to return home. In accordance with this position the General Secretariat declared neutrality in the struggle between the Bolsheviks and the Kaledin, and refused the Bolshevik troops passage to the Don.

Ukrainian soldiers could reasonably question why they had to wait in trenches, ordered by Petlyura to stay at their post, yet the Cossacks divisions could return home. Indeed only in October the All-Ukrainian Military Congress had took a negative stance toward the Cossack Congress being held in Kyiv, supported the Rada rejecting the Cossack proposal of a common struggle against the Bolsheviks and fought alongside the Bolshevik units. A meeting of the Military Revolutionary Committee of the South-Western Front stated in a resolution:

> Given the established fact of the counter-revolutionary movement on the Don and taking into account the fact that the Ukrainian Central Rada contributes to the sending of the Cossack units to the Don, thereby strengthening the counter-revolution, helping to organize desertion from the front and demoralizing other parts, the MRC strongly demands that the Ukrainian Rada cease the passage Cossack parts on the Don and do not interfere with the advancement of the Soviet units.[104]

Vynnychenko in a declaration had made a de facto recognition by the Central Rada of the Council of People's Commissars as the government in Russia and it may have served as the basis of a rapprochement. The general tendency of the Ukrainian Republic was closer to the Bolshevik/Left-SR government than the reactionary Don Cossack regime. But this was not appreciated by the Russian Bolsheviks who impatiently hastened war with the Central Rada with an aggressive strategy to replace it.

5. The War within the Ukrainian Peoples Republic

The mounting militancy of the workers and peasants was reflected in the two major Ukrainian socialist parties the USDRP and UPSR. But this was not a factor the Bolsheviks in Ukraine or the government in Petrograd seemed to consider when shaping their tactics. The UPSR's Congress at the end of November put forward a radical program for immediate implementation by the Central Rada and General Secretariat, from abolishing private property in land to state-worker control over factory production. The UPSR saw no need to re-elect the Central Rada due to the impending transfer of power to the Constituent Assembly of Ukraine. Alongside it, the Central Rada was to convene an all Ukrainian congress of re-elected councils of workers', soldiers peasants deputies 'for the further systematic development of the class struggle in Ukraine'.

This program advanced by the largest party in Ukraine at that time represented a significant and organic development of the revolution. But as Maistrenko records the Bolsheviks continued to act separately in a sectarian manner, they were not prepared to wait but set out to convene their own congress of soviets with a view to displacing the Rada. This agitation exacerbated relations between the Central Rada and the Council of Peoples Commissars, provoking a defensive response even by the Ukrainian left-wing currents. It was viewed as an encroachment on the Ukrainian Republic they had just created. The Central Rada could feel strengthened by the popular mandate it received in the elections to the All-Russian Constituent Assembly. The results illustrated the popular base of the Ukrainian movement less than three weeks after the October Revolution. The Ukrainian socialist parties secured a decisive electoral victory:

Table 5   Extract of All-Russian Constituent Assembly Returns, 1917[105]

Province	Ukrainian Socialist Bloc	RSDRP Bolshevik	Russian Socialist Revolutionaries
Kyiv	1,256,271	59,413	19,201
Poltava	749,860	64,460	198,437*
Podolia	656,116	27,540	10,170
Volhynia	569,044	35,612	27,575
Katerynoslav	556,012	213,163	231,717
Chernihiv	484,456	271,174	105,565
Kherson	114,000	95,000	493,000*
Kharkiv		114,743	795,558*

* Ukrainian Party of Socialist Revolutionaries and Party of Socialist Revolutionaries (Russian) Bloc.

In Poltava province, the UPSR gained 80.5 per cent of the vote; whilst in Katerynoslav the most industrialized province with a large Russian populace, the Ukrainian socialist bloc secured 46.6 per cent of the vote. Overall out of a total poll of 7.6 million votes cast the Ukrainian parties gained 53 per cent of the popular vote, the Bolsheviks 10 per cent, Russian SR's 18.3 per cent and the Mensheviks 1.3. per cent.[106] The elections further illustrated the divergence cutting through Ukraine. Whilst 55 per cent of votes cast outside the ten largest cities went to the Ukrainian parties, in the cities the results were divided with the Ukrainian parties outvoted by the combined total of other groups.[107]

In his later analysis, Lenin emphasized that the Ukrainian socialists had not only secured large votes in the army on the South-Western and Rumanian fronts but in Ukraine as a whole "the Ukrainian Socialist-Revolutionaries and socialists polled a majority", concluding that "to ignore the importance of the national question in Ukraine.....is a great and dangerous mistake."[108] A restatement of this fact is pertinent in face of contemporary historical revisionism, symptomatic is Andrew Murray, a prominent figure in British labor who (ignoring 1917 completely) claims "the Ukrainian idea gave birth to three separate short lived republics between 1918 and 1921, statelets which made up for their considerable deficiency in mass support by the sponsorship of foreign powers"[109] Reality was otherwise.[110]

The Constituent Assembly elections highlighted that frustration with the Central Rada did not automatically translate into a rejection of the Ukrainian cause itself. It was also a triumph for socialism in Ukraine, and particularly the socialists closest to the Ukrainian peasant majority then promoting a radical turn.

It should however be noted that the period between these elections and those to the Ukrainian Constituent Assembly less than two months after, revealed a swing towards the Bolsheviks is parts of Ukraine. In Chernihiv province the SR vote dropped from 50.7 per cent to 14.6, conversely the Bolshevik vote increased from 34.6 per cent to 56.3 per cent.[111] Though whilst the overall results were disrupted by conflict, 171 of 301 deputies elected in regions that voted still saw a 70 percent vote for Ukrainian socialists and 10 percent for RSDRP(b).

The Bolsheviks were not unduly perturbed by election returns and looked rather to an All-Ukrainian Congress of Soviets to secure a popular mandate for power. The agitation of the Bolsheviks for the election of a new Central Rada and convening of a congress of soviets was increasingly seen as only measures auxiliary to the armed seizure of power. It did not go unnoticed that the RSDRP(b) had taken little part in the Central Rada, they had been indifferent and in areas hostile to the quest for national emancipation. Now without waiting for the organic development of the Ukrainian Revolution, without co-operating with the Ukrainian socialist parties, a section of the Bolsheviks simply set about convening their own congress of soviets in Kyiv on 4 December 1917.

On the ground conflict was already brewing with Symon Petlyura acting virtually at his own accord disarming Red Guards and workers militias, attempting to disperse workers and soldiers' councils. The USDRP acted to have Petlyura removed from the post of Secretary of Military Affairs, though he continued with his own agenda in Left-Bank Ukraine.[112]

A valuable insight as to how it was that two governments led by socialists could find themselves at war with each other is provided by an article by the USDRP in their paper *Robitnycha Hazeta* on their differences with the RSDRP(b):

> Until now, in many claims, we were aligned with the Bolsheviks. We and they have tried and are seeking immediate peace, redistribute landlords and other lands into the hands of our poor peasantry. We and they struggled and struggle for control over industry, and the division of products, for maximum taxation of large property and capital. We and they were against agreement of democracy with wealthy classes, against the coalition ministry, for the transition of power in the country and the state to the hands of revolutionary democracy, which alone can resolutely and boldly fundamental social and economic reforms, etc.
> Even then, when it seemed we were moving in one front against our common enemies, we never lost the way, we stood for a Ukrainian Democratic Republic and Federation (Union) with the other areas of Russia. They were totally against our aspiration. We, as ones expressing the interests of the Ukrainian proletariat , first in the history of the Ukrainian revolutionary movement, stood up for a revolutionary struggle for national liberation and national development of the whole Ukrainian people. Up to this time they, if not openly hostile, they were altogether indifferent to the vital national-cultural and political needs of our people and our proletariat.

> Our differences were always great. But now these political differences have stood out clearly. They became the agenda for the political struggle in Ukraine. And we have to fix the boundaries. Ukrainian social-democracy cannot stand on the position of the Bolsheviks in the matter of the organization of state power in Ukraine. We, all our people, in revolution created the Central Organ of all the real revolutionary workers democracy of Ukraine, the Ukrainian Central Rada. By our own strength, the strength of our peasantry, workers and soldiers. We created for it unheard-of strength and might. We created out of it a centre not only of national, but also of political existence, we tied up with it all our hopes and yearnings of the working people of Ukraine. We protected it from the harshest blows, which the counter-revolutionary and imperialist Great-Russian bourgeoisie wanted to inflict on the Central Rada But in the heaviest hours of the organized democracy, the Bolsheviks were not with us; they were in the enemy camp. In the hours of a hardest counter-revolutionary attack on Ukraine, the Bolsheviks did not stand decisively for the defense of Ukraine, for the support and the strengthening of the Central Rada. They were silent, and by this itself, they were in the enemy camp. Because they are centralists, because they are against the Ukrainian democratic republic, because they are against the Federation. We know well all the inadequacies of the organization of the Central Rada. But we decidedly must say that the Rada was organized by the workers, peasants and soldiers in their own congresses, that the Rada was composed almost entirely out of representatives of these classes.
> We know all the inadequacies of our General Secretariat. It did not satisfy all the needs and hopes of our workers democracy. Strong fetters of the Provisional government and the hostility from Russian democracy put a brake on all the work of the General Secretariat. But when all the fetters fell, when their hands were untied, when the enemies were overcome, and overcome by the forces of the same Ukrainian democracy which in Kyiv had defended the Bolsheviks from a decisive bloody defeat, now we were standing on the road of creative workers-power work. At that very moment the Bolsheviks unexpectedly proclaimed a struggle against the Central Rada, revealing the real thoughts which they had up till then concealed, their real relation to the matter of national rebirth of our people.
> Against the Rada, they would set up the power of the Soviet of Workers and Soldiers Deputies". At this moment, when the Rada and the Secretariat begin immediately to convene the Ukrainian Constituent Assembly, when, after a short time, the Constituent Assembly of Ukraine will take the place of the Rada, at this time the Bolsheviks will convene their Regional Congress of Workers', Soldiers' and Peasants' Deputies of the Organization of Power on Ukraine.' Consequently, this Congress would be against the Central Rada. Against this Congress, we put the slogan of the Constituent Assembly of Ukraine.[113]

The approximately three hundred soviets in Ukraine however were not at all unified behind the Bolsheviks approach.[114] Councils of workers', soldiers' and peasants' deputies had emerged in Ukraine in March, and by the end of 1917 these new revolutionary authorities had been created in all large and small cities of Ukraine and many villages. Certain Bolsheviks and later Soviet historians contended that in December 1917 no soviets supported the Central Rada, reality however was more complex.[115] Workers councils and some district and provincial congresses of the Soviets of Peasants' Deputies did support the Central Rada whilst simultaneously demanding the implementation of the Lenin government's Decrees on Peace and Land. However, in the Councils of Workers 'and Soldiers' Deputies in the winter of 1917-1918, the leadership in the majority transferred to the Bolsheviks and Left Socialist Revolutionaries through re-elections. Yet the All-Ukrainian Congress held on 4 December 1917 proved to be a strategic catastrophe for the Bolsheviks.

The RSDRP(b) was not united on the issue of the congress itself, the Russophile 'Kateynoslav current' of the RSDRP(b), ignoring the populace around them considered the industrial regions not part of Ukraine. They convened a rival congress of soviets of Kryvyi-Rih and Donets Basin in Kharkiv. As result a large number of soviets ignored the invitation to the congress in Kyiv. Nevertheless soviets of key centers were represented, however the efforts of the Bolsheviks to ensure authority of the urban soviet delegates failed when the Central Rada took over the congress mandating commission. The Central Rada sent about 2,000 of its supporters to the congress 670 peasants and 905 from the military.[116]

Indicative of feelings on the eve of the Congress was the recollection of Yukhym Medvedev leader of the Kharkiv organization of left Ukrainian Social Democrats. On the train journey from Kharkiv to Kyiv there were many delegates from Ukrainian regiments, unions and other bodies—some sang revolutionary songs and others national, their revolutionary unity almost turned to violence when they began discussing political topics—they had not even reached the congress yet.[117]

The USDRP pre-meeting of 40 delegates to the congress voted overwhelmingly for the need for cooperation with the Bolsheviks and the organization of workers 'and peasants' power—only three voted against.[118] When Porsh arrived he was hostile to this decision and Vynnychenko appealed to them to avoid a split, the resolution by Medvedev were taken over by some USDRP leaders and disappeared. At the congress the Ukrainian SR Arkady Stepanenko took the chair from the Bolsheviks who lost control of the event they had convened.[119]

The whole event was ignited by a surprise ultimatum from the Council of People's Commissars to the Central Rada. Not only were the leading organs of soviet power in Russia unaware of this but neither were the Bolsheviks in Ukraine who were left embarrassed.[120] The Russian government whilst recognizing the Ukrainian Peoples Republic charged it with 'conducting behind a screen of national phrases, a double-dealing bourgeois policy', disarming soviet troops whilst giving Don Cossack troops passage yet denying transit to anti-Kaledin troops.[121] The ultimatum caused uproar; the Congress accused the Council of People's Commissars of hypocrisy, 'the Commissars permit self-determination only for their own party, while all other groups of peoples and nations they, like the tsarist government, want to keep in subjugation by armed force.'

In an atmosphere of recriminations the Congress expressed its complete support for the Central Rada and appealed to Russian workers soldiers and peasants not to allow such a war on Ukraine. What followed the congress of soviets was increased internal fragmentation, with two rival bodies claiming the government of the Ukrainian Peoples Republic. In the end 124 delegates representing 41 soviets, left in protest and moved to Kharkiv, a city which was instructive of the overall complexity and fluidity of the revolutionary process in Ukraine.

There the Mensheviks, Russian SR's and also the Ukrainian Social Democrats and Social Revolutionaries who were organized in the Kharkiv Free Ukrainian Rada, were all on the left of their organizations. Workers power was established in the city in October through a Kharkiv Province Military Revolutionary Committee as a 'union of all the revolutionary-democratic forces', with red guards and workers militias upholding it.

Unity was undermined in November when the RSDRP(b) gained greater influence in the soviet executive. Joined by a section of Ukrainian socialists the Kharkiv Soviet recognized the Petrograd government, welcomed the proclaiming of the Ukrainian Peoples Republic and called for the re-election of the Central Rada by a congress of soviets, and also the Ukrainian Constituent Assembly. There was however no desire for bloodshed between the local Ukrainian forces and Bolsheviks, the arrival of troops from Russia changed this. On 9 December these forces intervened and carried out an armed seizure of power which saw Bolshevik control established.[122]

In Kharkiv the delegates from soviets of the Kryvyi-Rih and Donets Basin combined with those from Kyiv in a new Congress of Soviets on 11 December. Representing 82 soviets, little more than a third of the 240 soviets in Ukraine the congress 'assumed full state power in the Ukrainian People's Republic' and declared the Government of Ukraine as the People's Secretariat, appointed by the Central Executive Committee elected by the congress.

Prominent in this first soviet government were a number of ethnic Ukrainian Bolsheviks such as Vasyl Shakhray, Mykola Skrypnyk and others also supportive of the Ukrainian self-government such Yury Lapchinsky. It also included a radical left split from the USDRP, the USDRP(left) led by Yevhen Neronovych and Yefim Medvedev who was head of the CEC. The congress in its declaration considered the Russo-Ukraine conflict 'a war the working masses did not want'.[123] In this they were right. However many at the time and later historians viewed the Peoples Secretariat as no more than camouflage for Russia's war on Ukraine. It is certainly true that Russia's recognition of the Kharkiv government was used to justify military intervention, it is nevertheless a fact that the first soviet government was established internally, it was not an appointment of Russia. The Secretary for Military Affairs Shakhray wrote:

> When open, armed struggle with the Central Rada began, Bolsheviks from all parts of Ukraine (its borders designated by the 3rd *Universal*) were of one mind in proposing that a Soviet centre should be established in Ukraine in opposition to the Central Rada, and not one responsible member of this party ventured to protest against the proclamation and establishment of the Ukrain-

ian People's Republic. On the contrary, in complete agreement with the programmatic demand of the right of every nation to self-determination, they openly or at least tacitly recognized this new republic, accepted it as a fact, stood on its ground. The will of the Ukrainian nation emerged, the Ukrainian people separated into a Republic in federative union with other parts of Russia. Good! We in this Republic will conduct a struggle for power not against the Ukrainian People's Republic, not against the Ukrainian people, not in order to strangle it. No! This will be a struggle within the Ukrainian People's Republic for power --this will be a class struggle....[124]

The emergence the Peoples Secretariat was not the only expression of strength of the radical left at this time, Maistrenko records that from within the Central Rada moves took place to replace the government of the Ukrainian Peoples Republic. This is a revealing episode of the strength of support for the emergent Borotbisty, for whilst nationalist historiography emphasizes the democratic mandate of the Central Rada from the Constituent Assembly elections, it ignores just who was elected.

The UPSR's had emerged as the most popular party, of the 120 deputies elected from Ukraine the UPSR formed a faction of 81 deputies in the Russian Constituent Assembly.[125] In their ranks it was the left-wing current, the future Borotbisty who predominated; one of a number of indicators that they had secured broad support amongst the Ukrainian masses.[126] After the dissolution of the Constituent Assembly by the Bolsheviks, these Left UPSR deputies returned to Kyiv aiming to establish a new government with the left-wing of the USDRP. Their plan was discovered and six UPSR leaders arrested and the UPSR left excluded from the Rada.[127]

None of this strengthened the position of the Central Rada which was facing an existential crisis. Soviet power was established in one town after another, province by province, Kharkiv, then Katerynoslav then Poltava. To see this solely as an 'invasion' is an erroneous portrayal. Local Red Guards, workers militias and Ukrainian soldiers actively carried through uprisings of the local population. An array of Ukrainian regiments either remained neutral or participated in the rebellions. A distinct regiment of Red Cossacks was organized by Shakhray and Vitaly Primakov from Ukrainian soldiers and workers growing to three thousand strong.

Russia deployed to Ukraine a ten thousand strong force under the command of Vladimir Antonov-Ovseyenko. Both Soviet and state-nationalist historiography has shrouded this conflict in mythology, focused on such episodes as the Arsenal Uprising of workers and soldiers and the Ukrainian students who opposed the soviet forces at the Battle of Kruty, in fact the war was one of paradoxes. An explanation for the ease of the Bolshevik victory can be seen in the desertion of about 300,000 peasant-soldiers from Ukrainized regiments, returning to their villages to carry through the agrarian revolution.[128] Others simply sided with Bolsheviks or remained neutral. Vynnychenko wrote that if 'Alexander the Great or Napoleon came to life and wanted to help the Central Rada or General Secretariat, even that would not bring relief', they had failed to grasp the 'spirit of times'.[129]

The Central Rada came out for more radical socialist policies when it declared independence of Ukraine on 9th January, 1918. The Fourth *Universal* declaring for 'the socialization of the land' and 'Forests, waters and all mineral resources -- the wealth of the Ukrainian working people -- are transferred to the jurisdiction of the Ukrainian People's Republic'. But the announced formation of 'a people's militia' to fight 'all enemies of the peasants'-workers' Independent Ukrainian Republic' did not change the reality. The Central Rada was unable to muster troops for its defense, it was not so much defeated by military forces as undermined by its own policies.[130] As Vsevolod Holubnychy concluded: 'This reminds one of Lypynsky's comment that the 'Ukrainian socialist parties "gave away" the land "in order to be politically popular". Unfortunately they did not give away enough therefore were not sufficiently popular. And in this way they failed, while Lenin succeeded.'[131]

Soviet troops swept across Ukraine from Kharkiv taking Kyiv on 26 January 1918. By this point however the Ukrainian Revolution was already in a malaise and the role of Soviet Russia and the Central Powers in Ukraine deepened it through the substitution of internal elements by external forces, the revolution consumed itself.

The Peoples Secretariat having proclaimed itself the sovereign government of the Ukrainian republic, soon discovered this was not a view shared by Russia or its emissaries. The view of Petrograd was of a subordinate relationship of Ukraine to Russia, the views harbored by some leading Bolsheviks towards Ukraine are revealed in a telegram sent by Stalin the Peoples Commissar for Nationalities: 'Enough playing at a government and republic. It's time to drop that game; enough is enough'.[132]

The commander of soviet forces that advanced on Kyiv was the anti-Ukrainian N.A. Muravyov who refused to accept the authority of the Peoples Secretariat which he viewed as guilty of 'narrow nationalism'. Antonov recorded that in Poltava Muravyov adopted 'the tone of a conqueror, and entered into a sharp conflict with the local soviet and roused all the Ukrainians against him.'[133]

The Peoples Secretariat was further undermined from within the ranks of the RSDRP(b) itself, no sooner had the People Secretariat set up in Kyiv when a **Donets-Kryvyi Rih Soviet Republic** was proclaimed separate from Ukraine led by Artem. The RSDRP(b) took a similar divisive approach towards Ukraine with the formation of an Odessa Soviet Republic and a Taurida Soviet Socialist Republic in Crimea. This divisiveness lasted until a Second All-Ukraine Congress of Soviets held in Katerynoslav in March 1918 declared it part of Ukraine. A fact overlooked by the contemporary supporters of the so-called Donetsk Peoples Republic.

This Russian chauvinism within the forces deployed in Ukraine gave the conflict the character of a Russo-Ukrainian war over and above the actuality of the crushing of autonomous Ukraine. This impacted on the Ukrainian socialist parties causing anger, divisions and in parts paralysis.

In the Central Rada frustrations and relations reached breaking point just as a mass workers uprising took place in Kyiv the USDRP resigned from the General Secretariat. On 17 January a new Council of Ministers was formed dominated by the centre-right of the Ukrainian Socialist Revolutionaries led by Vsevolod Holubovych. The beleaguered government was now increasingly reliant on military forces such as the Free Cossacks whose conservative leadership was opposed to the socialism of the Rada itself.

Illustrative was the workers uprising in January in Kyiv commonly known as the 'Arsenal Uprising'. It arose from below and was not an elitist Party initiative, raids and terror by the Free Cossacks partly alienated and provoked the rebellion. The 20,000 demobilized soldiers in the City remained neutral. The Sich Riflemen the Rada's most reliable troops formed a soldiers committee and sought an agreement with the Bolshevik revolutionary committee. Only Russian chauvinism of a Bolshevik leader prevented it and ensured their use against the uprising.[134] The uprising was suppressed at great loss of life, 400 insurgents and 300 Rada forces killed, there was over a thousand wounded, all fueling further polarization and resentment. Shortly after Muravyov's forces took Kyiv imposing a mass terror against Russian officers and Ukrainians without distinguishing between supporters of the Rada or soviet rule. An estimated two thousand were executed. The account of Moisei Rafes a leader of the Jewish Bund in Ukraine of the period is damming:

> The ideology of the military leaders of the first Soviet authority in Ukraine could not attract sympathies even of the local adherents of Soviet Power. 'Order No.14' of Muravyov which spoke of freedom he brought 'from the far north' on the blades of bayonets, gave sufficient grounds for talk of an 'occupation socialism'. The violent struggle against the entire Ukrainian people behind whom the Ukrainian CR [Central Rada] was seen, the excesses of the first days, the lack of respect for the local authority – the councils of workers deputies – all this contributed to substantial criticism.'[135]

As Kyiv was poised to fall, lured by the appeal of the Germans the delegation representing the Ukrainian People's Republic signed a separate peace treaty at Brest Litovsk on 27 January 1918. There was a price for the 200,000 German and Austrian troops driving the Bolsheviks out of Ukraine, and it was measured in grain, wool, flax, oil product and other raw materials. The advancing Germans did not occupy all of Ukraine until late April being forced to fight through serious resistance from Red guards and other pro-Soviet forces.

When the Central Rada reconvened in Kyiv it sought to continue as it left off, issuing an appeal stressing all laws and freedoms established by it remained in force. An appeal promised that the Germans "come as our friends and helpers for a short time in order to help us in this difficult moment; they have no intention to change our laws or regulations, [or] to limit the independence and sovereignty of our republic."[136] However German and Austrian forces were soon roaming the countryside requisitioning from the peasantry by force, considering the government of the UNR as unreliable 'left opportunists' the Germans ousted it and installed the conservative Hetman Pavlo Skoropadsky.[137]

Skoropadsky, an aristocratic landlord and former Tsarist officer established an authoritarian 'Ukrainian State' supported by the Union of Landowners and other conservative forces. The government of the Hetmanate included members of the Russian Constitutional Democratic Party and Russian monarchists. Vynnychenko considered the coup d'état 'only completed and crystallized in a precise form that which existed during the time of the Central Rada'; on its return to Kyiv its revolutionary essence was dissipated.[138]

Maistrenko's account of the 'Ukrainian State' brought into being by the German backed coup is particularly valuable in light of the current fashion for the Hetmanate in some quarters.[139] In 2017 large bill posters appeared in Ukraine celebrating Skoropadsky as a hero of the Ukrainian Revolution; he has been praised by both former President Yuschenko and President Poroshenko. This revisionism is airbrushing out of history the actual experience of the Hetmanate, which set about reversing the gains of the revolution, restoring land to the large landlords and factories to the capitalists.[140] The Hetmanate granted "a free hand in trade and raw materials procurement," to the occupying Austro-German forces that set about extracting all they could by force of arms from the countryside.[141] Their brutality discredited the UNR and even more Skoropadsky's Ukrainian State in the eyes of the workers and peasants, who came to view them as foreign occupants and at the very least counter-revolutionary.

The retrogression that gripped Ukraine in 1918 was soon met by a wave of resistance as insurgency spread across the countryside in May and a workers strike wave broke out in July. The Borotbisty basing themselves on the 'revolutionary centers' of workers and peasants set about organizing partisan detachments. This insurgent socialism drew upon the vernacular revolutionary traditions of

Ukraine. During 1918 this popular resistance would cost the German Imperial Army 20,000 dead, a fact largely ignored by Ukrainian's official celebrations of the period.

The consequence of Brest Litovsk was a continuation in Ukraine of the war with the Germans long after Russia concluded peace. The Hetmanate proved to be a defining moment, sharpening the process of differentiation in the Ukrainian revolution. Prior to the final defeat of the Peoples Secretariat a Second All-Ukrainian Congress of Soviets took place in Katerynoslav on 17 March 1918 with 1100 delegates; the congress adopted a declaration of independence of the Ukrainian Republic. This confirmed an important landmark as regards the trend of the Ukrainian Revolution, with both authoritative bodies in Ukraine the Central Rada and Central Executive Committee of soviets having come to the position of an independent Ukraine.[142] At the same time in the eyes of many workers and peasants an alternative articulation of national emancipation was now necessary.

The Brest-Litovsk treaty cut Ukraine off from events in Russia, sheltering it from the excesses of 'War Communism' and the erosion of soviet democracy in sharp contrast the idea of soviet power as an expression of the workers and peasants' self-organization thrived in Ukraine. It was an idea carried forward by a diverse current that stood on a soviet platform and sought to realize it within an 'independent Ukrainian socialist republic'. This current included the UPSR (Borotbists), the USDRP (Independents) and the current of Bolsheviks represented by such figures as Shakhray, Mazlakh, and the Federalist Opposition of Lapchinsky.

Mykhailo Hrushevsky former leader of the Central Rada wrote in 1920 of the Borotbisty that when 'they led an uprising under the slogan of a Ukrainian Republic that would be independent yet Soviet and friendly toward the Bolsheviks and Soviet Russia, the masses flocked to their banner....'[143]

One criticism of the Ukrainian pro-Soviet parties is that whilst the contest remained an internal affair they were defeated by their socialist opponents. The evidence of this is seen in the revival of the Ukrainian Peoples Republic headed by the Directory of

Vynnychenko and Petlyura in November 1918—not the soviet republic they envisaged. That in fact the balance shifted towards soviet parties by the Russian Red Army.[144] This critique relies on the presumption that democratic channels existed for such choices to be freely made when the participatory democracy of 1917 was not revived within the UNR. Instead conservative elements including from the Hetmanate were its inherent partner. It was Petlyura's militarists, who were engaged in pogroms and indiscriminate repression of the labor and peasant movement, who emerged as the face of the revived UNR, not Vynnychenko's "labor principle" or the democracy of the Ukrainian socialists.[145]

The Ukrainian Soviet Socialist Republic could not have attained power in March 1919 without a shift internally. A measure of the decline in the popularity of the Directory was the collapse of its armed forces from over 100,000 in December 1918 to a mere 21,000 in just over a month.[146] Having broadly supported the Directory during the 'November Ukrainian Revolution', the peasants, who were dissatisfied with its policies, rapidly went into opposition. Extensive evidence reveals considerable support for the Borotbisty and pro-soviet currents in their fight with Petlyura's evaporating forces.[147] The Red Army which advanced on Kyiv did so in circumstances in stark contrast to the earlier war with the Central Rada. When Arthur Adams writes that, "Peasant carts carried the Soviet infantry rapidly across the great steppes of the Dnepr's Left Bank", he provides an apt description of this conjuncture.[148]

The situation in spring 1919 could not have been more favorable for a convergence between the Ukrainian and the Russian Revolutions, and reconciliation of the internal elements. The creation of a Ukrainian republic based on councils with a plurality of parties was a viable possibility. Why then despite these favorable circumstances was their conception of Ukraine not fully realized?

An explanation can be found in the antagonism that continued between what Ukrainian Marxists described as the internal and external forces. The tendency of the internal forces was apparent in the struggle of the Central Rada for self-government, in the proclamation of the independent Ukrainian People's Republic; and in the striving to create an independent Soviet Ukraine. In contradiction, the tendency of the external forces strove to subordinate Ukraine to Russia and retard the internal forces.[149] It is an example of a clash between what Hal Draper later described as the democratic 'socialism from below' versus the elitist 'socialism from above'.[150] The agency of this external, 'socialism-from-above' was in this case the Russian Communist Party (Bolsheviks).[151]

This overarching conflict created a dual centre inside Ukraine which caused a state of instability in the revolution. This duality also revealed an inherent weakness of the Borotbisty. Maistrenko writes that though they were "strong in the countryside, they failed in their bid to control the revolutionary movement in the cities, where they were powerless to compete with the Bolshevik influence."[152] But it would be a mistake to believe there was a uniform hostility of urban workers towards the Ukrainian movement. Indeed in May 1918 the All-Ukrainian Workers Congress representing half a million workers, whose delegates were overwhelmingly non-Ukrainian, favored a struggle for "an independent Ukrainian People's Republic".[153]

In tracing the fate of the Borotbisty, Maistrenko introduces the reader to a pivotal aspect of the revolution which has been surprisingly overlooked by labor historians. In 1919 the crisis that arose after the First World War was at its peak, the "whole existing order" wrote British Prime Minister Lloyd George "is questioned by the masses from one end of Europe to the other". In Hungary a social democrat-communist alliance proclaimed a Soviet Republic, followed by the Bavarian Soviet Republic and in June the Slovak Soviet Republic. The Ukrainian question became a decisive factor in helping decide their fate for it was a bridge to the resurgent European socialism.

The Soviet Republic which was erected in Ukraine was described by the Borotbisty in a complaint to Lenin, as being like an "expansion of a 'red' imperialism (Russian nationalism)", giving the impression that "Soviet power has fallen into the hands of hardened Black Hundreds preparing a counter revolution".[154] Appointed by decision of Moscow, the head of the Soviet government was Christian Rakovsky. Well known for his later opposition to Stalinism his catastrophic rule in Ukraine is understudied and ignored by his biographers.[155] Recently arrived from the Balkans this self-styled specialist on the national question announced that the Ukrainian question barely existed anymore, the peasantry had no national consciousness, and the national movement was simply the invention of the intelligentsia as a means to obtain power.[156] These views of Rakovsky combined with the existing 'left communist' and Russophile currents were a recipe for disaster. The new Constitution of the Ukrainian SSR was never implemented; Ukraine remained, and was considered by the government, a regional unit of Russia.[157] The republic was ruled through appointed committees, soviet power as such did not exist and the pro-soviet Ukrainian, Jewish and non-Bolshevik Russian socialist parties were sidelined by the regime.[158]

Maistrenko wrote that the Bolsheviks had "more chances than the Jacobins to continue the national revolution, in other words to organize the creative impetus of the masses which was directed towards the construction of a new society".[159] One of those chances was in 1919 by the calls for the reconstitution of Soviet Ukraine as a genuinely independent and self-managed republic. This was being demanded not only by the Ukrainian socialists, but the Red Army commander on the Ukrainian front Antonov-Ovseyenko, and significantly by the leadership of the Hungarian Soviet Republic.[160] The appeals of Hungary's leader Bela Kun for an independent Soviet Ukraine with a coalition government of the Borotbisty, USDRP (Independents) and the Bolsheviks was spurned by Rakovsky; prophetically Kun concluded: "Forcing Rakovsky on the Ukrainians against their wish, in my opinion, will be an irreparable mistake".[161]

The experience of this and preceding episodes of the Ukrainian Revolution brings into question what has been a long accepted explanation for the fate of the Russian Revolution: the primary role of external factors in its degeneration and rise of Stalinism. Coupled with this assessment is the contention that unfavorable circumstances imposed on the Bolsheviks a restriction on options available to them. Yet on reading *Borotbism*, can we really agree that this fully explains the fate of the revolution? Even if one accepted the view that the one-party state in Russia arose from lack of Bolshevik allies this cannot explain events in Ukraine. Here the Borotbisty, unlike the Russian Left-SRs, did not go over to open revolt; whilst many of the other socialists who did were in part pushed and in part pulled by a situation created by the Russian Communists themselves. A multi-party democracy based was denied the opportunity to exist in Ukraine. Any objective reader must surely conclude that Lenin's insistence that the Borotbisty be accused of a "counter revolutionary mentality" was without any basis in fact.

For Lenin success of the Bolshevik project was predicated on extending the revolution westward. The entire approach of socialism-from-above in Ukraine contributed to undermining the very perspective on which the October Revolution was based. In the summer of 1919 Bolshevik rule in Ukraine disintegrated, resulting in the occupation of large areas of by the Russian Volunteer Army. The appalling policies and practices of the western backed 'Emergency Government' of General Denikin with its pogroms; repression and chauvinism are rarely recognized. They provide an indictment of the Russian liberal intellectuals who headed its Political Center. Barely distinguishable in their nationalism from the conservatives and militarists, their main objective was the preservation of the "one, indivisible Russia" and the restoration of Russia as a 'great power'.[162]

What is striking about this key juncture is that despite despair with the Rakovsky regime there was not a collapse or decline in support for the pro-soviet parties. Indeed the opposite occurred. In the case of the Borotbisty they witnessed a surge in support. Without the red partisans in Ukraine the Red Army could not have repulsed Denikin's offensive into central Russia.[163]

6. What might have been and legacy of the Borotbisty

In 1920 the depleted, exhausted pro-soviet forces defeated the Russian Volunteer Army and the Polish invasion. The resulting Riga peace treaty re-partitioned Ukraine; five million Ukrainians remained under Polish rule. Maistrenko concludes that the "struggle for a sovereign Ukrainian SSR was decided in the negative not by the internal development of Ukrainian political life but by the external pressure of administrative organization."[164] But the failure to establish a fully independent Ukraine in 1920 is neither the end of the history of the Borotbisty nor would it provide an adequate assessment of the Ukrainian Revolution. The dialectics of the revolution resulted in what Bojcun describes as "less than the Ukrainian socialists wanted to win. Yet it was more than the Russian socialists had been willing to concede."[165]

Prior to 1917 there existed only 'southern Russia'. The revolution had swept away the old social order and forged the Ukrainian SSR, a "clearly defined national, economic and cultural organism".[166] It became the framework for a significant struggle between the centralist Russophile element, and the '*Universal* current' of Ukrainian communists. Those communists of the oppressed nations succeeded securing the policy of *korenizatsiia* (indigenization) a program of 'positive action'. Whilst this gain was fragile, Ukrainization heralded an unprecedented national renaissance in the 1920's.

Prominent ex-Borotbisty energetically carried forward Ukrainization viewed as a "weapon of cultural revolution in Ukraine".[167] Maistrenko places this "final expression" of the Borotbisty in the context of the then intense conflict to shape the USSR. As such Ukrainization was not only the engine of efforts to assert autonomy and liquidate the vestiges of colonialism but a manifestation of opposition to ascendant Stalinism.[168] It brought "the Ukrainian people to the threshold of nationhood by the end of the decade".[169] But the dynamics of Stalinist centralism and its inherent partner Russian chauvinism destroyed the last vestiges of equality between the republics. The Ukrainian communists and intelligentsia were annihilated.

The reader of Maistrenko's *Borotbism* cannot but be moved by what is an historical tragedy and provoked by the questions that it poses to long accepted explanations of the fate of the revolution.

The Russian Bolsheviks were invariably dominated by the erroneous belief that the October Revolution demonstrated once and for all the path that every subsequent revolution must follow. They operated on the mistaken assumption that their model in some sense represented the prototype for socialist transformation, and they held to the utterly unfounded conviction that if only others had a communist party based on their democratic centralist model and under their authority. It was a model that was rejected by virtually all of classical Marxism and of social democracy in the Russian Empire. The consequence was a thoroughly sectarian attitude to the Ukrainian Revolution and other parties who were eventually destroyed. Socialism was re-defined as rule by "the party" rather than rule by the working class.

The contrast between the revolutionary cooperation of the socialists of the empire in 1905 and experience of 1917–1921 is stark. From the 1870s when Ukrainian social democracy had emerged to 1917, socialism in Ukraine had grown from a few intellectuals to nationwide dimensions. If the Ukrainian Revolution had developed organically unimpeded by other forces it would have inevitably seen the Ukrainian People Republic under the leadership of the radicals of the Ukrainian Socialist Revolutionaries and Ukrainian Social Democracy. If the Russian centralism of the Lenin government and sectarian character of the Bolsheviks had not prevented constructive participation in the Ukrainian Revolution, they would have enhanced this process and reinforced the formation of the Ukrainian republic. The division between peasantry and the urban working class could have been transcended, the pioneering Jewish National Autonomy would have continued to develop and Ukraine's Jewish community may have been spared the tragedy which was to follow.

The question of what might have been opens up many possibilities, Ukrainian socialism was not absorbed and marginalized by Ukrainian nationalism it was destroyed by external forces. A fate shared by Jewish, Polish and other sections of Russian socialism. The Bolsheviks endeavor to found their own Communist Party of Ukraine became a maneuver, a sub-unit of the Russian Communist Party. The CP(b)U far from representing a culmination of previous developments within the socialist parties in Ukraine was instead an artificial creation. The objective effect of the formation of the CP(b)U and a one party-state model imposed on Ukraine was the destruction of the entire previous socialist tradition which the Borotbisty was part. We may recall a neglected speech in Zurich in 1914 where Lenin had said:

> What Ireland was for England, Ukraine has become for Russia: exploited in the extreme, and getting nothing in return. Thus the interests of the world proletariat in general and the Russian proletariat in particular require that the Ukraine regains its independence.[170]

How well Lenin should have remembered Marx's statement that "the English Republic under Cromwell met shipwreck in Ireland. This shall not happen twice!" It did, in Russia's Ireland.[171]

Illustrations

Above, a picture from 1910 of the Maistrenko family, Ivan third from right aged 11. Below, Zina and Ivan in the revolutionary period.

Above left: Maistrenko with Volodymyr Vynnychenko in France in 1951. Above right: The URDP's *Nasha Borotba* [Our Struggle] which published Maistrenko's *Bolshevist Bonapartism*, which was published in English in 1948. Below right: *Vpered* [Forward] carried regular articles by Maistrenko.

Introduction 73

Left, Maistrenko's NKVD form releasing him from prison. Above, Maistrenko (far-left) with the Bandura band during World War Two. Below, Maistrenko with Hryhory Kostiuk after the war.

Biographical Sketch of Ivan Maistrenko

Ivan Vasylyovych Maystrenko (1899–1984), also known under the pseudonyms of Dalekyi, Zernytsky and Babenko, was born in Opishnya in Poltava region of Ukraine.

In Opishnya almost all of the population was of Cossack descent, Ivan's graduation certificate from school read "Ivan Maistrensko, son of a Cossack".[172] His parents were of Cossack ancestry from the Zinkivskyi district of Poltava, his mother Ulyana Lukivna was from a better off family in the village of Mali Budyshcha. Ivan's grandfather, Sava, was a landless rural weaver whose son Jacob managed to become a parish clerk, he in turn was able to assist Ivan's father Vasyl. Thanks to this, he succeeded in gaining the post of the manager of the state vodka store; this enabled him to ensure his children were educated in gymnasiums (general-education secondary schools) and seminaries. Nine of the children grew up (three others died when young), Ivan was the fifth.

In his memoirs *The History of my Generation* Maistrenko saw his own family as an illustration of the changed pre-revolutionary and new post-revolutionary life. His elder sister Halya epitomized the pre-revolutionary generation, being educated in a Tsarist school, linguistically Russian, admiring Russian cultural figures.[173] In contrast his younger brother Jacob influenced by the revolutionary age became a Ukrainian writer in Kyiv. His sister Marusya became a passionate Ukrainian patriot and at the age of twenty seven fell in the violent turmoil of the national rebirth in Poltava in 1920.[174]

After graduating from High School in 1914, Maistrenko entered the M.Gogol Teacher's Seminary in the village of Velyki Sorochyntsi, it was here that he began political activity becoming acquainted with illegal literature and joining the underground Socialist Youth Union—which had centers in Poltava and Kharkiv regions. The organizer of this circle was the future Borotbist leader Andriy Zalivychy, a prominent figure in the Ukrainian Revolution and a founder of the Ukrainian Party of Socialist Revolutionaries in 1917.[175] In December 1915 the Tsarist authorities broke up the young socialist organization, arresting Zalivychy.

After the overthrow of Tsar, the seventeen year old Maistrenko took an active part in the revolution. Maistrenko's experience of the revolution was not in the capital Kyiv so often the center of accounts, but in the towns and villages of Poltava gubernia. He was elected to the executive of the local branch of Prosvita, the Ukrainian educational and community association. In Opishnya, Maistrenko became one of the organizers of the local branch of the Ukrainian Party of Socialist Revolutionaries and the All-Ukrainian Peasant Union.[176] At Easter 1917 he was an organizer of the Ukrainian rebirth in Opishnya, where three thousand marched behind a portrait of Taras Shevchenko, with red socialist and blue-and-yellow Ukrainian standards.[177]

Having completed his studies at the seminary in the summer of 1918, Maistrenko became a lecturer-librarian in the village of Drabinovka in Kobelyaky district of Poltava region. At this time officers from the local wealthy families of the area returned from the war, Maistrenko recalled them as typical White Guards with an all-Russian attitude who did not feel themselves as Ukrainian.[178] Maistrenko undertook not only cultural but illegal political activity against the regime of Hetman Skoropadsky and the German occupiers, aligning himself with the radical left of the UPSR who became the Borotbisty in the summer of 1918.[179]

When the uprising against the Hetmanate began, Maistrenko was a member of the local revolutionary committee formed in Kustolivsky, he played an active role in the formation of the 'Kobelyaky Red Republic'.[180] Maistrenko described himself at that time as by 'nature a fanatic and a dreamer, he attempted to reconcile the Ukrainian struggle for national liberation with international communism.'[181] The strong Borotbist organization in Kobelyaky acted autonomously, calling themselves the 'Ukrainian Communist Party' even before the UCP(Borotbisty) was formed, Maistrenko becoming the party secretary of the 'Kobelyaky Communists'.[182]

In the late summer of 1919 as the Russian Volunteer Army under Denikin advanced towards Poltava a Red Partisan regiment was formed by the Kobelyaky Communists in which Maistrenko was appointed political commissar.[183] During autumn and winter of 1919 Maistrenko crossed over the front line on numerous occasions on missions to the Ukrainian socialist underground in areas occupied by the Whites. He had repeated close shaves with the White Guards, on one occasion when his hotel room was searched in Kyiv he managed to use the fact he was wearing a religious medal given as a gift by an uncle who was a monk, to convince them he could not be a communist.[184]

Maistrenko recalled speaking proper Ukrainian was often enough to convince White guards that he was neither a Bolshevik nor a Denikinite, though his ability to speak good Ukrainian did not prevent him being arrested by a Galician regiment of the UNR Army who suspected him of being a White agent. On another trip across enemy lines he often stayed with Jewish families. On one occasion they were frightened at his presence, until he began quietly singing the 'Internationale' to himself, knowing only someone close to the socialist cause would know the song may help reassure his hosts.[185]

In the chaos of the war with the Russian Volunteer Army Maistrenko's regiment became integrated into the Third Galician Corps of the army of the Ukrainian Peoples Republic, and then moved again to an autonomous red partisan unit. On learning this Maistrenko returned to his home of Opishnya, which was under occupation by White forces. At home his brother Petro had sought to convince him that the country needed a strong authority like General Denikin, but he was himself in turn conscripted to the Red Army and became commander of an armored train.[186]

In the last days of the Denikin occupation Maistrenko was living under false identity using the name of a childhood friend Mykola Vasyliev. But his papers lacked a picture. When he went to Poltava to get one taken he was arrested by a White officer from his village who claimed to know the real Vasyliev and recognized Maistrenko as a former member of the revolutionary committee. Under arrest Maistrenko managed to eat his false papers without being seen. The White officer however could not remember Maistrenko's real name, another officer entered who by coincidence was engaged to the sister of the real Vasyliev. This officer too could not remember who Maistrenko really was. Then he was taken before a panel of white officers, two testified he was not Vasyliev, at this point Maistrenko now confessed as to his true identity but insisted he was not a revolutionary. He was then asked to explain his history. Maistrenko explained that many members of his family were students and his older brother was also an army officer. After this he was asked "what are your convictions", to which he answered "I am a Ukrainian". He intentionally did not specify what kind of Ukrainian, whether he was a former Hetmanite supporter, a supporter of the UNR or a Ukrainian communist. To Maistrenko's relief some of the officers cheered with delight, fortunately for him the officers were Ukrainian intelligentsia who had been conscripted by the Volunteer Army. One of them even confessing he had been a Red Partisan commander and could Maistrenko reconnect him with the partisans.[187]

After the retreat of the Volunteer Army from Poltava region Maistrenko returned to Kobelyaky in December 1919 where he was leader of the local organization of the Ukrainian Communist Party (Borotbisty). At that time, the Borotbists enjoyed considerable authority among the Ukrainian population especially in the countryside, and posed a left-wing alternative to Bolshevik hegemony in Soviet Ukraine. At a meeting on February 23, 1920, Maistrenko gave a speech as representative of the UCP(b) in which he accused the CP(b)U of a dishonest policy on the territory of Ukraine, which was the reason for the uprisings in 1919 and the development of counter-revolution led by Denikin.[188]

Following the dissolution of the UCP(b) in March 1920, Maistrenko followed the section of the Borotbists who joined the CP(b)U. This gave him access to Soviet and Party positions and on April 8, 1920, he was elected secretary of the county executive committee of the Soviets.[189] Maistrenko attended the Fourth All-Ukrainian Congress of Soviets in Kharkiv on May 16–20, where his Borotbist views brought him into conflict the Bolshevik leadership. At the CP(b)U pre-congress meeting Maistrenko clashed with Grigory Zinoviev over the Ukrainian national question.[190]

Zinoviev had boasted that an English delegation to Moscow had stated that British workers wanted to join Soviet Russia.

Maistrenko saw this as demagogy and asked Zinoviev to explain whether the British Soviet state would also be part of Soviet Russia. It was clear to Maistrenko that Zinoviev did not believe this and as such why then should Ukraine remain part of Russia.[191] Maistrenko recalled that: "I understood the poverty and actual anti-Marxism of his ideas on the national question. And that is why I felt even more correct on the Ukrainian question."[192]

Maistrenko was already disillusioned with the CP(b)U and during his time in Kharkiv he met with dissident Bolsheviks including Lapchynsky leader of the Federalist Opposition and Kasianenko who had belonged to the USDRP(Left) group in 1917.[193] On July 22, 1920, Maistrenko and his supporters in Kobelyaky resigned from the CP(b)U and joined the Ukrainian Communist Party known as the *Ukapisty*, launched by the left-wing of the Ukrainian Social Democrats.

The Bolshevik leadership retaliated against this growth of the *Ukapisty* in Poltava region resorting to repressive measures. All the 'renegade Bolsheviks' were dismissed from their posts in the Soviet state apparatus. Maistrenko was at the UCP congress in Kharkiv at the time, when he returned as chairman of the Poltava UCP he and another comrade were sent to the Red Army. In response the UCP Central Committee sent a letter requesting his release, not knowing the difference between the UCP and CP(b)U, the commander released Maistrenko immediately.[194]

In the summer of 1920 Maistrenko attended the Second Congress of the UCP in Kharkiv. At this time the UCP had three thousand members which was large for an opposition party in Soviet Ukraine. Maistrenko noted that of the five who had attended the Congress from Kobelyaky, there were two Jewish members. This was unusual as most Jewish communists joined the CP(b)U at the time. Maistrenko recalled the fondness of these Jewish UCP members for him, one of them, Zhuravytsky was the nephew of the pro-independence Bolshevik Serhiy Mazlakh, co-author of the influential *On the Current Situation in Ukraine* with Vasyl Shakhray.[195]

At this time the UCP was a legal party and obtained some support from the Ukrainian SSR government. At the Fourth Congress of Soviets of Ukraine, three members of the UCP Central Committee (Richytsky, Avdiyenko and Mazurenko) were included in the All-Ukrainian Central Executive Committee. Maistrenko was elected as candidate member of the UCP central committee, at this time he changed his pseudonym from Ivan Daleky to Ivan Zernytsky. During 1920–1922 Maistrenko worked for the UCP in Kharkiv, it was period of great hardship with famine in Ukraine arising from drought and crop failure exacerbated by the Soviet government transferring large amounts of grain to Russia. Maistrenko wrote of his impoverished conditions:

> All of us were eating in Kharkiv at the canteens of KCA (Kharkiv Consumers' Association). The dinners were horrible: a soup made of sodden dry cabbage (dry cabbage is extremely unpalatable) and a spoonful of pearl-barley gruel. There was no fat either in borsch or in gruel. I was eating similar soups and gruels in 1930-s in the Siberian imprisonment.[196]

Half-starved Maistrenko was helped by some former Borotbists he knew who got him a job as a secretary at the editorial staff of the CP(B)U Central Committee newspaper *Selyanska Bidnota* [The Poor Peasant] also edited by a former Borotbist.[197] In the winter of 1920-21 Maistrenko became very ill with typhoid fever; insomnia and anxiety haunted him for years. Afterwards he developed paranoid delusions from his earlier witnessing of peasant resistance to grain requisitioning:

> I continued to believe that the insurgents had taken me prisoner and were brutally torturing me. At that time the insurgents were stopping trains going to Kharkiv (especially between Iama and Lyman) escorting communists out of the cars and executing them. The rumour was that when insurgents captured Red Army soldiers carrying out grain requisitioning, they cut the soldiers' bellies open while they were still alive and filled them with grain. Although I was opposed to the Bolshevik government in Ukraine, psychologically I felt on their side at the front; I also had a UCP membership card, and the insurgents certainly did not understand which Communist party was Bolshevik and which one was Ukrainian, just as most Bolsheviks did not.[198]

The UCP Central Committee set itself the task of winning the proletariat of the Donbas to the platform of an independent Soviet Ukraine. Maistenko was sent to the Donets Basin as a Secretary of the UCP provincial committee in Donetsk.[199] The UCP had three party centers in the Donbas: in Luhansk, Yenakiyeve and Bakhmut.[200] Maistrenko's memoir of Luhansk at this time are poignant reminder of that area as a Ukrainian territory:

> Everywhere the UCP committees were quartered in the buildings of "Prosvita". In Luhanske the members of "Prosvita" were mostly also UCP members. Almost all of them were local workers. In Luhanske the majority of population were Ukrainians, but the language spoken in the city was mostly Russian, as well as in Kharkiv. The difference was that many Ukrainian villages surrounded the latter; Luhansk, in addition to the Ukrainian villages, was surrounded by a great deal of coal (mostly anthracite) mines with newly arrived Russian workers (Khrushchev was one of them). The Ukrainian "Prosvita" seemed to me an isle amidst the Russian sea. The fact that the UCP committee was quartered in the "Prosvita" building, had in-depth sense and even certain symbolism. Mostly the workers of Luhanske were the members and visitors of "Prosvita". Many of them were former USDRP members. I say "former" because the USDRP, as a state party of the UNR fighting Bolsheviks, never legally existed in Ukrainian SSR territory. But its members in Luhansk considered themselves to be UNR supporters, though of some Left-wing deviation.[201]

Maistrenko organized in all the UCP centers in Donbas the last that he visited being Yenakiyeve which hosted a large steelworks. He lived there in poverty and to make ends meet he started a job digging ditches for a water supply system then started teaching Ukrainian language at the former gymnasia school as required by the People's Commissariat of Education.[202]

In the late autumn of 1921, Maistrenko returned to Kharkiv. He decided to leave the UCP at the beginning of the policy of Ukrainization and the cultural renaissance; he felt that that the UCP opposition to the New Economic Policy was unjustified in light of the state of the country completely ruined by the war.[203] Maistrenko re-joined the CP(b)U and recalled that:

> Personally I can say about myself, that I have visited all currents of communism in Ukraine: among the Borotbists, in the CP(b)U, in the faction of the federalists (the group of Lapchynsky) in the CP(b)U, in the UCP, finally, again in the CP(b)U. I was later embarrassed for such a youthful changeability. But now I think that it could not have been different. I sought, in the language of Vynnychenko, the complete liberation of the Ukrainian people—national and social.[204]

In 1925, after graduating from the Faculty of Economics of the Kharkiv Institute of National Economy, the Central Committee of the CP(b)U appointed Maistrenko to work on the Party papers *Selyans'ka pravda*, and the Ukrainian language organ of the Central Committee's *Komunist*. Maistrenko was active in taking forward the policy of Ukrainization assisted by his relationship with prominent figures in the Ukrainian cultural renaissance.

In 1929, on the initiative of the Ukrainian Soviet leaders Mykola Skrypnyk and Panas Lyubchenko, Maistrenko was sent to Odessa as deputy editor of the district newspaper *Odesskie Izvestia*. Maistrenko went to great efforts to create, a new Ukrainian newspaper — *Chornomors'ka komuna* [Black Sea Commune] — organ of the Odessa district KP(b)U.[205] The publication of this paper was an event of significance not only in the life of Odesa, but of Ukraine. In September 1930, Maistrenko was appointed editor of the *Chornomors'ka komuna*. Under his leadership this Ukrainian paper expanded into Odessa life its circulation growing from 70 thousand to 140 thousand.[206]

But Maistrenko found his position not without challenges from within the Communist Party itself. To his surprise from former members of the General Jewish Workers Bund who opposed Ukrainization. At the time Skrypnyk was struggling to reduce the number of Russian language schools in the Ukrainian SSR to that proportionate to the Russian population of Ukraine, advocating not only Ukrainian but Jewish schools. This was opposed by former Bundists who advocated Russian language schools for Jewish children. Their grounds of concern were that they did not want Jews closed into a narrow circle, but have access on an all USSR scale. Maistrenko was particularly surprised as the Bund had in the past disagreed with the Bolsheviks on the national question.[207] Maistrenko considered this resistance to Ukrainization by Jewish personnel of the CP(b)U could to a certain extent be explained by Ukrainian anti-Semitism. Maistrenko also emphasised that the years of the NEP and Ukrainization also saw the greatest rapprochement of Ukrainians and Jews particularly in mixed marriages, his brother Stepan moving to Odessa in 1929 to work as a journalist marrying the daughter of the Jewish writer Kvitka.[208]

During the period of Ukrainization Maistrenko played a key role in overcoming the legacy of Tsarist Russification turning Odesa into a cultural center of Ukraine alongside Kyiv and Kharkiv.[209] He created in addition to the newspaper *Trybuna robsel'kora* an illustrated weekly *Shkval*, a monthly literary journal *Metalevi dni*. A leading figure of the renaissance the poet Volodymyr Sosiura described Maistrenko as the 'knight of Ukrainian culture on the Black Sea'.[210] In the end as the overall environment began to change with ever growing Stalinism, the local elite who hated Ukrainization succeeded in having Maistrenko moved from the city.

In April 1931 Maistrenko returned to Kharkiv where the Central Committee of the CP(b)U appointed him to the post of Deputy Director of the All-Ukrainian Communist Institute of Journalism (VUKZH).[211] It was the time of the defeat of Ukrainization, growing Stalinist terror and onset of the 1932–33 'Holodomor', the man-made famine in Ukraine. Maistrenko considered this the era when: "honest communists were sent into exile and unscrupulous careerists and adventurers were promoted, various Krushchevs' and Brezhnevs' placed in leadership positions. They were pushed through the corpses of honest predecessors."[212]

In 1932–33 the famine swept the Ukrainian countryside killing millions of people. Maistrenko was emphatic it should not be forgotten that the famine was organized specially for Ukraine. In his memoirs he pointed out that peasants in the border villages of Russia did not experience the famine, even though they may well be Ukrainian themselves. In contrast Russian villages in Ukraine died of hunger, for example, the "Katsap" village Vasischeva near Kharkiv.[213] Maistrenko wote:

> In Old Cossack Poltava, swollen doctors fell ill in the hospital. And then they were given 300 grams of bread and cereals. A peasant who was arrested for theft received in prison 300 grams of bread and cereals and survived the 1933 famine, and his honest neighbor in the village died of hunger.[214]

Maistrenko sought to express opposition to Stalinism through his lectures on foreign literature by drawing parallels between classical tragedies and the current situation.[215] The use of Shakespeare and Balzac to draw associations with Stalin did not protect Maistrenko from the purges sweeping Ukraine. As a former member of non-Bolshevik parties (Borotbisty and *Ukapisty*) he was a target.[216] At first his case was put to a Commission, but it decided in his favour, then a Party meeting of the students to consider his expulsion from the CP(b)U also failed to expel him.[217] In one sense Maistrenko was content to be expelled as he did not want to be associated with the Stalinist terror, but he also knew expulsion meant arrest and he avoided this. Instead he was issued with a "strict reprimand, with a warning."[218]

The terror caught up with Maistrenko early on a winter morning of December 15, 1936, when a Lieutenant of the NKVD led him away carrying his confiscated books and papers with him. He was sentenced by the Kharkiv Regional Court on May 26, 1937, under Articles 54-10, part 1 of the Criminal Code of the Ukrainian SSR, to four years imprisonment He was not released until December 16, 1940.[219] His elder brother Peter was also imprisoned with him for the crime of making an ideological mistake in an agricultural textbook which he wrote.[220]

In the Kharkiv prison there were two hundred prisoners sharing a cell, sleeping on the floor. Prisoners gave lectures, Maistrenko lectured on Shakespeare's Macbeth; how the king seized the state power from the legitimate heirs; in fear of conspiracy he then murdered these legitimate heirs and all the opposition. His portrayal of Stalin by analogy was obvious.[221]

After two months of detention, the investigation into Maistrenko was handed over to G Bordony — one of the most experienced sub-commanders of the NKVD in Ukraine. However, despite two months of torture Maistrenko did not confess to being part of a 'right-wing nationalist Trotskyist counter-revolutionary organization' commissioned to commit a terrorist attack against the leaders of the Ukrainian people.[222] Meanwhile Pavel Postyshev the very leader Maistrenko was accused of conspiring to kill was removed from Ukraine. But Maistrenko was not released but convicted of counter-revolutionary agitation and sent to the Tomsko-Anshs'koho penal colony in the Tomsk region of Siberia. Maistrenko was later confined in Kharkiv prison for one and a half years, a move which may have saved his life.

In December 1940, Maistrenko was released. He joined his wife Zina and son Levko in Slovyansk, where he took up a role as an economist for the Maschormet machine building factory. Following the German invasion of the USSR in June 1942 he was not conscripted to the Soviet Army because of his political conviction under the Criminal Code. Such was the scale of demoralization by the Stalinist terror that Maistrenko recalled at this time he did not meet a single person who had a 'defensive patriotic position'.[223]

The situation was one of chaos in the period between the retreating Soviet forces and advancing Germans. Although there were those in the population who wished to be evacuated no assistance or transport was provided for them. Maistrenko's factory was not evacuated to the Urals, his wife Zina who was a Doctor however was evacuated. It was a cause of great upset between them that he did not join her but remained under the occupation with their son Levko. They would not make contact again until after the war when she visited Levko in New York.[224]

The entire populace that remained was then a subject of suspicion by the Stalinist state for the mere fact they lived under the occupation.[225] This led to incidents of collaboration and betrayal to the Gestapo by the NKVD. The communists in Slovyansk at the time were viewed as traitors and many were shot by the Gestapo after being informed on by NKVD agents.[226] The local partisans in Slovyansk were considered mostly opportunists working out who it was better to go with—Hitler or Stalin. Instead of moving to the rear of the front to attack the German forces, they carried out attacks on the civilian population. Maistrenko recalled a revealing incident when the local Ukrainian language paper published an article attacking the local partisan commander "Yenka" for his acts against civilians. In response the German Sonderführer went to the editorial office and instructed them nothing was to be written against "Yenka". This confirmed suspicion that "Yenka" was not only an NKVD agent but colluding with the Germans.[227]

In the early days of the occupation Maistrenko witnessed the tragedy of the Jewish residents of Slovyansk. A local doctor who was married to a Ukrainian officer came to him for advice.

Maistrenko told her to go to the east with her two children; everyone in Slovyansk knew she was Jewish. Yet she remained believing a promise by a friend in the city administration she could be given reliable documents to protect her. A few days later she came again to see him; terrified she was now wearing a yellow star and had been forced to clean the streets. Soon after Maistrenko saw her being taken from her home by the Gestapo after which she was killed along with a thousand other Jews at a quarry outside the city.[228]

The situation in Slovyansk became increasingly unbearable, it was a frontline city and under regular bombing. Meanwhile the Gestapo-NKVD terror was growing worse in the city. The head of the Ukrainian Police was an NKVD agent, who was himself having the local communists executed by the Gestapo. Many of the communists who had registered with the police were well known Ukrainians and were being killed first. All seventy CPU members who had registered with the authorities were executed before the Gestapo discovered the head of Police was an NKVD agent and shot him too.[229]

After this with Levko, and also his friend Hryhory Kostiuk and his wife, Maistrenko made home-made backpacks and sledges, and set off on foot towards Kyiv some six hundred kilometers away. It was the extremely cold winter of 1941 and Levko struggled to cope with the cold and hunger.[230] Travelling during the first Soviet counter-attack they were afraid of being caught in crossfire. Holding passports of Siberian political prisoners and passes in German and Ukrainian from Slovyansk, they expected to be shot on the spot if they were stopped by NKVD.[231] They received assistance from peasants and heard first hand how the German district chiefs treated the Ukrainian peasants worse than the landowners from the days of serfdom.[232]

Maistrenko arrived in Kyiv in early January 1942. He found accommodation, unheated and without electricity; all of Kyiv was dark except for buildings of the German authorities. Maistrenko found work as an inspector of prices in bazaars and restaurants.[233] A Kyiv City Administration had been established under the Mayor L. Forostovsky, Maistrenko observed that the city had initially illusions of a repeat of the Hetmanate of 1918, suddenly the city middle class began speaking Ukrainian.[234] The Melnyk wing of the Organization of Ukrainian Nationalists (OUN-M) had established control of the administration. This was short-lived, the Germans had different colonial plans for their Reichkommissariat Ukraine. The Germans set about ruthlessly crushing the OUN-M killing the leading figures at Babi Yar ravine, scene of the massacre of over 100,000 people including 33,771 of Kyiv's Jews in September 1941.

On their arrival in Kyiv Maistrenko and Kostiuk had visited the office of the newspaper *Nove Ukrayinske Slovo*, it was now in Russian and sought to justify the German occupation and distanced itself from any form of Ukrainian nationalism. The visitors had failed to realize the purge that had just taken place at the newspaper, Maistrenko also became increasingly suspicious that the NKVD were playing a similar role in Kyiv as in Slovyansk in turning over communists to the Gestapo. One such agent who informed on Communist Party members held a position at the personnel department at the city administration. Maistrenko had not hid his past membership or imprisonment, and in May he was arrested by the Gestapo. Believing his fate sealed he said farewell to 16 year old Levko.[235]

The Gestapo ordered him to write a confession of his membership of the Communist Party and Siberian imprisonment. His translator appeared to try to shield him from suspicion of association with Ukrainian nationalism, which was being purged by the Germans at this time. To his relief he was dismissed by the Gestapo back to a Kyiv whose middle class had reverted to a little Russian outlook and language.[236]

Maistrenko managed to secure a new job in Kyiv as director of a bandura band. It was a great relief for it was unconnected to the German authorities and he felt it even assisted in awakening national consciousness.[237] But precisely because of that the Germans treated it suspiciously, considered it harmful, and later they were punished.

In August 1942, the band went to Volyn which though part of Western Ukraine was included in the Reichskommissariat. In Rivne the Bandurists played a concert for Ukrainians in the local theater hall which was filled with nationally conscious youth, their enthusiasm seemed to lead Maistrenko into false confidence. At a following concert in the town of Zhidychyn near Lutsk he gave a speech before the concert advising Ukrainians 'do not trust any liberators, but build an independent life.' His speech was warmly received but costly for the bandura band who were ordered to return to Kyiv.[238] The band was now instructed to travel to Germany to give concerts for Ukrainian workers—the *Ostarbeiter* [eastern worker] slave labourers. This caused a great deal of consternation amongst the Bandurists who blamed Maistrenko and his speech for their misfortune.[239]

The band travelled by train to Germany, and over time they realized they not heading towards Berlin but to the north, in the direction of Hamburg. They were told they were being taken to concerts for Ukrainian workers in Germany.[240] But in fact they were taken to the Blohm and Voss shipbuilding and engineering company site by the port. There they found mostly young people from Kharkiv, in conditions similar to a concentration camp. Workers were not allowed to the city; even travel to work was under guard. Despite assurances they were there for concerts the band worked at the factory and only gave concerts for the local workers.

Maistrenko comparing the food and work to his time in the Siberian labor camp found that in Germany nobody got more than 300 grams of bread, whereas in Siberia they got 900 grams for those who achieved their work targets.[241] Some of the band now cursed Maistrenko for causing their expulsion from Ukraine. He kept silence feeling there may be some truth in their complaints, but he also knew from letters that Erich Koch the Reichskommissar had said Ukrainians should not engage in music, but work in agriculture to provide Germany with food.[242] As despair grew amongst them Maistrenko remembered an address given him by a supporter of the OUN in Kyiv of a newspaper for Ukrainian *Ostarbeiter* in Berlin. They managed to organize to send a letter pleading for help.

Finally, in November, someone came from Berlin to inspect the Bandura band and informed them they would be playing concerts. It was revealed that that there was a disagreement between the Gestapo and the Ministry for the Occupied Eastern Territories over what to do with them, the latter believing concerts may help improve *Ostarbeiter* efficiency. Thus compulsory music was added to the forced labor of *Ostarbeiter*.[243] Yet again fate shined favorably on Maistrenko and this bureaucratic dispute between the Nazi's resulted in him being saved from being worked to death.[244]

The Bandura band travelled all over Germany, including Austria witnessing the tragic life of the half-starved *Ostarbeiter*. At times Maistrenko saw kindness from the civilians towards prisoners, recalling in Düsseldorf seeing an old woman throwing a package of food to the *Ostarbeiter*. Alongside Jews and Poles it was only the eastern workers who were made to wear a symbol—a blue square with a white inscription "ost".[245]

As German defeat in the war became more apparent after Stalingrad feeling began to change amongst the *Ostarbeiter*. People were afraid they would not see their relatives again or be able to return to Kyiv. Once again Maistrenko was blamed, though he was conscious his own son Levko remained in Volhynia and this was a source of increasing worry for him. The uprising of the Ukrainian Insurgent Army (UPA) against the Nazi occupation was underway and Levko was a member of UPA.[246]

In one of those strange twists of history the Bandurists' made it to Berlin in September 13, 1943, where they performed in the residence of Hetman Skoropadsky against whose regime Maistrenko had participated in the rebellion in his youth.[247] After this the Bandura band were allowed to travel back to Rivne, and from there they were meant to travel to Kyiv. In Rivne Nazi terror had intensified with a series of public executions of Ukrainian prisoners. Maistrenko during the journey from Berlin to Rivne arrived at a city which was a fortress, the surrounding areas controlled by partisans of the UPA.[248] On returning to Western Ukraine Maistrenko observed that the "UPA dominated over the entire Western Ukraine and only the industrial centers and railroad stations were in the hands of the Hitlerites."[249] The situation contrasted sharply to Maistrenko's later experience of the Soviet press portrayal of Ukrainian "bourgeois nationalists" helping the Nazis fight against the USSR.

With the help of some local youth Maistrenko made contact with Levko and managed to meet him. He found his son in poor condition, winter was approaching and also Soviet forces, Maistrenko considered if his son remained he was at risk, the territory unlike the mountains was not suited to long-term partisan warfare. Maistrenko decided to take his son with him and arranged false-papers of the German Labor Front as a member of the Bandurists. They were just in time to help survive a Gestapo raid.[250]

The hopes of the Bandurists of returning to Kyiv turned to disappointment; the already depopulated city was being evacuated under the Germans scorched earth policy in the face of the advancing Soviet forces. Instead the Bandurists were sent west to Lviv in the District of Galicia, a unit of the Nazi run Generalgouvernement. Maistrenko observed that the area of the Generalgouvernement resembled peace time, it was "a completely different world compared to the Reichskommissariat. It is a much more normal life". On trams Maistrenko saw how the Poles refused to take a ticket as a kind of boycott of the German economy; it was spirit of solidarity that contrasted to the individualism that existed under Stalinism.[251]

Maistrenko and the Bandurists parted in Lviv, the band travelling around the Galician villages. In Western Ukraine there was still a Ukrainian community and life which contrasted sharply to the situation in the East. Maistrenko made contact with a range of people including the Ukrainian socialist Yavorsky who was also the editor of the paper *Lvivski visti*. Maistrenko was conscious that the Stalinist regime would return soon making it impossible for people to see in print the truth of the tragic events of 1933 in Ukraine. Maistrenko published a series of article on the famine in *Lvivski visti*, the editor told him "It is true, your article is written from a Marxist position" — which Maistrenko felt under the Nazi occupation was a dangerous statement — "But — the editor smiled back — "it's even good".[252]

In Lviv Maistrenko made the acquaintance of Nina Matuly who had been a CPU member Kharkiv and part of West Ukrainian community that was all imprisoned by the NKVD. Through her Maistrenko met former members of the Communist Party of Western Ukraine which had been closed down by Stalin. This included

Mykola Pavlyk who has been in a Polish prison for twelve years because he was Secretary of the Central Committee of the CPWU.

These Ukrainian communists had moved to the area after the partition of the Hitler-Stalin Pact. They recalled that the local apparatus was staffed by Stalin's men from the USSR they would not trust local revolutionaries. Slogans had been written on walls by local communists: "Comrade! Bolshevism – is not Communism", and "Bolshevism – Moscow Imperialism".[253] Maistrenko told these survivors of the fate of Ukrainian communists in Slovyansk and Kyiv, warning them to avoid the same provocation and not to become known to the Gestapo as the NKVD was also pushing them to kill them.[254]

Nina being of a mixed Ukrainian-Polish heritage also had close links with the Polish underground resistance; her sister was executed as part of the conspiracy to assassinate Hitler in 1944. At this time Maistrenko records violence intensifying in the city as the Polish underground killed Ukrainian activists, whilst in the villages the Ukrainian underground killed Polish activists; this was amidst the overall violence of war and occupation. Maistrenko wrote in his diary that one night in March 1944 alone, some nine hundred corpses were collected in Lviv.[255]

After publishing in a Ukrainian literary journal Maistrenko won a scholarship to write a book from the Ukrainian publishing house Krakow-Lviv, a comparative study of Ukrainian and European literature. But it was never written as the front moved towards Lviv, Maistrenko faced yet another impossible choice, of whether to risk moving with his son further west and somehow reach allied lines by the war's end or stay. He was determined 'never again to return to the Ostarbeiter camp, Stalinist Siberia or Nazi Hamburg.'[256] In March 1944 he left with Levko for Konigsberg in East Prussia where he gained a job as a language proofreader at a radio station.

Maistrenko was conscious that with the defeat of Nazi Germany looming the crimes of Stalinism should not be concealed by the victory over Nazism. He wrote several commentaries about the millions of victims in Ukraine in 1933 and murder of hundreds of thousands of communists. Maistrenko secured a further role on a

Ukrainian magazine *Dozvillya* for *Ostarbeiter* in Plauen, which he hoped would be soon in allied hands.[257] During the last days of the war life in the German city became unbearable; a bombing raid destroyed the city in March 1945. The air raids saved Levko from being forced into the Wermacht. After unsuccessfully claiming he had a heart condition he reported the next day to the barracks to find to his joy the RAF had destroyed it.[258] The City was liberated by the American forces on 16 April 1945 and Maistrenko moved with them after the city transferred to Soviet forces in July.

After the war Maistrenko was interned, along with the 200,000 Ukrainian refugees in displaced persons camps. There he made contact with other Ukrainians and became active in the émigré Ukrainian Revolutionary Democratic Party, becoming editor in 1946 of the Party journal — *Nasha Borotba*. The Party "set its task to create a Ukrainian liberation movement that would proceed from the modern Ukrainian reality"[259].

In 1948 the URDP split between a socialist left-wing that included Maistrenko, Vsevolod Holubnychy, Boris Levytsky and Hryhoriy Kostiuk and the more moderate wing of Ivan Bahryanyy. Maistrenko and his comrades would emerge as leading figures of Ukrainian scholarship in the post-war period.

The URDP left-wing began publishing in Munich *Nasha Borotba*, *Revoliutsiyny democrat* and the monthly paper *Vpered*, — a Ukrainian review for workers which ran from April 1949 until December 1959. It would become a voice for the socialist survivors of the generation of the Ukrainian Revolution and a record for their time. It remains a vital historical source to this day.

Maistrenko was one of their leading theorists and wrote under the pseudonym of Babenko. He wrote extensively for anti-Stalinist socialist publications, such as *Labor Action, New International* and *Fourth International*. In 1948 on his way to the Congress of the Trotskyist Fourth International in Paris, he met with Volodymyr Vynnychenko leader of the Central Rada in 1917. It had been a great regret to have missed a Central Committee meeting of the Ukrainian Communist Party attended by Vynnychenko in Kharkiv in 1920. Maistrenko published in *Nasha Borotba* one of Vynnychenko's last known works, which included a scathing rebuttal of narrow nationalism.[260]

Maistrenko and his *Vpered* comrades advocated principles of social ownership of the means of production, a planned economy and the construction of a classless society in an independent Ukraine. To be achieved by a new revolution in the USSR and the liquidation of the system of state capitalism. In 1948 the URDP published Maistrenko's analysis of Stalinism *Bolshevist Bonapartism*, in English and Ukrainian. In it Maistrenko considered that Stalin's ascendancy at the head of the bureaucracy represented not the victory of 'socialism' but a break with the revolution, the "Bolshevik Thermidor". Ukrainians were "deprived not only of their national independence, but even those elementary national freedoms which they had achieved during the first years of the revolution."[261]

> Not the spreading of communism is the task of the permanent Bolshevist war as the Stalinist propaganda columns read, but the introduction of the Russian state-capitalist system into foreign countries. This can be mixed up with socialism and communism only by he who consciously wants to discredit the liberation movement of the working people; but he actually aids imperialistic Russia, recommending her to those who are ignorant of the state of affairs as a socialist country.[262]

Maistrenko tried to form direct contact with the underground UPA, establishing correspondence with UPA theorists Petro Poltava and Osyp Hornovy. He considered this new "Ukrainian nationalism ceases to be nationalism, it switches itself to the positions of the revolutionary liberation movement of the working people, and thus it breaks more and more all the threads that have been knitted with the remnants of the reactionary-nationalist parties."[263]

Maistrenko and *Vpered* sharply opposed the narrow nationalism and totalitarianism of the Bandera wing of the Organization of Ukrainian Nationalists, and condemned their efforts to establish hegemony over the Ukrainian community abroad. This made life difficult for Maistrenko with the OUN(B) subjecting him to discrimination in the displaced persons camps and denouncing him as a communist and Bolshevik. They informed the American filtration service to stop his entry to the USA — as such he could not join his son Levko who moved to New York with Holubnychy.

This was a time when the Ukrainian émigré community in the west equated socialism with the Stalinist regime and had swung sharply to a right-wing nationalism. During the period of McCarthyism *Vpered* faced intense criticism for its socialist positions and the right-wing Ukrainians assisted by security agencies like the CIA harassed, black-listed and arrested supporters of *Vpered* who continued to speak out. This pressure increasingly marginalized *Vpered* as the right-wing consolidated their grip on the diaspora.[264]

They ceased publication of *Vpered* in 1959, but Maistrenko and his comrades were to be important for the Ukrainian new left which emerged in the diaspora in the 1960s. With the appearance of left journals *Dialoh* and *Meta* in 1977 they dissolved the URDP and supported the young socialists in their new journals. A new generation of Ukrainian socialists came to understand their historical past through the writings of Maistrenko and his comrades.[265]

Maistrenko continued his activities as a writer and publicist. He became the rector of the Ukrainian Technical and Economic Institute in Germany, founding their periodical publication. For a long time he did work for the Ukrainian editorial office of Radio Liberty, however they were uncomfortable with his stand in favor of Ukrainian independence which annoyed the Russian chauvinists at the station.

In exile Maistrenko wrote numerous articles and brochures on Soviet politics, economics, society and on socialist theory; his books are: *Bolshevik Bonapartism* (1948), *Borotbism, Chapter in the History of Ukrainian Communism* (1954), *The Crisis processes in the Soviet economy* (Ukrainian, 1955), *Agrarian policy of the Bolsheviks during fifty years of revolution* (Ukrainian, 1967) *The National policy of the CPSU and its historical development* (Russian, 1978), *History of the Communist Party of Ukraine* (Ukrainian, 1979) and his memoirs *The History of my Generation, Memoirs of a Participant in the Revolutionary Events in Ukraine* (Ukrainian, 1984).

Under the editorship of **Maistrenko** a number of Ukrainian socialist writings were republished, these included: *Documents of Ukrainian Communism* (Ukrainian, 1962), *On the Current Situation* by

Serhey Mazlakh and Vasyl Shakhray (1967, Ukrainian), *Russian Social Democrats and the National Question by Lev Yurkevych* (Ukrainian, 1969).

Maistrenko was a man of solid convictions that changed over time, but never betrayed. The well-known Ukrainian-Canadian scholar Bohdan Krawchenko noted that: "Until the end of his days, Maistrenko remained left and also a modern man, an unbridled fighter for the rights of his people".[266]

Maistrenko took a keen interest in socialist politics until his death aged 85 in Munich on November 18, 1984. He concluded his memoirs stating that whilst disagreeing with most socialist currents he believed the program of struggle for emancipation from all exploitation would be based on our understanding of Stalinism and the people's revolutions in the USSR.

Borot'bism

A Chapter in the History of Ukrainian Communism

by

Iwan Majstrenko

RESEARCH PROGRAM ON THE U.S.S.R.

The cover of the original 1954 edition of *Borotbism*

Introduction

IVAN MAISTRENKO

The aim of the present study is to trace in detail the history of *Borotbism*, its ideological origins and its evolution, and to assess the significance of the Borotbisty in the Ukrainian revolution and in the life of the Soviet Ukraine down to the purges of 1933.[a]

Before considering the main subject of the study, however, it will be useful to identify briefly the major political parties of the left which, together with the Borotbisty, played a role in Ukrainian history during the period under discussion.

The Communist Party (Bolshevik) of the Ukraine (abbreviated CP(b)U) had perhaps greater influence among the urban working classes of the Ukraine than any of the other parties to be mentioned, but its impact on the Ukrainian peasantry was negligible. Its strength, however, derived not from the support of the Ukrainian masses, but from the military and administrative apparatus which the Bolsheviks brought to the Ukraine from Russia.

The Ukrainian Communist Party (Borotbisty)(abbreviated UCP(b)) was a continuation of the Ukrainian Party of Socialist Revolutionaries (abbreviated UPSR). Toward the end of the year 1917 there emerged within the UPSR a distinct "Internationalist" group which was ready to subordinate specific Ukrainian demands to the interests of world revolution. In mid-May 1918, at the Fourth Congress of the UPSR, the Internationalists achieved a short-lived control over the entire party, but immediately following the congress the UPSR split into a left and a right wing. Controlling the party's organ *Borotba* [Struggle], the Internationalists, the left wing, adopted the name "Borotbisty." At the same time they moved ideologically toward Bolshevik communism, a move which was reflected in the new name for their party which they adopted in March 1919: "UPSR (Communists-Borotbisty)." In August of that

---

a   See note to the Foreword

year the party merged with the Ukrainian Social Democratic Workers' Party (Left Independents); to mark its clean break with the Socialist Revolutionary tradition, the party now took the name "Ukrainian Communist Party (Borotbisty)." Finally, in the spring of 1920 the Borotbisty merged, or "united" as it was then termed, with the CP(b)U, thus providing the latter with many outstanding leaders in the field of Ukrainian culture, men and women who played a prominent part in the CP(b)U and in the Ukrainian S. S.R. until the purges of 1933.

The Ukrainian Communist Party, the so-called *Ukapisty*[b], derived from the Ukrainian Social Democratic Workers' Party (USDRP), calling themselves for a while the Independent faction of that party. At first openly at war with the Bolsheviks, the *Ukapisty* became a legal opposition party only at the beginning of 1920. However, by that time all the important positions in Soviet Ukrainian political life had been filled by members of the older parties: in the industrial areas by the CP(b)U, in the smaller towns and villages by the Borotbisty. Thus the gains of the *Ukapisty* among the workers were insignificant, and they therefore played a less prominent role than the Borotbisty.

The party of the Ukrainian Anarchists, the followers of Nestor Makhno, which at first glance might appear to be an offshoot of international anarchism imported through Russia, was in reality a typically Ukrainian phenomenon. It had a large following among the peasants of the southern Ukraine.

The Ukrainian Party of Left Socialist Revolutionaries (*Borbisty*)[c] was in fact a Ukrainian branch of the Russian Party of Left Socialist Revolutionaries, which in turn was a descendant of the *Narodnaya Volya* (People's Will or People's Freedom). The *Borbisty* had some influence in Left Bank Ukraine (that part of the Ukraine east of the Dnepr River), primarily in the cities, but very little in the villages.

---

b   From the letters "u," "k" and "p," the first letter of each word in the full Ukrainian name of the party. — Ed.

c   The plural form of Borbist, derived from the name of the party newspaper Borba [Struggle], published at first in Russian and later in Ukrainian.

In addition there were several smaller groups: the Maximalists, the Revolutionary Communists and two leftist Jewish groups, the Communist *Bund* and the Jewish Communist Party. With the exception of the Anarchists, all the above-mentioned parties eventually merged with the CP(b)U.

1 Historical Antecedents

In approaching the history of *Borotbism*, which has its roots in the pre-revolutionary period, it is imperative to consider certain characteristics of political life in the Ukraine which have marked the development of Ukrainian political thought. A dualism pervaded this development from the beginning of the nineteenth century down to the establishment of Soviet rule in the Ukraine. During this entire period two types of political tendencies and organizations existed side by side. One type regarded itself as Russian and participated in political movements within the imperial framework; the other aimed to preserve and strengthen Ukrainian national individuality. The former included the Southern Society, the Russian populists (narodniki) and the Russian Social Democratic Workers' Party (RSDRP); the latter, the separatist Little Russian Society headed by Vasyl' Lukashevych, the Society of United Slavs, the Brotherhood of Saints Cyril and Methodius, the members of the society Hromada [Community], Mykhaylo P. Drahomanov, the Revolutionary Ukrainian Party (RUP), and the Ukrainian Social Democratic Workers Party (USDRP).[1] This dichotomy characterized Ukrainian political life right up to the Soviet period, when it finally disappeared. In the course of the 1917 Revolution, right wing political currents completely vanished from the Ukrainian scene, while Russian leftist groups in the Ukraine became Ukrainized.

A. Components of Ukrainian Political Thought

1. The Russian Influence

The influence of Russian political thought on the political life of pre-revolutionary Ukraine is to be explained not only by the influx of Russians into the Ukraine and by the partial Russification of the Ukrainian Zhmerinka intelligentsia, but by the enrollment of many conscious Ukrainian patriots in the Russian parties. These Ukrainians were primarily concerned with the abolition of autocracy, believing that as soon as democratic freedom was established in Russia a national rebirth of the Ukrainian people would follow automatically. "Having lost faith in the possibility of achieving anything through cultural activities," writes Professor Vasylenko-Polons'ka, "a number of Ukrainian patriots in the 1870's became members of the Russian revolutionary organization known as the Narodnaya Volya [People's Will or People's Freedom]." The leader of the Narodnaya Volya, Andrei I. Zhelyabov, was himself of Ukrainian descent. Other members of Ukrainian descent in the group included the poet P. Hrabovs'kyi, Sophie Perovska (a descendant of Hetman K. Rozumovs'kyi), D. Kibalchich, V. Debagoryi-Moriyevich, Ya. Stefanovich, and D. Lizogub.[2]

Such collaboration between Ukrainian and Russian revolutionaries, it might seem, would have ran counter to the Ukrainian struggle for liberation, but such leading Russian revolutionaries as Alexander Herzen and Mikhail Bakunin had been sympathetic to the Ukrainian struggle and had strongly denounced the imperialism of the tsars. For example, Bakunin had written: "Russian social revolutionaries aim first of all &t the destruction of our state....In order that a union [of Slavic peoples] may be established it is first necessary that the Russian Empire should fall to pieces."[3] It must also be borne in mind that the tsarist government, to use Dmytro Doroshenko's words, "persecuted even scholarly research devoted to the ethnographic and historical character of the Ukrainian people. Hence Ukrainian sentiment could be expressed only in belles-lettres, without the slightest impact on real life.'[4] Under such conditions attempts to cultivate Ukrainian culture appeared vain to everyone but those with an inexhaustible faith in the future, like the members of the Hromada. It is not surprising, therefore, that the more active elements among the Ukrainian intelligentsia turned away from the dull and seemingly hopeless cultural work undertaken by the members of the *Hromada* and by the Ukrainophiles (as Ukrainian patriots were then called) and that together with the Russian revolutionaries they attempted to pull down that "prison of peoples," the Russian Empire. In view of such close ties between the Russian and Ukrainian opposition to tsarism, it was natural that Zhelyabov proposed to Drahomanov, at that time the ideological leader of the Ukrainian revolutionaries, that he represent the *Narodnaya Volya* abroad.⁵

Indeed, by the end of the nineteenth century the Ukrainian revolutionary movement bore the stamp of Russian revolutionary thought. Of the representatives of the Ukrainian intelligentsia in the late 1890's, Doroshenko writes that "although they belonged to a new generation ... and were inspired by national ideals ... [they] had been brought up in the spirit of the all-Russian radical and social ideas and views, which exerted a powerful influence over even the most [politically] conscious Ukrainians.'⁶ "The pioneers of the Ukrainian national and political revival, ..." writes Isaak Mazepa in similar vein, "could not, in view of almost two hundred years of Russian rule over the Ukraine, escape from the influence of Russian political ideology."⁷ Ukrainians had come to believe that a political and social revolution, rather than peaceful cultural progress, offered the only road to Ukrainian liberation. At the same time, however, Russian revolutionary thought itself was under the influence of current western European ideas, then attempting to formulate basic laws which would explain the development of European nations. "In all circles of Russian society, and especially in socialist groups," according to Mazepa, "there was such wide enthusiasm for everything European that often political parties of tsarist Russia quite uncritically borrowed western European models for their ideas and organization.⁸ Ukrainians were therefore inclined to regard Russian political thought merely as an intermediary between themselves and western Europe.

It was the official barring of cultural development for Ukraine, according to Doroshenko, which led to the disillusionment of the young Ukrainian radicals of the 1890's and their negative attitude toward "all other solutions of the problem of a Ukrainian revival except in the form of a revolutionary movement."⁹ The fact that Ukrainian leaders regarded their ultimate goal as the same as that of the Russian revolutionaries led to yet closer ties with them. During the Revolution of 1905, when a split occurred in the ranks of the Revolutionary Ukrainian Party (RUP) (founded in Kharkiv in 1900), the leaders of the schism who took the Ukrainian Social Democratic Union (*Ukrainska Sotsiyal-Demokratychna Spilka*, referred to as the

Spilka) into the RSDRP believed that Ukrainian liberation would be decided not by national but by social factors and by the general political situation in the Russian Empire. "It is unnecessary to worry whether the Ukrainian people will feel nationally conscious," wrote one of the *Spilka's* leaders Oleksander Skoropys-Yoltukhovskyi. "The important thing is that they be politically and socially conscious. They cannot be anything but Ukrainian."[10] This atmosphere of trust in the Russian revolutionary democrats, which even the most radical Ukrainian revolutionaries shared, lasted down to and including the period of the Revolution of 1917. It was to leave its mark on *Borotbism*.

2. The Cult of the Peasant

The orientation of Ukrainian political thought toward the peasantry (which before World War I constituted over 80 per cent of the total population in the Ukraine) was evident as early as the 1840's in the Brotherhood of Saints Cyril and Methodius. The intellectual leaders of the Brotherhood "put forward as their task the cultural and social emancipation of the peasant masses.'[11] Indeed, it can be said that before the Revolution of 1917 the concepts of "Ukraine" and "Ukrainian" tended to be treated as synonymous with "peasant." Young Ukrainians from Polonized families, who in the 1860's devoted themselves enthusiastically to the Ukrainian national movement, were dubbed "peasant lovers" (*khlopomany*) by the Polish gentry.[12]

The peasantry was also the social basis of Drahomanov's teachings. In their "remote past," in the view of Drahomanov's Russian biographer David I Zaslavski, "he saw the democratic Cossack system and the *[Zaporozhskaya] Sech'* which, in its social economy, was close to that of the primitive commune."[13] According to the brochure *Mykhaylo Petrovych Drahomanov*, published in 1897 by a group of Ukrainian Marxist Social Democrats, Drahomanov's "ideal was a peasant state with anarchist production .. .." "His strong point was that his teaching compelled the people in Galicia and Russian Ukraine [*Naddnipryans'ka Ukraiha*] to turn to the peasant masses, neglected and downtrodden by the course of history."[14]

Likewise, the peasantry provided the social basis for the Ukrainian Radical Party, the first political party in Galicia, which was founded in 1890. According to the anonymous author of the contemporary brochure *Radyhaly i radykalizm* [Radicals and Radicalism],

> the party is founded on the basis of scientific socialism and accepts all the consequences of this premise. However the Party does not agree in every respect with the workers' socialist parties, for, while the latter are active among [urban] workers, the Ukrainian radicals work among the peasants.[15]

Similarly, the first Ukrainian political party in Russian Ukraine, the RUP, "devoted most of its attention to the village proletariat and the landless or impoverished peasantry," despite the fact that it had been created by Marxist socialists.[16] And when the *Spilka* united with the RSDRP in 1906, it endeavored within the RSDRP to work among the peasants "not only in the Ukraine but in other lands of the Russian state."[17]

Whenever Ukrainian political parties tried to ignore the peasants, they became small groups without any significant influence on Ukrainian political life. Such, for example, was the fate of the party led by Mykola Mikhnovsky, the Ukrainian People's Party, which seceded from the RUP in 1902. "It did not extend beyond the limits of a small group of intellectuals, and it played no significant part in the Ukrainian liberation movement. Neither did it have any influence on the internal evolution of the RUP itself."[18] A similar fate befell Ukrainian non-socialist liberal groups. Thus the Ukrainian Democratic Party, the Ukrainian Radical Party (a group which broke away from the first-mentioned party), the Ukrainian Radical Democratic Party (formed from elements of the two preceding parties), and the Society of Ukrainian Progressives (which was created to replace the last-named party) — all remained small groups of intellectuals. Their attempts to assume the then fashionable socialist coloring, represented by Mikhnovskyi's socialistic declarations and the renaming of the Society of Ukrainian Progressives in 1917 as the Ukrainian Party of Socialist Federalists (UPSF), were of no avail in strengthening them. They did perform an important function by providing centers for intellectual life, but they failed to attract a mass following.

Even after the Revolution of 1905, when it became possible to form opposition groups and when liberal parties were established in the Ukraine, the importance of appealing to the peasantry was generally recognized. It was for this reason that during the 1917 Revolution the Ukrainian landowners headed by Serhiy Shemet and his brothers Volodymyr and Mykola formed the Ukrainian Democratic Agrarian Party with a distinctly peasant coloring. Similarly, the leader of Ukrainian conservatism and monarchism Vyacheslav Lypynskyi (in exile from the summer of 1919) made his chief work, *Letters to Brother Agriculturists. .,* an appeal to the peasant.[19]

The cult of the peasant limited the appeal of the Ukrainian political movement in the Russified Ukrainian cities, the main politically developed centers. (Only after 1917, under the Ukrainian People's Republic which was created primarily by the support of the peasants, were the Ukrainian towns gradually de-Russified. Although the majority of the urban population was ethnically Ukrainian, most of the inhabitants did not regard themselves as Ukrainian. The de-Russification of the towns was to progress at an increasing tempo under the Soviet regime until 1933.) Thus the main stream of the RUP, the Ukrainian Social Democratic Party (USDRP), which in theory rested on the support of the workers, owed whatever mass following it had to the peasants. The creation of a strong peasant party in 1917, the Ukrainian Party of Socialist Revolutionaries (UPSR) brought about a decline of the USDRP's influence in the village. Indeed the main factor which was to divide the UPSR from the USDRP was the fact that the former was primarily a peasant party, while the latter was a workers' party. In 1917 the USDRP in Luhansk, the membership of which consisted chiefly of workers, passed the following characteristic resolution:

> In view of the fact that no Ukrainian SR organization yet exists for the Lugansk peasants who are in danger of being led away by the Russian SR's, the local USDRP has authorized some of its members to create in Lugansk a branch of the UPSR.[20]

The eventual success of the Borot'bisty was due to the fact that they had the support of the peasants; conversely, the Marxist workers' party, the Ukrainian Communist Party (Ukapisty), failed to achieve similar success.

3. Romantic Nationalism: The Search for Self-Existence

A characteristic aspect of all Ukrainian political life both before and during the Revolution was its enthusiasm for national romanticism, its appeal to Ukrainian history and tradition. These features were to add a distinctly nationalist coloring to such political trends of the extreme left as Ukrainian Communism and *Borotbism*, in spite of their internationalist programs. It is true, of course, that leftist movements of all oppressed peoples tend to be tinged with nationalism.

The national aspect became especially apparent in the case of those Ukrainian political figures who later seceded from the Russian to the Ukrainian camp. The "old Bolshevik" Vasyl' M. Shakhray, who after 1918 advocated the creation of an independent Ukrainian communist party, was to appeal in his writings to the national consciousness of the Ukrainians and other oppressed peoples. Another "old Bolshevik," Yuriy F. Lapchynskyi, later became an ardent advocate of Ukrainization, and a similar change occurred in Mykola O. Skrypnyk's views.

It is important to note that transferring from a Russian political party to its Ukrainian counterpart entailed a change of mentality and style on the part of the person concerned, despite the similar programs of the two parties. Not only was it characteristic of these Ukrainized Russian politicians to repudiate their previous stand on the national problem; inevitably they refashioned their entire political education according to new, Ukrainian needs. This was true both of the neophytes who left the Russian parties and, to a large extent, of all Ukrainian intellectuals who had been brought up in the Russian school of thought and who, upon returning to the Ukrainian fold, had to repudiate their past associations with Russians. It is true that most Ukrainian political parties were formed as counterparts in name and doctrine of Russian political parties. In the course of time, however, they became totally alienated from their Russian models, developing a different point of view on almost every important issue. It is significant that when the Borot'bisty declared their opposition to the leadership of the UPSR, they did not follow the example of the Russian Left SR's, but called themselves "Internationalists."

B. Ideological Precursors of *Borotbism*

1. Drahomanov: The Father of Ukrainian Political Parties

Mykhaylo P. Drahomanov is justly regarded as the father of Ukrainian political parties. A highly cultured man, Drahomanov "rose far above the level of all the Russian emigre's, occupying in Geneva a place comparable to that held by Lavrov in Paris.[21] Having been sent abroad by the Kyivan *Hromada* to protest the ban on Ukrainian publications and cultural activities in Russia, he initiated the periodical *Hromada*, in which he attacked the non-political thinking of the Ukrainians at home and of the Russian populists, pleading for an active, decisive and revolutionary struggle. This development took place in the 1880's, a time of darkest reaction throughout the Russian Empire following the assassination of Alexander II. The Ukrainians were so terrorized and oppressed that the very members of the Kyivan *Hromada* who had sent Drahomanov abroad for the express purpose of conducting political propaganda, in 1886 sent him a letter calling his activity "harmful to the Ukrainian cause." In their letter they recommended that he confine his activities to informing the world of conditions in the Ukraine and to writing for the legal Russian press.[22] When Drahomanov refused to comply, his voice from abroad, according to Dmytro Antonovych, "frightened more than it attracted."[23] Nevertheless, because Drahomanov remained undismayed, his work appealed to some of the young Ukrainians who now turned their backs on the cultural work of the Ukrainophiles and demanded a revolutionary solution of the Ukrainian problem. Operating side by side with the cultural circles, "Drahomanov circles" of students now read the writings of Drahomanov in secret gatherings.

The political impact of Drahomanov's ideas was first felt in Galicia where, under the relatively liberal Austrian constitutional monarchy, conditions were more favorable to political action than in Russian Ukraine. The result was the creation in Galicia in 1890 of the Ukrainian Radical Party, "the first modern Ukrainian party. Its program was one of non-Marxist, ethical socialism, of the kind that Drahomanov had always advocated."[24] In 1896 a year after Drahomanov's death, the leaders of this party commented:

> His ideas were not expressed in vain; they have become the foundation of the Ruthenian-Ukrainian Radical Party in Galicia and in Eastern Ukraine .... Under the influence of Drahomanov's writings and of French and German literature these young Ruthenians turned socialist.[25]

As has already been seen, this party recognized the need to turn to the peasantry. On the national problem, the program of the Radical Party called for "the independence of Rus-Ukraine, in order that, as in Khmelnytskyi's day, all oppression may be destroyed and just law and order established."[26]

In the 1890's, however, a "young" group was formed within the Radical Party which accepted a Social Democratic platform, that is, the Marxist doctrine oriented toward the workers rather than the peasants. This group provided the first Marxist critique of Drahomanov. One of its members, Yulian Bachynsky, in the work *Ukraïna irredenta*, published in Lviv in 1895, argued for an independent Ukraine on the basis of an analysis of economic development in eastern Europe.

2. Marxism Enters Ukraine

Events in Galicia had repercussions in Russian Ukraine. "The young Ukrainian progressives," chiefly those who had received their political education in "Drahomanov circles," writes Antonovych, "having observed Galician life, began to sympathize with the Radical Party. ..."

> In 1893-1894 the entire student Hromada in Kyiv, led by the young poet and student of philosophy Ivan Steshenko, began to lose interest in the cultural and non-political aspects of the Ukrainian movement and declared itself in favor of Ukrainian political radicalism.[27]

But there were also other reasons why the younger generation at the opening of the twentieth century turned to the creation of political parties. One was the influence of Marxism; the other, the development of industry.

By the end of the nineteenth century the increasing industrialization of Ukraine provided a fertile ground for Marxism in the new urban working class which was being created. With the failure of populism in the 1880's both in Ukraine and in Russia, Marxism seemed to many to provide the revolutionary solution. It is noteworthy that the first Marxist critic of the Russian populists in the 1870's had been Drahomanov's friend Mykola I. Ziber, a professor at Kyiv University. A Ukrainophile and a member of the *Hromada*, Ziber was also one of the first to translate Marx into Russian. The strength of the Marxist ideology in the Ukraine can be seen from the fact that of the five Social Democratic groups which participated in the formation of an all-Russian Social Democratic party at Minsk in 1898 three were from the Ukraine, although they regarded themselves as Russian.

Particularly noteworthy among the many Marxist groups which dotted the Russian Empire in the 1890's was the one formed in Kyiv under the leadership of Ivan Steshenko and Lesya Ukrainka, Drahomanov's niece, later a famous poet. The brochure *Mykhaylo Petrovych Drahomanov*, published in 1897 by this group, was devoted to a Marxist analysis of Drahomanov's ideas. It was this pamphlet which, as has been seen, defined "the strong point" of Drahomanov's teachings as the effect they produced of "compelling the people in Galicia and Russian Ukraine to turn to the peasant masses . ... " The "weakness" of Drahomanov's social and economic outlook, the analysis continued, was its

> failure to note that the peasantry is not entirely homogeneous. To begin thinking about the peasantry as a whole means very little. The modern class principle of sociology demands clarification as to which class of the peasants one is defending, for only then can sympathy for the peasants have concrete value.

Nonetheless, Drahomanov's ideas were praised:

> His honest and wise pen never tired of working for the Ukrainian cause; the Galician radical movement, in particular, owes him a great deal. His constant

reminder that Ukrainians must not stand in line behind the Russian radical groups, but must form their own national group to work among the people, has great importance even now.[28]

The activity of Drahomanov, the experience of the Galician Radical Party and the pronouncement of the young Marxists in Russian Ukraine, together with the increasingly revolutionary atmosphere at the turn of the century, all contributed to the creation of the first Ukrainian political party in Russian Ukraine. This was the RUP, formed on February 11, 1900 in Kharkiv, where the influence of the non-political Ukrainophiles was not so strong as in Kyiv.

C. The Experience of the Revolutionary Ukrainian Party (RUP)

A central role in the political life of Russian Ukraine in the early twentieth century was played by the RUP and its successor the USDRP (the name the party assumed at its congress in December 1905 following the splitting off of the *Spilka* group). The RUP is to be credited with the final development of the idea of a Ukrainian national revolution and with the formation of the definitive type of Ukrainian revolutionary. The latter was now reflected in the novels of Volodymyr Vynnychenko and Mykhaylo Kotsiubynsky and in the poems of Lesya Ukrainka and Oleksander Oles.

This generation was to live to see the Revolution of 1917 and the emergence of a younger generation, many of whom would enroll in the ranks of the Borotbisty. It is important, therefore, to analyze in some detail the ideas motivating die RUP and its offspring the USDRP and the *Spilka*; the difference between Ukrainian and Russian political parties in Ukraine was now clear, and these three parties were to influence the Borot'bisty.

1. The Problem of National Liberation

The idea of national liberation was central to the postulate of a Ukrainian revolutionary party independent of the Russian parties. In the half decade 1900–1905 the RUP was agitated by a heated debate over the question whether an independent party was necessary or not. On the one hand, the tradition of the nineteenth century called for a united front with the Russians in the struggle against the tsarist autocracy. On the other hand, by the turn of the century it was becoming increasingly evident that Russian opposition to the regime did not necessarily include approval of the liberation movements of the non-Russian peoples of the Empire. Russian non-socialist liberals were prepared to make only small concessions, in the cultural field, while the socialists, despite their talk of self-determination-Lenin even advocated "self-determination up to secession"[29]—were in fact denying this right in other sections of their programs.[30] Moreover, after 1905 no Russian socialist made such extreme statements on the subject as had Bakunin. It was becoming apparent that the liberation of the non-Russian peoples would have to be the concern of these peoples alone, not of the Russian revolutionaries: hence the necessity for the creation of Ukrainian political parties.

2. Formulation of the National Program

The first platform of the RUP, published in 1900 under the title *Samostiyna Ukraina* [An Independent Ukraine], was drafted by the nationalist Mykola Mikhnovsky. In this document the aim of the party was stated to be "one, indivisible, free, and independent Ukraine from the Carpathians to the Caucasus." The platform sharply criticized the non-political Ukrainophiles of the older generation. "Ukraine is for the Ukrainians," it stated, "and we cannot lay down our arms as long as one enemy is left in our territory .... Forward, since we can neidier hope for any favors nor look back."[31] In 1902, however, the socialist leaders of the RUP declared in their theoretical organ *Haslo* [Watchword] that the final goal of the party was "an independent Ukrainian Republic of the working masses, with socialized means of production, nationalization of the land and a dictatorship of the proletariat."

Repelled by this Marxist approach, Mikhnovsky withdrew in 1902 to form his own party, the Ukrainian People's Party, which, as has already been observed, remained small because it failed to take account of the peasantry. The following year *Haslo* admitted that "the idea of Ukrainian independence has its value, but we must recognize that this program betrays the lack of a socialist outlook .... "³² The "Proyekt prohramy RUP" [Draft Program of the RUP], printed in 1903, claimed therefore that "the RUP shares the basic principles, aims and tactics of international Social Democracy." The draft program clearly defined the social demands of the party and, on the national problem, set the attainment of autonomy with a separate legislature as the party's practical minimum demand.³³

It should be pointed out that after 1905 the USDRP was obliged, for tactical reasons, to take this same half-way position in its plank on the national problem. Mazepa explains this approach to the national problem by the Ukrainian parties in the following manner:

> If we compare these declarations of Ukrainian political organizations and political leaders of the period prior to the Revolution of 1917 with the declarations and programs of other subjugated peoples, we are bound to observe the great difference between those nations with a *historical* and mature state consciousness and Ukraine, which lacked that consciousness. Thus the Poles, for instance, always aimed at the restoration of the Polish state within its historical boundaries, including even Lithuania, Byelorussia and half Ukraine. Similarly, the Irish in their struggle against England stressed their historical rights to an independent state. In Ukraine the loss of state consciousness was the result of the prolonged domination of Russian education. Therefore Ukrainian political ideas after the Revolution of 1905 only reach[ed] halfway [to independence] .... The idea of complete Ukrainian independence could gather strength only after the downfall of the tsarist regime .... Meanwhile, the era of Ukrainian political history which begins with Drahomanov and ends with the Revolution of 1917 was a *period of transition* from the cultural to the political phase in the development of our regeneration.³⁴'

3. Nationalism Splits the RUP

Although some Ukrainian revolutionaries underestimated the importance of the national problem, the debate on this issue finally brought about a split within the RUP at its Congress in December 1904. One group, led by Mariian Melenevsky (pseudonym Basok), began negotiating with the Russian Social Democrats with a view to a possible merger of the two parties. Another group within the RUP, headed by Mykola Porsh, demanded that the party program include an appeal calling for the independence of the Ukraine. Such a clause, Melenevsky's group believed, would isolate the RUP from the Russian Social Democrats and the Jewish *Bund*. But no official conclusion was reached, for on January 12, 1905 when the revolution was gathering momentum, Melenevsky's group issued a declaration calling the majority of the RUP "bourgeois radicals." Taking the name "Ukrainian Social Democratic Union" (the *Spilka*), this group regarded itself as consisting of "proletarian elements" and declared that "a centralized proletarian party for Russia as a whole" was a necessity; thereupon it announced its willingness to join the RSDRP "on the basis of autonomy." The statute by means of which the *Spilka* was accepted into the RSDRP stated: "The Ukrainian Social Democratic Union is a part of the RSDRP and aims at the organization of the Ukrainian-speaking proletariat."[35]

4. The Lesson of the Spilka

During the Revolution of 1905 the *Spilka* proved to be more active among the Ukrainian peasant masses than the RUP (USDRP); it welcomed agrarian unrest among the peasants and supported the partition of the large landed estates. The RUP (USDRP), on the other hand, following the tradition of western European socialists, condemned the spontaneous peasant uprisings in a resolution at its Congress in December 1905 as "the product of petty bourgeois instincts which are attempting to turn back the wheel of history-to the small holding system; therefore [the uprisings] are completely reactionary."[36] Later events showed that this peasant movement was not so much a turning back the clock of history as a mobilization of the masses against autocracy. It is noteworthy that in the elections to the Second State Duma, which convened in 1907, the *Spilka* elected fourteen members while the USDRP elected only one.

Although the *Spilka* hoped to become the only fully Ukrainized Social Democratic organization in Ukraine, in effect the RSDRP treated the *Spilka* not as its local branch in the Ukraine, but as a peasant section. It even suggested that the *Spilka* become a peasant section of the RSDRP for the whole of whole of Russia.[37] Fedenko has written that:

it would be quite superficial and historically incorrect to regard the collaboration of the RUP members with the Russian Social Democrats as "national treason." One has to understand the conditions which prevailed in Ukraine at that time and the feelings of these Ukrainian politicians of the *Spilka* who collaborated [with the Russians]. Aside from a somewhat "naive cosmopolitanism,". . . they were also motivated by the hope of extending socialist ideas in a Ukrainian form over the entire Ukraine....[38]

The leader of the *Spilka*, Melenevsky, in his open letter "To Comrades from the Ukrainian Social Democratic *Spilka* and the Ukrainian Social Democratic Workers' Party,' published in the Ukrainian SD monthly *Nash holos* [Our Voice] in Lviv in 1912, wrote that the *Spilka* had merged with the revolutionary current and had become an inseparable part of it; it had become the soul of the revolution throughout the greater part of the Ukrainian territory.[39] By being Ukrainian and carrying on its mission in the Ukrainian language, it contributed much to the socio-political and national education of the masses.

It is significant that the two most prominent leadets of the *Spilka*, Melenevsky and Skoropys-Yoltukhovsky, did not return to the USDRP after the dissolution of the *Spilka* but went over to the nationalist camp. During World War I they formed in Vienna the "Union for the Liberation of the Ukraine" which propagated dismemberment of the Russian Empire and the establishment of a Ukrainian state. The history of the *Spilka* therefore confirms the thesis advanced earlier, that beginning with the second half of the nineteenth century Ukrainian participation in Russian political parties was motivated not by a denial of Ukrainian aspirations, but by a desire to encompass the downfall of autocracy in the shortest possible time. Nevertheless, the leaders of the Spilka, like the Borotbisty and *Ukapisty* who were to follow them, failed to realize that by becoming dependent upon the Russian parties they had lost their freedom of action, especially in one vital sector—the national liberation of the Ukraine.

2 Origins of the Ukrainian Party of Socialist Revolutionaries (UPSR), Predecessor of Borotbism

A. Ideological Background of the UPSR

Although the Ukraine in the early twentieth century was primarily an agricultural country, and although the peasants formed the solid core even of some Ukrainian Marxist parties, there was no separate Ukrainian peasant party in Ukraine before 1917, such as the party of Socialist Revolutionaires (SR's) in Russia. The revolutionary movement in the Ukraine, as in Russia, developed under the double influence of populism and Marxism. The generation of the 1840's through the 1870's—from the Brotherhood of Saints Cyril and Methodius to Drahomanov—had been guided by populist ideals and aims. Following the period of reaction in the 1880's, a new generation reared on Marxism came to the fore in the last decade of the nineteenth century. From this time on, down to the Revolution of 1917, Marxist and Social Democratic ideas played the leading roles in the political life of Socialist circles in Ukraine. However, after 1905 populist ideas enjoyed a revival, which was to contribute to the formation in 1917 of a strong party for the peasants, the UPSR, side by side with the USDRP.

The UPSR did not possess a uniform and clear-cut ideology, for it was influenced by many sources. Zhyvotko offers the following explanation for this fact:

> At a time when socialist thought in the West was based primarily on the materialist conception of social growth, and in particular on Marx's philosophy of history, in the East [it] developed along two paths: 1) as a materialist (monistic) outlook which provided the foundation for Social Democracy, and 2) as a pluralist view of social development, expounded by populism, which after an idealist and critical-stage ... soon provided the stimulus for the creation of the Party of Socialist Revolutionaries (All-Russian), which held its first congress in 1897 in Voronezh. The same ideology inspired the Armenian party "Dashnaktsutyun [Unity]," the Georgian Party of Socialist Federalists and the Ukrainian Party of Socialist Revolutionaries.[1]

The influence of populism in Ukraine, although significant, was weaker than in Russia. There were at least two reasons for this.

In the first place the Russian populists leaned heavily on certain theories concerning Russia's destiny which had been developed by Slavophiles. But toward the end of the nineteenth century Slavophilism became tinged with Russian national Panslavism, a development which greatly limited its appeal to Ukrainians.

Secondly, Russian populism accepted from the Slavophiles their theory of the significance in Russia's development of the peasant repartitional commune (*mir*) as the germ of the future structure of Russian society. The Ukraine, however, lacked the *mir*, which had become the cornerstone of the philosophy of the Russian populists and their intellectual descendants, the SR's.

Therefore, although brought up on Russian populist ideas, the Ukrainian SR groups at the beginning of the twentieth century made important revisions in these ideas to fit their own needs, revisions based on the teachings of Drahomanov, on the publications of the emigre Mykola Zaliznyak, who translated much western European socialist literature into Ukrainian, and on the Ukrainian revolutionary press which was influenced more by liberal and Social Democratic than by populist ideas.[2]

Of the UPSR in 1917 Shapoval has stated that it

> grew spontaneously and comprised a wide range of intellects, temperaments, tastes, and habits. To expect that all should merge into one specific type within the period of a year was impossible. Therefore, although all had a single aim, the roads were many.

Thus the UPSR, when it was formed in 1917, had the character of a non-Marxist peasant party. It was not, however, anti-Marxist, as were the Russian SR's who for years had waged ideological battle against the Russian Marxists.[3]

B. The First Attempts at Formation of Ukrainian SR Groups Before 1917

The first mention of a Ukrainian SR group occurs in connection with the split in the RUP, brought about by that party's evolution toward Social Democracy.ᵈ Mykyta Shapoval, the most prominent leader of the UPSR, has stated that he "knew of an attempt to create an organization of Socialist Revolutionaries as early as 1903.[4] In his autobiography he relates that

> in 1903 we followed the [Russian] Socialist Revolutionary program. In order to check on the basic premises of the ideology, [Oleksander K.] Mytsyuk was sent from Prokhorovka to Kyiv where he saw the Social Democrat student [Volodymyr] Vynnychenko. On his return he told us his impressions, and we decided that the SR program was the best.[5]

In the following year Shapoval formed the Committee for the Defense of Ukraine, which organized the destruction of monuments commemorating Russian domination over the Ukraine. But it was only while in prison in 1906-1907 that Shapoval, "upon reading Lazarev's Zemlya i volya [Land and Liberty], finally became convinced of the truth of the Socialist Revolutionary platform."[6] By 1909 Shapoval was "ready to fight for revolutionary populism.'[7]

Arkadiy Zhyvodko, anodier well-known figure in the UPSR, believes that

> the first signs of organized Ukrainian Socialist Revolutionary life were evident in 1903-1904 when some members of ... the RUP, upon leaving that party ... began to form circles of Ukrainian Socialist Revolutionaries. On the whole, however, Ukrainian Socialist Revolutionaries, as a separate political trend, were scarcely in evidence before 1905. It was in 1906 that separate circles of Ukrainian Socialist Revolutionaries became evident in a more precise form.[8]

Zhyvotko cites evidence from police reports to the effect that "in 1907 an organizational congress was held by the Ukrainian Socialist Revolutionary Party, and its program approved."[9] He also mentions a manifesto, dated August 1911, which declared that

> in 1906 two parties came into existence almost at the same time: the Ukrainian Party of Socialist Revolutionaries and a militant organization called "Ukrainian People's Defense Ukrainska Narodnya Oborona."
> In 1907 "UNO" held its last congress which, aside from preserving its militant function, accepted the program of the Ukrainian Socialist Revolutionaries and thus merged with them. Since that time there has been one "Party of Ukrainian Socialist Revolutionaries" with a "Supreme Council" at its head.

---

d   See pp. 111-115.

The manifesto, signed by a "Supreme Council of the UPSR," closed with these slogans: "Long live the Revolution! Long live the Party of Ukrainian Socialist Revolutionaries! Long live Socialism! Fight for 'land and liberty'! Liberty to all peoples! For us—a Free Ukraine!'[10] Thus was Russian populism mingled with nascent Ukrainian nationalism. According to Zhyvotko, the Ukrainian members of the Second State Duma, (Dovhopol, Vasyl' Khvist and others) were connected with the UPSR and spoke on its behalf in 1907.

None of the members of the UPSR congress mentioned by Zhyvotko, however, are recorded in other extant sources, nor are there any other traces of UPSR activity or of a program at this time. Furthermore, Pavlo Khrystyuk, a prominent leader of the UPSR, has written that "until the great Ukrainian revolution [1917] the Ukrainian Party of Socialist Revolutionaries had no program of its own, although separate groups ... existed as early as the time of the first Russian Revolution in 1905-1906."[11] And finally, in his autobiography Shapoval makes no mention of the UPSR as a party before the Revolution of 1917. Thus, while it can be concluded that the UPSR did not exist as an organized, all-Ukrainian party prior to 1917, it is equally evident that embryonic SR groups existed long before 1917. There seems little doubt that the manifesto mentioned by Zhyvotko was issued by just such a group.

C. The First SR Groups and Party Program

Shapoval mentions that in Kyiv in the period 1905-1907 a circle of Ukrainian SR's, including Serhiy O. Yefremov and Mykola Zaliznyak, attempted to form a party. Following the failure of the 1905 Revolution, Zaliznyak organized an SR group abroad. An agrarian terrorist group of SR's had been led by Mytsyuk in the province of Poltava in 1903-1904, while a similar group was organized in 1907 by Volodymyr Chekhovsky in the province of Chernihiv. Shortly before World War I an active group of revolutionary populists, including Shapoval, Tovkachevs'kyi, Bohats'kyi, and Yevshan, centered in Kyiv around the journal *Ukrainska khata* [Ukrainian Home], which was publish.ed from 1909 to 1914. The extent of this group's activity consisted of "criticizing 'bourgeois populism' and advancing a program of political, cultural and economic 'maximalism'." Similar groups of Ukrainian SR's were formed in Kharkiv, Moscow and Petrograd during World War I.[12]

Both Zhyvotko and Khrystyuk make note of another Kyivan group of SR's, one which in 1913 began to publish the illegal journal *Borotba* [Struggle]. This publication, with financial aid from Ukrainian SR's in Moscow, survived until May 1, 1915. It was edited by Mykola Kovakevsky with the participation of A. Polons'kyi, S. Yefremov, Levko Kovaliv (a future member of the Borotbist Central Committee), V. Prokopovych, A. Nikovs'kyi, Pryhar', and the poet Oles'.[13] It has not been possible to establish whether there was any direct contact between this group and the group under the influence of *Ukrainska khata*. The lack of evidence suggests that there were differences of opinion among the local groups, a fact which helps to explain the absence of a unified policy among the Ukrainian SR's.

It was Kovalevsky who made the first major attempt to draw up a program for the UPSR. First published in Borotba, the program was revised and in January 1916 "circulated widely as a pamphlet" under the title "Draft Party Program of the Ukrainian Socialist Revolutionaries, Endorsed by the Kyiv Group of Ukrainian Socialist Revolutionaries.'[14] The "ideal" form of government, according to the program, would be "an alliance [*soyuz*] of free national and territorial federations to be governed by a combined [*spil'nyi*] parliament," but "in view of the current socio-political situation" the program demanded only "the convening of a Ukrainian constituent assembly [*ustctnovchyi soym*] which would establish the national and territorial autonomy of the Ukrainian people." further, the program favored "nationalization of the land," while in the field of international relations it declared the party to be "a free member of that large socialist family – the International."

Two of the members of the *Borotba* group – Kovalevsky and Kovaliv – attended a congress of Ukrainian socialist parties which convened illegally in Moscow in January 1915. Although Ukrainian SR's and SD's at the congress debated the possibility of merging all existing groups into one Ukrainian socialist party, no agreement was reached. Following the congress, Ukrainian SR's met amongst themselves. Besides Kovalevskyi and Kovaliv, those present included Mykola Shrah and Mykhaylo Poloz (like Kovaliv, a future member of the Borotbist Central Committee). In connection with the Moscow meeting, Khrystyuk mentions two organizations in Borispol and Novo-Basan' in the province of Poltava which were founded by the peasant Odynets' (a future Borotbist), administrative exile from the province of Chernihiv.[15]

In the period 1915-1916 smaller but no less active groups of SR's worked in the cooperatives and other Ukrainian organizations such as the Youth Union (*Yunats'ka Spilka*) and the Ukrainian Socialist Committee, in which the subsequently prominent Borotbist Andriy Zalyvchyi distinguished himself.[16] Especially active in the province of Poltava, the Youth Union included among its members from Poltava the following future Borotbisty: Oleksander Lisovyk, Matena-Bohayevych, Andriy Khvylya, the Demyanovsky brothers, Viktor Chuhay, Mynko, Vilenberg, and Daleky. Almost all the UPSR youth in the province of Poltava were to follow the Borotbisty.

3 Ukrainian Party of Socialist Revolutionaries in 1917

A. From the First to the Second Congress of the UPSR

1. The First Congress of the UPSR

To follow the ideological evolution of *Borotbism*, it will be useful to glance briefly at the activity of the UPSR in the revolutionary year 1917. The UPSR was formally organized as a political party at its First Constituent Congress, which convened in Kyiv, April 4-5 (17-18), 1917. The party was made up principally of three groups: village organizations; urban students, workers and clerks; and individuals who had withdrawn from the party of Russian SR's. Although it might have seemed likely that the most valuable contribution would be made by the last mentioned group, by virtue of its previous experience, nevertheless leadership actually passed into the hands of younger members like Mykyta Shapoval who organized the Congress and formed the first Central Committee of the party. Shapoval himself, however, was co-opted to the Central Committee only a month later. Those elected to the presidium were Mykola Kovalevsky, Levko Kovaliv (later a Borotbist), Pavlo Khrystyuk, and Volodymyr Zaliznyak.[1] The young leaders showed considerable talent and even brilliance, but because of the inexperience the UPSR, numerically the strongest Ukrainian party in 1917 with its one million members, was incapable of forming a government under the Ukrainian People's Republic. "In its ideology, temperament and tactics," according to Volodymyr Vynnychenko,

> the UPSR on the whole satisfied the revolutionary aspirations of the Ukrainian peasantry. Within its ranks were some talented and active men sincerely devoted to the ideas of the Revolution; but it was young, without organizational experience and without definite party schooling or tradition. Built on the program and tactics of the Russian Socialist Revolutionaries, it had no time to adapt this borrowed platform to the national needs and therefore felt insecure and unstable. The peasant masses followed it willingly, with complete

trust, but it lacked sufficient intellectual and organizational power to assume leadership [in the Rada] on the basis of its numerical superiority.[2]

In principle the Central Rada and its government, the General Secretariat, were formed on the basis of a coalition of three parties: the UPSR, the largest party in the Rada; the USDRP, smaller but politically more experienced; and the UPSF, liberal and national-democratic in outlook, appealing largely to the intelligentsia and calling itself "socialist" only to be in fashion. In fact, however, the General Secretariat became a coalition of the USDRP and the UPSF; the representative of the UPSR had no real influence. In selecting its candidates for ministerial posts, the UPSR inclined toward professors or specialists in the particular field rather than its foremost leaders. Perhaps the best analysis of the UPSR's tactics at this time has been provided by Shapoval:

> Our fatal flaw was that we lacked leadership of our own .... We had the masses behind us and we had our slogans, but we did not have leaders capable of transforming these slogans into organizational form .... The membership of the UPSR was drawn from all classes — the intelligentsia, the quasi-intelligentsia, the peasants, and a scattering of workers. Yet the educated group among them all was very small .... Some of the UPSR members who held ministerial posts were typical representatives of the quasi-intelligentsia; at best they would make good bureaucrats or managers, but they were not statesmen.[3]

In a word, during the Revolution the UPSR played the role of a youth movement, having the virtues of enthusiasm, but also the drawbacks of inexperience. The two major questions debated by die First Congress of the UPSR were the land and national problems, particularly the latter. Although there was a distinctly separatist group present, the Congress passed the following resolution on the "national question:

> At a time when great work is being carried out by the free peoples of Russia, the constituent congress of the Ukrainian SR's considers that the greatest need of the Ukrainian people is the immediate realization of broad national and territorial autonomy for Ukraine, the guarantee of the rights of national minorities and the immediate institution of a territorial Ukrainian Constituent Council in order to work out the bases and forms of autonomy and to prepare for elections to the Ail-Russian Constituent Assembly .... At the same time the

> Congress... regards a federative democratic republic as the best form of government for the Russian state, the establishment of which the UPSR will demand at the All-Russian Constituent Assembly.

All attempts "to delay the creation of a Ukrainian Constituent Council," the resolution continued, would be regarded by the UPSR "as a continuation of the old imperialist policy of oppression and domination which had been pursued by the Moscow tsars and Russian emperors in Ukraine." The party demanded that the Russian Provisional Government "declare its attitude toward Ukrainian autonomy" and requested that "Ukrainian soldiers [in the Russian army] be concentrated in separate regiments."[4]

On the question of land reform, the UPSR did not, because of the economic state of the country, demand the immediate socialization of the land, but it did

> insist that all land in Ukraine belonging to the state, the imperial family and private landowners be placed in a Ukrainian Land Reserve and be distributed (for use), through communal organizations, among the peasants.[5]

However the question of compensation to owners was evaded with the vague phrase that "expenses incurred by land reform must be borne by the state."

Further, the Congress debated a proposal to merge all socialist parties in Ukraine, but no conclusion was reached. In its demands concerning the status and rights of workers, the resolutions of the party's First Congress differed little from those of the other socialist parties, in particular the party of Russian SR's.[6]

2. The Growth and Influence of the UPSR

Following the First Congress of the UPSR, the party began to issue a weekly newspaper entitled *Borotba* [Struggle]. The enrollment en masse of peasants, soldiers and workers into the party proceeded rapidly; the UPSR worked through the Peasant Union (*Selyanska Spilka*) and the local peasant unions, which were non-political trade organs for the peasantry, embracing several million persons.[7]

The First All-Ukrainian Peasants' Congress. The results of the activity of the UPSR among the peasants found expression at the First All-Ukrainian Peasants' Congress, held in Kyiv during late

May and early June 1917 (old style). The Congress was attended by 2,500 delegates elected on the basis of one representative from each volost peasant union and two representatives from each county and provincial peasant union.[8] Although the SR's Khrystyuk and M. Osadchy were among the members of the presidium of the Congress, whose delegates were for the most part members or sympathizers of the UPSR, the men most prominently mentioned in the proceedings are the Social Democrat's Vynnychenko and Borys Martos, a fact which indicates the inexperienced leadership of the UPSR.

On the national question, the "Independents" at the Congress were quite belligerent, advocating "a complete break with Moscow and the immediate proclamation of an independent Ukrainian republic."[9] One delegate even called upon the Ukrainian people "to take up arms for their freedom." The Congress voted to endorse the demands of the Central Rada for Ukrainian autonomy and the reconstruction of Russia as a federative state. It also went on record as favoring a convention of all non-Russian peoples of the former empire and the Ukrainization of all public administration in Ukraine.

It must be borne in mind that by autonomy and federation the Ukrainians meant full equality with Russia, not some form of subordination; yet the masses avoided the use of the slogan "independence," since it suggested alienation from other peoples. A characteristic feature of the 1917 Revolution was its tremendous optimism and its faith in "liberty, equality and brotherhood." It was a striving for cooperation among equals; hostility toward other peoples was regarded as betrayal of the Revolution. The struggle was against Russian imperialism, not against the Russian people. The recognition of the Russians as equals was manifested in the relations between the Ukrainian and Russian peasant organizations. Both sides accepted the All-Ukrainian Council of Peasants' Deputies as the only "ruling body" for the Ukrainian peasantry which would brook no Russian interference. Should occasion arise, the Ukrainian Council would consult with its counterpart, the All-Russian Soviet of Peasants' Deputies, on matters of common interest.[10]

In contrast to the resolution on the land problem adopted by the First Congress of the UPSR, the First All-Ukrainian Peasants' Congress voted for total abolition of the right of private ownership of land. All land was to be transferred, without compensation, to the Ukrainian Land Reserve and distributed among those who would themselves work it, in allotments sufficient for the sustenance of a family but not in excess of what a family could cultivate by its own labor. The decision on communal farms was especially significant:

> In view of the fact that farming through joint effort conserves labor, requires fewer implements and creates an opportunity for the better cultivation of land and the use of machinery, it is desirable to place large farms in the hands of agricultural associations, as centers of the future socialist economy.[11]

This decision was dictated by the desire to preserve the high agronomic technical level of large estates in Ukraine.

The resolutions of the First All-Ukrainian Peasants' Congress "were confirmed by countless smaller province, county and volost peasant congresses" and became, especially the preamble, "a primer which every peasant knew by heart and to which he held fast."[12]

The June Conference of the UPSR. Immediately following the First Peasants' Congress, the UPSR held a conference in Kyiv, June 3-6 (16-19), 1917. The resolutions adopted indicate how far the party had moved to the left. The conference demanded "the initiation of peace negotiations to end the war without annexations or reparations," and pressed for the resignation of the Russian coalition government on the ground that it was "incapable of concluding peace and introducing the necessary socio-economic reforms"; the party favored the formation of a government in Petrograd which would include "representatives of revolutionary democracy." The resolutions of the Ukrainian Peasants' Congress on the land problem were also endorsed.[13]

The First All-Ukrainian Workers' Congress. Aside from the USDRP, the UPSR was the only party represented at the First All-Ukrainian Workers' Congress, held in Kyiv, July 11-14 (24-27), 1917, but the party representatives walked out when the Social

Democrats rejected their demand for the abolition of private ownership of land.[14] In all current problems the UPSR was more responsive to the emotions of the masses than the USDRP. As day by day the Revolution became more radical, the UPSR moved further to the left. The absence of a firm policy based on a considered analysis of events was, on the one hand, a weakness of the UPSR, since the party was forced to rely on purely pragmatic measures; on the other hand, the absence of doctrinal strictures in a time of revolution saved the UPSR from the pitfalls of prejudice and error inherent in any rigidly formalized doctrine.

B. From the Second to the Third Congress of the UPSR

1. The Second Congress of the UPSR and its Turn to the Left

The Second Congress of the UPSR convened in Kyiv, July 15-19 (28-August 1), 1917, shortly after the July days in Petrograd. The resolutions put forward by this well attended and stormy congress show a further trend to the left. The main points of the resolution on land reform, which in general agreed with the program of the Russian SR's, were 1) the irrevocable abolition of the private ownership of land, which was not to be the object of purchase or barter; 2) the granting of land to the peasants, for their use, subject to control of the village, volost, county, provincial, and national land committees elected by the toiling people by secret and direct ballot; 3) the allotment of land not in excess of the working capacity of a family but sufficient to maintain it; 4) the transformation of large estates into model farms under the management of agricultural associations; 5) the allotment of state funds for the temporary support of those who incurred financial loss as a result of land reform; and 6) the right of the Ukrainian Constituent Assembly to make the final decision on land reform.[15]

On political and national issues, too, the Second Congress of the UPSR went beyond the First Congress. "While standing on the principle of revolutionary socialism and subscribing to the international class struggle of the toiling masses of all nations," the party now considered that "the common goals of humanity" could be achieved "only along national paths"; it "consciously defended] the national heritage of all nations." Moreover, the national problem, it held, could be solved "only under a socialist regime." The party supported everything which would

> foster the class consciousness and international solidarity of the masses, satisfy the socialist principle of the equality of all nations before the International and guarantee the right of each nation to self-determination, that is, the widest political freedom — the complete sovereignty of nations.
> ... the UPSR stands for the transformation of the present warring imperialist states into a federation of democratic republics, established on the basis of the national-territorial principle, with an international guarantee of the rights of minorities .... The limits of sovereignty of the federal union should be established, through voluntary agreement among the sovereign nations forming the federation, in accordance with the interests of the masses of each nation concerned.

And finally it was deemed imperative

> to demand the transformation of the Russian state into a federation of national-territorial republics with equal rights and with the guarantee of the rights of the national minorities within each republic. As for Ukraine, it should join this federation, along with other nations, as a democratic republic within its ethnic boundaries, regardless of its present state allegiance.[16]

It is important to note that the UPSR regarded Ukraine as having equal rights with other nations and that the federation which Ukraine would join was conceived as a voluntary union, not necessarily limited only to the other peoples of the former Russian Empire.

Despite the heated debates among the various factions within the party, at this early stage in the Revolution the resolutions of the Second Congress were approved "almost unanimously" and incorporated into the party program. According to Khrystyuk, the leading figure at the Second Congress, there were at that time three contending groups within the party: the Moderates; the Confederalists, primarily from Right Bank Ukraine, advocates of independence; and the Internationalists, primarily from the Left Bank from the provinces of Poltava and Kharkiv, who, because they were "under the strong influence of the Russian SR's and the Russian socialist intelligentsia in general," emphasized social and economic issues. It was from the Internationalists that the Borotbisty were to emerge. It should be noted that of the seventeen members elected to the Central Committee by the Second Congress, two were future Borotbisty—Mykhaylo Poloz and Panchenko.[17]

Those were days of the rising tide of revolution in Ukraine, although conditions were not yet so stormy as in Russia. The large landed estates were still intact, and the factories undisturbed. But because of delay in executing the necessary reforms and because of the inability of the Rada to form a sound state apparatus within so short a time or to combat Bolshevik propaganda effectively, the Rada's control over the country gradually weakened. In the words of the Left SD Mykhaylo S. Tkachenko, a prominent Ukrainian political figure of the day, "the splendid Ukrainian organization began to waver."[18]

2. Influence of Bolshevik Ideas on the Ukrainian Revolution and on the UPSR

The Second Session of the All-Ukrainian Council of Peasants' Deputies. Immediately following the unsuccessful Kornilov coup in Petrograd, the Second Session of the All-Ukrainian Council of Peasants' Deputies convened in Kyiv, September 2-5 (15-18), 1917 under the auspices of the UPSR. A resolution addressed by the Council to the Petrograd Provisional Government advised "all Russian democracy" that "the very elements hostile to the Ukrainian liberation movement were to be found in the Kornilov circles" and that the latter's "information" was influencing Petrograd in its Ukrainian policy. The resolution further demanded Ukrainian autonomy by calling on Petrograd to recognize the General Secretariat of the Rada.[19] A second resolution favored continued activity of the councils (soviets) of soldiers', workers' and peasants' deputies throughout Russia and Ukraine, since they had played such an important part in suppressing the Kornilov revolt. It recommended that the Provisional Government do everything in its power to bring the immediate cessation of the war" and "the con-of peace among the belligerent nations." At the same time the Second Session advocated the strengthening of the peasant unions as "the only organizations capable of safeguarding the achievements of the Revolution against the evil designs of the bourgeoisie.'[20]

In the economic field, "control over industry" was recommended for the purpose of establishing price control over scarce commodities, banning the production of luxury goods and regulating "the distribution of essential goods— mainly through the cooperatives." Factories "neglected by their owners" should be reopened and food distribution transferred from the food committees, which had been formed at the beginning of the Revolution but which now contained "few democratic elements," to the newly elected "democratic zemstvos.[21] As for agricultural problems, the Rada was requested "to confirm the rights of the land committees and to authorize them to fix land wages and rents." Toward this aim, the Second Session resolved to expel the Don Cossack, Caucasian and other military detachments from Ukraine, "since they had been quartered in Ukraine on order of the counterrevolutionary generals to protect the interests of the landowners.'[22] In addition, it was decided that "the transfer of large model estates to agricultural associations for collective farming may be carried out only with the approval of village communes and [only] when there are people willing to undertake collective farming."[23] The idea of model farms had originally been proposed by specialists from the intelligentsia, but because of the attempted Kornilov coup the masses had become suspicious of all educated persons and their plans; hence the provisional clause in the resolution on model farms.

With regard to the coming elections to the All-Russian Constituent Assembly, the Second Session advised the Peasant Union to "vote in a bloc with the UPSR and USDRP, but with the latter only if the SD's recognized the land program of the Peasant Union.'[24]

The Third All-Ukrainian Military Congress. At the time of the Bolshevik coup in Petrograd (October 25 [November 7]), the Third All-Ukrainian Military Congress was meeting in Kyiv, October 20-29 (November 2-11), 1917.[25] Although the majority (1,300) of its delegates were supporters of the UPSR, political parties at that time were not so much in control of the masses as carried away by them.²⁶ This was especially true of the young, inexperienced UPSR.

Members of the French, Belgian and Rumanian military missions attended the Third Military Congress as guests. "In order to combat anarchy," the Congress demanded that the Central Rada and the General Secretariat, "supported by the Ukrainian revolutionary army, assume full power in the entire territory of Ukraine." The Bolshevik demand that all power in Ukraine be transferred to the councils of workers' and peasants' deputies was opposed, since in Ukraine this would "mean the transfer of power to the hands of non-Ukrainian democracy." Nonetheless, the Congress did not regard the Russian Bolshevik coup in Petrograd as "anti-democratic"; on the contrary, it promised "to make every effort to prevent Ukrainian soldiers from fighting against the representatives of the interests of the toiling people." But on the national problem the Congress did criticize the position of the Russian Bolsheviks; it asked that the Rada "immediately proclaim a Ukrainian Democratic Republic within the ethnic boundaries of Ukraine."²⁷

In the military sphere, the Congress rejected the idea of a permanent Ukrainian army, but favored the creation of a people's militia and the complete Ukrainization of the army and navy with the transfer, until demobilization, of Ukrainian sailors from the Baltic to the Black Sea. And in the realm of religion, the Congress proposed the formation of "a free Orthodox Autocephalous Church, disestablished from the state...with a congregational constitution [*sobornyi ustriy*] and a liturgy in the Ukrainian language..."²⁸

Clearly, some of the points in the resolutions of both the Second Session of the All-Ukrainian Council of Peasants' Deputies and the Third Military Congress were borrowed from the Bolsheviks. Although the Bolsheviks did not control these congresses, their ideas and propaganda were slowly infiltrating the Ukrainian masses.

The Third Session of the All-Ukrainian Council of Peasants' Deputies. On November 7 (20), 1917 the Central Rada published its Third *Universal* (manifesto) proclaiming the Ukrainian People's Republic, in federation with Russia. The General Secretariat added a supplementary explanation on land reform, while a circular from

Minister of Agriculture Martos promised that farms of up to 50 desyatins would remain intact.[29] It was with this decision in mind that the Russian Bolsheviks accused the Rada of protecting the interests of wealthy peasants.

In welcoming the Third *Universal*, the Third Session of the All-Ukrainian Council of Peasants' Deputies, which convened in Kyiv, November 18-23 (December 1-6), 1917 took into account the results of the elections (held November 12 [25], 1917) to the All-Russian Constituent Assembly. On the average, 70 per cent of those eligible had voted; in the province of Poltava from 90 to 95 per cent. To Lenin the election results clearly revealed that

> in November 1917 the majority of the votes in Ukraine went to the Ukrainian Socialist Revolutionaries and Social Democrats, who together polled 3,900,000 votes as against 1,900,000 cast for the Russian SR's. The total votes cast amounted to 7,600,000.[30]

In favoring "a provisional, central federated government for Russia" consisting of all socialist parties — from the Bolsheviks on the left to the People's Socialists on the right — the Third Session condemned the Bolshevik coup in Petrograd. At the same time it proposed that the national governments should be represented in the central government at Petrograd and peace treaties concluded with the participation of delegates from the Ukrainian People's Republic, but that Ukrainian soldiers in the Russian army should remain in uniform until the signing of such a treaty.[31]

In response to the promise made by Martos to keep intact farms of up to 50 desyatins, the Third Session demanded that the Central Rada issue a decree abolishing the right of private ownership of land. On the other hand, when the session expressed its opposition to the holding of new elections to the Central Rada, as demanded by the Bolsheviks, the Ukrainian peasants showed in effect that they had not lost faith in the Rada; they regarded the Russian Bolshevik attacks upon it as a continuation of Kerensky's centralist policy.[32] In as much as the Bolshevik slogans advocating a soviet form of government for Ukraine were finding favor throughout Ukraine, Khrystyuk believed that the Bolsheviks would have been much more successful had they attempted "to form a strong

Ukrainian communist party in Ukraine," one which would have included "suitable elements" among Ukrainian revolutionaries.

> Such tactics would not have inflamed national passions; as a matter of course, they would have shifted the center of gravity from the national to the socio-economic field, the class struggle, which would have been precisely in the interests of a rapid development of the Revolution.[33]

Similar ideas advanced by Ukrainian socialists who were prepared to give power to the Bolsheviks, but only if they were Ukrainians, will appear later.

C. From the Third Congress of the UPSR to the Liquidation of Ukrainian Revolutionary Democracy

1. The Third Congress of the UPSR and the Party's movement toward the Soviet position

It was against the background of these events that the Third Congress of the UPSR convened in Kyiv, November 21–24 (December 3–6), 1917 with 500 delegates attending, many from the front lines. The Congress adopted the following agenda:

> I) the current situation; 2) directives to the deputies elected to the All-Russian Constituent Assembly; 3) the Constituent Assembly of Ukraine; 4) the party and the Peasant Union; 5) additions and corrections to the party program and party statute.[34]

As had the Third Session of the All-Ukrainian Council of Peasants' Deputies, the Third Congress of the UPSR welcomed the Third *Universal* and favored the creation of a federation of democratic republics of the peoples of the former Russian Empire. However, the views of the Internationalist wing of the party are evident in the statement that "the national aspect of the revolution in some measure is beginning to imperil, further successful development of the social and economic class struggle. .;.; and is dictating a policy .of social conservatism" 'which "might destroy" the support given to the Rada by the peasants and workers.'[35] Khrystyuk, a participant of the Congress, relates that the Internationalist wing, well represented, sharply disapproved of the Rada, accusing it of over-emphasizing the national struggle at the expense of social and economic issues, thus endangering the political and national gains made by the Ukrainians. As a result, the Congress passed a special resolution outlining legislation which the UPSR would attempt to put through the Rada:

1) abolition of the right of private ownership of land; 2) state and workers' control over industry; 3) cultural autonomy for the national minorities in Ukraine; and 4) nationalization of some branches of industry, especially factories which had ceased operation.[36]

In its attitude toward the form of the future Ukrainian government, the Congress was ambivalent. While favoring an all-class parliament (the Ukrainian Constituent Assembly), it also supported a "central all-Ukrainian *class organ*" (an all-Ukrainian council of peasants', workers' and soldiers' deputies). It seemed to envisage the coexistence of these two bodies, for the latter was to serve as the foundation for the Ukrainian Constituent Assembly. It was therefore demanded that the Rada form "territorial centers — councils of workers', peasants' and military deputies." Toward this end, the Congress advocated the withdrawal of non-Ukrainian armed forces from Ukraine and their replacement by Ukrainians and the concentration, in purely Ukrainian regiments, of all Ukrainians serving in the Russian army. It also called for the convention of an all-Ukrainian council of soldiers' deputies and for new elections to all the local peasant, soldier and worker councils.[37]

The new Central Committee elected by the UPSR at its Third Congress included several members of the Internationalist wing, future Borotbisty — Mykhaylo Poloz, Panas Lyubchenko, Hnat Mykhaylychenko, the poet Vasy P M. Ellansky, Siverov-Odoyevsky, Oleksander Ya. Shumsky, Andriy Zalyvchy, and Levko Kovaliv. Shapoval, a member of the center, later recalled in emigration that the majority of the Central Committee

> favored a socialist revolution in accordance with the resolutions of the Third Party Congress, while the minority favored a bourgeois revolution. The debate over the future Ukrainian government clearly illustrated the fact that the UPSR was split into three main groups: a) the Left, in favor of a socialist revolution in union with the Bolsheviks; b) the Center, in favor of an independent Ukrainian social revolution and negotiations with the Bolsheviks; and c) the Right, in favor of war against the Bolsheviks and a bourgeois-democratic revolution. The leaders of the Left were Poloz, Mykhaylychenko, Ellansky, Shums'ky, Kovaliv, and others; of the Center—[Mykola] Shrah, [Ivan] Lyzanivsky, [yu] Okhrymovych, [Nykyfor L] Hryhoryiv, myself, and others; of the Right-[M.] Saltan, [Mykola] Chechel', [Vsevolod] Holubovych, [O] Zhukovs'kyi, [Oleksander] Sevryuk, and others, led in fact by the non-party man [Mykhaylo S.] Hrushevsky.
> The main struggle was between the Right on the one side and a combination of the Left and the Center on the other. The forces of all three groups were approximately equal, but the Left and the Center together formed a majority, which was in favor of... a peace treaty with Moscow.[38]

This clear-cut division, however, was not so apparent at the time. The real difference was between the left (the Internationalists) and the non-left, yet even this division was not a fixed one, for often members of the right advanced very leftist suggestions. During the first cabinet meeting of the government headed by the SR Vsevolod Holubovych in mid-January 1918 (old style), the program of "power to the councils" was proposed, while a few weeks later the same government called the German army into Ukraine. This action not only compromised the party but also, more than anything else, showed the political immaturity of the party leadership.

2. The Impact of the Russo-Ukrainian War

The Third Congress of the UPSR had outlined a plan for the convening-of an all-Ukrainian congress of councils of workers', peasants' and soldiers' deputies. Without waiting on the initiative of the Rada to convoke such a congress, the Ukrainian Bolsheviks called one on their own to meet in Kyiv, December 4–6 (17–19), 1917. Although this congress was attended by 2,500 delegates, only about sixty of them were Bolsheviks. It was precisely at this moment that the Bolshevik government in Petrograd issued its ultimatum to the Rada, in effect a declaration of war on Ukraine.[39] This move at once changed the atmosphere of the Congress, giving it a national emphasis. "No [other] Ukrainian congress was so enraged against the

Bolsheviks," writes Khrystyuk, an eyewitness, "as this one, which was convened on Bolshevik initiative." Even the Ukrainian Bolsheviks were taken aback by the Petrograd ultimatum. Consequently one of their leaders, Vasyl M. Shakhray, attempted to explain the ultimatum as "a misunderstanding," assuring the Congress that the Ukrainian Bolsheviks, who "had just as much right to call themselves Ukrainians as the representatives of other parties," would do their utmost to bring about a peaceful settlement.[40] But his assurances were of no avail.

In "appealing to the peoples of Russia to prevent the possibility of a new, shameful war," the First All-Ukrainian Congress of Councils declared that "while the Council of People's Commissars is negotiating peace with General Hindenburg, it has presented the democracy of all the peoples of Ukraine with an ultimatum and threatens war." Just as had the Third Session of the All-Ukrainian Council of Peasants' Deputies two weeks previously, the First All-Ukrainian Congress of Councils disapproved of the Bolshevik coup and demanded that all socialist parties be included in the new Petrograd government.[41]

Here two attitudes manifested themselves — the romantic revolutionary and the Bolshevik realist. To the romantics the Bolshevik negotiations with Hindenburg and simultaneous war against Ukraine seemed paradoxical, a betrayal of the Revolution. But the Russian Bolsheviks, being weaker than the German army, regarded the negotiations as a necessity; yet they also viewed the war against the young and weak Ukrainian republic as a necessity, because the Congress of Councils repudiated them. It was almost a certainty that the elections to the Ukrainian Constituent Assembly, set for December 27 (January 9), would lead to the rejection of any collaboration with the Bolsheviks. Furthermore, it would have been more difficult for the Bolsheviks to combat a Ukrainian Constituent Assembly than to fight the Rada, which still bore the stamp of revolutionary improvisation. The Bolsheviks had no reason to believe that a compromise with the Rada was possible; the latter had already exhibited open hostility toward the Bolshevik regime on several occasions.

It is true that the Russian Bolsheviks momentarily hesitated, calculating whether another policy toward Ukraine might be more advantageous. They were about to return the Ukrainian national treasures, preserved in Russian museums, and even to transport Ukrainian military units to Ukraine from Russia.[42]

But the Bolsheviks insisted that the Rada recognize the supremacy of their Council of People's Commissars, predicating their demand on the Rada's Third *Universal*, which, as has been seen, formally acknowledged the federation of the Ukrainian People's Republic and Russia. In the final analysis however, the war was initiated because the Bolsheviks and the Rada could not find a common meeting ground. Moreover, the Bolsheviks also hoped to attract sympathizers from among the Ukrainian people, who were not solidly united behind the Rada. Here they met with some success, although the Bolshevik occupation of Ukraine under Mikhail Muravyov, the Red general, made them extremely unpopular with the masses.

The peculiar relationship between the Ukrainian Rada and the Bolshevik Council of People's Commissars now divided the Ukrainians into two camps. One camp was inclined to seek understanding with the Bolsheviks at any price, while the other placed its hopes in the military support of the Entente or the Central Powers. Faced with the fact that the First Congress of Councils in Kyiv had turned against them, the Bolsheviks, plus some of the members of the Kyiv City Council of Workers' and Soldiers' Deputies, withdrew to Kharkiv, where on December 14 (27), together with the Congress of Soviets of the Donets and Krivoi Rog Regions, they formed a rival congress which elected a central committee and declared the Rada dissolved.[43] It is this congress which has gone down in Soviet history as the First All-Ukrainian Congress of Soviets of Workers', Peasants' and Soldiers' Deputies.

The first Russo-Ukrainian war led to a major crisis within the ranks of Ukrainian revolutionaries; it brought about an internal transformation of the UPSR and accelerated the growth of that party's Internationalist wing. It also demonstrated the weakness of Vynnychenko's government. On January 9 (22), 1918 the Rada issued its Fourth *Universal*, proclaiming the complete independence of the Ukrainian People's Republic.⁴⁴ Under pressure from the UPSR, the Rada included in the proclamation a clause concerning the socialization of land and industry and the state control of banks. Nevertheless the Ukrainian SR's demanded Vynnychenko's resignation. The left wing of the Central Committee of the UPSR, in contact with the Russian Left SR's (who had entered a coalition with the Bolsheviks), demanded the creation of an SR government in Ukraine and an immediate truce with the Russian Bolsheviks. The more moderate members of the UPSR, on the other hand, advocated a coalition with the left wing of the USDRP. However, events moved faster than political plans. The Bolsheviks advanced into Ukraine, the government of Vynnychenko resigned and the UPSR was asked to form a new government. But the party was being torn asunder by two warring factions.

3. Failure of a Left SR Coup and of a Right SR Government

Shapoval has observed that the left wing of the UPSR considered the war with Soviet Russia "simply a mistake and a misunderstanding"; from their point of view the Rada had moved too far to the right, and at the same time they "found it difficult to reach an agreement with the more moderate sections of the party." In fact the Central Committee, despite several days of meetings, failed to agree either on a platform or on a cabinet. During this period of indecision the left wing "even considered... a political coup to overthrow the Rada and proclaim a soviet government in Ukraine... ." Due to their hesitation, however, most of their leaders—Poloz, Mykhaylychenko, Siverov-Odoyevs'ky, and Shumsky—"were arrested on orders of the Social Democrat Kovenko, the city commandant in Kyiv." They were released soon afterwards, and, "in the end, the Socialist Revolutionary Vsevolod Holubovych was entrusted with the formation of a new government."⁴⁵

Vynnychenko's version of this basic conflict within the UPSR has a slightly different emphasis. "Among the very members of the Central Rada and the General Secretariat were men who recognized the hopelessness of the struggle for the type of government we wanted," yet who realized that a defeat "by force of arms" "would jeopardize the gains of the national revival," for in that event the government "would pass into the hands of non-Ukrainian nationals." Therefore they were prepared to see new elections to the Rada; they would "accept the slogan 'all power to the Soviets' and were even ready for a coup,.,.. if only it were brought about by *Ukrainian* forces." Both Vynnychenko and Shapoval agree that the group which planned the coup, through their contacts with Russian Left SR's, "reached an understanding with the Council of People's Commissars on the establishment of a Ukrainian soviet government. ..." It was evident, adds Vynnychenko, that "they would also have come to an agreement with the Kharkiv People's Secretariat," that is, a Bolshevik group, "in order to ensure a national character to a soviet government. ..."[46]

It is clear from these events that the antagonisms within Ukrainian political life at that time were not so deeply ingrained as those within Russia. This was due in part to the fact that there were relatively few Ukrainian bourgeois capitalists or large landowners, and in part to the fact that all Ukrainian parties were united in the desire to preserve the national gains of the Revolution. The concessions which some of the Ukrainian parties were prepared to grant their rivals in order to conserve national sovereignty are characteristic of the whole Ukrainian revolution.

Khrystyuk once said that the UPSR was more revolutionary than the USDRP, but this was true only while the Revolution was in full swing; as soon as the peak was passed, the UPSR as a whole moved to the right of the USDRP. The best illustration of this rightward tendency was provided by the policy of Holubovych's government in treating with the Central Powers.[47]

The failure of Holubovych's government to halt the advance of the Bolsheviks into Ukraine can be explained by 1) the inadequacy of the Rada's reforms, 2) its feeble administrative structure and the absence of a standing army, 3) the Russification of the Ukrainian towns, 4) the greater military potential of the Russians, 5) the unemployment and famine in Russia which prompted an attack on the rich Ukraine, 6) the presence in Ukraine of Russian armed forces which had been fighting on the German front and which were therefore at the rear of Ukrainian units fighting against the Bolsheviks, and 7) the absence of natural geographical boundaries between Ukraine and Russia. In addition to these factors, the Central Powers virtually placed Ukraine in the position of an occupied country, preferring rather to aid Ukraine through the employment of their own troops than to release the Ukrainian units of the Austrian army or the Ukrainian prisoners-of-war in Germany.[48]

Despite Bolshevik attempts to foment civil war in Ukraine on a class basis, the war remained largely a national one — Ukraine versus Russia. It was no accident that the Bolshevik troops entering Kyiv were greeted not by a Ukrainian but by a Russian Right SR, Ryabtsev, or that tsarist gendarmes lay slain side by side with Red Guards in the Prague Hotel, which had passed from Red to Ukrainian hands during the street fighting. The Bolshevik army, led by Muravyov executed several prominent Ukrainians, including even the Left SR's (Zaslavskiy, for example) who had negotiated with the Council of People's Commissars.

Chiefly because of the national character of the war, a faction of the Ukrainian Bolsheviks formed an opposition against their leaders. In December this faction published a leaflet in Kyiv entitled "Concerning Social Democracy in Ukraine," in which they accused the Ukrainian Social Democrats and Socialist Revolutionaries of having formed a pact with the bourgeoisie. They declared that the Bolshevik party was alien to Ukraine and therefore, to defend the proletariat, advocated the formation of a new party.[49] Later, after Muravyov went over to the Whites, these Bolsheviks attempted to dissociate themselves from the behavior of the Red troops in Ukraine.

The first campaign of the war between Russia and Ukraine was one of the factors leading to the German occupation of Ukraine in the spring of 1918. On April 28, the German army dissolved the Rada and on the following day instituted a government under Hetman Pavlo Skoropads'kyi. Revolutionary democratic government in Ukraine had come to an end.

4 The Borotbisty Under the Hetmanate

Ukrainian political life during the Hetmanate was in part conducted underground; this was especially true of the UPSR and of all peasant organizations. 'Revolution had brought radical changes in the agrarian life of the country—the abolition of private ownership of land and the partition, in some measure, of the large landed estates. By dissolving all land committees and restoring the right of ownership and sale of land, the Skoropadsky regime re-established prerevolutionary conditions.

A. Worker and Peasant Opposition to the Hetman Coup

1. The Second All-Ukrainian Peasants' Congress

The proclamation of April 29, 1918 by the Hetmanate was coolly received by the masses and by practically all Ukrainian political parties. Opposition was registered at the Second All-Ukrainian Peasants' Congress, which convened illegally in the Holosiiv Forest near Kyiv, May 8–10.[1] Despite the arrest of many delegates en route to the Congress, more than twelve thousand delegates from virtually all villages in Ukraine gathered at the Congress, in which the Ukrainian SR's played a prominent role. The Congress resolved 1) not to recognize the Hetman regime, 2) to demand the restoration of the Ukrainian People's Republic, 3) to appeal to the German people and their government to support the Ukrainian claims, 4) to demand the convocation of the Ukrainian Constituent Assembly, 5) to form local armed groups which would, upon instructions from the center, start an uprising, and 6) to appeal to the workers and democratic organizations in Ukraine to unite with the peasants in support of the aims of the Revolution.

The proclamation to the Ukrainian peasantry, which the Congress distributed illegally in hundreds of thousands of copies, read:

> Brother peasants! Land and freedom are in peril! A black cloud has spread over our land and would...keep the peasants in poverty and ignorance.

Let us all rise up against counterrevolution! We will die, but we will not surrender our land and freedom!

2. The Second All-Ukrainian Workers' Congress

The second All-Ukrainian Workers' Congress convened, also illegally, in Kyiv, May 13–14.[2] The majority of the delegates were representatives of Russian and Jewish workers. The Congress adopted a series of resolutions which advocated 1) the restoration of the Ukrainian People's Republic, 2) the creation of a Ukrainian Constituent Assembly, 3) the transfer of the land to the people, without compensation to owners, 4) the institution of an eight-hour working day and workers' control over production, 5) the guarantee of all liberties proclaimed by the Third and Fourth *Universals*, and 6) the equality of all nationalities in Ukraine. The Congress declared that the Hetmanate was "the beginning of a struggle by the world bourgeoisie against the revolutionary aspirations of the working masses of the whole world. Suppression of revolution in Ukraine will be followed by suppression of revolution in Russia." The proposal of the Bolshevik delegates to call on the workers to fight for the establishment of a Soviet Ukraine, however, was rejected by the Congress.

Robitnycha hazeta [Workers' Gazette], the USDRP's organ in Kyiv, heralded the Congress as "the first united demonstration of the proletariat of Ukraine which refused to orient itself toward Moscow and Petrograd and declared itself ... in favor of the Ukrainian [People's] Republic.'[3] The question arises: Why did the Russian Mensheviks and Jewish Bundists at the Congress vote for an independent Ukraine? The Russian Cadets (Constitutional Democrats) and other rightist parties which supported the Hetmanate spoke openly, at their own party congresses, of the temporary nature of Ukrainian statehood. The answer lies in the fact that an independent Ukraine had by this time become an integral part of the Revolution. The Second Workers' Congress certainly would not have supported this idea, had it not felt compelled to recognize the demand for the existence of a Ukrainian state.

B. The Fourth Congress of the UPSR and the Split

1. The Fourth Congress

The Fourth Congress of the UPSR, the last congress of the still united Ukrainian SR's, convened illegally in the vicinity of Kyiv, May 13–16.[4] Because many of the party's leaders were under arrest or in hiding, only thirty-four or thirty-five delegates were able to assemble. The agenda for the Congress included 1) reports from the party group in the Central Rada and from the party Central Committee, 2) the current situation and 3) party tactics. According to Shapoval, a participant in the debates of the first two days, there were three openly hostile groups at the Congress:

> During the first two days, there were reports, debates and resolutions. The discussion of the question of whether the Rada could be regarded as an organ of revolution was especially heated. The Left was already disposed to follow the Bolshevik line; it repudiated the Rada and proposed a resolution which condemned it in the strongest terms. However, the majority voted for the resolution of the Center. The Right supported the Center. The resolution criticized the Rada but did not reject it. The [new] Central Committee was elected on the third day. Because some of the delegates of the Right and the Center were absent and because some of the members of the Center were included in the list of the Left, a paradox occurred: the list presented by the Left received a majority by one or two votes. Thus the Central Committee fell into the hands of the latter! . . . Asked whether the Central Committee would follow the directive[s] indicated in the resolutions, the new men of the Central Committee gleefully replied that they would not. That response prompted the Center to declare that they were creating a separate faction of their own within the UPSR. The split was a fait accompli.... Thus the largest revolutionary party of Ukraine was destroyed only a year after its Constituent Assembly.[5]

The differentiation which Shapoval made between a center und a right wing was not manifest, according to Khrystyuk, until after the Congress. Khrystyuk, the major source for the Congress, speaks only of a division into a left and a right wing, each of which was almost equally represented. The representatives of die right wing insisted that the breathing space offered by the Hetmanate should be used "to organize the masses and raise their cultural level and their class and national consciousness." Motivated by a desire to preserve the Ukrainian state as one of the greatest gains of the Revolution, they favored participation in a future parliament (State

Council), if one were to be convened by the Hetman, and believed that the UPSR should collaborate with the USDRP and UPSF "for the purpose of placing the government in Ukrainian hands."

The left wing delegates, on the other hand, regarding the Revolution as incomplete, stressed the importance of its social and economic aspects. They protested the "national, state-minded and evolutionary" policy of the party's right wing and "the undermining" of the class struggle by the non-political and cultural work of the party heads. To prepare the peasants and workers for an uprising against the Hetman regime, they called for a party underground organization.

The following excerpts from speeches delivered by members of the left wing anticipate the split that was to rend the party following the Congress. (To protect their identity the speakers were referred to by numbers.)

> Comrade 6. The present state of affairs is the result of the policy of the Central Committee and the government. The Hetmanate is a further outgrowth of that policy. In following the road of unity with counterrevolutionaries in the Rada, the UPSR has brought about the downfall of the government of the moderate parties. It is with this in mind that we must judge the present situation. Two irreconcilable wings have developed within the UPSR. . . . The first was pro-German; the second, if it had had the troops, would have fought the first. To criticize the government was not enough; it should have been destroyed by armed force. The government was supported by all but its own people. The name "Socialist Revolutionary" was adopted by persons other than Socialist Revolutionaries. When comrades say that we must establish a democratic bourgeois republic, this clearly characterizes that wing. We must separate. In matters of tactics, perhaps we will agree with the right wing, but our presuppositions and our psychology are different. ... It is clear that one or the other must leave the party.
> Comrade 17. The principal reason for the bankruptcy and weakness of the party lies in the fact that it is not socialistic. Those who stood for merely a national revolution have joined it. Under the banner of the party they joined the [Rada] government to establish Realpolitik. Those who summoned the Germans were little interested in the revolution. They stifled our revolution and have delayed its outbreak in Germany. They wanted to save the state at any price. Social issues were of secondary importance. Now they are ready immediately to abandon the [demand for] socialization of the land. We are now divided into two groups—the Internationalists and the Statists. We are not against the German people; we are simply against the policy of the present government.

Comrade 18. We have two trends in our party—the revolutionary and the evolutionary. The latter is revolutionary [only] in the nationalist sense. This is evident from its work both in the government and in the Rada. All this obscures the class struggle. In those organizations which remain legal we should work legally. But at the same time we should also develop revolutionary activity. Our principal work will be done underground.

Because of the division of the Congress into left and right, each wing offered a resolution "on the present situation, tactics and appraisal of the past activity of the party." The resolution proposed by the right wing stressed the following points:

> 1. In the past revolutionary year [some of the demands] of the party...have been realized... The party has found strong support in the revolutionary enthusiasm of the masses...Yet the fact that the party relied mainly on revolutionary enthusiasm was also its weakness; for when the revolutionary enthusiasm of the masses began to subside, it became-clear that the party lacked other, more stable foundations which would enable it to remain the leader of the masses and at the same time check the triumphant course of reaction and moderate the ebbing of the revolutionary wave.
> 2. The [Hetman] coup of April 29 does not reflect the configuration of the [social] forces in the country. From the point of view of social evolution it is abnormal. Power has been usurped by elements which have no support in the country. Therefore, one of the current tasks of party tactics is the fight...for the democratization of political and social life in Ukraine. . . .
> 3 The period of political stagnation should be utilized to strengthen the party so that at the earliest reappearance of the revolutionary wave the party will emerge better prepared and stronger.
> These tactics should apply equally to national and social policy, since the turn of events in Ukraine represents a threat to both the national and the social gains of the Ukrainian Revolution.

The resolution proposed by the left wing, the future Borotbisty, was the first document in which they clearly formulated their position.

> 1 The Fourth Congress of the Ukrainian Party of Socialist Revolutionaries takes cognizance of the fact that since the last (Third) Party Congress the Central Committee, the parliamentary representatives and the party members who participated in the [Rada] government have deviated from the path which was clearly defined by the ideological program, the tactical postulates of the party and the very foundations of international socialism. As a result, the party has become ideologically bankrupt and has abetted counterrevolution in Ukraine. Having lost popularity among the masses, the party has completely discredited its name ....
> 2 Recognizing that the toiling peasants and workers of Ukraine, deprived of their gains, should continue to marshal their forces for the final victory over

reaction and hoping that the revolutionary movement in Ukraine, as an organized force, will become an integral part of the world revolutionary movement, the Congress recommends:

 a. initiating a wide campaign among the masses in order to prevent spontaneous outbreaks by the people, which weaken the revolutionary forces of democracy;

 b. granting priority to an active organized struggle in the tradition of Socialist Revolutionaries;

 c. dissociating the party clearly from all socialist and non-socialist political trends in Ukraine which by following a conciliatory policy, obscure the tasks of class struggle;

 d. striving unswervingly for the consolidation of all revolutionary socialist forces in order to achieve the final victory of socialism through class struggle.

The resolution offered by the right wing received a slight majority.

The draft resolution on the land question advocated abandonment of the policy of socialization and proposed, instead, that land be granted to the peasants "for their lifetime and their posterity,'" but without right of sale. However, this resolution, together with the resolution on the past record of the Central Committee and the party's representatives in the Rada, failed to receive the necessary majority.

Khrystyuk believes that the victory of the left wing in the elections of the new Central Committee can be explained by the fluid composition of the Congress, a fact which was in turn the result of its conspiratorial nature. The members of the new Central Committee, according to Khrystyuk, consisted almost exclusively of leaders of the left wing—Levko Kovaliv, Andriy Zalyvchy, Hnat Mykhaylychenko, Arkadiy Prykhodko, Vyacheslav Lashkevych, and K. Korzh, a candidate. Mykola Shrah and the candidate Mykola Chechel were members of the right wing.[6]

Several weeks after the Congress, the Central Committee announced the dissolution of the UPSR, ignoring the resolutions which had just been approved. From then on the party existed only illegally. The party newspaper Borotba [Struggle], previously a daily, became an underground weekly. The members of the left wing of the UPSR eventually became known, therefore, as "Borotbisty," that is, supporters of Borotba. In the new party registration the Central Committee accepted members only from the left wing. It is true that a new registration was long overdue. In 1917 membership in the UPSR had numbered more than a million, but this was largely a paper membership; the majority had registered collectively, during mass political meetings. To have left the party in such a state of unchecked and uncontrolled mass membership during the Hetmanate would have exposed it to dangerous provocation.

2. Aftermath of the Congress

Opposition of the Non-Left. The opposition to the left-controlled Central Committee announced the formation of a "Provisional Organizational Committee of the Central Faction,'? which included Shrah (who withdrew from the new Central Committee), Chechel', Saltan, Ivan Lyzanivskyi, Volodymyr Zaliznyak, Holubovych, and Okhrymovych. The Central Faction addressed the following declaration to all party members:

> .... As is well known, there has existed in the party for some time a wing which has called itself "Internationalist" or simply "Left Bank men." This was a small group which had its strongholds chiefly in some towns in Poltava and Kharkiv Provinces. The ideology of this group differed and differs in many respects from the basic ideology of the party. This was particularly evident with respect to the idea of [creating] a state. While the majority of the party believes that the national liberation of the Ukrainian people, through the creation of an independent Ukrainian state, is a necessary prerequisite for the success of their struggle for social and political liberation, the afore-mentioned group has underestimated the problem of the national state, regarding the idea of Ukrainian (but not Russian) statehood more or less as both factions of the Russian Socialist Revolutionaries have regarded and still do regard it. This was the first fundamental difference.
> Another point of difference lay in the understanding of the methods of class and mass struggle. While in the opinion of the majority of the party the best method was the political and professional organization and education of the masses and an organized struggle over a longer period of time, regardless of whether the revolution was advancing or receding, the afore-mentioned group paid little attention to work among the masses and....emphasized insurrectional tactics exclusively. By way of analogy it might be said that the majority of the party approximated the position of European socialism, while the above-mentioned group was close to the position of Russian Bolshevism...
> In this connection, the group showed great reluctance to accept any minimum program, while the elements which today compose the Central Faction of the UPSR have always defended the view that the party program must be realized

by both revolutionary struggle and evolutionary activity; therefore, a minimum program and its gradual realization cannot be regarded as incompatible. These were and still are our main differences.

The declaration went on to announce that, because it had been impossible to overcome these differences at the Fourth Congress, the party had split into two equal factions. The newly elected Central Committee had placed the party in an extremely difficult position; hence the need arose to create a center composed of all who did not share the former's views. The declaration further asserted that it was "necessary once for all to clarify the problem as to whether our party should, in the class struggle, adopt the methods of European socialism or follow the road of Russian anarchic insurrectionism." It closed with an expression of confidence that the majority of the party would join the Central Faction and that at the next party congress this action would be confirmed.[7]

The left-controlled Central Committee responded to this declaration by resolving "1) to consider the creation of a 'Central Faction' as inadmissible, and 2) to forbid party members from participating in its formation"....The tone of the resolution was that of a different party.[8]

Whether or not final victory would lie with the left wing or with the Central Faction hinged on the political situation of the moment. The course of events indicated a definite tendency toward the left, toward agrarian revolution which had been interrupted by the Hetman regime. The Hetmen regime itself provoked a leftward reaction which threatened to unleash civil war. The growing wave of peasant discontent favored "anarchic insurrectionism," not "European socialism." It is not surprising, therefore, that not long after the split in the UPSR the Borotbisty acquired a large following, while the right wing of the old UPSR narrowed to a small circle of government elite."[9] Even during the Fourth Congress the Borotbisty showed greater vitality than the right wing. While the Congress was compelled to move from one place to another, the Borotbisty attended its sessions more regularly and were a more disciplined force than the right wing, and hence were successful at the critical moment, the election of the new Central Committee. They controlled the party apparatus at the Congress, for illegality and underground work were their forte.

According to Shapoval, at the time of the party split the leaders of the right wing were Mykola Kovalevs'ky, Holubovych, Saltan, and Sevryuk; those of the center included Shapoval himself, Nykyfor Hryhory, Lyzanivsky, and Shrah.[e] The right wing had been dominant during the period of the Central Rada. The center, despite the efforts of Shapoval and Hryhoryiv during the period of the Directory[f], was never successful in playing a leading role, perhaps because Shapoval himself, like so many SR's, emigrated to the West very early.[10]

The split of Ukrainian society into legal and illegal camps. On May 24, four moderate Ukrainian parties, including even the Ukrainian Democratic Agrarian Party which had actively supported the Hetman coup, sent a joint statement to the Hetman government protesting its "anti-Ukrainian and antidemocratic policies." The regime was therefore forced to rely entirely on the support of the right Russian parties, the Cadets and Monarchists, which in Ukraine represented the Russified upper stratum of society. Hence the course of the regime was set to the right, despite the fact that the German authorities declared that the government should include representatives of the Ukrainian socialists and should follow a leftist policy.[11]

The Hetman government and administration included many former tsarist officials, from ministers at the top to members of the village police at the bottom. They offered their services as "specialists," only too happy to leave insecure Petrograd for hospitable Kyiv. The policy of the new "Ukrainian State" (the official title which superseded that of "Ukrainian People's Republic") aimed at the destruction of the revolutionary gains. A strict censorship of the press was imposed, public meetings were restricted, strikes were banned, and the eight-hour day was abolished. A compulsory work program was introduced for urgent agricultural projects, which in

---

e   Cf. p. 135–136
f   See Chapter 5

practice meant that the peasants were forced to work on landed estates for wages established by special governmental commissions. State-fixed prices for grain also hurt the peasants. The German occupation army despoiled the country of its agricultural produce and raw materials. The peasants were compelled to restore to the landed estates everything which they had seized during the Revolution. To help the landowners collect the fines imposed against peasants who could not meet this demand, the Hetman government formed punitive detachments which terrorized villages and frequently executed peasants. According to records of the German general staff, by the end of the summer more than 20,000 German soldiers had been lost in combating peasant uprisings.[12]

These drastic measures only accelerated the polarization of Ukrainian political life. Vynnychenko offers the following characterization of the period:

> The Ukrainians were divided into two major camps—the legal and the illegal. The legal camp comprised all parties which had formerly been in the Central Rada—the SD's, SR's, SF's, Independents, and other groups...The illegal camp included left Ukrainian SD's (Independents) and left Ukrainian SR's, who had broken away from their legal parties. They sharply criticized those SR's and SD's who had negotiated with the Germans, the Hetman government and the Russian bourgeoisie.... .
> Unfortunately, the left camp was too weak to marshal Ukrainian democracy.... The chief Ukrainian political leaders remained in the legal camp. In spite of....the criticism levelled at them by their leftist comrades, they attempted to save whatever they could.[13]

The illegal camp held that real national sovereignty for Ukraine could be achieved only through social revolution. In their view, Ukraine could never become a bourgeois state, because it lacked Ukrainian landowners and industrial capitalists. They accused the legal parties of siding with the Russian bourgeoisie, since they supported the latter's protégé the Hetman.

The legal camp stood for the preservation of the Ukrainian state at any price. Later the parties within this camp were to justify their revolt against the Hetmanate by the fact that the 1 latter proclaimed a federation of Ukraine with Russia (November 14, 1918), thus betraying the idea of Ukrainian independence. They regarded the collaboration of the Borotbisty with the Russian Bolsheviks, Left

SR's and Anarchists its national treason. In an attempt to Ukrainize the Hetman government and to control it from within, the legal Ukrainian opposition parties formed the Ukrainian National Union (*Ukrainsky Natsionalnyi Soyuz*), headed by Vynnychenko. It was charged with the defense of Ukrainian independence, both at home and abroad, and the establishment of a parliamentary system of responsible government.[14] It is noteworthy that such an opposition body existed only in Kyiv. The German occupation army and the Hetman regime precluded a wide activity on the part of the National Union. In the provincial cities, especially where German troops were garrisoned, no such organizations were possible. On the other hand the revolutionary mood of the oppressed peasantry tended to favor illegal parties, especially the Borotbisty who, according to Khrystyuk, possessed the most effective political organization of the day.

C. The Program of the Borotbisty

1. The Platform of the New Central Committee

One document from this period shows the Borotbisty to be, ideologically, a completely new political group: the "Platform, of the Central Committee of the UPSR." Before presenting the main features of this Platform, it will be useful to define some of the terminology current at that time. The term "democracy" in the vocabulary of the UPSR was used in the social and economic, not the political and constitutional, sense. The "democratic" forces were the peasants and workers; only those movements were "democratic" which recognized the interests of the toiling masses. In Borotbist documents the term "statehood" was largely a negative concept, acquired under the influence of the Russian Left SR's, the Anarchists and perhaps, too, Drahomanov. However, it is important to emphasize that, although "artificial state boundaries," "independence as the ultimate goal" and efforts "to create national states (inevitably connected with imperialist tendencies)" were condemned in Borotbist publications, "the right of Ukraine to equal partnership among states" was taken for granted.

The Platform, having acknowledged the temporary triumph of counterrevolution in Ukraine, went on to analyze the reasons for this development. These were found to be 1) the absence of strong mass organizations in Kyiv and throughout the country; 2) the one-sided, nationalist policy of the Rada, which had delayed social reform and aroused suspicion among the peasants, thus adding fuel to Bolshevik propaganda; 3) the destructive Bolshevik war against Ukraine, which had demoralized the toiling masses, paved the way for separatist and nationalist tendencies and for collaboration with the Germans, and brought an end to revolutionary organizations in Ukraine; 4) the influence of the "international bourgeoisie," in particular the German bourgeoisie, on the Hetman government; 5) the "infamous" alliance of the Hetman regime with German militarism which "was compromising the very idea of the Ukrainian liberation movement and the Ukrainian socialist parlies"; and 6) the lack of support from international revolunonary socialist forces and the Second International.

"International' reaction," the Platform declared, "in taking advantage of the military unpreparedness of the [Ukrainian] Republic and the weakness of its democratic organizations, has openly aided the bourgeoisie in their struggle against land and other reforms." This reaction, it was stated, aimed 1) to transform Ukraine into a colony, 2) to abrogate those rights secured by the Treaty of Brest-Litovsk, 3) to transform the independent Ukrainian government into a dependency subservient to Berlin, and 4) to prevent revolution in Germany. The Platform expressed faith in "the inevitable revolutionary solution to chaos in the world by international democracy."

> the success of the struggle which the toiling masses are waging . . . for their political, national and socio-economic liberation will be possible only if the struggle is supported by the politically mature democratic organizations in Ukraine and is conducted in close contact with the democracies of other countries to which Ukraine has been bound by the course of historical events.

It is noteworthy that this Borotbist pronouncement contains no regrets over the separation of Ukraine from Russia and makes no direct reference to Russian revolutionary movements. The Platform expressly stated that, "in coordinating its work with international revolutionary democracy," the Central Committee would "maintain the closest of ties with the socialist parties of Germany, Austria-Hungary, Great Russia [sic], Poland, and other neighboring countries, and [would] inflexibly pursue class tactics."

The Hetman regime was severely censured, yet at the same time the Platform warned against premature and ill-organized peasant uprisings. As for the German occupation, the Central Committee would "combat demagogic slogans which were calculated to stir national enmity and which called for an armed uprising against the Germans," but it would "advocate a struggle on the domestic class front."

The Central Committee was of the opinion that government by councils of workers' and peasants' deputies would be "possible only for the short period of actual revolution," after which "government should be transferred to local self-governing organs....and to a central parliament, the first of which must be the Ukrainian Constituent Assembly." Finally, it was considered "imperative that the Ukrainian Constituent Assembly be convened in the shortest possible time."

2. The Weapon of Terror

Appended to the Platform was the Central Committee's resolution of June 3, 1918 on domestic tactics. In addition to dissolving all legal organizations of the party, 'the resolution sanctioned the use of terror against "the most influential and most iniquitous representatives of reactionary despotism in the capital and in the periphery as well as against the representatives of international counterrevolution in Ukraine." The resolution continued in the following words:

> Political terror is germane to the view of revolutionary socialism concerning the role of the individual in history. It is justified by the recent revolutionary past and by present events. ... .Systematic terror, together with other forms of mass demonstration (such as strikes, peasant unrest and sabotage), is of enormous importance; it disorganizes the enemy. Moreover, terror aids propaganda and agitation; being an open means of warfare which is manifest before the eyes of all the people, it destroys the authority of the government and engenders new revolutionary forces. ... Finally, terrorist activity by an illegal revolutionary party is a means of self-defense and protection against harmful

influences, spying and betrayal. Terrorist activity ceases only with victory over reactionary despotism and with the full restoration of all political and civil liberties.[15]

The phrase "terror is germane to the view of revolutionary socialism..." was borrowed from the program of the Russian SR's. In 1918, the year of greatest terrorist activity throughout Russia, Russian Right SR's assassinated Volodarski and Uritski in Petrograd and attempted to assassinate Lenin in Moscow. To sabotage the Treaty of Brest-Litovsk, the Russian Left SR's assassinated Count Mirbach, the German envoy in Moscow, and General Eichhorn, the Commander-in-Chief of the German army in Ukraine. The Anarchists bombed the building of the Moscow City Committee of the Russian Communist Party (Bolshevik), killing several people, among them Barbara Yakovleva, the secretary of the Bolshevik Moscow Committee. The cult of terror evoked by revolutionary ardor and by the unruly and violent masses of demobilized soldiers was intensified in Ukraine by the severity of the German occupation and became an accepted part of the revolutionary times.

The leaders of the UPSR (Borotbisty), like the Russian Left SR's and Anarchists with whom they were closely allied, were also carried away by the wave of terror. Terror was glorified by the two Borotbist poets Vasyl Chumak, at the time nineteen years old, and Vasyl Blakytny, a member of the Central Committee. It is therefore understandable that the Borotbisty, unlike the right wing of the UPSR, did not participate in reformist institutions such as the National Union and the zemstvos. A few months of the Hetman regime was sufficient to deepen considerably the gulf between Left and Right Ukrainian SR's. It was in this period that the Borotbisty severed all ties with Ukrainian parliamentary democracy, never to re-establish them.

3. The National Question

While the right wing of Ukrainian democracy sought to compromise with the Hetmanate and the Germans, the Borotbisty attempted to establish contact with revolutionary socialist groups in

Europe, especially in Germany. They believed that world revolution was at hand and, rapt in their apocalyptic visions, had no time for the prosaic endeavors by the Ukrainian liberal and right socialist groups to bring about a democratization of the Hetman regime.

The position of the Borotbisty was clearly evident in an article entitled "Appeasers, published in their underground organ *Borotba* in August 1918.[16] The article discussed a recent memorandum of the zemstvos to the Hetman which pleaded with the government to protect democracy and the Ukrainian nation. (The zemstvos were led primarily by moderate socialists, the most active of whom was Symon Petlyura.) "The gentlemen of the zemstvo have forgotten just one thing," the Borotbisty declared, that "Mister Hetman is a usurper and a tool of the Black Hundred, a mortal enemy of the Ukrainian people. If they have forgotten, then they are simply prepared to make... a pact with the devil himself and to aid reaction."

The second issue of *Borotba* carried a long article entitled "The Ukrainian National Union,"[17] which offered a discussion of "the party point of view on the problem of the nation and the state":

> During world war, at a time when the supremacy of the bourgeoisie is threatened by revolution, the best means of defense...of the...*status quo* against the growth of socialist action is the involvement of the working people in all kinds of national-statist orientations. Among the "great power" nations the function of such disruptive tactics has been performed by various theories of "historic missions" "racial destinies," etc., as well as by pseudo-liberating slogans which have screened the aggressive and imperialist intentions [of these powers]. Among the "smaller," the "non-historic" nations the bourgeoisie painstakingly spread and support separatist and independent tendencies and inculcate into the masses the desire to build national states, a desire which is not only foreign but hostile to the independent class policy of the proletariat.
> The various illusions of the proletariat, which are linked with the growth and strengthening of a national state, lead to the worst kind of opportunism, to collaboration between classes and to an unnatural unification on the "national-state" front which allows the dominant classes to appease the revolutionary spirit of the people by means of. . . insignificant "reforms," thus restraining them from [carrying out] a wide *find* planned struggle for the complete transformation of the present social structure. However, social concessions, the complete liquidation of revolutionary efforts and the substitution of civil peace for the class struggle do not ameliorate the national problem. National oppression is detrimental to the masses, not only because civil liberties are destroyed in an atmosphere of national restrictions, but above all because

[it] keeps the people in ignorance, prevents the development of class consciousness and diverts the attention of the masses from the cause of all enslavement—social inequality. In the fight by oppressed people for their total liberation, the national (just as the political) struggle must therefore be regarded as a means [to an end]; it must not replace the class struggle. All the more inadmissible is the substitution of a national struggle for the ultimate goal—the institution of a socialist order in which alone the realization of full and total, sovereign [sic] freedom is possible.

At a time when the consciousness of national injustice must play the role of a revolutionary agent, bourgeois politicians with all their efforts are propelling the proletariat toward a statist ideology, deceiving it with promises of national liberation through the creation of a national state. The enthusiasm shown for the slogan of national statehood destroys the solidarity of international toiling democracy and substitutes the conservative slogan of the state for the revolutionary idea of the nation, thus giving the national bourgeoisie a monopoly in the exploitation of the masses within the country and in an imperialist-aggressive policy abroad.

The state was and is the instrument of this exploitation, the means of subjugation of the majority by the minority, and the centralized national state even more so than the federative. Therefore socialist [policy] must strive to win back, step by step, the recognition of [the rights of] national collectives and to endow them with an important share of the functions of a modern state, until their transformation into a federation of "autonomous national-personal (extra-territorial) alliances" [*natsional' no-personal'nykh (eksterytoriyalnykh) spilok*].

Having set forth this theory, the article continued with an attack on the National Union:

> Our understanding of the national problem, dictated by the fundamental postulates of international revolutionary socialism, ... draws a sharp line between the UPSR, on the one hand, and the national-democratic, bourgeois and pseudo-socialist parties and organizations which make up the so-called "Ukrainian National Union" [on the other].
> Both the naked idea of "creating a strong independent Ukrainian state" [incorporated in the Statute of the Union], ... concealed only by the fig leaf of commercial liberalism, ... and the tactics of the Union, which have hitherto been demonstrated in obsequiousness toward the German government and in shrewd political combination which follow the goal of *contemporary Ukrainian reaction*, instead of fighting it, not only preclude the possibility of participation in the "Union" ... by the UPSR, but make it the task of all party organs and members of the party *to conduct a determined struggle against the influence of the "Union" on the toiling masses,,,.* ,
> The UPSR is deeply convinced that the Ukrainian people basically has nothing in common with the Ukrainian State; there is no difference whether it is a monarchy, as today, or a bourgeois republic, the dream of our national-patriots. While struggling for social and political liberation, for the opportunity for a wide development of its national, people's culture, *the proletariat of Ukraine,*

like every other proletariat under capitalism, *has no country*. It must simply win one for itself, and do this not in alliance with "its" national bourgeoisie, but in a fierce struggle against it, within the great world-wide struggle of the oppressed against the oppressors for the destruction of the contemporary order and the establishment of socialism.

This revised program of the UPSR (Borotbisty) had several new characteristics. First, it used as its argument "the class struggle of the proletariat" and repeated the Marxist dictum that "the proletariat has no country." This meant that the UPSR (Borotbisty) had shifted from its earlier populist, peasant-oriented platform to that of the Social Democrats, or more accurately (by the fall of 1918) to that of the Communists. Second, to "the conservative idea of the state," the new program opposed "the revolutionary national idea." This was obviously not Marxism, which has a place for the state at one stage of social development. For the Borotbisty, the national idea at that time was by no means secondary, even though they made national liberation dependent on social liberation. They refused, however, to recognize the fact that, in addition to the problem of national liberation, there also existed the problem of national sovereignty.

The third issue of *Borotba*, in October, continued the polemic against the Ukrainian democratic right, on the occasion of the proclamation of the right to self-determination announced by the Western powers.

> Under the historical conditions of life in Ukraine the idea of national liberation was advanced simultaneously with the idea of social liberation. But in the course of this struggle, particularly in the most recent times,...the Ukrainian socialist parties have made the problem of the national state the first item on their agenda... .
> ...Supported by foreign circles and governments in their behind-the-scenes combinations to strengthen the Ukrainian Hetman state, they discredit and cynically profane the very idea of national liberation in the eyes of the toiling masses, *thrusting them into the clutches of those Russian left socialist parties which showed quite clearly during the revolution their lack of understanding of the national problem and their imperialist-centralist chauvinism.*[18]

The Borotbisty, as can be seen, were seriously concerned with the fate of the Ukrainian national revolution and feared that the

Ukrainian right socialists by their policy would drive the Ukrainian masses into the Bolshevik camp.

D. Movement of the Borotbisty Toward a Non-Bolshevik Soviet Platform

1. The Kharkiv Province Party Conference

Although the Borotbist program just discussed was already far to the left, there developed under the Hetmanate an opposition faction within the UPSR (Borotbisty) which advocated an even more radical course. A group in the Kharkiv organization of the UPSR (Borotbisty) prompted a discussion of that section of the party Platform which stated that "the transfer of power to the councils of workers' and peasants' deputies is possible only for the short period of the revolutionary overturn,"¹ following which the function of government was to be delegated to a parliament through the Constituent Assembly.

During the party conference in Kharkiv Province, held July 14-15, 1918 a group within the UPSR (Borotbisty) sharply attacked this point of view and advanced the slogan "all power to the councils of toiling democracy." A resolution to that effect was rejected, whereupon the group withdrew from the party and issued the following statement:

> During the recent period of the revolution the UPSR has compromised itself in the eyes of the toiling people, a fact which became especially evident after the October coup. In place of a coalition government, the October coup advanced the slogan of government by the toiling revolutionary democracy. This slogan was adopted by the revolutionary socialist party [sic] of Russia, but it found support among only a few members of the UPSR. The position of the party as a whole until then was not clear; in fact, the right wing in the party overwhelmed the left. As a result the Central Committee, as well as the Council of Ministers and the Central Rada, in which Ukrainian SR's participated, pursued a nationalist policy and rejected the toiling elements of Ukraine, leaving them to the Bolsheviks. This policy was stretched to the limit when the so-called UPSR concluded an alliance with the German imperialists in order to stifle socialist revolution in Ukraine.
>
> Since the formation of the Hetmanate, the UPSR of the left wing recently succeeded in dissolving the infamous leadership of the party and founded a new,

illegal party of reliable persons who hold firmly to the principle of revolutionary socialism. However, once again the elected illegal Central Committee held to a non-revolutionary platform, having adopted the tactics of appeasement and coming out, at this difficult hour of the revolution, for the slogan of a Constituent Assembly, while the proletariat and the toiling peasantry of Russia are fighting for a government of Soviets. Because of the direction taken by the new Central Committee, some old members of the UPSR, traitors to the toiling people, [re]joined the party, while members who stand for a government of Soviets are expelled from the party. We think, therefore, that the "Platform of the Central Committee," which recognizes the slogan of a Constituent Assembly as the only revolutionary slogan, is a platform of appeasement. In this difficult period for the revolution it is necessary to stand on the principle of the class struggle and not to organize the toiling masses in parliamentary institutions in which the bourgeoisie, as well as the toiling elements, will participate.

We, Ukrainian SR's of the left wing, therefore deem it impossible to remain longer in the party. We leave the party which has advanced not along the road of revolutionary socialism, but along the road of the Russian Right SR's and Mensheviks — the road of appeasement.[19]

This declaration shows the great influence of the Russian Left SR's, which is not surprising in view of the fact that radical ideas from Soviet Russia were penetrating all the more into a Ukraine terrorized by occupation, in particular into the region bordering on Russia.

2. The August Conference of Party Emissaries

The differences within the UPSR (Borotbisty) were also manifest at the All-Ukrainian Conference of Party Emissaries, held August 19–22, 1918.[20] It was attended by party agents from the provinces of Kyiv, Podolye, Volyn', Kherson, Poltava, Kharkiv, and Chernihiv, the chief representatives of the Central Committee for internal, external and military affairs, and the representative of the literary section of die Central Committee and the secretary — in all fourteen members. The agenda for the conference included 1) reports from local delegates, 2). party organizations, 3) party apparatus, 4) party relations with other parties and trade unions, 5) military organizations of the party and their relation to other sections of the party, 6) party counterintelligence and its organizations, 7) the next party congress, and 8) current business. The agenda alone shows to what extent the Borotbisty had expanded their range of interests and strengthened their organizations since the Fourth Congress of the UPSR.

The Conference devoted its attention primarily to a discussion of the question of whether the UPSR (Borotbisty) was a new party or the old UPSR regenerated. Blakytny (under the pseudonym Brat) argued that "we have merely revived our old party, the UPSR, which was steered in an alien direction by our March guests" (a reference to the mass influx of new members following the February Revolution of 1917). Lashkevych (using the pseudonym Baron) said that "we are a new current in the old party." (In 1919 Lashkevych was to leave the Borotbisty and go over to the Bolsheviks.) In reality, the new UPSR was very different from the old UPSR, which after the Second Party Congress[g] had expressed itself in favor of parliamentary democracy and a bourgeois revolution, relegating socialist revolution to the distant future.

The debates on the class basis of the UPSR (Borotbisty) showed how far the party had departed from its recent past. Many of the speakers pointed to the necessity of expanding party work in the cities, even advocating that the urban proletariat should become the focal point of their attention. As one of the speakers using the pseudonym Otello put it, in reporting on party organizations and the party apparatus, "we should conduct a broad and active campaign among the working class in order to combat the monopoly of influence which the Social Democrats and Bolsheviks have over the factory proletariat."

Considerable attention was also given to the place of a national state in the socialist revolution and to the party's relations with the state-oriented Ukrainian socialist parties and to the Russian Bolsheviks and Russian Left SR's. The majority held the view that the solution of the national problem was as important as that of the socio-economic problem. However, the national state as a mere slogan and as an end in itself was rejected. The position of all other Ukrainian parties was i ondemned as counterrevolutionary. At the same time the (onference voiced disapproval of the tactics of the Russian Holsheyiks and Left SR's with respect to the national

---

g   See pp. 128–130

question, particularly the Ukrainian problem. Modzhyuk (possibly a pseudonym of Mykhaylychenko), declared:

> It is impossible for us to cooperate with the Communists (Russians) who set themselves against the socialists and represent a statist party, fighting for [the preservation of] the Russian state, or with the Russian Left SR's, who follow the Bolsheviks.

Blakytny argued that "we cannot unite with these parties because they are communist, while we are socialist.... ". Yet eighteen months later, Blakytny was to become the most ardent advocate of union with the Bolsheviks.

It is of course impossible to regard these pronouncements of the young Borotbisty as their definitive political views. Most of them were not yet thirty. The important fact is that they had departed from their recent past and were looking to the future.

* * *

Meanwhile events in Ukraine moved rapidly. Disregarding the serious discontent, the Hetman regime became even more oppressive. The fines which peasants had to pay landowners were so arbitrary that the Austrian military forces refused to assist in their collection until the alleged damages had been supported by evidence. A congress of landowners and wealthy peasants, meeting in Kyiv in early November, opposed the compulsory redistribution of land, arguing that it abolished the" right of private ownership of property, "the cornerstone of the very existence of the state.'[21]

Faced with defeat in the West and the threat of internal revolution, official German policy began to favor a union of Ukraine with a non-Bolshevik Russia. Fedir A. Lyzohub, Prime Minister of the Hetman government, in an interview with the newspaper Berliner Tageblatt, pointed to the Pereyaslavl Treaty of 1654 as the ideal form of alliance between Ukraine and Russia. The Hetman government was forced to surrender Rostov-on-Don, Taganrog and the Donets region to the White Don government.[22]

In consequence, resistance to the Hetman regime was intensified and the National Union redoubled its efforts to persuade the

Hetman to appoint a new, pro-Ukrainian government. But following the outbreak of revolution in Germany on November 7, the White Russian ministers in the Hetman government insisted that the Ukrainian army be placed under the command of the Russian general Anton Denikin. When the Hetman issued the declaration announcing federation of Ukraine with Russia on November 14, the Ukrainian ministers resigned, because the government banned a meeting of the National Union scheduled for November 17. Simultaneously the National Union, forming a new Ukrainian government, the Directory, called for a general uprising against the Hetmanate, in which both wings of the old UPSR played a prominent role.

In the words of Mazepa, the Hetmanate was, on the whole,

> an artificial delaying of the revolutionary movement which ... reached the peak of its development toward the end of 1917 and the beginning of 1918. The peasants scarcely had time to take over the land from the landlords when a new regime began...to give it all back.... This was the main reason for the continued growth of the revolutionary spirit among the masses.[23]

Visty Rady, Organ of the Poltava Council of Workers, Soldiers and Peasants Deputies

Partisan detachment in the anti-Hetman uprising in Mirgorod, Poltava province, 1918

Hetman Pavlo Skoropadsky and German officers.

Funeral of victims of the Hetman Skoropadsky's regime in Mirgorod, Poltava Province in December 1918

5 The Borotbisty in Revolt Against the Hetmanate and the Directory

A. The General Uprising Against the Hetmanate

Local uprisings against the Hetmanate had occurred as early as the summer of 1918, led by the Anarchist Nestor Makhno, a brilliant partisan leader in the province of Katerynoslav, by the Borotbist Mykola Shynkar in Zvenigorod District of Kyiv Province and by the Bolshevik group in the border region between Ukraine and Russia.[1] The moderate Ukrainian parties at that time had attempted to guide the Hetmanate toward democratic rule; not until the Hetman proclaimed federation with Russia on November 14 did they break completely with the regime.

On November 13, the Ukrainian National Union in secret meeting formed a Directory of the Ukrainian People's Republic, choosing a cabinet which consisted at first of three, later of five, members: Vynnychenko (SD) as Chairman, Fedir Shvets' (Peasant Union), Symon Petlyura (SD), Panas Andriyesky (Independent Socialist), and Andriy Makarenko (Independent, representative of the railwaymen's association).[2] In the period between the formation of the Directory and the final downfall of the Hetmanate on December 14, the USDRP formed in illegal Ukrainian Military Revolutionary Committee in Kyiv, which, according to Vynnychenko, "represented the Directory in Kyiv. ....and was responsible for the conduct of the uprising ... in the capital."[3]

The Directory's call, on November 15,[h] to revolt against the Hetmanate was taken up by hundreds of thousands of peasants; soon the whole of Ukraine was engulfed in a sea of revolution.

A few days before the uprising against the Hetmanate,

> P[anas] Lyubchenko, having learned from N[ykyfor] Hryhoryiv that the center [of the UPSRj -would participate in the organization of an uprising, declared that the Central Committee [i.e., the Borotbisty wished to keep in touch with the Organizational Committee. . . . Lyubchenko also disclosed the fact

---

h   See pp. 181–183 for Bolshevik activity in this period.

that the Central Committee had decided to carry out an act of terror against General Skoropadsky, since it held the view that an uprising should begin [in this way] and not directly, as had been planned by the insurrectional center of the Ukrainian National Union. However, the uprising forestalled the plans of the Central Committee....[4]

It is almost certain that an uprising initiated with assassination would not have been so relatively peaceful and bloodless as the coup of December 13–14, organized by the Directory's Revolutionary Committee in Kyiv. Oleksander Shulhyn has described it as not a revolution, but simply a transfer of power from the Hetmanate to the Directory.[5]

"During the uprising," recalls Khrystyuk, who was then negotiating for the center group of the UPSR,

> Poloz (from the Central Committee of the Party) arrived at Fastov for lengthy talks with N. Hryhoryiv concerning party unification and joint action, stressing that there was no basic divergence of views between the two wings ....However, after talking to S[ymon] Petlyura, Poloz changed his mind about joint action, declaring that Petlyura's position could not be accepted by the Central Committee and that he, Poloz, did not believe it would be possible to carry out a revolutionary socialist policy [in collaboration] with Petlyura; therefore the Central Committee would take action against the Hetman, independently of the Directory.[6]

When the Military Revolutionary Committee, in which the various Jewish parties were represented in addition to the USDRP, staged its successful coup against the Hetmanate in Kyiv during the night of December 13–14, 1918 the Borot'bisty failed to send their forces as promised.[7] This was their third unsuccessful revolutionary intervention in an urban area. Earlier the Directory's call for an uprising, according to Moisei G. Rafes, a prominent leader of the Jewish Bund, had been "supported by underground organizations of Communists and Ukrainian Borotbisty scattered across the country."[8] In the city of Poltava[i] the Borotbist Matena-Bohayevych had led an unsuccessful uprising, while the Borotbist-led uprising in Chernihiv ended in failure and the death of the able Central Committee

---

i   For an account of the uprising against the Hetmanate in Poltava Province, expecially the unit led by Pyatenko in the volost of Kustulovo, see Appendix I, p. 280.

member Andriy Zalyvchy. The Borotbisty were in close liaison with the other parties of the left—the Borbisty, the Anarchists and the Bolsheviks—through the Provincial Insurgent Committee (*Huberniyalnyi Povstctnsky Komitet*, (abbreviated HAPKA), rather than with the National Union. It is therefore understandable that the Borotbisty were not represented on the Military Revolutionary Committee in Kyiv.

It would be a mistake to conclude that all Ukrainians who participated in the general uprising against the Hetmanate shared the Directory's platform. Aside from the regular army units won over from the Hetman, such as those under the command of Colonel Peter Bolbochan, and the Sichovi Striltsi regiment, which had been recruited from former prisoners-of-war of Galician origin, the Directory controlled only a few of the minor insurgent detachments: those commanded by Shepel in Podolye Province, Anhel in Chernihiv Province and Ihnatyev-Mysevra in Poltava Province.[9] The program of the insurgent peasant masses was, in fact, far more radical than that of the National Union. Fedenko, a historian sympathetic to the National Union, writes that "although the Directory's call to arms was obeyed by hundreds of thousands of peasants and workers, they now sympathized to a large extent with the Bolshevik slogans of Soviet government and dictatorship. " The masses had come to believe the propaganda spread by the leftist parties to the effect that "Skoropadsky's regime was the consequence of the Rada's policy." Thus "many insurgent detachments, headed by the Atamans [military chieftains] Hryhoryiv, Makhno and Zeleny, declared their support for a soviet government."[10] Unlike the minor insurgent bands mentioned above which had no concentrated party support, behind these three atamans there stood the strongly leftist political leadership of the Borotbisty, the Anarchists and the Ukrainian SD's (Independents), respectively.

In the general uprising against the Hetmanate the forces of the Directory and the armies newly won over from the Hetman carried the yellow and blue flag, the recognized colors of the Hetmanate, while the Borotbisty flew a red banner.[11] This was perhaps the first manifestation of hostility toward the Directory. There were occasions when Ukrainian insurgents carried both banners; such was the case in the united bands led by the Left SR (*Borbist*) Serdyuk and the Petlyurist Ihnatyev-Mysevra, who cooperated in the general uprising against the Hetmanate. In more restricted circles, however, Serdyuk spoke of a separate political platform. 'Vynnychenko cites a telling peasant comment on the rise of the Directory: "Lo, there goes Petlyura after the Hetman; she will show him. Glory be to God, there will be no more of this Ukraine."[12] The suspicious attitude adopted by the illiterate peasant masses toward the Ukrainian state influenced the Russian Bolsheviks, who began to assume that there was little or no national consciousness among the Ukrainian people. However, Bolshevik policy in Ukraine, based on this false assumption, later suffered several serious setbacks.

The role played by the National Union in overthrowing the Hetmanate should not be underestimated. Only those close to the government circles and in contact with the Hetmanate army could have seized Kyiv so quickly and compelled the Hetman to abdicate. Moreover, only a coup led by such well-known figures as Vynnychenko and Petlyura from the moderate socialist parties could have achieved the necessary psychological victory over the Hetman and the well-to-do peasants who, despite misgivings over the collapse of the Hetmanate, supported the Directory.[13] It was therefore to be expected that the Directory, headed by the popular Vynnychenko, would become a government representing all revolutionary Ukraine.

B. Disaffection with the Directory

1. Failure of the Directory's Military and Foreign Policy

It soon became evident that the real rulers of Kyiv and the provinces were the military groups, which the Directory could not control. "During the night of December 23, an armed group raided the offices of the Central Bureau of Trade Unions [in Kyiv], destroying all books and records concerning the elections to the [city] council.... Early on December 25, the first Communists were executed by another armed group.'[14] The Central Bureau of Trade Unions was raided four times. A special regiment under the command of the

Ukrainian SD Kovenko was dispatched on punitive expeditions to towns where councils of workers' and peasants' deputies had been formed. Some members of the Central Committee of the USDRP, the predominant party in the government of the Directory, "did not sleep at home for fear the military forces might arrest them without trial."[15] "The bodies of workers killed by unknown assailants were found in Kyiv almost every day..." At the same time "the Hetmanites... had a wonderful time in Kyiv...."[16] The numerous anti-Jewish pogroms, in which some of the Directory's high-ranking atamans participated, added to the complete disgust with which the Directory was regarded by both Ukrainian and non-Ukrainian democrats. It was not surprising that the forces of the Directory rapidly dwindled.

> When the Directory was installed in power, it had an army of of 30,000 strong near Kyiv alone. Its strength throughout Ukraine reached 100,000. The army ... which entered Kyiv was admired by all for its discipline and good bearing. ... The fact that over 300 million rubles were spent on the army during these six weeks should also be borne in mind.... Yet a week before our expulsion from Kyiv...there were only 21,000 men in the entire Ukraine on all fronts, including all garrisons and reserves.[17]

The foreign policy of the Directory was as unpopular with the masses as the arbitrary violence of the military. At the request of the French forces in Odessa the volunteer Russian White Guards were dispatched to the Don.[18] The Directory's orientation toward the Entente and the unpopular war against Soviet Russia, which in fact had been forced upon it by Soviet Russia (the Directory finally declared war on January 16, 1919), helped to undermine the prestige of the Directory with the people. Only the Directory's isolation from all groups of the peasantry could "explain the overwhelming success and rapid advance of the Soviet armies up to the time of Ataman Hryhoryiv's first shift of allegiance to the side of the Soviet government." It was this act which "led to the [Soviet] occupation of Odessa and the expulsion of the French."[19] In the end, the Directory's policy of compromise "aroused opposition from both the Right and the Left."[20] The army rank and file went over to the Bolsheviks, while the officers joined the Whites. "If our own peasants had not risen against us," Vynnychenko concludes, "The Russian

Soviet government would have been powerless against us."[21] Against this background of rapid change, the Borotbisty emerged as the most numerous and influential Ukrainian political party of the day.

2. Peasants' Congresses Under Borotbist Influence

During the uprising against the Hetmanate and in the period of the Directory the influence of the Borotbist platform was manifest in nearly all the resolutions passed by peasant congresses, despite the fact that some Borotbist leaders were received unfavorably.[22] For example, Shumsky's plea for a more critical attitude toward the Directory met no response at the Kyiv Province Peasants' Congress, held December 21–24, 1918. Yet, although the peasants still trusted the Directory, a resolution adopted by this Congress favored a "Ukrainian Toilers' Republic" and "reforms ... which would strengthen the position of the toiling classes — the peasants and the workers." The Congress also demanded that the Hetmanate generals and officers should be punished severely and that all foreign armies should leave Ukrainian soil as soon as possible. Both requests, of course, were sharply at variance with the Directory's policy. In a similarly ambivalent vein, the district peasants' and workers' congress in Zolotonosga, Poltava Province, on January 4–5, 1919 expressed confidence in "our revolutionary government, the Directory," yet at the same time demanded that "private ownership of land be abolished." But the Directory continued to tolerate private ownership of property. Moreover, the district congress demanded that "the army must be, for the time being, a class army, that is, it must consist exclusively of the revolutionary toiling element." Many other peasant congresses expressed open hostility toward the Directory, and as a result their meetings were sometimes banned.j

---

j   For example, see the account of the clash between Bolbochan and the Borotbist Roman Matyash at the peasants' congress in Poltava Province, Appendix I, pp. 283–284.

The growth of Borotbist influence is particularly evident in the resolutions adopted by the Executive Committee of the All-Ukrainian Council of Peasants' Deputies at its session of January 14–15, 1919. The Council demanded that

> the Directory... issue a decree within the next twenty-four hours transferring power in the volosts, districts and provinces to the... councils of peasants' and workers' deputies .... The central government should be in the hands of the All-Ukrainian (united) Congress of Councils of Peasants' and Workers' Deputies. ....

The Borotbisty further persuaded the Executive Committee to declare that "*the provinces of Kharkiv, Poltava and part of Chernihiv and Katerynoslav have repudiated the government of the Directory.*"[23] Aside from the Borotbisty, the center of the UPSR and the Independent wing of the USDRP attempted to exert an influence in the countryside; however the latter was too small a group, while the former did not adopt a platform of "all power to the councils" until January 28, 1919. It can therefore be said that in this period peasant Ukraine was best represented by the Borotbisty.

C. Final Attempts to Reunite the UPSR

Despite the split at the Fourth Party Congress in May 1918, the reactionary policy of the Hetmanate caused the Central Faction of the UPSR to move to the left. When its Organizational Committee in Kyiv expressed general agreement with the program of the Borotbist Central Committee, the former held two official sessions with the Central Committee's representatives.

One of the major issues raised during the negotiations for reunion was that of federation. The Central Committee, Mazurkevych reported for the Borotbisty, recognized "federation as the ideal."[24] It was not against an independent Ukraine"; nevertheless, "it desired agreement with the Muscovite revolutionary parties, including the Bolsheviks." The Borotbist conception of federation was not that of a step toward independence but of a step, after independence, in the direction of international union. Only equal and independent nations could form a federation; therefore, in their view, independence was a prerequisite for federation. Since the Borotbisty frequently are regarded as federalists, it is important to bear this conception in mind. This approach "was satisfactory to the members of the Organizational Committee," which in fact found "no serious differences in principle" between the two committees.

The negotiations now shifted to a discussion of organizational control of the party. The Organizational Committee "insisted that the Central Committee's resolution concerning the dissolution of the party should be annulled." Speaking for the Central Committee, Mazurkevych and Shumsky informed Nykyfor Hryhoryiv of the Organizational Committee that "the Central Committee demanded the immediate dissolution of the Organizational Committee." Afterwards, individual members of the center, "except those compromised through their 'conciliation' policy, would have the right to register in the Central Committee's organization." To this Hryhoryiv replied: "Either register all members of our group or we will remain as a separate party organization of the center." On this point the negotiations were deadlocked, but it was agreed that Hryhoryi'v should continue to talk with Lyubchenko, and that O. Shadyliv (for the center) should talk with Zalyvchy (for the Central Committee). However, Zalyvchy died in Chernihiv, and Lyubchenko and Hryhoryiv, shortly before the uprising, were unable to agree on joint action against the Hetmanate in view of the Borotbisty's desire to initiate the uprising with an assassination. The Borotbisty also disliked Petlyura's approach to the plan for an uprising. Still, Lyubchenko "expressed a desire to bring party unification to a satisfactory conclusion, a hope which Hryhoryi'v shared."

Once the Directory's forces had entered Kyiv on December 14, unity talks were resumed.

> In charge of the press, Hryhoryiv provided the Central Committee with paper and printing facilities in Kyiv. . . . Members of both groups met in an atmosphere of mutual confidence. Negotiations for unification proceeded especially satisfactorily after the center began publishing in Kyiv its organ Trudova respublika [Toilers' Republic], which represented the platform of the soviet tendency within the center. N. Hryhoryiv conferred with II. Mykhaylychenko, P. Khrystyuk with A. Prykhod'ko, and O. Zhukovs'kyi with Shynkar'. . . . Hrushevsky also voiced his approval. However, the bid for unification again

failed. The acting head of the Organizational Committee, Yanko, was at that time so openly pro-Directory that he was more hostile toward unification. M.Yu.Shapoval, himself a member of the Organizational Committee, was working for "unification" of the center of the Party with the Ukrainian National Union. The Party "leaders" [i.e., the center] therefore took a sharp turn to the right. The Directory's policy also precipitated a crisis. The Central Committee's organ was banned; left SR's, now regarded as equivalent to Bolsheviks, were arrested. ... A situation arose in which-one group, the center, was in the National Union, in the Directory and in the government and was hence fully responsible for its policy, at the same time tolerating the terror directed against another group, the left, which was forced to go deep underground. The logic of events had brought about a complete divergence in fact, if not in word. The problem of unification.., was thus buried.

The friendly atmosphere of the negotiations had been conditioned by the fact that not only the center of the UPSR, but many other political and military leaders were sympathetic to the idea of a soviet form of government for Ukraine. Indeed, faced with the leftist sympathies of the masses, the Directory attempted to adapt itself to their wishes. Vynnychenko (SD), Shapoval (Center SR) and Viktor Mazurenko (SD Independent), all represented in the government, "advocated that Ukraine be proclaimed a soviet republic, thereby hoping to neutralize Russian Bolshevik propaganda in Ukraine."[25] The tendency was so strong — the Russian Bolsheviks had initiated their second invasion of Ukraine in late December 1918[k] — that the Independent wing of the USDRP broke with that party at its Sixth Congress, January 10-12, 1919 and adopted a soviet platform, although, in contrast to the Borotbisty, it continued to have relations with the Directory, hoping to win the latter over to its own policy.[26] And in late January the center of the UPSR also "accepted the soviet platform on the basis of the so-called 'labor principle'."[27] As Volodymyr M. Chekhovs'ky, Prime Minister and Foreign Minister of the Directory, declared at the Sixth Congress of the USDRP, "the soviet system and Bolshevism are two different things."[28]

It is difficult to appraise the sincerity of the Borotbisty in their negotiations for party unity. Political reality forced the two wings of the party further apart. The decision was made in the outlying

---

k   See pp. 181-183

areas of the country, where enmity between Borot'bist and Directory military units erupted in open battle.[29]

D. Borotbist Ties With Pro-Soviet Parties

Borotbist influence in the towns and the capital was much weaker than in the country. As has already been indicated, the three attempts to exert an influence in urban areas during the actual final uprising against the Hetmanate had been unsuccessful. Rafes provides a glimpse of Borotbist activity in Kyiv after the Directory had entered the capital. While the Ukrainian National Union was conferring over the formation of a cabinet, the Military Revolutionary Committee, preserved as a "civic" organization, "convened a parallel conference of delegates of all the socialist parties, including the Bolsheviks and their allies the Ukrainian SR's (Borotbisty)."[30] After Vynnychenko had received the delegation of the United Jewish Socialist Party, which sought to establish contact with the government, the Central Committee of the USDRP called a conference of the central committees of all socialist parties, including the Borotbisty, which met on the night of December 28–29. Rafes labeled it a "historic" conference, because afterwards the left socialist groups concluded that agreement with the Directory was impossible and that it would have to be overthrown.'[31]

> The representative of the Ukrainian Socialist Revolutionaries (Borotbisty) was most insistent on this point, having carefully analyzed the policy of the Directory and having underlined the danger of repeating the errors of the Central Rada from the viewpoint of the interests of the development of the young Ukrainian nation.[32]

In the face of the second Russian Bolshevik invasion of Ukraine, Chekhovsky acting for the Directory, in late December prepared "an extraordinary diplomatic mission" including representatives of all influential parties for the purpose of conducting peace talks with Moscow. Poloz, the Borotbist representative, declared that "his party was ready to take part in the trip to Moscow only to obtain information."[33] It is clear that the Borotbisty did not want to be identified with the Directory.

At this time the Bolsheviks controlled the Kyiv City Council of Workers' Deputies with 85 per cent of the votes. The Ukrainian SR's, in addition to the United Jewish Socialist Party and the Bund, were admitted as members of the Council's Executive Committee, as Rafes indicates, "because of their role throughout the country," despite their small numbers in the Council itself. There can be no doubt that Rafes had in mind only the Borot'bisty. "All the parties thus favored a decisive struggle for a soviet government and, comprising an illegal Executive Committee, participated in the preparation of armed strife against the Directory in Kyiv.'[34]

To thwart pressure from the left, the Directory convened a Toilers' Congress (*Trudovyi Kongres*), an attempt at a parliament, which opened in Kyiv, January 23, 1919.[35] "The decision to call the Toilers' Congress," writes Mazepa, "was an obvious concession to Bolshevik slogans. The landowners and the financial and business circles, which had supported the Hetmanate were excluded...." In spite of this, both the workers (Ukrainian and non-Ukrainian) and the peasants greeted the elections to the Congress passively. The rightist groups were no less satisfied with the Congress, even though the idea of parliamentary democracy triumphed over that of soviet government. The left parties, for the most part, boycotted the elections to the congress. There were no Bolsheviks represented, and of the 593 delegates, the theoretical total, only "about thirty were sympathetic to the idea of a soviet government, all of them Left Ukrainian Socialist Revolutionaries (Borotbisty) or Independent Ukrainian Social Democrats." Neither in its elections nor in its organization was the Congress representative of the revolutionary masses, declared the USDRP (Independents) in a statement delivered during the Congress; freedom of agitation had been forbidden, and no soldiers took part in the elections. While the Directory, in convening the Congress—the statement continued—wished to satisfy both socialist and imperialist ambitions, it had in fact failed to satisfy either. This was the consensus of all the left parties, including the Borotbisty. The speeches by members of the pro-Soviet parties-the Borot'bist Korniy Taranenko, the SD Independent Zinovyev and the Bundist Rafes—"were greeted by shouts and whistling.[36] The slightest reference to the necessity of concluding peace with Soviet Russia or to transferring power to the workers' and peasants' councils aroused deep resentment. ..."

While the Congress was in session the Bolshevik Kyiv Committee circulated among the delegates a statement supposedly containing "the conditions of an agreement between the Directory and the Allies." Allegedly, the Directory had agreed to join a Russian federation, fight against Bolshevism and place its armed forces under the joint command of a staff to consist of a Frenchman, a Russian, a Pole, and a Ukrainian. Further, a volunteer Russian army was to be formed in Ukraine. In return for this, the Allies were ready to admit the Ukrainian People's Republic to the Paris Peace Conference. The Bolshevik statement asserted that the information had been obtained by Bolshevik counterintelligence at considerable cost.[37]

Actually the statement corresponded to the demands of the French which had been presented to the representatives of the Directory in Odessa. No agreement was reached, but the rumors, deliberately spread by the Bolsheviks, were effective; according to Rafes, "the Congress terminated under the impression that the Directory had come to terms with the Entente, and this only served to isolate the Directory." The delegates of the left walked out of the Congress the day before it closed, issuing a proclamation which accused the Directory "of responsibility for the war against Soviet Russia and of plotting with the imperialist governments of the Entente." The parties of the left, the declaration continued, "once more declare that the Congress has no right to speak in the name of the toiling masses of Ukraine. . . . [We] are leaving the Congress and disclaim any responsibility for its resolutions and their possible consequences."[38]

The consolidation of the left socialist parties, which the USDRP failed to achieve in favor of the Directory at the end of December, was thus effected at the end of January against the Directory under the leadership of the Bolsheviks.

E. Inherent Weakness of the Borotbisty

Although the Borot'bisty understood the mood of the peasantry and therefore had a large following in the villages, in failing to consolidate their rural forces they were unable to profit from their position. The UPSR as a whole

> failed to seize control of the peasant rebellions, largely because the party failed to plan an uprising against the Hetmanate on an all-Ukrainian scale and to create an all-Ukrainian revolutionary-political center necessary for such a revolt. The party had neither sufficient strength, authority, nor the organizational and technical ties with the insurgent elements on an all-Ukrainian scale to do this.[39]

Most peasant rebels joined a chieftain not because of his political platform, which they could not understand, but because of his personality. The peasants trusted Makhno, not his anarchism; they followed Zeleny, not the Social Democratic platform which he represented. This fact in turn inflated the personal ambitions of the individual rebel leaders, who usually began their careers as agents for some political party and ended as self-styled heroes, repudiating their party. Such was the case with Hryhoryiv, who started out as a minor unknown Borotbist, later rising to the position of a great popular leader, conducting his own policy. There is no doubt that this phenomenon, known in Ukrainian history as otamanshchyna [chieftainry], limited the political significance of the uprisings, causing them to descend in many instances to mere expressions of dare-devilry and sometimes even lawlessness.

On the other hand, although the Borotbisty acted independently of the Directory and were strong in the countryside, they failed in their bid to control the revolutionary movement largely because they were weak in the cities, where they were powerless to compete with Bolshevik influence. The Borotbisty attempted to become a party of the urban proletariat but were unable to do so. To do this they would have had to re-educate the Russified workers of the cities, and this required more time than was at their disposal. Just as the Russified bourgeoisie inclined toward Denikin, the Russified working class (tended to look to Red Moscow.[40] In fact, all Ukrainian political parties lacked adequate support among the

Ukrainian urban population. The workers' councils in Ukrainian towns were, as Shakhray said, "facing Petrograd, with their backs turned on Ukraine." This may be an exaggeration, but it was nevertheless suggestive of the chief weakness of the Ukrainian revolution.

The Borotbisty were thus deprived of an independent role in the history of the Ukrainian revolution. To become the deciding force, they needed the support of the Ukrainian urban proletariat; instead, by leading the poor peasants and village proletariat to support the program of "power to the councils," they allied themselves with the Bolsheviks. Given the relative forces of the two contending parties, this situation could only lead to the eventual surrender of the Borotbisty to the Bolsheviks.

By accepting the platform of the Bolsheviks, however, the Borotbisty forced them to live up, at least partially, to the slogan which proclaimed the free development of each nation. In this way the Borotbisty paved the way for the Ukrainization of the working class and of the Ukrainian cities which began in the 1920's under the Soviet regime.

6 The Second Period of Bolshevik Rule in Ukraine

A. The Bolshevik Approach to the Ukrainian Problem

During the period of the Directory and the advance of the Soviet Red Army into Ukraine, Borotbist policy veered toward the Bolshevik platform. In order to understand the situation which faced the Borotbisty in late January 1919, it is necessary briefly to trace Bolshevik participation in the uprising against the Hetmanate. With the collapse of German power in the fall of 1918,

> the Council of People's Commissars [in Moscow] decided on November 11 to direct the Revolutionary Military Council of the [Russian Soviet Federated Socialist] Republic to launch an attack within ten days in support of the workers and peasants of Ukraine who were rebelling against the Hetman.[1]

For this purpose a Revolutionary Council, consisting of Georgii L. Pyatakov, Volodymyr P. Zatonsky, J.V. Stalin, and Vladimir A. Antonov-Ovseyenko, was established in the Kursk frontier area on November 17, 1918.[2] At the same time a Provisional Workers' and Peasants' Government of Ukraine headed by Pyatakov was formed.

The servants of an empire are often more aggressive in the dominions than in the mother country. It was Pyatakov who provided the theoretical justification for the empirical attitude of the Russian Bolsheviks in Ukraine who regarded everything Ukrainian as counterrevolutionary and destructive of all-Russian proletarian unity.[3] On the national question Pyatakov shared the views of the German Social Democrat leader Rosa Luxemburg, who regarded the national struggle for independence as detrimental to the interests of the proletarian revolution.[4] A man of extraordinary will power, Pyatakov engineered conflicts between the Directory and the Council of People's Commissars in Moscow. In opposition to the Borotbisty, the Ukrainian SD Independents and even some local Bolsheviks, he advocated a policy of direct intervention by the Russian Red Army.

Pyatakov and his associates did not believe that the Bolsheviks would gain a following among the workers and peasants in Ukraine. On November 11, 1918 Yakov A. Epshtein (pseudonym Yakovlev), a Katerynoslav Bolshevik, declared that "although the workers and many of the peasants, especially in Chernihiv Province, are on our side, there is no basis for thinking that a [pro-Bolshevik] revolutionary movement can arise, let alone succeed, in Ukraine without the support of considerable forces of the Red Army."[5] And in fact the Ukrainians rebelled against the Hetmanate under both democratic and leftist Soviet slogans.[1] A centralist at heart, Pyatakov tolerated the existence of a Ukrainian Soviet government, but firmly opposed any compromise with Ukrainian realities or with the Ukrainian left wing pro-Soviet parties.

In the Bolshevik view — the view which is today official Communist policy — the rights of men and nations are relative rather than absolute; they arise in the process of transition from old to new social conditions. These rights, according to the Bolsheviks, manifested themselves clearly for the first time during the French Revolution, yet the stage of development of the forces of production in eighteenth century France made their full realization impossible. In order to win complete freedom, the theory runs, it was necessary to destroy the existing, antiquated social forms. History had assigned this task to the working class, whose aims were to be realized by the Bolshevik Party. Everything would have to be subordinated to this goal, since its realization was the prerequisite for other liberties, among them the freedom of subjugated peoples who could never achieve real equality under the old social conditions. For the Bolsheviks, the national problem was therefore of secondary importance. Lenin stated that the Bolsheviks did not support every national movement of liberation, but only those which advanced the struggle for the liberation of the proletariat.[6] This was the basic ideological distinction between the Bolsheviks and the Borotbisty. (It is important, however, to bear in mind the fact that the Bolsheviks never openly repudiated the equal rights of the Ukrainian peoples.)

---

1   See pp. 167-170

The Bolsheviks became strong in Ukraine primarily because they had the support of the Red Army. Yet this fact does not completely explain their success. They controlled 85 per cent of the seats in the Kyiv City Council of Workers' Deputies during the Directory.m Bolshevik influence was equally strong in the Donets Basin and the urban areas of the provinces of Kharkiv, Katerynoslav and Odessa. The fact that the Bolsheviks commanded the vital political centers, the cities, was enough in itself to make them powerful in Ukraine. In the final analysis the proximity of Ukraine to Red Russia precluded successful competition with the Russian Bolsheviks, who regarded Ukraine as merely one more battlefield in the Civil War.

B. Borotbist Efforts to Form a Government

The Borotbisty stood for the complete equality of Ukraine and Russia. Guided by their belief in the inalienable rights of personal and national freedom, they too had the proletarian revolution at heart, for social liberation was the realization of man's right to equality. But that was precisely why they attacked the national policy of the Bolsheviks which, in their view, obstructed the strengthening of soviet government in Ukraine. They accused the Bolsheviks of abetting, by their policy, Petlyurism and making this movement popular even with social classes which ought to have been on the Soviet side.

Taught by the experience of the Muravyov period of Bolshevik rule in Ukraine in early 1918,n the Borotbisty in January 1919 worked for "a) the organization of a separate national Ukrainian army, b) an independent and separate administration of the Ukrainian economy, and c) an intensification of Ukrainization."[7]

1. The Borotbist Central Revolutionary Committee

Khrystyuk mentions a Borotbist Chief Revolutionary Committee, consisting of Shynkar, Mykhaylychenko, Blakytny, Shumsky,

---

m See pp. 176–177
n See pp. 139–144

Lytvynenko, and Lashkevych, which participated in the organization of the uprising against the Hetmanate. Dissatisfied with the Directory's policy, the Committee, in league with the Russian Bolsheviks, directed an uprising against the Directory throughout Left Bank Ukraine.[8] As far as can be ascertained, this is the same committee, with a slight modification in name, as the Borotbist Central Revolutionary Committee which became active in mid-January: "the Ukrainian SR's [Borotbisty], vacillating between the Directory and the Bolsheviks, were an important political group which formed the so-called Central Revolutionary Committee, headed by Hnat Mykhaylychenko."[9]

Rafes devotes considerable attention to the conflict of this Borotbist center with the Bolsheviks and the attitude which the Jewish Bund adopted toward it.

> The formation of Pyatakov's government in Kharkiv consisting solely of members of the Communist Party was highly embarassing to all of us. We regarded it as... an attempt to ignore all other groups at the risk... of causing friction with that part of the peasantry which... supported the Borotbisty. In the middle of January, because of this friction, the party of Ukrainian SR's (Borotbisty) created its own government, the "Council of Revolutionary Emissaries," paralleling the [Bolshevik] Kharkiv government. This was no mere gesture, since the Borotbisty carried on extensive work and mustered large partisan units. The creation of this second government was also very disturbing to us (the Bund). [As a result] the Bureau [of the Bund\ called a special meeting which adopted the following attitude toward this conflict:
> "Having heard the declaration of the "Council of Chief Revolutionary Emissaries," formed by the party of Ukrainian SR's (Borotbisty), the meeting... has come to the following conclusion:
> "1) The formation of this center solely by the party of Ukrainian SR's (Borotbisty), which draws its support exclusively from the Ukrainian peasantry, and without agreement with the other parties which accept the platform of Soviet rule, in particular the Communist Party, is a sign of growing friction between the urban proletariat and the poorer strata of the peasantry....
> "2) Under the difficult international circumstances in which the fight for the establishment of Soviet rule is being and will continue to be waged during the initial period following its institution, this fight is being aggravated in Ukraine by the national differences between the city and the village and conceals in itself consequences extremely dangerous for the whole revolution in Ukraine. Thus, the task of all adherents of Soviet rule is to make every effort to liquidate the imminent conflict, by means of agreement among the revolutionary socialist parties.
> "3) As an organization which relies on the support of the urban proletarian masses, the Bund, in this conflict, cannot in any event tie itself with the center

formed by the Ukrainian SR's (Borotbisty). In endeavoring to achieve an agreement, it should limit itself to the propagation of its platform among the working masses and, by the influence it thus gains, to the continuation of its revolutionary activity in the organs of the "Executive Committee" [of the Kyiv City Council] in close contact with the political organization of the Communists."[10]

Thus the minority party, the *Bund*, troubled as it was by the conflict between the Bolsheviks and Borotbisty, came to support the stronger side, the Bolsheviks.

2   Attempted Use of Hryhoryiv's Army

The first item on the Borotbist political agenda in their endeavor to establish a soviet, but non-Bolshevik government in Ukraine was the formation of an independent Ukrainian Red Army. The source of manpower and military skill for such an army was to be the partisan army of Ataman Hryhoryiv, who had succeeded in uniting under his command many Borotbist partisan detachments in southern Ukraine which had kept aloof from Bolshevik influence after the uprising against the Hetmanate.

Ukrainian historians who maintain that Hryhoryiv betrayed the Directory overlook his role as a Borotbist partisan leader and forget that the Borotbisty never recognized the Directory. "Before the uprising against the Directory," according to one Soviet source, "Hryhoryiv was, it would appear, a district emissary of the [Borotbist] Central Revolutionary Committee."[11] This would indicate that in the Borotbist movement Hryhoryiv was, politically, a new man, since the rank of district party emissary was certainly low for a military leader of his caliber.

There is only one set of documents available which shed light on the cautious, although under the circumstances quite daring, attempt of the Borotbist Central Revolutionary Committee to contend with the Bolsheviks in the creation of a Ukrainian Red Army. The documents record the negotiations between Hryhoryiv and the Soviet high command in the last days of January 1919, when the Bolshevik Red Army was already deep in Ukraine.[12] The following telegram from Hryhoryiv to the Bolshevik Revolutionary Committee in Aleksandrovsk (now Zaporozhye) initiated the negotiations:

> I, the Ataman of the partisans in Kherson Province and Taurida wish to speak with the representatives of the governmental authority in Aleksandrovsk and transmit very important information to it. Will a representative of this authority speak with me?
> I shall at once advise you of my platform, if the authority in Aleksandrovsk is democratic, not Cadet. Therefore listen: with the capitulation [of the Directory] on January 25 [1919] new style, soviet rule has been proclaimed in Ukraine. The Directory has fallen. To replace the Directory a new government has been formed of Left SR's [Borotbisty] and Ukrainian Bolsheviks. Members of the new government include Hnat Mykhaylychenko, Mykola Shynkar', Kolosfov], Shums'kyi, Vasyl' Blakytnyi, Vyacheslav Lashkevych, and Mykola Lytvynenko. Revolutionary headquarters of the Central Revolutionary Committee is located in Kharkiv. Do you know about this?
> All twenty of my partisan units are fighting against the independents [i.e., nationalists] and the supporters of the world bourgeoisie; we are against the Directory, the Cadets, the English, the Germans, and the French, whom the bourgeoisie have brought to Ukraine. We are not against the toiling people of Germany or France or other states; we fight only those who protect the bourgeoisie. The toiling peasants and the workers are with us.
> Right now a declaration of the Council of Revolutionary Emissaries to the Ukrainian people, the peasants and the proletariat is being printed. Keep in touch with Apostalovo by telegraph; tomorrow the declaration will be transmitted for distribution among the people. Councils and land committees must be introduced everywhere. I am now sending a delegation to Aleksandrovsk to verify the type of government which is being established in that area.

Having described the strength and distribution of his forces, Hryhoryiv continued:

> Vynnychenko, it is said, went to Soviet Russia to conduct negotiations, but his mission was too late; several representatives of the new government in Ukraine proclaimed soviet rule in order to avoid strife within democracy and in order to achieve that which our weary and betrayed toiling people have so long awaited. Our motto is: all power to the councils and dictatorship of the proletariat.[13]

The Soviet historian of these events contends that Hryhoryiv was "confused" over recent political developments:

> Mykhaylychenko, Blakytnyi, Shums'kyi, and other leaders of the Ukrainian SR's [Borotbisty] were organizers of the Central Revolutionary Committee in opposition to the Directory, but were not members of the provisional Revolutionary Government (Bolshevik), although the Central Revolutionary Committee sent Blakytnyi (Ellans'kyi) and Marchenko (Lashkevych) to negotiate an agreement with the Bolsheviks.

At first glance it might appear that Hryhoryiv really was ignorant of the political developments. His reference to a new Soviet, Borotbist-controlled government in Kharkiv, headed by Mykhaylychenko, seems to strengthen this view. However, a later telegram from Khristian Rakovsky to Georgii V. Chicherin, Soviet Commissar of Foreign Affairs, makes it clear that a government headed by Mykhaylychenko did exist in Znamenka, very near Hryhoryiv's headquarters. From Hryhoryi'v's reference to Kharkiv, it can thus be argued that he intentionally filled the new Kharkiv Bolshevik government with Borotbisty. In any event, other available evidence confirms the view that Hryhoryiv, while negotiating with the Bolsheviks, was not improvising, but was acting in accordance with someone's definite plan.

Having relayed its conversation with Hryhoryiv to the high command of the Kharkiv group of Soviet armies, the Aleksandrovsk Revolutionary Committee received the following telegram from Vladimir Kh. Aussem:

> To the Military Revolutionary Committee in the city of Aleksandrovsk.
>
> Having heard the report by the representatives of your committee on the negotiations between your delegation and Ataman Hryhoryiv, I have to inform you that the high command of the Ukrainian Soviet Red Army can enter into negotiations or agreements only upon these conditions: unconditional recognition of Soviet authority in the Ukraine as represented by the Provisional Workers' and Peasants' Government which is in Kharkiv and [which] is headed by Comrades Pyatakov, Kotsyubyns'kyi, Rakovsky, Artyom, and others, and subordination to the high military command of the Soviet Red Army of the Ukraine.
> Should these conditions be acceptable, it is suggested that Ataman Hryhoryiv appear in person or send his representatives to the city of YeKaterynoslav for negotiations, which will be conducted with him by Comrades Dybenko and Petrenko, on behalf of the military command, and by someone to be authorized, on behalf of the government. The representatives should be accompanied by a member of the Aleksandrovsk Revolutionary Committee, safeguarded by special pass to be issued by the afore-mentioned Revolutionary Committee. It is understood that the representatives will be guaranteed safe conduct.
>
> Commandant of the Kharkov group of troops of the Soviet Army: Aussem.
> Senior Adjutant: Shulzhenko.

From the tone of Aussem's telegram it is obvious that the Bolsheviks, while recognizing the importance of Hryhoryiv's partisan army, felt sufficiently strong to demand his complete submission.

The progress of the negotiations can be followed in the record preserved of a direct wire conversation between Hryhoryiv and the authorized Bolshevik representative, Petrenko, on February 1, 1919:

> *Hryhoryiv*: I am Afaman Hryhoryiv.
> *Petrenko*: I am Chief of Staff of the special group, Petrenko.
> *Hryhory'iv*: Good afternoon, Comrade Petrenko. What has my delegation achieved and when can I expect it back? *Petrenko*: You alone are responsible for the delay. We are awaiting your reply. Do you agree to recognize the Revolutionary Military Council of the Ukrainian Soviet Army as the only military center?
> *Hryhoryiv*: Such a council should be formed from representatives of our center and yours. We have almost the same platform as you and have our own Central Revolutionary Committee. In my opinion it would be most advisable to unite our armies and high commands into one; it would be a little awkward to subordinate one army to the other. As of today we have approximately 100,000 men on all fronts: 30,000 partisans, and the remainder regular units.

The fast-moving military events of February 1, 1919 were turning to the advantage of the Bolsheviks. The Directory's army was in retreat before the Bolsheviks, advancing on Kyiv. In view of this, Hryhoryiv's figure of 100,000 men under his command was probably an exaggeration.

The conversation between Petrenko and Hryhoryiv continued as follows:

> Petrenko: Comrade Hryhoryi'v! We do not want to resort to propaganda and agitation. I think you must realize the present situation. There is in the Ukraine the Provisional Workers' and Peasants' Government, which consists of Bolsheviks and Left SR's [Borot'bisty].[14] It is headed by Rakovsky. Of the Left SR's I know so far only one. Do you wish to recognize this government and accept the supremacy of the Revolutionary Military Council appointed by it? We have nothing else to talk about. Compromises and contacts will be established later in the party centers upon agreement between the Bolsheviks and [Left] SR's.
> Hryhory'iv: Our movement consists almost entirely of [Left] SR's, except that my chief of staff and his aide are Bolsheviks. In order to halt the advance of the English, French, Germans, and Cadets, whom I have been fighting for four days, we should combine our front. You must realize that yesterday and today I fought stiff battles against forty-two echelons of [Ukrainian] nationalists and

Galicians. In Znamenka, I myself, my staff and our partisans are ready to extend to you a brotherly hand, but without authority from our center, with which I have been out of touch for the second day, I wish to regard our agreement [obyednannya], or more exactly my agreement with you, as tactical [operatyunym].

I agree to your conditions and recognize your supreme command, provided that in future the problem concerning unification of the higher command rests with your center and ours. I think that your command and ours will reach an agreement, since we shall not argue over the [problem of] authority. Power should belong to the people through their elected representatives; our supreme authority and yours are temporary and revolutionary. The permanent government will be formed not by us or by you, but by the people. What do you say to this?

Petrenko: The Congress of Soviets which will be held early in March will elect the government. You will learn more details about this in the declaration of the Workers' and Peasants' Government. I shall now report your agreement to our command. With your delegation we shall begin to discuss the shortening of the front. The rest we shall leave to the party centers. . . .

The results of his conversation with Hryhoryiv, Petrenko now reported to Aussem by telephone:

Chief of Staff Petrenko, on the phone: I wish to inform you that agreement with Ataman Hryhoryiv was reached at 1500 hours today. Ataman Hryhoryiv has accepted our conditions, has recognized the supreme authority of the Provisional Workers' and Peasants' Government and the military command of the Revolutionary Military Council, stipulating the possibility of further negotiations between his center, that is, the Left SR [Borotbist] government, and our center. He commands forces in the area from Aleksandrovsk to Kherson and Nikolayev, along the right bank of the Dnepr. He is in complete control of the Nikolayev-Znamenka railway line, just outside Nikolayev at Novopavlovka station. . . .

Aussem: Once Hryhoryiv has accepted our terms, it will be possible to begin regrouping his units. Have him tell us just what units he has and give us exact, not fantastic figures. The point about future negotiations with his center or, as you put it, the SR government, is rather vague. There is no such center, at least not in Kharkiv, as he says in his first telegram. Vasyl' Blakytnyi is here, but he doesn't know about the center.[15] Please tell him this and do not agree to conduct any negotiations with the center.

Petrenko: When I transmit to you the contents of our telephone conversation with [Hryhoryi'v], the picture will become clearer. Blakytny's name appears under the declaration of people's commissariat to the Ukrainian people and soldiers."[16] We have [a copy of] this declaration, and Averin knows of it too. The delegation cannot furnish exact details of its forces, since these are partisans. The Central Revolutionary Committee, as the supreme authority is known, is located in Znamenka. It is said that there are in all 20 units, 23,000 men strong, with some artillery and a considerable number of machine guns.

Hryhoryiv's chief of staff was not, as he said a Bolshevik, but the very popular partisan leader Yurko Tyutyunnyk.[17] Moreover, the Borotbist Central Revolutionary Committee was in Znamenka, the location of Hryhoryiv's headquarters.

His account of being cut off for two days was merely a political maneuver. The Borotbist Central Revolutionary Committee did not want to participate directly in the negotiations, since it was already holding talks with the Bolsheviks in Kharkiv. Hryhoryiv's negotiations must therefore be regarded as a diplomatic move by the Borotbisty in an attempt to impress the Kharkiv Bolsheviks with Borotbist military strength. However, because the bargaining power of the Borotbisty was small, Hryhoryiv readily accepted Bolshevik supremacy, albeit conditionally. He had the choice of joining either the then popular Red Army or the unpopular army of the Ukrainian People's Republic. By siding with the Bolsheviks he had little to lose: on the one hand he retained command of his forces, while on the other hand Bolshevik support enabled him to carry out a successful campaign against the French and Denikin's Volunteer Army in the south. On March 9, 1919 Hryhoryi'v retook Kherson, on March 12, Nikolayev, and on April 4, Odessa, thus becoming a popular hero fighting under the slogan "Drive the Entente into the sea!"[18]

Finally, there is Rakovsky's telegram concerning the Bolshevik agreement with Hryhoryi'v to the Moscow Commissar of Foreign Affairs Chicherin:

> Moscow. To Chicherin. Copy to Lenin, Trotsky, Sverdlov.
>
> On February 1, an agreement was reached between representatives of our army, which is operating on the border of Katerynoslav and Kherson Provinces, and Ataman Hryhoryiv. He is a Ukrainian SR who commands considerable partisan forces and is operating in Kherson Province on a continuous front as far as Nikopol*.
> Hryhoryi'v has recognized the supremacy of the authority of the Provisional Workers' and Peasants' Government of Ukraine and the Command of the Revolutionary Military Council, leaving it to the Ukrainian SR government, established on the right bank of the Dnepr, to negotiate a political agreement with us.
> Two representatives of the Ukrainian SR's, Elansky and Blakytny are here, but negotiations have not yet begun.[19]

Rakovsky.

To confront the Bolsheviks with an already existing Borotist controlled Ukrainian soviet government, supported by a Borotbist-controlled Ukrainian red army, was the only move open to the Borotbisty. The documents indicate beyond the shadow of a doubt that the Borotbisty attempted to do this, but the balance of military and political forces was not in their favor. The more experienced administrative and military personnel of Ukraine had withdrawn to the west with the Directory, leaving the Borotbisty exposed to the organized machine of the Russian Bolsheviks. The Borotbisty had little control in the cities, and, had they declared war on the Bolsheviks in the winter of 1919, their large following in the villages would probably have refused to support them. The masses would not have understood why two parties with the same political platform—Soviet rule—should fight one another, especially when the threat of intervention by the Allies in the south and by the Directory in the west had yet to be removed.

A minor but contributing factor to Borotbist failure was their hostile relations with the Independent wing of the USDRP which were rooted in ideological differences. In attempting to shake off the tag of idealistic populism in their evolution toward communism, the Borotbisty lived through a period of ideological eclipse. The Ukrainian SD Independents, having gone through the same Marxist school as the Bolsheviks, could withstand them better then could the Borotbisty, whom the Independents regarded with contempt. The Borotbisty, on the other hand, feeling more closely identified with the masses, looked on the Independents as friends of the Directory, and hence bourgeois. Collaboration between the two Ukrainian parties of the left was thus impossible.

C. Implementation of Bolshevik Occupation Policy

The decline in prestige of the Ukrainian state among the masses as a result of Hetman rule, together with the advice of Bolshevik leaders in Ukraine, was undoubtedly behind Lenin's remarks at the Eighth Congress of the Russian Communist Party (Bolshevik) in

March 1919 that "Ukraine is separated from Russia by exceptional circumstances; the national movement has not taken deep roots there. Even if it did exist, the Germans stamped it out.'[20]

Prior to the arrival of the Bolshevik Soviet government from Kharkiv, the Bolshevik-controlled Executive Committee of the Kyiv City Council, contending with a host of Ukrainian problems, named four Borotbisty among the special commissars appointed to take over the various ministries vacated by the Directory: Mykhaylychenko (Foreign Affairs), Panas Lyubchenko (War), Taranenko (Rationing), and Klunnyi (Agriculture).[21] However, the Soviet government headed by Rakovsky, who replaced Pyatakov, had no intention of granting concessions to the Ukrainians; Ukraine was then regarded primarily as a source of food.

The Bolshevik habit of mechanically measuring all conditions by the Russian yardstick can be seen at work when the Bolsheviks, crudely and without even the transitional period which had existed in Russia, attempted bodily to transplant the system of War Communism to Ukraine. (In Soviet Russia the whole system of War Communism — complete nationalization of industry and land, abolition of the free market, confiscation of the peasants' surplus produce, and compulsory employment — reached its peak in 1919.)

The cardinal factor in Bolshevik occupation policy in Ukraine during the first months of 1919, however, was the existence of famine in Russia. In the wake of the advancing Red Army, the Moscow press wrote jubilant articles designed to appeal to the famished population. For example, the Moscow City Soviet on February 6, 1919 issued the following proclamation:

> Comrades! The victory of the uprising of workers and peasants in Ukraine opens the way to save the workers and toiling masses of Russia from famine and economic disaster. The Ukrainian Red Army of workers and poor peasants has regained from the German imperialists and the local landowners, kulaks and bourgeoisie very large reserves of grain, meat, fats, sugar, salt, fodder, coal and in general everything from the want of which the population of our cities is starving, suffering and dying. Food reserves exceed tens of millions of poods. They offer salvation to us, our families, our children, and the entire cause of the proletarian revolution. . . . Deliverance from famine and disaster is in our bands. It is near.[22]

Moscow's agents invaded the Ukrainian villages to supervise the requisition of foodstuffs. Khrystyuk describes how this worked out in practice:

> The Workers' and Peasants' Government stripped Ukraine... of everything it could lay its hands on—bread, sugar, meat, factory machine tools and equipment, farm implements, furniture from buildings, even musical instruments. ... By a simplified system of requisitioning, the Red Army men seized from Ukrainian peasants everything that could be removed—grain, cattle, poultry, plows, even women's clothes.[23]

On February 26, 1919 Pravda wrote:

> Ukraine now has approximately 250–300 million poods of extra grain. . . . Before spring, Ukraine can deliver some grain, about 200,000 poods of frozen meat, 200,000 poods of salt, 300,000 poods of dried fruit, a large quantity of potatoes, almost seven million poods of sugar, some confectionary products, and small quantities of millet.[24]

As Aleksandr G. Shlikhter, then Commissar of Food Supplies of Ukraine, wrote in 1928, "every pood [of food] was soaked in blood." According to his calculations,

> the government acquired by July 1 not fifty million poods, but only eight and a half million. However, even three-quarters of this [amount] remained in Ukraine and was rationed to proletarian centers (primarily to workers of the Donets Basin) and to the Red Army. Only about two million poods were sent to Moscow and Petersburg].[25]

Neither the principles of the communist program concerning the equality of nations, nor the Directory's proposals (in January) for peace and trade with Russia, nor the outbreak of revolution in Hungary (in mid-March) could check the onslaught of the hungry Russians from the north.[26] Pyatakov's thesis denying the existence of a national problem in Ukraine was ideological balm for the Moscow strategists, since it fitted in with the momentary needs as well as the desires of Soviet Russia.

No less catastrophic than the food requisition policy was Bolshevik agrarian policy in Ukraine. The government held back about three million desyatins, or 25 per cent of the land fund (former state-owned land, forests, sugar-beet farms, and large estates which were transferred to agricultural communes). To obtain the remaining 75 per cent of the land, the peasants had to seize it themselves.[27] 'Here, too, Bolshevik policy gave less consideration to the peasantry in Ukraine than it had in Russia.

The failure of the Bolsheviks to solve economic problems in Ukraine was compounded by their blundering national policy. They simply refused to recognize Ukraine as a nation, not only politically but even culturally. Rakovsky declared at a meeting of the Kyiv City Council on February 13, 1919 that the attempt "to institute Ukrainian as a state language was reactionary and entirely unnecessary. . . . One is told to remember the peasantry, but the peasants also regard themselves as Russians.'[28] He repeated the old Russian contention that the Ukrainian cause and the very idea of a Ukraine were the invention of Ukrainian intellectuals. (Within five years Rakovsky was to become a staunch defender of the rights of the Soviet Ukraine.) Rakovsky was criticized for his views by representatives of all the pro-Soviet parties. The Left Bundist Rafes warned: "Woe to that party, woe to that government which does not consider all the peculiarities of the country."[29] The negative stand on the Ukrainian question taken by Rakovsky, a Rumanian who had been in Russia only since 1918, was the result of Russian influence, especially that of the Soviet administration in Ukraine which was predominantly Russian and openly hostile to Ukrainian culture and ideas. The Soviet administration requisitioned buildings of Ukrainian cultural institutions for state purposes and excluded the Ukrainian language from public use.[30] In practice the administration was even more anti-Ukrainian than the government.

The foregoing factors provide an explanation of the un-yielding Bolshevik attitude toward all pro-Soviet Ukrainian parties, the fury of the plundering Red Army and the persecution of everything Ukrainian. In the nature of things it would have been extraordinary had there been no reaction to the state of affairs engendered by the implementation of Bolshevik occupation policy.[31]

D. Borotbism in Crisis

1. Internal Party Differences

The inability of the Borotbisty to form their own government caused a serious crisis within their ranks. The Kyiv branch of the party resolved at a meeting held during the first half of February that,

> Because ideologically and tactically the Communist Party (Bolshevik) of Ukraine has recently come very close to the Ukrainian Party of Socialist Revolutionaries [Borotbisty],[32] the Central Committee of the UPSR [Borotbisty], in the interests of the world socialist revolution and particularly of Ukraine, should call a Party Congress for the purpose of solving the problem of the possible forms of joint activity by both parties-the UPSR [Borotbisty] and the CP(b)U.[33]

At a second meeting later in February, the Kyiv group proposed outright merger in the following resolution:

> 1) Since there appear to be no great differences of opinion between the UPSR [Borotbisty] and the CP(b)U in matters of basic tactics; 2) taking into account the desire of the party rank and file to add to the name "UPSR" the word "Communist," or suitably to rename the UPSR altogether; 3) warning the party that with its separate existence, in opposition to the leaders of the CP(b)U, events and the party's support from "reliable" elements inevitably will lead it into the camp of counterrevolution; 4) taking into account that there already exists the nucleus for a real communist party, linked organizationally with communist parties of other countries and [ideologically] with their correct positions; 5) regarding it as a duty to support these positions as much as possible; and 6) considering it a duty to avoid that disorganization within the UPSR [Borotbisty which might arise if individual members or separate groups were to join the CP(b)U – the meeting, in the interests of a successful development of the socialist revolution, has resolved: To demand that the Central Committee of the Party enter into negotiations -,with the Central Committee of the CP(b)U with a view to uniting the UPSR [Borotbisty] with the CP(b)U and effecting this merger successfully at the Fifth Congress of the UPSR [Borotbisty].[34]

"Not only ideological but practical considerations as defined in point three of the resolution," Khrystyuk writes, "played an important role in the desire to merge.'[35] As was expected, the Borotbisty called for a merger with the Bolsheviks at their Fifth Congress, held in Kharkiv, March 6–8, 1919. It was at this Congress that the Borotbisty once again changed their party name, this time to "Ukrainian Party of Socialist Revolutionaries (Communists-Borotbisty)."[36]

The danger of disorganization which was feared by the Kyivan Borotbisty became acute when Vyacheslav Lashkevych, a member of the Central Committee and of the Council of Revolutionary Emissaries, Serhiy Pylypenko and many other party members individually joined the CP(b)U.[37] Despite this threat, a merger of the Borotbisty and the Ukrainian Bolsheviks was impossible in March 1919. Not only did the Borotbisty as a whole still believe in their separate existence; the CP(b)U, flushed with victory, was not interested in bringing them into the CP(b)U or the Bolshevik government.

2. Rejection by the CP(b)U

The unification plea of the Borotbisty (and of the *Bund*) was formally rejected by the CP(b)U at the latter's Third Congress in Kharkiv, during the first week of March. By a small margin of votes, 101 to 96, the Congress adopted the resolution "On the Attitude Toward Petty Bourgeois Parties" proposed by the CP(b)U's left wing.[38] The following passages are relevant to the Borotbisty:

> 1. At a time of growing and intensified civil war in Ukraine, and in anticipation of an inevitable and violent kulak counterrevolution in the villages, no agreements with such parties as the Right SR's, the Independent Ukrainian Social Democrats and others are admissible....
> 2. Taking into account the fact that the victorious development of the proletarian revolution in Ukraine has deprived such strata of the petty bourgeoisie as urban craftsmen and the middle peasantry of any hope of realizing their program and has proved the impotence of their political parties, and [the fact] that in the course of events these parties (the Left *Bund* and the Ukrainian SR's [Borotbisty]) are compelled either to accept the platform of Soviet rule or to attempt to merge with our party:
> the Third Congress considers that, despite their acceptance of Soviet rule, these parties are incapable of accepting the program of the dictatorship of the proletariat with all its consequences and that therefore *their representatives must not be given any responsible posts in the councils*. The Congress particularly emphasizes the fact that it is inadmissible to include them in the government

of Ukraine, which should consist solely of *representatives of the Communist Party*, the only leader of the toiling revolutionary masses.[39] Concerning attempts of the petty bourgeois parties (the Left *Bund* and Ukrainian SR's [Borotbisty]) to unite with our party, the Third Congress of the CP(b)U has decided not to admit any groups in the ranks of our party and to accept [new members] only... in accordance with the [party] statute."[40]

Accordingly, no Borotbisty were admitted to the Bolshevik-controlled government, although the Third All-Ukrainian Congress of Soviets, which was well attended by the Borotbisty, elected several Borotbist deputies to the Central Executive Committee.[41] To be sure, practice differed in local government. Unable to fill all positions in the local councils, the Bolsheviks were compelled to accept Borotbist participation. "Having failed to reach an agreement with the CP(b)U despite great concessions, the UPSR [(Borotbisty-Communists)], like all other Ukrainian soviet parties," Khrystyuk pointedly observes, "logically should have declared war on the CP(b)U and become an illegal organization. [But] the party inclined... toward agreement at any price.[42]

E. Joint Action Against Hryhoryiv

1. Bolshevik Detente with the Borotbisty

The Bolsheviks had scarcely installed a central government in Ukraine when their multiple disregard of Ukrainian interests brought on widespread rebellion. By April 1919 the Bolsheviks had lost *de facto* control over large areas of Ukraine. From then on, as even the Bolshevik historian M. Kubanin admits, "the revolutionary committees and councils existed only nominally and were in fact controlled by one or another ataman or underground organization."'[43] The population ignored the Bolshevik government's orders and lived under the protection of underground insurgent centers. Atamans Hryhoryiv, Zeleny and Makhno all led their partisans in active rebellion.

Only when faced with open revolt throughout Ukraine did "the need to unite all revolutionary forces against counterrevolution prompt the Central Committee of the CP(b)U to adopt a resolution admitting the [Borotbisty] into the Ukr.-S.S.R. Council of

People's Commissars."[44] The CP(b)U in May waived its March resolution against admission on direct orders from the Central Committee of the Russian Communist Party (Bolshevik). "All soviet parties... were admitted to the Central Executive Committee. Representatives of the Ukrainian SR's Communists (Borotbisty) were included in the presidium of the Central Executive Committee and in the Council of People's Commissars of Ukraine.'"[45] Borotbisty who were brought into the government included Mykhaylo Panchenko (later replaced by Shumsky) as People's Commissar of Education; Lytvynenko as Commissar of Finance; Lebedynets' as Commissar of Justice; Poloz" as Chairman of the Supreme Council of National Economy; and Yakovlev us deputy head of the Cheka in Ukraine.[46] In these areas of government the Borotbisty, although not active, were in a position to resist cultural Russification,o check the economic plundering of Ukraine and abate the campaign of terror then being conducted against Ukrainian intellectuals, perhaps despite the presence of Yakovlev.[47] The posts of Deputy People's Commissar of Internal Affairs, Food, and Communications were also held by Borotbisty. However, Poloz was the only member of the Borotbist Central Committee in the government, and no key commissariats were in the hands of the Borotbisty. Moreover, as Rafes aptly comments, "this change in the center was scarcely reflected in the countryside, where the old policy remained in force. . . .'"[48]

2. Hryhoryiv's revolt against the Bolsheviks

D. Petrovsky, another Bolshevik historian, supports the view that the attempt to placate the Ukrainian pro-Soviet parties was already late.[49] In the period April 1–May 1, 1919 there were 93 uprisings; in the period May 1–15, 28 uprisings; and in the period June 1–19, 207 uprisings.[50] The insurgent partisans were the same peasants who two and three months earlier had welcomed the Bolsheviks. Ukrainian peasants, poor and rich alike, joined in battle against the Russian Bolsheviks. "The first large rebellion," occurring in early May and, led by Ataman Hryhoryi'v,[51]

---

o See Appendix 4.

spread rapidly through three provinces, destroying a great part of [Bolshevik] successes and facilitating the advance of Denikin. . . . Not only did the proletariat mobilize its forces, but the petty bourgeois parties came out against Hryhoryiv.... The RSDRP [Mensheviks] and the Bund rallied their forces in opposition to Hryhoryi'v and Denikin. The Left SR majority [i.e., the Borotbisty] and the [Ukrainian] SD Left "Independents" also arrived at a decision [to fightj against the Hryhoryiv adventure. . . . Only two parties supported Hryhoryiv . . . the Ukrainian Left SR-Activists[52] and the SD "Independents-Activists."[53] By decree of the Council of Workers' and Peasants' Defense they were declared to be outside the law and subject to the red terror.[54]

Reduced to one partisan detachment, Hryhoryi'v wrote to the government of the Ukrainian People's Republic on June 28, 1919:

> We broke away from you because you were conducting a petty bourgeois domestic and foreign policy which allowed the Entente powers to exploit our people and their wealth. We broke away from the Communists and we fight them because 90 per cent of the people do not want communism and do not recognize the dictatorship of a party or dictatorship of an individual. In our view, it is necessary to have proportional representation of the nationalities in the councils. . . . Tell us and the whole Ukrainian people what kind of rule you are bringing to Ukraine, for people say that you have an agreement with the Entente powers and that the National Union, which in our view is a nest of the "Black Hundred," still exists. . . . As for the land problem, socialization of the land is the only acceptable solution in Ukraine. . . . We are in contact with the All-Ukrainian Revolutionary Committee [of the USDRP (Independents)]. Rumors about [our ties with] Denikin and Kolchak are all lies.[55]

In general Ataman Hryhoryiv remains an enigmatic figure. Some even refuse to believe that he was ever a Borotbist. It is most probable that, like so many of the partisan leaders of the day, he was an independent ataman whom no party, either Borotbist or Bolshevik, could discipline. After his break with the Borotbisty he acquired some notoriety for his, anti-Jewish pogroms. In July during an attempt to reach an understanding with Makhno, Hryhoryiv was shot at Makhno's headquarters. The reason is unknown, but presumably personal rivalry was involved.[56]

In January the Borotbisty had counted on the forces of Hryhoryiv to organize an independent Ukrainian Red Army, but his May his active opposition to Bolshevik rule made him their enemy. Except for Hryhoryiv's about-face and the anti-Bolshevik uprising led by the Borotbist Shchohryn, the Borotbist party as a whole remained loyal to the Bolshevik government.[57] Their participation in the government and active aid against the anti-Bolshevik partisan uprisings had a double effect upon the party. While on the one hand the party became even more pro-Soviet, on the other hand it lost some its adherents. That the party's influence among the peasants was still considerable, however, became evident during the All-Ukrainian Congress of Volost Executive Committees in Kyiv in June 1919, at which the Borotbisty controlled Approximately 50 per cent of the delegates.[58]

The forces of the Ukrainian People's Republic, approaching from the west, and the armies of General Denikin, moving in from the south and east, occupied Kyiv on August 31, 1919. This date can therefore be considered as marking the formal end of the second period of Bolshevik rule in Ukraine. Khrystyuk justly remarked of the period that

> the groundwork for the [Soviet] government in Ukraine was prepared by the growth of the Ukrainian revolution, but the government itself rested, . . . ideologically, ... on the Russian Communist Party and, materially, on the Russian [Red] Army and Russian [bureaucracy]. . .[59]

Borotba, daily of the Central Committee of the Ukrainian Party of Socialist-Revolutionaries, 1917

News of the Poltava Soviet, published by the Council of Workers and Soldiers Deputies in 1917 calls for 'All Power to the Soviets'.

'Long Live the Ukrainian Peoples Republic!' Announces the paper of the Ukrainian Social Democrats *Robitnycha Hazeta*, Nov. 1917.

'Long Live Free Ukraine', a demonstration in Kyiv during the upsurge of the Ukrainian Revolution in 1917.

Borotbyst, organ of the Poltava province committee of the Ukrainian Communist Party (Borotbisty)

Proletarska Borotba, Ukrainian Communist Party (Borotbisty), Zhytomyr

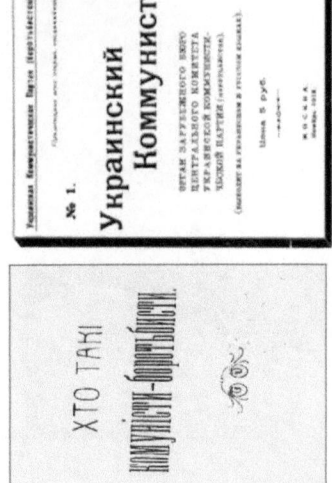

Who are the Communist-Borotbisty, pamphlet, and only issue of the Borotbist Moscow journal *Ukrainsky Kommunist*, 1919.

Borotba, organ of the Central Committee of the Ukrainian Communist Party (Borotbisty)

Levko Kovaliv

Mykhaylo Poloz

Hryhoriy Hryn'ko

Vasyl' Chumak

Memorial plaque in Zhytomyr

Hnat Mykhaylychenko

Oleksandr Shumsky

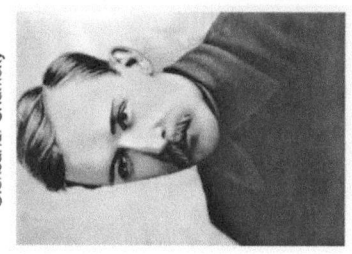
Vasyl' Ellan-Blakytny

7 Borotbisty in the Denikin Underground

A. Formation of the Ukrainian Communist Party (Borotbisty): UCP(B)

While the armies of the Ukrainian People's Republic were fighting in the approaches to Kyiv in August 1919, an important event occurred in the life of the UPSR (Communists-Borotbisty). The Central Committees of the UPSR (Communists-Borotbisty) and the USDRP (Left Independents) by joint decision announced the formation of a new Ukrainian political party in a covering letter of a memorandump which was directed to the Executive Committee of the Communist International. The Memorandum, primarily an appeal to economic factors rather than to ethical values, outlined briefly the peculiarities of the social and economic development of Ukraine which made incumbent the formation of a single communist center. The covering letter read as follows:

> To the Executive Committee of the Third Communist International
>
> By decision of the Central Committees of the Ukrainian Social Democratic Workers' Party (Left Independents) and the Ukrainian Party of Socialist Revolutionaries (Communists)* of August 6, 1919 both parties named have merged into one Ukrainian Communist Party (Borotbisty) with the motto "Workers of the World Unite!"[1]
>
> The act of merging into a single Communist Party two detachments of Ukrainian Communism, which until now have participated separately in the proletarian revolution in Ukraine, is a great, crowning moment in the development of the Ukrainian communist movement, which accurately expresses the real command of local social reality and at the same time is a new point of departure in the future organizational and ideological consolidation of communist forces in the towns and villages of Ukraine.
>
> The deep split within the ranks of the Ukrainian socialist parties and the dividing off of the communist forces, which grow organically out of the aggregrate of social and economic conditions in Ukraine, began immediately after the February Revolution of 1917 and, by the first siege of Kyiv by the troops of Soviet Russia, had reached such intensity and force that the representatives

---

p   See Appendix V.

of the left wing of the Ukrainian socialist parties were arrested and condemned to execution by the right wing, which then controlled all political life in Ukraine.

The subsequent course of the Revolution brought this split to its inevitable end; the left wing—that organic cell of Ukrainian Communism—irrevocably took up the struggle in the name of rule by Soviets as the only organizational form of the dictatorship of the proletariat.

The ranks of fighters united round the organizational center of Ukrainian Communism during the dark period of Hetmanate reaction; they were tempered in the heroic and ruthless struggle both against it and against the Ukrainian National Union, which disguised its counterrevolutionary nature with democratic phraseology.

The disorganization of the Hetmanate apparatus by vigorous action and the unmasking of the counterrevolutionary nature of the Ukrainian National Union before the eyes of the Ukrainian proletariat and peasantry led Ukrainian communist forces to the uprising against the Hetmanate, to the active control of that uprising, [including] the seizure of Poltava, Zhitomir, Zhmerinka, and other localities, and to the decisive struggle against the product of the National Union—the Directory—both at the head of insurgent detachments and at the "Toilers' Congress" convened by the Directory.

In the heat of this struggle for the greatest ideal of our age, the struggle in the name of rule by Soviets, the last threads are being cut, the last traces of former contacts with the compromising parties are vanishing, and the intrinsic nature of the organizational and ideological center of Ukrainian communist forces which has been strengthened in battle is outgrowing the bounds of old party names.

The struggle against the Hetmanate and the Directory was conducted shoulder to shoulder with the Communists-Bolsheviks of Ukraine. The deep realization of all the dangers [arising out] of the existence of two communist centers in Ukraine forced the organizational and ideological core of Ukrainian communist forces (the Communists-Borotbisty) to call, in March 1919, for the formation of an inter-party Soviet center at the moment of uprising and for organizational merger with the Communists-Bolsheviks.

The urgent need for the creation of a single Communist Center in Ukraine has not been understood and evaluated by the Communists-Bolsheviks of Ukraine.

The experience of the subsequent development of the proletarian revolution in Ukraine, the practical participation [of the Borotbisty] in the formation of the Soviet government and its fateful outcome have sharpened the awareness among the ranks of Ukrainian Communists of the urgent need to create a single communist center, which will grow organically out of the aggregate of social and economic conditions and peculiarities of Ukraine.

A consideration of this experience and the increased understanding of the next and most important task in the development of the revolution in Ukraine have led to the merger of two detachments of Ukrainian communist forces into one Ukrainian Communist Party (Borotbisty), which has assumed the leadership of the Ukrainian communist movement and its representation in the ranks of the Third International.

> Facing the eclipse of the second proletarian revolution in Ukraine, entering a period of the fiercest reaction in Ukraine, leading the entire party, and, together with it, going underground tin preparation] for a new struggle, the Central Committee of the Ukrainian Communist Party (Borotbisty) announces the entry of the party into the ranks of the Third International and sends warm greetings to the leaders of the proletarian revolution, assuring them that the hour is at hand when, forged together by one Communist Center, the workers and peasants of Ukraine will start a new uprising in the name of rule by Soviets, and a regenerated Ukrainian Soviet Republic once again will engage in open battle with the enemies of international communism. Kyiv, August 28, 1919.
>
> Central Committee of the Ukrainian Communist Party (Borotbisty).[2]

By implication the covering letter scored the Bolshevik leaders in Ukraine who fled to Russia with the retreating Red Army in the hope of eventually returning under the protection of a victorious Red Army.'[3] The meeting of the Central Committees of the two old parties at which this joint decision was made came to be regarded as the First Congress of the new UCP(b).

Both parties participated in the merger on a parity basis, although actually one large party, the UPSR (Communists-Borotbisty), was joined by a small left wing group of Kyivan SD Independents.

The left wing Independents had refused to follow the USDRP (Independents)" in the latter's active opposition to the Bolshevik-controlled government in the spring of 1919. When the USDRP (Independents) became an underground organization, creating an All-Ukrainian Revolutionary Committee which declared open warfare against Rakovsky's government, the left wing remained a legal organization.[4] Under the leadership of Pankiv and Hukovych, they became known as the Left Independents. Through their representative at the All-Ukrainian Congress of Volost Executive Committees in Kyiv in June 1919, the Left Independents officially conveyed their greetings to the Congress. They condemned the participation of the USDRP (Independents) in the anti-Bolshevik uprisings, yet at the same time criticized the excesses of Rakovsky's government. The Left Independents thus moved close to the Borot'bist position, and their merger with the Borotbisty was the logical consequence.

As Marxists who had long since accepted the doctrine of "the dictatorship of the proletariat," the Left Independents escaped the ideological crisis through which the Borotbisty passed. In the minds of the Borotbisty, as they came under the influence of Marxism in their movement toward communism, the heritage of populism seemed a political liability. Given this frame of mind, the Borotbisty found merger with the USDRP (Left Independents), though a small group, of considerable ideological and political significance. Through them, the new party, the UCP(b), rid itself of the populist heritage of *Borotbism*. At the same time the merger strengthened the opposition of Ukrainian leftist parties to the Bolsheviks. No longer did the Borotbisty feel compelled to demonstrate that they were as good Marxists as the Bolsheviks. They could now claim before the Communist International, and before the Ukrainian urban proletariat, that they were demanding for Ukraine no more than the sovereignty due every nation, while the Bolsheviks were actually subjugating Ukraine to Russia. The Borotbisty, it is clear, hoped that the Communist International would draw the proper inference—that for Ukraine, at least, they had become better Marxists than the Bolsheviks.

Lenin, who carefully followed the Borotbist moves, soon claimed the very opposite. On February 22, 1920 he wrote: "I emphatically insist that the Borotbisty be accused not of nationalism, but of counterrevolutionary and petty bourgeois mentality."[5] The implication was that even though the Borotbisty agreed with the Bolsheviks on the national question— which was not the case— they were unreliable as Marxists. The Borotbisty for their part, anxious to obliterate their populist past, treated the Left Independents as equals and accepted the Marxist slogan "Workers of the World, Unite!" With the infusion of new Marxist blood into the party, the Borotbisty hoped, revitalized, to re-enter the struggle against the Bolsheviks for a sovereign, communist Ukraine.

B. Two Views on the Formation of the UCP(B)

1. The "Dual Roots" Theory

The Bundist Rafes, writing during the Denikin occupation in 1919, oversimplified the Borot'bist point of view when he quoted one of their planks, "support for the national culture of young nations," to demonstrate that "the new party, in the words of its initiators, is based on a Marxist outlook, but differs from [the Bolsheviks] in its views on the national question."[6] The heart of the matter lay not merely in "the national culture of young nations" but in their equality and independence. Another former Bundist, Ravich-Cherkassky, writing as a Bolshevik in 1923, described the formation of the UCP(b) in the following words:

> At a time when Mazurenko, Drahomyretsky and other leaders of the Independents stirred up kulak rebellions and pogroms, a small but consolidated group split away... and created a new party of "Left Independent Ukrainian Social Democrats." This group was headed by Pankiv and Hukovych. The Borotbisty, as the Ukrainian Left SR Party, indisputably showed themselves to be revolutionaries during the struggle between the Bolsheviks and the Directory..., During the entire period of Soviet rule in Ukraine in 1919 the Borotbisty gradually, very slowly it is true, rid themselves of their traditional, semi-Petlyurist tendencies. Before that time considerable strata of the peasantry had been more or less under their influence. After the Third Congress of the CP[(b)]U branded them as petty bourgeois national-socialists, the Borotbisty, in seeking to influence the urban proletariat, began to polish up on the Marxist view of history, gradually destroying the vestiges of their SR prejudices. In August 1919 this process of adaptation to the *proletarian* revolution was crowned by the merger of the Borotbisty with the above-mentioned group of Ukrainian SD Left Independents. This merger of quantity and, relatively, even of quality undoubtedly increased the prospects of the Borotbisty to [acquire] the right to call themselves communists.'[7]

In his *History of the CP(b)U* Ravich-Cherkasski in 1923 advanced the idea for which he was condemned by official Soviet critics in the late 1920's that the CP(b)U was not a branch of the Russian Communist Party (Bolshevik), but a new communist party in Ukraine created by Bundists, Borotbisty, Jewish Communists, *Borbisty*, and *Ukapisty*, as well as by the Bolsheviks. By 1923 this theory of the multiple origin of the CP(b)U was also accepted by former Borotbisty, themselves members of the CP(b)U. On the other hand the

Bolsheviks, having once consolidated their power in the 1920's and having absorbed the other leftist parties, rejected the view that the CP(b)U was a confluence of many streams. Rather, they claimed that the elements in the CP(b)U of non-Bolshevik origin had quickly become assimilated. Insofar as the essential ideology of the CP(b)U is concerned, they were correct. Wielding undivided power, the Bolsheviks preserved their basic party doctrine. But the Borotbisty, and later the *Ukapisty*, nonetheless did influence the policy of the CP(b)U with respect to the national question (Ukrainization); when the Bolsheviks later decided to abandon this policy, they had to destroy all the former Borotbisty and *Ukapisty* within the CP(b)U.

The Borotbisty themselves considered their merger with the Left Independents to be an inevitable consequence of the Ukrainian revolution:

> As the Ukrainian peasantry was divided into kulaks and toiling peasants, and the latter into the well-off middle peasant and the hired laborer, . . . the Ukrainian Party of SR Communists, the party of the Ukrainian peasant proletariat, crystallized more and more out of the ill-defined, old opportunist party of the Ukrainian SR's. With a similar crystallization of the purely proletarian elements out of that mass of workers, intellectuals and petty bourgeoisie which had been under the influence of the USDRP, there arose the party of Left Independents, linked primarily with the industrial proletariat of Ukraine—the proletariat of the city. Since the interests of all proletarian groups were identical, . . . the splits in the USDRP and the UPSR ever more forcefully bore out the need to unify the communist forces in city and village.[8]

2. The Bolshevik Argument

In order to understand why the Bolsheviks, and Lenin in particular, took such a hostile stand toward the Borotbisty, especially toward their efforts to gain admittance to the Third International, it is necessary to consider briefly the Bolshevik argument. A synthesis of their argument, based on statements by Lenin and other prominent Bolsheviks, would run as follows: 1) The cardinal political difference between the Bolshevik party and all other Soviet parties was that the Bolsheviks had guided the Revolution to the Soviet platform, indeed had fostered and created the Soviet system, while all other parties had merely been drawn toward that platform. The correctness of this thesis was supported even by the Borotbist pronouncement that the UCP(b) had arisen as the result of a process of differentiation within the Ukrainian peasantry and urban proletariat under the impact of the Bolshevik Revolution. 2) Such an "empirical" explanation for the origin of *Borotbism*, whose radicalism was the product of revolutionary events, harbored the danger that an ebbing of the revolutionary wave among the masses might well impair that radicalism. 3) The Borot'bist proposition that the UCP(b) was the only center around which Ukrainian communist forces could crystallize was not valid; Chronologically, the Left USDRP (led by Neronovych) had been the first such center, while, besides the Borotbisty, another possible center was the Ukrainian Communist Party (the *Ukapisty*) which had held its constituent congress in Kyiv, January 22–25, 1920. *Borotbism* therefore represented but one stage in the crystallization of Ukrainian communist forces. The proper rallying center was the Bolshevik organization of the industrial proletariat, which were an integral part of Ukrainian life no less than the professedly Ukrainian movements. 4) It would be more correct to speak of the CP(b)U as possibly independent of the Russian Communist Party (Bolshevik), as had been suggested by the Ukrainian Bolshevik Shakhray, than to suggest the transfer of leadership of the Ukrainian proletarian revolution from the proletarian party, the Bolsheviks, to a party which at best could only aspire to the proletarian. 5) The existence of a large Russified urban proletariat in Ukraine made the formation of a purely Ukrainian government impossible during the difficult period of the Revolution. Such a government would inevitably be controlled by the peasants rather than by the workers, a circumstance which would destroy the fundamental aim of the Revolution-the dictatorship of the proletariat. 6) Even if other proletarian parties were to attempt to rise to the top in Ukraine, or if the CP(b)U itself were to attempt to become independent, Bolshevism would ruthlessly beat down such attempts, because the dictatorship of the proletariat in backward peasant countries could be realized only by means of a highly centralized communist party. 7) Given the existing conditions, there could be no talk of administrative equality between that territory (Russia) which contained the center of the Revolution and a territory (Ukraine) where the Revolution was directed by that center. Speaking at the Eighth All-Russian Conference of the Russian Communist Party (Bolshevik) on December 3, 1919 Lenin stated:

> Comrade [Dmytro Z.J] Manuilsky is greatly mistaken in thinking that we reproached them [i.e., the Ukrainian Bolsheviks] for separatism [*samostiinost'*] in the national sense, in the sense of independence [nezavisimost'] for Ukraine. We reproached them for their separatism in the sense of their not wishing to reckon with Moscow's views, the views of the Central Committee in Moscow. This word [*samostiinost'*] which was used in jest, had quite a different meaning.[9]

This method of granting nominal independence to non-Russian peoples while in actual fact subordinating them to Moscow, "the center of world revolution," was later applied by Stalin in gaining control over the so-called satellite states of Eastern Europe.

The Russian Bolshevik attitude toward the Borotbisty is best illustrated in a draft resolution entitled "Our Attitude Toward the Borotbisty," sketched probably by Lenin himself, concerning the liquidation of *Borotbism*. Found among the Trotsky papers preserved at Harvard University, it bears the date May 1919:

> The bloc of our Party with the Borotbisty had as its aim to attract to a sustained Communist policy a young political party in the socialist structure of Ukraine, still so poor in experience.
> In making this experiment, our Party had clearly in mind the fact that it might have directly opposite results, namely that it might hasten the degeneration of the Borotbisty into a militant party of counterrevolution, with the splitting off from it of its most honest and conscious socialist elements.
> In either case, the drawing of the party of Borotbisty into governmental responsibility—by hastening the political evolution of the party, would have a progressive meaning, since it shortened the period of indefiniteness- and formlessness of political groupings and relationships.
> 4. At the present time it can be confirmed with full conviction that the Party of Borotbisty has evolved to the right, i.e., to the side of degeneration into an intellectual political group, basing itself mainly on kulak elements of the villages and on swindler-scoundrelly elements of the city, including also the greater part of the working class [sic]. . . .
> 7. Under the guise of a struggle for Ukrainian independence, which found its expression in the Ukrainian Soviet Government, the Borotbisty have carried on a disorganizing struggle against the necessary union and unification of the economic apparatuses serving the interests of both countries. By this they help economic chaos and threaten to undermine all the work for economic construction in Ukraine and in Russia.

8. Especially criminal, however, is the work of the Borotbisty in the military field. In the guise of a struggle for an independent Ukrainian army, the Borotbisty support the partisan bands,by word and deed opposing them to the Red Army, and are multiplying thereby the elements of bandit chaos which are leading Ukraine to the brink of chaos. Under the conditions of a far from completed struggle in Ukraine with internal and external counterrevolution, the encouragement of partisanism [the organization of the armed forces into independent guerrilla detachments—B.W.], which has already surrendered the Worker-Peasant Ukraine into the hands of the hated enemy, is nothing but subservience to the bandits of imperialism and the delivery of a treacherous stab in the back to the Soviet Power. . ...

11. It is incumbent upon the leading elements of our Party and of the Soviet Power in Ukraine to open a most serious, attentive and energetic campaign against the party of the Borotbisty, exposing its intelligentsia-careerist, chauvinist and exploiter-kulakist character.

12. Attention must be especially paid to all those cases where Borotbisty directly or indirectly support corrupted partisans and undermine the authority and strength of the Russo-Ukrainian [Rossiisko-Ukrainskoi] Red Army. . . .

13. It is incumbent upon the corresponding Soviet organizations not to leave unanswered even one single chauvinist, anarcho-kulakist declaration of the Borotbisty. It is necessary by means of merciless exposure to make the genuinely alert section of the toilers who follow the Borotbisty aware of the fact that the road of this Party is the road to the inevitable ruin of Soviet Ukraine.

14 It is necessary to reckon with the fact that a certain number of pure socialist elements have so far stayed in the ranks of the Borotbisty because of the official Communist banner of this Party and its external revolutionary phraseology. . . .

15. By means of all the measures indicated above, i.e., by means of a broad and energetic exposure of the chauvinistic politics of the Borotbisty, by means of the attraction into our own ranks of its best elements and the merciless dispersion of the Makhnoist and Petlyurist elements in the ranks of the Borotbisty, our Party must in a short time prepare the conditions for driving the Borotbisty out of the ranks of the government, and for the complete liquidation of the Borotbisty as a recognized Soviet Party. ..."[10]

It is well to recall that in May 1919 Ataman Hryhoryiv launched his attack against the Bolsheviks. The caustic tone of the resolution can be partially explained by the bitterness which the Bolsheviks felt toward the Borotbisty at that time. A supplementary decision at the very end of the resolution mentions that "the moment of liquidation is to be determined by the Politburo [in Moscow] and communicated to the Ukrainian Revolutionary Military Council."[11] But the "moment of liquidation," as planned by Lenin, never came, because Bolshevik control came to an end in the summer of 1919 with the advance of Denikin's armies.

There is a revealing comment on the covering letter of the Borotbist memorandum written probably by Georgii Zinovyev, the head of the Russian delegation to the Communist International and editor of its journal:

> *From the editorial office*: At the Congress of the Communist International in Moscow in March 1919, Ukraine was represented by the Communist Party of Ukraine—CPU (Bolshevik). Only this party, the proletarian organization in Ukraine which has behind it about twenty years of work, now belongs organizationally to the Communist International. The Executive Committee of the c[ommunist] I[nternational] regards it as its duty to demand that only one communist party, comprising all communist forces, should exist in every country. The Communist International will also demand this in Ukraine.[12]

Thus the Janus-like policy of the Bolsheviks stands fully revealed. To the outside world the Bolsheviks appeared as recognizing Ukraine as a separate country whose representative in the Communist International had the same rights as other communist representatives, but behind the closed doors of inner party counsel Moscow accepted the Rakovsky dictum that Ukraine was the invention of a few intellectuals.

The reply of the Communist International to the Borotbist memorandum was made public only in 1920, after the Denikin period, and will be considered later.q Here it will be sufficient to note that during the Denikin occupation of Ukraine the Borotbist Central Committee commissioned a special delegation headed by Hryhoriy Hrynko and Levko Kuvaliv—the Foreign Bureau (*Zarubezbnoye Byuro*)—to present the Borot'bist brief before the Communist International in Moscow.

C. Borotbist Opposition to the Denikin Regime

Only the people's despair under the second Soviet Russian occupation of Ukraine can explain the success of Denikin's drive in Left Bank Ukraine in the summer of 1919. Denikin's military superiority to the army of the Ukrainian People's Republic was due first to the fact that he had better troops—so numerous were the tsarist officers

---

q   See pp. 244-247

in the Volunteer Army that at times regiments consisted entirely of officers—and second to the fact that it was recognized by the Entente and well supplied by Great Britain. To a people exhausted by the ravages of civil war the coming of Denikin, perhaps because of his monarchist orientation, evoked memories of a prerevolutionary peaceful life. However, even the first days of the new regime proved disappointing. Supported by Russian landowners and former tsarist financiers and industrialists, the regime aimed at a complete restoration of pre-revolutionary conditions. In the wake of his army came landowners to reclaim their property; factories, mines and various enterprises were returned to the old proprietors. The social contrasts now became unbearable.

To make matters worse a new reign of terror was instituted, this time against the poorer peasantry, the Jews and the Ukrainian patriots. Once in Kyiv, Denikin issued "An Appeal from the Commander-in-Chief to the Population of Little Russia", using the derogatory "*Malorossiya*" which had been the traditional tsarist term for Ukraine.[13] The Denikin regime refused to recognize the right of national autonomy, let alone national independence. Ukraine schools were closed, libraries destroyed, and Ukrainian leaders executed without trial. Three years' progress in the national field was wiped out. The Cadet N.I. Astrov, an official of the Denikin government pointed out that

> violence, torture, pillage, drunkenness, odious behavior of governmental representatives in local areas, the impunity of criminals, the weak, clumsy people, the cowards and the debauchees in local areas, people who brought with them old vices, old ignorance, laziness, and arrogance—all discredited the new government.[14]

1 The Borotbist Underground in Kyiv

The conditions created by the Denikin occupation were ideal for underground activity. The Central Committee of the CP(b)U dissolved the party as a separate organization on October 2, 1919, thus admitting the fiasco of its policy which had brought about its downfall.[15] The Bolshevik underground was far weaker than it had been under the Hetmanate. Even Soviet sources admit this. The Rear Echelon Bureau (*Zafrontbyuro*) of the Central Committee of the

CP(b)U sent only 800 party workers into the underground, all of them young and inexperienced.[16] According to a Soviet historian of the Denikin period, D. Kin, the Bolshevik underground in the Kyiv area was "very weak." The Borbisty did some work, but "the Borotbisty were much more effective.'[17] A Borbist member of the underground, Sergei D. Mstislavski (pseudonym of Maslovski), recalls that "we did not see any great need for propaganda. Agitation spread, so to speak, 'of itself through the efforts of the Volunteer authorities; what words could surpass the forcefulness [*yarkost'*] of their 'agitation by deed'[!]"[18]

The Central Committee of the UCP(b), located in Kyiv, re-established the system of party emissaries which the Borotbist underground had instituted during the period of the Hetmanate.r In an unguarded moment Mykhaylychenko, one of the most important members of the Borotbist Central Committee, was seized:

> On November 7 and 8 Hnat Mykhaylychenko, . . . Hryhoriy Kostryuchenko, apprehended with papers addressed to headquarters of the Twelfth Army (concerned with coordinating a drive on Kyiv from without and from within), Vasyl' Chumak, and Klyavdiya Kovaliva were arrested and executed on the spot. This was the first serious setback in the entire period of the underground. The loss of Hnat Mykhaylychenko was particularly serious. He was a man of complete integrity, a true revolutionary, an excellent worker, and a talented writer. The setback of the Borotbisty we [i.e., the *Borbisty*] explained as the result of their carelessness; they "exposed" their underground for the few days of the October seizure of Kyiv [by the Red Army]. Their committee held an open meeting in the premises of the former Borotbist club (on the corner of Prorizna and Pushkin Streets). As a matter of fact, our underground workers were also expected to be at the meeting, but, warned that the Soviet forces had begun a retreat, they did not attend. Those who attended the meeting were somehow seen and followed. The circumstances of their arrest could have led to further disclosures. . . had it not been for the haste shown by [Denikin's] counterintelligence.[19]

Mstislavski points out that Denikin's counterintelligence moved rapidly because of the reappearance of the Borotbist underground organ *Borotba* in early November:

> . . .every line of ... Borotba was aflame, an unconditional call to revolt. The Borotbist underground, manned mostly by young people, lived the days of

---

r   See pp. 161–162

illegal struggle on the whole with great enthusiasm, great buoyancy and joy. These qualities also marked the newspaper which was permeated with a militant spirit and confidence in victory despite literary deficiencies. Borotba described the progress of the international movement in a leading article summing up the results of the "Communist Revolution"....

At this very hour, the revolution in Eastern Europe, having experienced its most critical moment, is now recovering from the blow and going over ... to the attack: The Volunteer Army and the Petlyura regime are disintegrating and rotting.... The fighting spirit of the Red Army is rising. The revolutionary wave in Ukraine is growing....

The revolution is in full swing.

"The struggle is reaching its climax. In order the sooner to finish the fight, in order that all men may the sooner turn their swords into ploughshares and heal the wounds inflicted by the imperialist war and forced civil war, communism calls on all workers, all the oppressed and downtrodden to arms, to battle. Under the red banner of International Struggle — Workers of the World, Unite!"[20]

The first two orders issued by the Borotbist Central Committee deserve to be reproduced in full:

Order No. 1

Workers and Peasants.

The tsarist generals, the hirelings of the English and other capitalists, have proclaimed mobilization. Their own forces, the forces of the Volunteer hirelings and the landowners' White Guardist officer-sons, and the rich cossacks from the Don and Kuban' are no longer sufficient. Even with their aid they have no hope of defeating the revolutionary workers' and peasants' army and the red insurgents. Therefore they proclaim compulsory mobilization, so as to destroy the workers' and peasants' revolution through you and your forces, to regain their lordly rights with your calloused hands and to leave you, your children and brothers, who have already shed rivers of blood, in the slavery of capitalism.

This shall not be.

At this moment when the capitalists of Europe are barely holding out against the wave of revolution; when the Red Army by its own forces has smashed Kolchak and the Don Cossacks and is mercilessly beating the Volunteers; when Voronezh, Oryol, Kursk, and Chernihiv have been reoccupied; when the Red forces stand before Kyiv and the whole Ukraine is aflame with rebellion — you will not go against your brothers, you will not aid your enemies, you will not obey the mobilization.

> *In the name of the Revolution* we proclaim the mobilization ordered by Denikin's forces to be inoperative, and all who help to carry it out enemies of the workers and peasants.
> Workers and peasants! The mad dog of capitalism, dying, is employing all means to prolong its noisome existence. Take up arms, kill it off. In a free land we shall freely build the kingdom of Labor, Peace and Equality — the kingdom of Socialism.
>
> Chief Emissary of Combat Military Affairs of the C[entral] C[ommittee] of the UCP(b).
> (signature)[21]
>
> Order No. 2
>
> For the Special Section of the Combat Emissariat of the C[entral] Committee] of the UCP(b)
>
> All committees, emissaries, party members, and sympathizers are ordered to collect information (lists and addresses) about the Volunteers and those who support the mobilization of the White Guardists, and to send it immediately to the appropriate organs of the Special Section.
> The emissaries of the Special Section are ordered immediately to establish revolutionary terrorist courts (consisting of village elders [*starosty*], volost elders [*statshiny*], chairmen and secretaries of house committees, etc.) to try active assistants of the White Guard Mobilization.
> Active aid in the mobilization as well as complicity in the White Guard organization is subject to punishment up to and including immediate execution, on a level with provocation and the transmission of information about Communists and their sympathizers.
>
> Chief of the Special Section of Combat Emissaries.
> (signature)[22]

To demonstrate that this was no "empty threat," a postcript to Order No. 2 read: "For treason, supplying information to the White Guards and provocation, death sentences were carried out in the case of the following persons: H. Mashenko, Derusyvtsev, Sminkovs'kyi, K. Kolyachenko, R. Maynes, and Karnachev.[23] The two orders were in Russian and Ukrainian, while the rest of *Borotba* was in Ukrainian. *Borotba* had a distribution in Kyiv wide enough for the orders to make an impression on the population. "The success of [Order No. 2] was in no small measure also due to the fact that it was reprinted in the newspaper *Kiyevskoye ekho* [Kyivan Echo] (November 8/21) as an exposure of 'Bolshevik atrocities'"[24]

One of the commonest methods used by the Borotbist underground in Kyiv in combating the Whites was the employment of brigades of "panic-mongers" to spread rumors through the bazaars. Although several *Borotbisty*, Borbisty, Bolsheviks, and Bundists were executed toward the end of the Denikin regime, this did not adversely affect underground activity, at least that of the UCP(b), partly because those seized had not been active, but primarily because the village was the main base of the underground movement.

2. Borotbist Activity Among the Partisans

The course which the Denikin regime took helped to unite all opposition parties, even those hostile to one another. The Bolshevik underground leader Svenitsky-Zheleznyak reported the following characteristic event:

> A congress of the initiatory-revolutionary group of Novo-Moskovsk District was held September 26 (old style). Under the influence of separatist elements, a resolution was adopted on the establishment of a socialist bloc of all "left" parties, including even the Petlyurists, for the purpose of fighting the Whites. -The congress elected a revolutionary committee which was half Petlyurist and half Makhnoist. . . .[25]

The Borotbisty kept in close touch with the Makhnoists, the *Borbisty* and the Bolsheviks. Such relations benefited all concerned, especially the Bolshevik organizations, which had a good supply of money and arms but lacked direct contacts-as Kin frankly admits-with the village, the main base of revolutionary operations.

> Of the large partisan detachments of the soviet typ'e led by [non-Bolsheviks] mention should be made of the one under the Borotbist [Yakiv] Ohiy, 250 men strong (according to data of mid-September), which operated in Poltava and later in Kremenchuk Districts; that under Kotsura in the region of Chigirin; that of the Borotbist [Kost'] Matyash in Poltava District; and that of [Todos] Taran in Kremenchuk District.
> All these detachments were in touch with the Poltava Provincial Revolutionary Committee, which was made up of three Communists, one Left SR [i.e., *Borbisti* and one Borot'bist (who actually did not work for he was shot en route to Kremenchug). The Communist Shavryn, Kolosov's deputy, was also on the Committee, [prom Shavryn's orders] it is evident that non-party insurgent units operated at least in agreement with if not in complete subordination, to

the Provincial Revolutionary Committee. On December 16, 1919 Shavryn ordered Ohiy, the commander of the insurgent Soviet brigade, and Matyash, Klymenko and Skyrta with their detachments to undertake the seizure of Kremenchug. On the same day Shavryn issued operation orders to Kotsura, commander of the Fourth Russian Ukraine Regiment, and Petrov, commander of the insurgent Soviet unit in the Soloshitski area. . . .[26]

This passage shows clearly the close contact maintained between the partisan units and underground party organizations, yet it contains several inaccuracies. The forces of Ohiy and Matyash formed one, not two units. In addition, Kin exaggerates the role of the Poltava Provincial Revolutionary Committee. The present author was frequently in Poltava at the time and had a thorough knowledge of the local underground, but cannot recall ever having heard of the Committee. In any event even the Bolshevik units did not regard such committees seriously, since their terrorized leaders had little real influence in the underground. The work of such committees was confined to supplying the partisans with arms and money, although as a matter of fact even these were more frequently obtained in battle with Denikin's forces. It is most unlikely that the non-Bolshevik partisan leaders Ohiy, Matyash and Serdyuk obeyed orders of the Poltava Revolutionary Committee. On the other hand it should be pointed out that they were hardly in a position to quarrel with the Bolshevik underground, because by mid-December the Red Army was already deep in Ukraine.[27]

The unpopularity of the Bolshevik underground with the Ukrainian people was pointed out by the Bolshevik underground leader Pavlo I. Popov in his report of October 21, 1919 to the CP(b)U's Rear Echelon Bureau:

> The idea of Soviet governmental rule is very popular with the peasants, more so than any other would be, but the approach of the Soviet armies they fear like fire; they dream of their "own" Bolsheviks. The notion that "Petlyura made a pact with the Bolsheviks" is popular (I heard it mentioned many a time while passing through Kyiv and Radomyshl' Districts).[28]

More information about Borot'bist partisan activity is available in Kin's study:

> The insurgent movement was wide-spread in Kherson Province, especially in the districts of Nikolayev, Kherson, Yelisavetgrad [now Kirovohrad—Ed.],

and Aleksandriya. Here a prominent role in organizing the insurgent movement in the villages was played by Left SR's *Borbisty* and Ukrainian SR's Borotbisty. ... In the village of Bashtanka (Poltavka)... an uprising was initiated in mid-September... by peasant Communists and Borotbisty.... The [Bolshevik] Odessa Committee reported that "in connection with the intensified insurgent movement, a military-insurgent provincial headquarters was established on a parity basis upon agreement with the Left *SR's-Borbisty* and the Ukrainian SR's-Borotbisty. ..." In Podolye the Provincial Revolutionary Committee, the Communist Provincial Committee, the Left SR's [i.e., *Borbisty*], and the *Ukapisty* [i.e., Borotbisty] joined in calling for an armed uprising against the Whites.... The commander of the Kyiv district was the well-known Petlyurist bandit Anhel and the commander of the Poltava district was Ataman Pyatenko, a former member of the Poltava Province Executive Committee which operated also in Kyiv Province. ... In the Motovilovka-Boyarka[-Budayevka]-Vasil'kov-Fastov area an Insurgent Committee was created headed by the former Borotbisty Kotsyuba and Koshevyi.[29]

Particularly noteworthy is the activity of the Bolshevik partisan leader Kolosov. During the Hetmanate he had led a force of 6,000 partisans in Katerynoslav Province; he was also mentioned in Ataman Hryhoryiv's telegram to the Bolshevik Revolutionary Committee in Aleksandrovsk as a member of the Council of Revolutionary Emissaries, that stillborn Borotbist government.s In the Denikin period Kolosov, along with Svenitsky-Zheleznyak, Yurvyn, Zhupanov, and Bukhovs'kyi, was a member of the Revolutionary Military Council of Left Bank Ukraine and Southeastern Right Bank Ukraine.[30]

Kolosov shortly succeeded in organizing an insurgent center in the area of the so-called Samarsky Forests.... He established the headquarters of the second brigade in the region of Kekaterynoslav... and that of the third brigade in the region of Poltava.... Kolosov later formed two more brigades in the region of Slavyansk... and in the region of Aleksandriya.... Comrade A. Novyts'ky, in charge of the agency of the [Bolshevik] Rear Echelon Bureau, wrote in one of his letters [dated November 28, 1919]' that Kolosov... fell under the influence of Petlyura's followers... [and] that he was popular among the insurgents.
Kolosov's report before the Rear Echelon Bureau of the Central Committee of the CP(b)U fully confirms Novytskyi's description [of him], although Kolosov attempted to demonstrate that he was master of the Petlyura followers, not they of him.[31]

---

s   See p. 186-187

A Bolshevik like Kolosov who fell under Petlyura's influence was, for all practical purposes, an ally of the Borotbisty.

Ravich-Cherkassky provides more information about Borot'bist underground activity:

> With Denikin's arrival [in Kyiv], Petlyura withdrew to Volyn and Podolye Provinces.... Borotbist forces were concentrated in these same areas. In close contact with the Bolsheviks, the Borotbisty fought against Petlyura, stirred up an uprising among Petlyura's troops and, jointly with the Bolsheviks, organized a Revolutionary Council in Volyn Province, to which several thousand men of Petlyura's army transferred their allegiance. [Ataman] Volokh was appointed their commander....
>
> In general it is impossible to deny that in Right Bank Ukraine, especially in Volyn' and Podolye Provinces, the Borotbisty had a well organized party which supplied that entire area with literature and underground workers during the Denikin period; however, they showed no clear-cut tendency to seize power without the Communists [i.e., the Bolsheviks]. Despite very strong Borotbist influence in this area, the Revolutionary Council consisted of [only] one Borot'bist, three Bolsheviks and one non-party man. It is true that the Bolsheviks in Volyn did not at that time display particular firmness; two Bolshevik members of the Revolutionary Council went over to the Borotbisty.[32]

The last sentence of the above passage is very telling; it contradicts the statement that the Borotbisty "showed no clear-cut tendency to seize power without the Communists." That such a tendency did exist will be evident from material to be discussed presently.[†] The Borotbisty were only a minority on this Revolutionary Council, a situation due to tactical rather than any other considerations, but it is almost certain that some of the Bolsheviks on the Council were Borotbist agents. This method of infiltrating the Bolsheviks was used by the Borotbisty in other localities after the downfall of Denikin. In Kobeliaky a scandal broke out when the local Bolshevik committee uncovered a Borotbist agent among its members and expelled her from the Party. To be sure, the Bolsheviks, too, had their agents amongst the Borotbisty. Yet for obvious reasons the former Bundist Ravich-Cherkassky exaggerates the loyalty of the Borotbisty to the Bolsheviks. A late-comer to the CP(b)U, Ravich-Cherkassky was attempting to demonstrate that Ukrainian Bolshevism was a composite of many component streams.

---

† See pp. 236–241

* * *

By the end of December 1919 the Denikin regime was in a state of total collapse, more from internal opposition than from the external pressure of the Red Army, which pursued the Whites southward to the Black Sea with almost no resistance. The Borotbisty played a major role in the disruption of the rear of Denikin's army. This is clear from the single fact that strong Borotbist organizations sprang up across the country as Denikin retreated. Bolshevik organizations also appeared, but they were created only under the protection of the advancing Red Army. Indeed the Borotbist and Bolshevik organizations sometimes clashed."[33]

The self-dissolution of the CP(b)U in early October had demonstrated, perhaps most clearly, that in 1919 the CP(b)U was a force alien to the Ukrainian revolution, without ties with the majority of the population. It was as if the Bolsheviks by this act had openly admitted that they considered an all-Russian offensive to be their only hope of overthrowing Denikin. Had the support which Denikin received from the Entente been rendered to Petlyura, it is doubtful that such an all-Russian campaign would have succeeded.[34]

8 The third Period of Bolshevik Rule in Ukraine

A. Bolshevik Re-Examination of the Ukrainian Problem

1. Bolsheviks Face To Face with the Ukrainian Problem

The defeat of General Denikin in the fall of 1919 forced Moscow to face the urgent problem of what Bolshevik policy in Ukraine should be. The issue was the more crucial, because the Borotbisty now emerged as a dangerous rival of the CP(b)U. The experience of 1919 demonstrated to the Bolsheviks the consequences of ignoring Ukrainian aspirations. In their approach to the Ukrainian problem the Bolsheviks became much more cautious than they had been during the war against the Directory.

In early 1920 the Bolsheviks sought earnestly to effect a compromise between the principle of self-determination, a pre-requisite for Soviet success in non-Russian territories, and the centralization of power, which alone could ensure the survival of Bolshevik rule. Any infringement of the principle of self-determination tended to lend to the war, when waged in non-Russian territory, a national character and to turn not only hostile social classes but whole nations against the Bolsheviks, except for small groups of the Russian proletariat and petty bourgeoisie. The continuation of open warfare became difficult both materially and morally, for it exposed the contradiction between the Bolshevik program (self-determination) and Bolshevik practice (Red imperialism). The fact that Bolshevik centralism in non-Russian territories inevitably became tinged with Russian nationalism served only to make matters worse. The existence of this dilemma was brought out trenchantly by the old Ukrainian Bolshevik

Zatonsky in a speech before the Tenth Congress of the Russian Communist Party (Bolshevik) in March 1921:

> It is important to distinguish between necessary centralization and primitive Russian jingoism [*rusopyatstvo*]. The term is not mine, but Comrade Lenin's, which he used unfortunately only at the end of 1919. for the first time, at the Party Conference. ... We must expect an intensification of the national struggle. ... We must expunge from the minds of comrades the idea that soviet federation means necessarily Russian federation. ...[1]

It is obvious that for the Bolsheviks the national problem in Ukraine had become of the utmost importance: first, because Ukraine was, after Russia, the largest Soviet republic and, second, because the Russian chauvinists in Ukraine were more uncompromising than those, for instance, in Turkestan or the Caucasus. They simply would not accept the idea that Ukraine could be a separate nation.

2. The Guiding Hand of Lenin

Lenin showed the greatest elasticity and ingenuity in finding formulas to reconcile the contradictory principles of self-determination and centralism. He was the author of all Party and government resolutions on national policy in Ukraine at that time. Speaking at the Eighth Conference of the Russian Communist Party (Bolshevik) on December 3, 1919 Lenin affirmed the indivisibility of Bolshevik power in Ukraine and defined the aim of the Party to be an alliance with Ukraine peasantry and the destruction of the Borotbist party, just as in the case of the Russian SR's.

> If some comrades declared that I had recommended a block with the Borotbisty, they are in error. I here compared the policy which must be applied toward the Borotbisty with the policy which we applied toward the [Russian] Right SR's. In the first week after October [the 1917 coup], at peasant congresses we were then accused among other things of not wanting to use the forces of the peasants after once having seized power. I said [then]: We took [over] your program as a whole for the purpose of utilizing the peasant forces; we want this, but we do not want an alliance with the SR's. Therefore Comrade Manuilsky is as extraordinarily in error as Comrades [Yakiv] Drobnis and [Andrei S.] Bubnov, in alleging that I recommended a bloc with the Borotbisty. My idea was to point to our need for a bloc with the peasantry of Ukraine; in order to realize this policy we should not conduct the dispute with the Borotbisty in the way it is being conducted....
>
> The question is: Do we need a bloc with the Ukrainian peasantry, do we need a policy such as we needed at the end of 1917 and for many months in 1918? I maintain that we do; therefore the greater part of the state farms must really be parcelled out. We must fight against the large farms, we must fight against

petty bourgeois prejudices, we must fight against partisan warfare [*partizanstvo*] The Borotbisty talk a great deal about the national question, but they do not mention *partizanstvo*. We should demand that the Borotbisty dissolve the Union of Teachers-even if it uses the Ukrainian language and the official Ukrainian state seal—in the name of the same principles of proletarian communist policy in the name of which we dissolved our All-Russian Teachers' Union, since it has not applied the principles of proletarian dictatorship, but has defended the interests and applied the policy of the petty bourgeoisie.[2]

Lenin's comparison of the Borotbisty with the Russian Right SR's was inaccurate. The SR's were an anti-Soviet party, while on the contrary the Borotbisty defended the Soviet platform. In addition, Lenin's example of the Ukrainian Teachers' Union shows the contradictions into which the Bolsheviks were forced in their attempts to solve the national problem in Ukraine. The Teachers' Union in Ukraine, unlike the Teachers' Union in Russia, was no mere trade union; it was an association of those who strove for the national liberation of their country. The dissolved Teachers' Union in Russia was merely replaced by another Russian organization with a different class composition. However, in Ukraine the Bolsheviks replaced the dissolved Teachers' Union with an association of Russian teachers, Communist and non-Communist, which was interested in the preservation of an indivisible Russia, even though Red.

Equally ambivalent was Lenin's "Letter to the Workers and Peasants of Ukraine Concerning the Victory over Denikin," dated December 28, 1919. It reads in part:

Until Ukraine is completely liberated from Denikin, the All-Ukrainian Revolutionary Committee... will be its government before [the convening of] the All-Ukrainian Congress of Soviets. Side by side with the Ukrainian Communist-Bolsheviks, Ukrainian Communists-Borotbisty work as members of the government in this Revolutionary Committee. The Borotbisty differ from the Bolsheviks chiefly in that they stand for the unconditional independence of Ukraine. The Bolsheviks do not make of *this* an issue of disagreement and disunity; *in this they* do not see any obstacle to united proletarian work. Let there be unity in the struggle against the capitalist yoke and for the dictatorship of the proletariat; over the question of national borders and federal or other ties between states, Communists must not disagree. Among the Bolsheviks there are advocates of complete independence of Ukraine, advocates of a more or less federal tie and still others in favor of a complete fusion of Ukraine with Russia.

These questions should not create insurmountable differences. They will be decided by the All-Ukrainian Congress of Soviets.-'[3]

Lenin was here speaking not to the Party, but to the Ukrainian masses. It would have been too dangerous to tell them that the Bolsheviks opposed a bloc with the Borotbisty and in fact favored a dictatorship of the Russian Bolshevik Party over the peasants. Hence Lenin played down the possibility of disagreement, so much so that he recognized as Communists those who "are in favor of complete fusion of Ukraine with Russia," although in March 1919 at the Eighth Congress of the Russian Communist Party (Bolshevik) he had branded such Communists as chauvinists who must be fought.[4]

In his "Letter" Lenin referred to such Communists in a much milder tone:

> That is why we Great Russian Communists must be ready to make concessions in our differences with the Ukrainian Communists-Bolsheviks and the Borotbisty, when the differences concern the state independence of Ukraine, the form of its union with Russia and the national problem in general. All of us Communists—Great Russian, Ukrainian, or of any other nation—must be uncompromising and inflexible in matters concerning the basic problems of the proletarian struggle which are identical for all nations—the problems of proletarian dictatorship, the rejection of conciliation with the bourgeoisie and the preservation of the unity of those forces which are defending us from Denikin.[5]

Lenin's "Letter" purposely avoided all controversial issues, leaving their solution not to the armed insurgent masses, but to narrow party counsel. Not without reason, Lenin was afraid to admit fully to the Ukrainian masses the differences between the Bolsheviks and the Borotbisty. The essence of his argument was that (1) the Bolsheviks would somehow manage to solve the Ukrainian problem, even though some Bolsheviks were demanding Ukrainian independence while others were advocating an undivided Russia; (2) the Party must form a bloc with the Ukrainian peasantry and isolate the Borotbisty (absorbing some of the Borotbisty and dispersing the rest); and (3) toward this end, the masses must only be told that differences between the Bolsheviks and the Borotbisty were secondary. In point of fact the primacy of Bolshevism would be ensured through its administrative and military arm.

B. Bolshevik Resolutions

1. The Russian Bolsheviks

The first and most fundamental document which reflected the new Bolshevik policy in Ukraine was the resolution of the Central Committee of the Russian Communist Party (Bolshevik) "On Soviet Power in Ukraine," later approved by the Eighth All-Russian Party Conference, held December 2–4, 1919:

> Inflexibly applying the principles of the self-determination of nations, the C[entral] Committee] deems it necessary to emphasize once again the fact that the CC stands for the recognition of the independence of the Ukr.S.S.R.
> Considering the necessity for a very close union of all Soviet republics in their struggle against the threatening forces of world-wide imperialism as indisputable to every Communist and every conscious worker, the R[ussian] C[ommunist] P[arty] takes the position that the determination of the forms of this union will be decided finally by the Ukrainian workers and toiling peasants themselves.
> On the basis of the decisions of the A[ll-Russian] C[entral] Executive] Committee] of June 1, 1919 and of the C[entral] E[xecutive] C[ommittee] of the U[kraine] of May 18, 1919 the relations between the Ukr.S.S.R. and the R.S.F.S.R. are defined at the present time as a federative tie.
> In view of the fact that Ukrainian culture (language, schooling, etc.) has been suppressed for centuries by tsarism and the exploiting classes of Russia, the CC of the RCP imposes upon all members of the Party the duty of facilitating in every way the removal of all obstacles to the free development of the Ukrainian language and culture. Inasmuch as nationalist tendencies are observable among the backward section of the Ukrainian masses as a result of the oppression of many centuries, members of the RCP are obligated to treat them with the utmost patience and tact, counteracting [these tendencies] with a word of comradely explanation of the identity of interests of the toiling masses of Ukraine and Russia. Members of the RCP in the territory of Ukraine must in deed adhere to the right of the toiling masses to study and speak in their native language in all Soviet institutions, in every way opposing attempts by artificial means to reduce the Ukrainian language to a secondary plane, striving on the contrary to transform the Ukrainian language into a weapon of communist education of the toiling masses. Steps should be taken so that all Soviet institutions have a sufficient number of employees conversant in the Ukrainian language and so that in the future all employees will be able to make themselves understood in Ukrainian.
> It is essential to guarantee the closest contact of Soviet institutions with the radical peasant population of the country; to do this it should be the rule that, in securing a decisive influence over the representatives, of the peasant poor, the majority of the representatives of the toiling peasantry be drawn into the revolutionary committees and Soviets immediately upon their formation.

In view of the fact that in Ukraine, to an even larger extent than in Russia, the peasantry makes up the overwhelming mass of the population, the task of the Soviet government in Ukraine is to gain the confidence not only of the peasant poor but of the wide strata of the middle peasantry, whose real interests tie them most closely to Soviet rule. In particular, in preserving the fundamental principles of our food policy (state grain purchases at fixed prices and compulsory assessment) the implementation of this policy must carefully conform to the conditions of the Ukrainian countryside.

The next task of our food policy in Ukraine should be to extract grain surpluses, on a *rigidly limited scale*, [in an amount] necessary to feed the Ukrainian poor [peasants], the workers and the Red Army. In extracting surpluses special attention must be given to the interests of the middle peasantry, rigorously distinguishing them from the kulak elements. Counterrevolutionary demagoguery which instills in the Ukrainian peasantry the idea that the aim of Soviet Russia is to export grain and other food products from Ukraine to Russia must be unmasked.

The enrollment on the broadest scale of the poor and middle peasantry into administrative rule in all spheres should be imposed as a duty on the agents of the central governmental authority, all party workers, instructors, etc.

In order to establish genuine rule by the toilers, steps must be taken immediately to prevent the inundation in Soviet institutions of elements of the Ukrainian urban petty bourgeoisie, which are alien to an understanding of the conditions of life of the broad peasant masses and which frequently parade under the banner of communism.

The condition under which such elements can be tolerated in both Party and Soviet institutions must be preliminary verification of their efficiency and devotion to the interests of the toilers *in action*, above all at the front in the rank and file of the army in the field. Everywhere and under all conditions such elements must be placed under rigid class control of the proletariat.

In view of the fact that a large quantity of the arms in the hands of the Ukrainian rural population is — as experience has shown — inevitably concentrated in the hands of the kulak and counterrevolutionary elements because of the lack of organization of the poor, and that this leads to actual domination of the bandit kulaks rather than dictatorship of the toilers, the very first task of Soviet construction in Ukraine is the removal of all arms and their concentration in the hands of the workers' and peasants' Red Army.

7. Agrarian policy must be conducted with special attention to the interests of the land economy of the poor and middle peasantry.

1) The goal of agrarian policy in Ukraine should be: 1) Complete liquidation of proprietor landownership, re-established by Denikin, with the transfer of land to those without land and poor in land.

2) Establishment of state farms only on a strictly necessary scale, conformable to the vital interests of the associated peasants.

3) In the amalgamation of peasants into communes, artels, etc., rigid application of the party policy which rejects all compulsion in this respect, leaving [amalgamation] exclusively to the free decision of the peasants themselves and rigorously guarding against any and all attempts to introduce the principle of compulsion.[6]

The tactics behind this resolution, according to Valentyn Sadovsky, a once prominent leader of the USDRP,

> were dictated by the belief that the level of political and national development of the Ukrainian masses was very low. It took into account the fact that the politically immature masses would be attracted by promises of concessions without noticing that these concessions were only temporary and conditional.'7

The resolution silently condemned the Russian Bolshevik policy of 1919 in Ukraine and revised its most important tenents— those dealing with the national, the land and the food problems. A new feature introduced was the barring of the urban petty bourgeoisie, hostile to the Ukrainian peasantry and Ukrainian national liberation, from work in the new Soviet administration. It was precisely this group which had provided the major support for the Bolshevik occupation of 1919. (In Ukraine the Bolsheviks lacked the support of those classes which were loyal to them in Russia.) However, during the Denikin occupation this group almost in its entirety lied to Russia rather than go underground. The resolution under discussion thus denounced them for previous spineless-ness and proposed that their loyalty to the regime be tested by service in the Red Army.

Notwithstanding the intentions of the Bolsheviks to keep "bourgeois philistinism" (*meshchanstvo*) out of the new Soviet government in Ukraine, the philistines could not be Converted into idealists and nationally tolerant Bolsheviks overnight. They persisted in their Russian jingoist attitude, making enemies of Ukrainian peasants and intellectuals. Once the Borotbisty had joined the CP(b)U, they made a determined effort to exterminate such "bourgeois philistinism" within the party and the administration, but their struggle, led by Blakytny, ended in failure.u

2.　The Ukrainian Bolsheviks

In line with Russian Bolshevik activity, the CP(b)U issued a series of official directives and proclamations on national policy in

---

u　See pp. 265-269

Ukraine. Of these, the appeal "To All Party Organizations of the CP(b)U," issued December 15, 1919 by the Central Committee of the CP(b)U, should be singled out. It admitted that the Red Army's retreat in the face of Denikin's summer advance had led to the Ukrainian Bolsheviks' "mass emigration to Russia." The atrophy of Bolshevik party life in Ukraine which had ensued, the appeal continued, had been exploited by other parties, in particular the Borotbisty, to strengthen their influence. This was the more feasible, since the Bolsheviks had hastened to enroll in the Red Army, while "the Borotbisty who considered themselves a Soviet party, showed no inclination to help Soviet Russia in its difficult straggle and attempted to exploit Denikin's victory to discredit our Communist Party as a party hostile to the Ukrainian workers and peasants." With the collapse of Denikin, "party life must be roused from its state of lethargy through common effort." Toward this end, in addition to the All-Ukrainian Revolutionary Committee, a small "party center" was being established consisting of Rakovsky, Zatonsky and Kossior— members of the Central Committee of the CP(b)U; and Petrovsky and Manuilsky—co-opted from the All-Ukrainian Revolutionary Committee.[8]

Though admitting the flight of Bolshevik party functionaries (*apparatchiki*), the appeal made a virtue of desertion, calling it to aid to Soviet Russia, but in the same breath censured the Borotbisty for carrying on an underground struggle. The appeal anticipates that approach to Ukraine which later found application in Stalin's policy.

The re-establishment of Soviet governmental authority in Ukraine was the subject of the manifesto "To the Workers and Peasants of Ukraine," issued in early December by the All-Ukrainian Revolutionary Committee.[9] It was this committee, as Lenin later in the month pointed out, which was to be the government until the convening of the next (Fourth) All-Ukrainian Congress of Soviets. The manifesto was signed by the three Ukrainian Bolshevik members of the Committee: G.I. Petrovsky (Chairman), Zatonsky and Manuilsky. Notable by his absence was Pyatakov, who had been active under similar circumstances in the fall of 1918.ᵛ Hrynko and Ye. Terletsky, who had been a member of the first Ukrainian Soviet government, were later brought into the Committee to broaden its base.¹⁰ However, the parity of one representative each granted the two non-Bolshevik parties did not reflect their respective strength. The Borotbisty were in every way the stronger party, but because the *Borbisty* were virtually a Russian party they were more palatable and less dangerous to the Bolsheviks.¹¹

The Ukrainian people, declares the manifesto, "becomes a free master of the Ukrainian land. . . . The free and independent Ukrainian Socialist Soviet Republic has risen again." While the need for the free development of Ukrainian culture was mentioned, primary attention was focused on "the unbreakable alliance of Ukraine and Russia, the pledge of which is the united Russo-Ukrainian Red Army." Another passage straightforwardly states that "the Ukrainian Red Army has merged with the Russian Red Army." The "unbreakable alliance" is referred to as "the union of the free Ukrainian peasants with the workers and peasants of Russia."

With regard to the land problem, the manifesto declares that in 1919 "ten million desyatins [of land belonging to large estates] had not been distributed to the peasants, because strong soviet government in the villages had been lacking." The slogan of the day now became "Seize the landowners' land." As for the national policy, the aim remained, as in 1919, "the establishment of Ukraine in close association with Russia," even though the document ends on the contrasting note of "Long live the independent-Ukrainian Soviet Republic!"¹²

Sadovsky's interpretation of the resolution by the Central Committee of the Russian Communist Party (above, page 169) applies equally to the All-Ukrainian Revolutionary Committee's manifesto. In the manifesto the calculated attempt to play upon the political ignorance of the masses was concealed even less skillfully.

---

v   See pp. 181–182

3. The Borotbist-Ukrainian Bolshevik Agreement

Of signal importance was an agreement signed in Moscow, December 17, by the Central Committees of the CP(b)U and the UCP(b):

> We, the undersigned representatives of the Central Committee of the CP(b)U and of the Central Committee of the UCP (Borotbisty), entering into interparty collaboration in the All-Ukrainian Revolutionary Committee, have made the following agreement in the name of our parties:
> The directives drafted at the Conference of the RCP, upon the proposal of the delegation of the CP(b)U are accepted as the basis of collaboration.
> The Ukrainian Communist Party (Borotbisty) endorses unconditionally the manifesto of the All-Ukrainian Revolutionary Committee and, together with the representatives of the CP(b)U in the Revolutionary Committee, will carry out the program outlined in the Manifesto.
> Inasmuch as all work of the All-Ukrainian Revolutionary Committee is subordinated to the main task of the struggle against the united forces of Russian and international counter revolution, represented at this moment by Denikin, Kolchak, Petlyura, and all other enemies of the workers' and peasants' government, both sides signatory to this agreement pledge themselves to support with all their efforts the Russo-Ukrainian Red Army in the-execution of its tasks of annihilating once for all the forces of imperialist world reaction.
> Therefore we pledge ourselves to root out all attempts to disperse the forces of the united revolutionary front against the White Guard army, especially condemning all agitation which advocates the organization in Ukrainian territory of separate military formations of former partisans and disbanded Petlyurist army men and troop separation of the Ukrainian from the Russian Red Army. We pledge ourselves to fight mercilessly any agitation which disorganizes the front and aids counterrevolution.
> Signed: Kh. Rakovsky, D. Manuilsky, G. Petrovsky, and S. Kossior for the Central Committee of the Communist Party of Ukraine (Bolshevik); L. Kovaliv and H. Hryn'ko for the Central Committee of the Ukrainian Communist Party (Borotbisty).
>
> Moscow, December 17, 1919.[13]

In the light of the negotiations for admission of the UCP(b) to the Communist International conducted in Moscow by Kovaliv and Hrynko in the late summer of 1919, it is very difficult to account for the agreement reached with the Bolsheviks. It was in the period December 1919 January 1920 that the Borotbisty tried, for the last time, to create a Red Army of their own, independent of Moscow. It is hardly likely that Hrynko and Kovaliv differed from other members of the Borotbist Central Committee on this matter. Kovaliv, an old member of the Central Committee, refused to go along with the majority of his party in joining the CP(b)U in 1920.

As far as the present author can recall, Kovaliv and Hrynko's mission to Moscow was considered a failure by the rank and file Borotbisty. Kovaliv's open letter to all members of the UCP(b), published at the time as a separate pamphlet, offered no solution; rather it was an appeal for per-serverance.[14] The letter was the object of irony and criticism among the Borotbist leaders. Yet in spite of altercations between the Borotbisty and the Bolsheviks, the Borotbisty were not accused of breaking the Moscow agreement.

Only once, in a pamphlet published by the political section of the Russian Twelfth Army, did Zatonsky censure the Borotbisty for inconsistency and for exaggeration of their differences with the Bolsheviks which he believed was dangerous to the Revolution.'[15]

One is forced to conclude that the Borotbisty were consciously playing a double game in the hope that they would eventually gain the upper hand over the Bolsheviks and thereby be able to break the agreement. From previous experience the Borotbisty knew that the Bolsheviks were not to be trusted in regard to agreements and treaties. They must also have known of Bolshevik plans to destroy the UCP(b). Therefore they had nothing to lose. In their last desperate move for supremacy in the Soviet Ukraine, the successful formation of an independent Ukrainian Red Army, they reasoned, might open the doors of the Communist International at which they now knocked in vain.

C. Final Borotbist Attempt To Organize A Ukrainian Red Army

What gave substance to the array of anti-Borot'bist Bolshevik resolutions and proclamations was the final attempt on the part of the Borotbisty to build an independent Ukrainian Red Army. In such an army, as they conceived it, the service of non-Ukrainian nationals would be allowed. They even envisaged a joint high command with the Russian Red Army. The Ukrainian Red Army could send its units to aid the Russian Red Army in combating such common enemies as Kolchak in Siberia or Yudenich outside Petrograd. However, it would always retain its Ukrainian character and command, and its official language would be Ukrainian. Here was the crux of the Borot'bist demand. Their aim was not, as the Bolsheviks charged, to split the revolutionary forces; they wanted merely an alliance of these forces, which would be separate ethnically and culturally, not fused into a single Russian army.

1. Interlude with Makhno

While still underground during the Denikin occupation, the Borotbisty, represented by Lisovyk, Hrudnytsky and Kostyantyn Matyash, formed a military pact with the Anarchist Makhno during a conference with Volin, Makhno's political adviser, and Chubenko, Makhno's adjutant. A resolution agreed upon stated: "It is necessary to combine the [partisan] units in order to organize an independent insurgent Ukrainian army, so as to thwart the party dictatorship of the RCP (Bolsheviks)."[16] By the time Lenin accused the Borotbisty of supporting the partisans, the transformation of the Soviet Red Army from a conglomeration of units into a regular army was well advanced. The Borotbisty, on their part, also realized the importance of a regular army: seeking the support of partisan units was merely a tactical maneuveur; such units were to provide the foundation for a regular army. To be sure, Makhno also hoped to profit by the alliance, but as a means to strengthen his own partisan movement.

2. Alliance With Ataman Volokh

A much more significant move in the Borotbist attempt to form a separate army was their alliance with Ataman Volokh. Volokh, a burly phlegmatic man, with a bearded, pock-marked face, was a figure out of Repin's painting "The Zaporozhian Cossacks." An officer in the army of the Ukrainian People's Republic, Volokh was nevertheless a sympathizer with the SR's, perhaps even a member of the UPSR. He manifested his leftist views on more than one occasion. In March 1919 he had staged a revolt at the front lines of the Ukrainian People's Republic. A Revolutionary Committee of the

Southwestern Ukrainian Front, consisting of Bolsheviks, Borotbisty and representatives of military units, was formed in Vapnyarka, March 23. The Committee accepted a Soviet platform and in consultation with the military commanders appointed Volokh to replace the supreme commander of the front who had been favorable to the French in Odessa. At the same time the Committee began truce negotiations with Rakovsky's government. A truce was arranged, but it was later violated by the Bolsheviks.[17]

At the end of 1919 Volokh repeated his performance. Together with two other atamans he formed a pro-Soviet triumvirate. The Volyn' Province Insurgent Committee was transformed into the Volyn Regional Revolutionary Council, headed by the local Borotbist Koval. At the "head of the *Haydamak* brigade, Volokh arrived in Lyubar, where Petlyura and the government of the Ukrainian People's Republic were established.[18] Volokh's detachment flew a red flag, with the inscription "Long live Soviet power in Ukraine." A message was sent to Petlyura, asking that he resign. In reply, Petlyura's officer cadets were ordered to disarm Volokh's detachment, but most of them including some of Petlyura's personal guards, went over to Volokh. Early on December 2, Volokh's troops seized Petlyura's headquarters and the treasury.[19] Petlyura, his ministers, army staff, and others, under the protection of the *Sichovi Stril'tsi*, fled to Nova Chortoriya.[20] The Central Committee of the Borotbist party, at this time located in Zhitomir, "established contact with Volokh as soon as they learned that Volokh, together with some of the troops, had left the army [i.e., of the Ukrainian People's Republic]."[21] It is possible that an understanding between Volokh and the Borotbisty had existed even earlier. Yet Tyutyunnyk claims that[22]

> At first Volokh had no intention of joining the Red Russians. Having seized actual power, Volokh, so as to give everything an appearance of legality, wanted to compel the government and all who fought for Ukrainian independence to recognize the Soviet form of government. . . .

Tyutyunnyk evaluates Volokh's action in Lyubar in the following way:

> 1) Great impudence and carelessness displayed during the preparatory period; 2) no specific goal or clear-cut plan; 3) inability to exploit the revolt. . . ;

4) a want of courage to force the entire army to recognize the fact of the coup; and 5) a lack of understanding of Red Moscow's policy toward Ukraine.

However, Tyutyunnyk is not harsh with Volokh himself; he does not believe that Volokh wanted to destroy the government center of the Ukrainian People's Republic. ."No one was executed by Volokh, even though it was said that 'Petlyura went in one direction and Volokh in another'."

Volokh crossed the lines of the Red Army and sent a delegation in search of the Borotbist Central Committee in Zhitomir. When his envoys asked the local committee of the CP(b)U where the Borotbisty could be found, they were told that none were in Zhitomir, although the Borotbist Central Committee was located next door. Volokh's envoys thereupon went to the headquarters of the Twelfth Red Army in Korosten. Volokh was enraged when his men reported back the Bolshevik proposal that Volokh "lay down his arms within twenty-four hours."

> Just then, the Borot'bist delegates Shumsky, Nemolovsky and Savytsky reached Volokh from Zhitomir. . . . The Borotbisty were equally infuriated by the tactless behavior of Volokh and the Revolutionary Council.

They criticized Volokh's undiplomatic move in conducting negotiations with the enemy, the Bolsheviks, "not from a neutral *one, but on the enemy's very doorstep. "

> With Poloz's blessings, a Revolutionary Committee of Right Bank Ukraine was formed consisting of three persons: Nemolovsky, Voytsekhivsky and Savytsky. . . with Volokh as Commander-in-Chief. At the same time a Revolutionary Committee existed in Left Bank Ukraine. . . . These Revolutionary Committees conducted a completely independent policy. The leaders of the Borotbist party Poloz, Shumsky and Ellansky were not members of the committees, for fear of spoiling their red careers which they hoped to earn in Moscow [should their plans miscarry]. If the Revolutionary Committees succeeded in forming a sizable [military] force, the Borotbist leaders would proclaim themselves a Socialist Government of Ukraine. . . . Without waiting for the Russians to disarm them, Volokh and the newly formed Revolutionary Committee decided to seek a "neutral zone". ... In a declaration to his red troops, . . . Volokh stated: "We shall drive across the entire Ukraine and unite all active Ukrainian forces. We shall begin to build our own Independent Socialist Soviet Republic!"

Mazepa comments as follows:

The Borotbisty started to form their army "on the spot," without the consent of the Russian Bolsheviks.[23] In order to separate itself from the Russian Bolshevik army which was advancing from the north, the newly formed Revolutionary Committee, together with Volokh and his army, immediately followed in the footsteps of our army [i.e., of the Ukrainian People's Republic] into Kyiv Province. . . . Behind the army of the "Winter Campaign,"[24] Ataman Volokh and his "red army" reached Uman'. While still in the Lyubar area, he had made contact with the Borotbisty; now having reached the Uman' area, he attempted to win over Cossacks and officers from the army of the Winter Campaign. However, the results of his action were of no benefit to the Borotbisty. . . .[25]

The Sixth Detachment of the Zaporozhian Division, stationed in Uman', was won over to Volokh when the delegation of the Borot'bist Revolutionary Committee, headed by Serhiy Savytsky, came to that city. On January 10, 1920 Savytsky sent the following communication to Tyutyunnyk:

> Comrade Yurko! The Revolutionary Committee of Right Bank Ukraine stands on the platform of an Independent Socialist Soviet Ukrainian Republic with its own national red army, its own finances, etc. An alliance with Soviet Russia is possible only in combating the enemies of both republics. *We are building an army on the spot.* The Russians will have to accept the existence of a Ukrainian Red Army as a fact, and they will change their hitherto prevailing policy toward Ukraine. However, in order to do this, some sort of agreement must be reached with you. Think it over, Comrade Yurko, and give me your answer.
>
> Yours,
> Savytsky   January 10, 1920[26]

In reply Tyutyunnyk proposed that Savytsky contact the general staff of the army of the Ukrainian People's Republic. Savytsky, of course, could not do this. He was prepared to negotiate with Tyutyunnyk, Ataman Hryhoryiv's former chief of staff, but not with Tyuyunnyk's present superiors, the army general staff of the Ukrainian People's Republic. Tyutyunnyk, who knew Savytsky personally, considered him "a great patriot who believed that the success of Ukrainian liberation depended on the outcome of the world revolution." Tyutyunnyk's account continues:

> Units of the Russian 44th Division entered Uman' January 12, 1920. "Misunderstandings" between the Russians and the Borotbisty began to arise immediately. The red Russians completely ignored the red Borotbisty and gradually prepared to liquidate the "irregular bands," as they called Volokh's red

troops. As early as January 14, the head of the Revolutionary Committee of Right Bank Ukraine, Nemolovsky, complained of the ungrateful Russians in a letter to the editorial office of *Visti Revkomu Umanshchyny* [News of the Revolutionary Committee of the Uman' Area] (Number 3), which read as follows: "Comrade editor! Number 1 of your Bulletin contains an article 'On the Eve of the Entry of Red Units into Uman'.' It is written in such a way as to suggest that the city of Uman' was occupied by *irregular troops*, but regular troops (the Red Army) moved in from Khristinovka.

"I request that the next issue of the News correct this and announce that Uman' is occupied by *regular Ukrainian troops*, not by partisans. The official Ukrainian Communist Party (Borotbisty) is in charge of these troops.

"I. Nemolovsky, in charge of the political section of Ukrainian Red Troops."

. . . this letter was printed, . . . although the District Uman' Revolutionary Committee organized by the Russians had no intention of being subordinated to the Revolutionary Committee of Right Bank Ukraine. It was a moment of crisis between those elements which were on the point of reneging and those which wanted to remain orthodox Borotbisty with a national coloring. . . .
"Misunderstandings" occurred. . . in all areas of Ukraine. Although in the center the Borotbisty were allegedly an official party, in the periphery the Russian elements often paid no attention to the "yellow and blue Communists," as they called the Borotbisty. The local population began to place its hopes in the Borotbisty, in opposition to the Russians. This, in turn, created difficulties for the local representatives of the "Soviet [Bolshevik] Power." Almost simultaneously with the "misunderstandings" in Uman', the Kanev Revolutionary Committee issued the following order:
"In view of the dissemination of provocative rumors in the city and district of Kanev, ... we admonish the population of the city and the district that there are no misunderstandings between the [two] revolutionary parties the Ukrainian Communist Party (Borotbisty) and the Communist Party of Ukraine (Bolshevik). These parties. . . are organizing a government of Soviets of Peasants' and Workers' Deputies in Ukraine in complete agreement. Anyone spreading provocative rumors will be remanded before the Military Revolutionary Tribunal.

"Head of the Kanev District Military Revolutionary Committee, Fedorenko.
"Chief of the Information and Agitation Section, Kryzhanivsky.
January 20, 1920, Kanev."

The Russians. . . spread rumors among the *Haydamaky* that . . . [in Lyubar] Volokh took all the gold for himself and the [Borot'bist] Revolutionary Committee, and only silver and copper were left for the *Haydamaky*. [The Bolsheviks] were definitely gaining control of the government; Volokh and the Borotbisty resisted, but to no avail.
In the meantime the *Haydamaky* saw that an Independent Socialist Soviet Ukrainian Republic did not exist. Singly and in groups the "Ukrainian red troops" started to join our army [i.e., of the Ukrainian People's Republic]. The

entire "red" cavalry, under Colonel [?] Legin, deserted [Volokh] and joined the Zaporozhian Division. . . . The *Haydamaky* became very bitter; they planned to attack Volokh and the Revolutionary Committee of Right Bank Ukraine and then, having repented, come over to our army.
Seeing the hopelessness of creating a Ukrainian Army, . . . the Borotbisty and Volokh decided to dissolve their "troops" and abandon their plans for the creation of a Socialist Ukrainian Republic.
Remnants of the *Haydamaky* were forcibly incorporated into the 44th and 60th Russian Divisions. The Revolutionary Committee of Right Bank Ukraine quietly died. . . . The entire Volokh incident had an adverse effect on the future of the Borotbisty. Some of the party leaders, such as Shumsky, Poloz, Ellansky, and others, became renegades, . . . while others were forced to go underground. The party of left appeasers died.[27]

A few words should be said about the subsequent fate of Volokh. As a member of the UCP(b), he too joined the CP(b)U. However, the Bolsheviks did not use him in his old profession of military leader, but attached him to the propaganda train of Petrovsky, the Chairman of the Ukrainian Executive Committee. He was executed in the early 1930's during the collectivization drive.

3. The Trotsky Order

The Borot'bist struggle for an independent Ukrainian army, despite its failure, did leave an imprint on Moscow. A secret order, issued by Trotsky, concerning Moscow's military policy in Ukraine contains the following relevant points:

> The task of military organization in Ukraine. . . consists in creating red Ukrainian units out of Ukrainian workers and Ukrainian peasants, who do not exploit hired labor, with a Ukrainian command and Ukrainian language. [A prerequisite] is the disarming of the kulak and completely bandit elements of the village and city. . . irrespective of whether or not they go under the name of Petlyurists, Makhnoists or any other name. . . .
> When the ground has been cleared of banditism, it will be possible immediately to lay the foundation for a Ukrainian workers' and peasants' red army, at the outset only a few model regiments strong. . . .
> All attempts by any political group in Ukraine to find support among insurgent units or to make the latter the basis of a separate army must be branded as military sabotage and treason to the Socialist Ukrainian Republic.[28]

The last paragraph was obviously directed against the Borot'bist and Makhnoist efforts to organize just such an army. Tyutyunnyk considers Trotsky's order "an attempt to form Janissary regiments in Ukraine," although he assumes that the Borotbisty might have known of Trotsky's plans and hoped, perhaps, to control any such regiments. However, no Janissary regiments were created. The only tangible outgrowth of Trotsky's order was the establishment of a Ukrainian military academy for officers in Kharkiv, but it was regarded with suspicion and dissolved in the early 1930's. Had Ukraine succeeded in creating an army of its own, the reign of terror in the 1930's, when millions of people died of starvation, would have been impossible.

D.   The Growth and Dissolution of the UCP(B)

1.   The Spread of Borot'bism Among the Masses

Some information on Borotbist activity in the post-Denikin period can be obtained from the work of Ravich-Cherkassky:

> In the last days of December [1919] the [Borotbist] organs *Proletarskaya pravda* [Proletarian Pravda, in Russian] in Kharkiv, *Chervonyt styah* [Red Standard] in Kyiv and *Ukrains'kyi proletar* [Ukrainian Proletarian] in Katerynoslav began to appear. The first was edited by Kalyuzhnyi, the second by Hukovych and the third by Lisovyk. Their central organ was *Borotba*, published in Kyiv. On January 20, they called a conference of Left Bank Ukraine in Poltava, which was attended by representatives from the provinces of Poltava, Kharkiv, Chernihiv, Katerynoslav, Kherson, and Taurida.
> The Borotbisty, competing with the Bolsheviks, now sought the support of the urban proletariat, but they met with complete indifference, which they explained as due to the assimilation [i.e., Russification] of the proletariat, Ukrainian by nationality. . . . the Borotbisty argued with the Bolsheviks in heated discussion at [public] meetings and in the press against the policy of the CP(b)U. . . . The representatives of the UCP(b) in Moscow—the Foreign Bureau [*Zarubezhnoye Byuro*]—regarded their chief task as "the representation of [their] party at the center of the world communist revolution and the placing of the fundamental problems and next tasks in the development of the revolution in Ukraine on the agenda of the Executive Committee of the Comintern." Hrynko, a member of the Foreign Bureau, emphasized in the press an extremely important fact, which "the leaders of the proletarian revolution, and in particular Comrade Lenin," had treated with respect to the issues raised by the Borotbisty. Lenin severely condemned the "Russian jingoistic" [*rusapetskiye*] work methods of the Communists in Ukraine.[29]

As far as the present author recollects, *Proletarskaya Pravda* was not a Borotbist but a Bolshevik newspaper. This surmise is borne out by the fact that the paper continued to appear through the 1930's. It is simply not conceivable that the Bolsheviks would take over a Borotbist title. When the Bolsheviks created a newspaper for mass consumption in Kharkiv in the 1920's, they did not call it *Robitnycha hazeta* [Workers' Gazette], which had been the name of the USDRP organ, but *Robitnycha hazeta-proletar* [Workers' Gazette-Proletarian], Besides the newspapers mentioned by Ravich-Cherkassky, the Borotbisty published *Borotbyst* in Poltava (edited by Hordiy Kotsyuba and Mykola Khrystovyi and several issues of the district paper *Kobelyatsky Borotbyst* [Kobeliaky Borotbist]. *Krasnoye znamya* [Red Banner] was the only Borotbist newspaper published in Russian.

There is good evidence that the Borotbist point of view enjoyed some support within the CP(b)U itself. In February 1920 a group in opposition to the policy of the CP(b)U published a pamphlet, entitled *Draft Resolution on Party Policy*, in which it pointed to the divergence between party policy and the demands of the Revolution. It criticized the leaders of the CP(b)U for their failure to understand that the social revolution in Ukraine could be brought to a successful end only with the help of the Ukrainian proletariat. "After the national oppression of the Ukrainian people under the Romanovs and Habsburgs," the pamphlet declared, "all attempts to control the destinies of the country from without will inevitably intensify the growth of nationalism." The pamphlet also demanded that the CP(b)U become an independent member of the Communist International and cease being a branch of the Russian Communist Party (Bolshevik).[30]

Perhaps the most significant symptom of the spread of *Borotbism* was the attitude of the Ukrainian intelligentsia. Having lost all hope of seeing Ukrainian independence achieved through the instrument of the Ukrainian People's Republic, many Ukrainian intellectuals cast their lot with the Borotbisty. This new influence also affected students and other young people. Following the Bolshevik example, the Borotbisty in early 1920 formed their own youth organization, the Communist Youth Union (Komunistychna Yunats'ka Spilka). With thousands of members across the country, the Union was stronger numerically than the Borot'bist urban organizations.

Despite the growth of *Borotbism* and its popularity among the masses, the failure to create a Borotbist-controlled Red Army boded ill for the whole movement. The desertion of the old Borotbist partisan leader Ohiy, who broke away from the detachment which he led together with Kostyantyn Matyash and Lisovyk, was a sign of the coming defeat.w

2. The Bolshevik Ring Around the Borotbisty

The dark outlook for the future undermined the faith of individual Borot'bist leaders. Two of them, Shumsky and Blakytny began to favor amalgamation with the CP(b)U.

> The right-nationalist wing was against unification [with the CP(b)U, . . . [while] the revolutionary elements inclined toward merger. The rightist elements which had played a leading part within the UCP[(b)] remained stubborn. Negotiations with the Executive Committee of the Comintern over amalgamation were conducted by the right Borotbist Poloz.[31]

Two resolutions by the Executive Committee of the Communist International contributed to the further decline in morale among the Borotbisty. The first resolution, published in Ukraine by the Central Committee of the CP(b)U January 30, 1920 read as follows:

> A session of the Executive Committee of the Communist International, devoted to the Ukrainian question, was held in Petrograd, December 22, 1919. The meeting was attended by representatives of the Central Committees of the CPU (Bolshevik) and the Ukrainian Communist Party (Borotbisty). After hearing and discussing reports by the representatives of these parties, the Executive Committee passed the following resolution:
> 1) Ukraine was represented at the First Congress of the Communist International solely by the CPU (Bolshevik), which the Congress recognized as the authorized representative of the Ukrainian proletariat.
> 2) It became clear from the report of the representatives of the UCP (Borotbisty) that this party, which seeks admission to the Third International, adheres in its activity to the principles of the Third International and accepts completely the program of the RCP (Bolshevik), but because of its recent formation it does not yet have sufficiently strong support among the urban and

---

w   See Appendix 1, pp. 176–177.

village proletariat of Ukraine and has not yet succeeded in making itself sufficiently known or in correctly applying the principles of the Third International.

3) Before replying to the petition of the UCP (Borotbisty) asking for admission to the Communist International, the Executive Committee believes that it has the duty of raising the question of the unification of all communist forces in Ukraine in one party, starting from the principle that in every country there should be a single communist party and bearing in mind that the cause of the communist revolution in Ukraine demands complete unity in the ranks of those who protect the interests of the Ukrainian working class and toiling peasantry.

4) While considering the conference of December 22 as the first step toward clarification of the differences of opinion existing between the CPU (Bolshevik) and the UCP (Borot'bisty), the Executive Committee proposes that the Party of the Borotbisty submit, in addition to its memorandum, the fullest possible reply (in written form) to the following questions:
a) its attitude toward the land problem,
b) its attitude toward the national problem (in particular, toward national culture and the [Ukrainian Teachers'] Union),
c) its attitude toward the establishment of a common Red Army (in particular, toward the problem of the partisan movement),
d) its attitude toward the creation of a special economic- center,
e) its attitude toward Soviet Russia.

5) In order to eliminate the disagreements between both parties and to help them toward amalgamation, the Executive Committee of the Communist International has formed a temporary Ukrainian Commission, under the Communist International, which consists of representatives of both parties (two delegates each), under the chairmanship of the chairman of the Communist International. The commission will deal with controversial issues on request of either of the parties or on decree of the Executive Committee of the Communist International.

Chairman of the Executive Committee
of the Communist International,
Petrograd G. ZINOVIEV.
January 5, 1920[32]

It was now clear that all Borot'bist efforts to gain admission to the Communist International would fail.

Final rejection came in the second resolution, published in Ukraine on February 29:

> . . . the Executive Committee of the Communist International has unanimously decided:
> 1) The Executive Committee of the Communist International regrets finding that the party of Borotbisty, which calls itself a communist party, in reality

departs from the principles of communism in several extremely important questions.

2) Agitation in the Borotbist party's organs is conducted against the Red Army, which helped to liberate Ukraine from the Denikin yoke. Such agitation can only be labeled counter-revolutionary, since experience has fully shown that defense against imperialism is impossible without a united, regular, battle-tested Red Army.

3) In demanding the immediate formation of a separate national army, the Borotbisty are forced to seek support among the demoralized nationalist elements of the former Petlyurist forces and among kulak elements in the villages and the urban petty bourgeois, democratic intelligentsia. In this way they actually abandon the merciless struggle against the chauvinist elements of the petty bourgeois groups, a struggle which is binding on every truly internationalist party.

4) Because of this purely petty bourgeois deviation, the Borotbisty began to conduct further open agitation against Communists of other nationalities, in particular Russian Communists, who work in Ukraine. This agitation has nothing in common with the principles of the Communist International and is reminiscent of the darker aspects of activities by the parties of the Second International.

5) The Executive Committee of the Communist International considers that the closest brotherly alliance should exist among those republics in which soviet rule prevails. The Executive Committee of the Communist International is cognizant of the fact that the R.S.F.S.R. at the Seventh All-Russian Congress of Soviets in the resolutions of the All-Russian Central Executive Committee and in other official decisions of the Soviet Republic recognized unconditionally the independence of Soviet Ukraine and expressed its readiness to join in the closest brotherly association with the Ukrainian Soviet Republic. The Central Committee of the Communist International is convinced that Ukraine can withstand the pressure of the imperialists and their hirelings only by the closest economic and military alliance with Soviet Russia.

6) In view of all this, the Executive Committee of the Communist International is obliged *to refuse admission of the party of Borotbisty into the Communist International.*

7) The Executive Committee of the Communist International considers that no one will prevent the true communist elements among the Borotbisty from joining the ranks of the CPU (Bolshevik), the party which fully recognizes the independence of the Soviet Ukraine, which has been active in Ukraine for almost twenty years and which has united the most stable elements of the Ukrainian proletariat, adding a glorious page to the history of the liberation battle of the world proletariat, through its heroic struggle against the imperialist plunderers.

8) The Executive Committee of the Communist International cannot but regard the desire to create a second, parallel party in Ukraine as an attempt to split the ranks of the workers. The Communist International demands that in every country there exist only one communist party. All honest followers of communism ought to join the ranks of the solid Ukrainian party — the CP(b)U. We call upon all workers of Ukraine to do this.

Chairman of the Executive Committee of the Communist International, G. Zinovyev[33]

Since the Borotbisty held the Communist International in high esteem in their press, the second resolution came as a severe blow. It amounted to a call for dissolution.

The second resolution, drafted in all probability by Zinovyev himself, contained several inaccuracies and falsifications. First, it was not true that the Borotbisty were agitating against the Red Army; they wanted to collaborate with it. But to prevent the Russification of Ukrainian soldiers in a single Russian Red Army they also wanted a separate Ukrainian army. The fact that the Communist International in this issue sided with the Russian Bolsheviks proves that it was supporting the centralist idea of a single Russian army, in this respect differing not one iota from the tsarist army. Second, it was equally false to say that the Borotbisty "agitated against Communists of other nationalities, in particular Russian Communists." In their own ranks the Borotbisty had Communists of Russian, Jewish and other national origins. The Russian Communists were attacked not on the ground that they were Russian, but that they were imperialist. Even sharper were the Borotbist attacks on such Ukrainian Bolsheviks as Pyatakov, Zatonsky and Manuilsky. Third, the Borotbisty, just as much as the Communist International, wanted a "close brotherly alliance" with Soviet Russia, but they meant genuine alliance, not subordination. Finally, the Communist International's resolution was misleading in its claim that Soviet Russia "recognized the independence of the Soviet Ukraine." Had this really been the case, the Borotbisty would have had no differences of opinion with the International.

3. Dissolution of the UCP(B)

Just how great an authority the Communist International was for the Borotbisty can be judged from the following exchange of communications which spelled out the formality of dissolution and amalgamation:

Comrade Zinoviev received the following telegram March 16, 1920:

"In the name of the entire party, the All-Ukrainian conference of Borotbist Communists sends warm greetings to the Chairman of the Communist International, Comrade Zinoviev. The conference has voted unanimously to elect Comrade Zinoviev as honorary chairman. The presidium. Blatytny [sic]."

In reply Comrade Zinoviev sent the following telegram: *Kharkiv. To the All-Ukrainian Conference of Communists-Borotbisty.* I heartily thank you for your telegram and, on behalf of the Executive Committee of the Comintern, take this opportunity of saying to you:

Communists of all countries who are following the fate of the Ukrainian revolution would be happy to learn that in Ukraine from today there exists only one communist party, which is leading the workers and toiling peasants of Ukraine to complete victory in close alliance with the Russian Socialist Soviet Federated Republic [sic].

The Executive Committee on its own initiative proposes, comrades, that you enter the ranks of the Communist Party of Ukraine (Bolshevik), the party which for a quarter of a century has paved the way for the present victories.

The Communist International is convinced that the unity of all activities of Communists in Ukraine is not only imperative but possible.

Zinoviev.

From the editors: The editors note with satisfaction that the Ukrainian "Borotbisty" Communists have actually joined the ranks of the Communist Party of Ukraine (Bolshevik). Therefore we now have a single communist party in Ukraine. To this party we send our greetings.[34]

The UCP(b) was dissolved by majority vote at its Second Congress in March 1920. A sizable opposition to dissolution, led by Poloz, Panas Lyubchenko and Mykhaylo Panchenko, remained true to the old populist ideals, not only on national but on ideological grounds. As for Shumsky and Blakytny, the most ardent advocates of amalgamation with the CP(b)U, it was currently rumored among the Borotbisty that they had negotiated with the Bolsheviks prior to the Second Congress unknown to the Central Committee. In the end, however, Levko Kovaliv and Mykhaylo Panchenko were the only members of the Borotbist Central Committee who refused to join the Bolsheviks; they remained without party affiliation.

No more than the Bolsheviks did the Borotbisty wish a repetition of the Muravyov occupation of 1918 or the events of 1919. Patriotism and a desire to avoid a further downfall of Soviet government in Ukraine motivated the Borotbist decision. They could no longer take up arms openly against the Bolsheviks, nor could they go underground, since this would place them in the same camp with the Ukrainian People's Republic, with which they would not compromise. The one practical means remaining, in their view, was to resist the CP(b)U within the existing Soviet framework, through a reliance on the support they enjoyed among the Ukrainian people.

The Borotbisty held fast to their communist position, dictated by national as well as by social factors, that a sovereign Ukrainian state was possible only within the communist camp. As a young communist party, the Borotbisty could not criticize the Bolshevik social program; for that matter, they were not concerned with it. They did not subscribe to the ideal of a separate Ukrainian communist ideology; they wanted only to secure for Ukraine equal rights with other nations within the framework of international communism. This could be achieved, according to the Borotbisty, only if the Ukrainian, not the Russian, Communists were masters of Ukraine.

In concentrating on their fight for national equality, the Borotbisty were careful to conform to the Bolshevik social program."[35] They thought that by this tactic it would be made impossible for the Bolsheviks to accuse them of "bourgeois reactionism." Since the Bolsheviks had in principle recognized Ukraine's right to independence, the Borotbisty attempted to take them at their word. The Bolsheviks, on the other hand, well understood and neutralized the Borotbist strategem by playing down the national question in their debates with the Borotbisty; by emphasizing social problems they brought into question the communist orthodoxy of the Borotbisty. That was why Lenin, in his "Remarks on the Draft Resolution of the Executive Committee of the Comintern," wrote on February 22, 1920: "I emphatically insist that the Borotbisty be accused not of nationalism, but of counterrevolutionary and petty bourgeois mentality..."[36]

But Lenin's efforts to condemn the Borotbisty on these grounds failed; in Ukraine their dissolution and merger with the CP(b)U were interpreted as the consequence of their nationalism not their bourgeois outlook. By opposing the Bolshevik solution to the national problem, *Borotbism* served as the earliest experiment in this field within the Soviet state system. The experiment ended in failure and tragedy for its exponents, but it revealed the inability of Bolshevism to solve the national problem.

E. Divers Views on the Dissolution of the Borotbisty

Ravich-Cherkassky, although defending the CP(b)U which he had joined in 1919, realized that Bolshevik centralist policy in Ukraine was in need of correction. The following is his account of the dissolution of the UCP(b):

> Finally, in the beginning of March, the Executive Committee of the Comintern, after lengthy consideration, rejected the Borotbist petition for admission to the Third International. This decision had a sobering effect on the Borotbisty. They had to place on their agenda the question of the discontinuance of a communist party which was [declared to be] outside the Communist International. The quasi-Petlyurist elements in the UCP(b) in the provinces of Poltava, Kateynoslav, Volyn', and other areas could not reconcile themselves to this. However, for the UCP(b) retreat into the past was cut off with no road ahead. The UCP(b) had but one way out—by shaking off its nationalist elements and by further purifying its Marxist, revolutionary consciousness, to enter the ranks of the CP(b)u with unfurled banners.[37]
> The simultaneous existence of two [communist] parties, the CP(b)U and the UCP(b), in Ukraine could not but affect the tactics of both. If under the influence of the proletarian revolution in Ukraine and the fierce criticism of the CP(b)U the Borotbisty more and more pulled themselves together and took the road of Marxism, irreconcilable revolutionism, communism, and internationalism, the CP(b)U itself was not uninfluenced by the UCP(b). It was largely due to the influence of the UCP(b) that the 'Bolsheviks underwent an evolution from a "Russian] C[ommunist] P[arty] in Ukraine" (the proposal of Kviring's followers at the Taganrog Conference) to a genuine Communist Party of Ukraine.[38] The "federalist" tendency within the CP(b)U was the wedge which the Borotbisty drove into the CP(b)U. Not in vain did Hrynko, in conversation affirming the important role of the Borotbisty in the revolutionary communist movement in Ukraine, refer to the "note" of the federalists "which clearly formulates the very necessity of establishing, not in words but in deed, a Ukr.S.S.R. with a complete apparatus of proletarian power in all branches of life."
> This was the situation in which both parties, the CP(b)U and the UCP(b), followed the inevitable historical process out of dire necessity, moving closer together while engaging in sharp debate, the one straightening out its communist line, the other adapting itself to the peculiarities and specific conditions of socio-economic and national-cultural life in Ukraine.[39]

Ravich-Cherkassky failed to mention only one thing, namely, that a separate CP(b)U in fact did not exist. It was a Ukrainian branch of the Russian Communist Party (Bolshevik), controlled not by the Communist International but by the Central Committee of the RCP(b) which later tried and deported Ravich-Cherkassky, which purged and destroyed all the former Borotbisty and which proclaimed that the CP(b)U was as inseparable from the RCP(b) as was Ukraine from Russia. A more critical commentary on the Borot'bist dissolution came from the pen of Hrushevsky in the fall of 1920:

> Faced with the choice of either merging completely with the Russian Communists or becoming... an opposition party,... the Borotbisty decided... to join the RCP[sic], Such a statement was issued by their representatives (Shumsky and Elansky) in Kharkiv and was later confirmed by a majority vote at the party conference at the end of March of this year. However, this resolution provoked sharp opposition within the party.
>
> This opposition, like that of the Independent SD's who accepted the Soviet platform and even the name "communist" ("Ukrainian Communist Party") but who did not consider it necessary to merge with the Bolshevik Party, disagreed with Bolshevik centralist policy. In its view, the tendency of the Bolsheviks to uphold at all costs the hegemony of Russian Communists in Ukraine and to govern Ukraine without Ukrainians, depriving it of all independence and making it completely dependent on Moscow, is incorrect and harmful.[40]

A sharp condemnation of the Borot'bist decision was uttered by the leader of the SR center Nykyfor Hryhoryiv, who shared with the Borotbisty a common populist heritage. In an open letter to Khrystyuk commenting on his willingness to return to the Soviet Ukraine, Hryhoryiv criticized the policy pursued by Khrystyuk and Hrushevsky for the following reasons:

1. Negotiations with the Moscow Bolsheviks, if not supported by our organized force, will lead to nothing;
2. The reckless and uncritical search for favors will take us down the road of the "Borotbisty," that is, we will be told: "if you agree with us then join us; if you do not want to join us, then you disagree with us; that means that you are our enemies, and enemies we shall fight";

3. To go over to collaboration with the Moscow Bolsheviks without any safeguards for the interests of the Ukrainian working masses means sheer appeasement of the victors, a new Moscophilism and abandonment of party ideals.... The revolutionary position of the "Borotbisty" and their emphasis on social [principles] I regarded and still regard as correct, but their merger with the CP(b)U and their renunciation of the party program I consider a mistake. Only the exertion of considerable organized pressure could correct this mistake. I shall continue to defend this view, but I do not approve of separate defections, singly or in groups (like the Borotbisty) and I shall fight them, since I regard them as harmful not only to our party but to the development of socialism in general.... While sharing the [Borotbist] position ideologically, I did not approve of their tactics, which were false and not in the public interest. Having torn themselves away from the masses, they had to merge with the CP(b)U.[41]

The Borotbisty viewed the situation differently. They did attempt to build a stronger organization, starting from the premise that their own army was a prime consideration. Although they failed, their decision to merge with the CP(b)U, in the hope of influencing it from within, gained for them a decade of grace to continue to resist centralist Russian policies.

Noteworthy in this connection is Lenin's pronouncement on the Borotbisty expressed at the Ninth Congress of the Russian Communist Party (Bolshevik), held March 29–April 4, 1920:

> Comrade Bubnov said... that the Central Committee was guilty of strengthening the Borotbisty. This is a most complex and tremendous question, and I think in this most important problem, where intricate maneuvering was needed, we came out the victors. In the Central Committee when we [i.e., Lenin] spoke of maximum concessions to the Borotbisty, we were laughed at and told that we were not straight in our dealings with them. But one can attack one's adversary directly [only] when there is a straight line with him. Once the enemy decides to zigzag, we must pursue and catch him at every turn. We promised the Borotbisty a maximum of concessions, but on condition that they pursue a communist policy. In this way we proved that we are not guilty of the slightest intolerance. That our concessions were right was proved by the fact that all the better elements of the Borotbisty have now

joined our Party. We have reregistered that party; instead of a Borotbist uprising which would have been inevitable, we have brought into our Party, under our control and with our recognition, due to the correct policy of the Central Committee superbly executed by Comrade Rakovsky, all the best of the Borotbisty, while the rest have vanished from the political scene. This victory is worth several good battles. To say, therefore, that the Central Committee was guilty of strengthening the Borotbisty is not to understand the political line in the national problem.[42]

A reply by Bubnov, who was at that time working in Ukraine, came in the following form:

I ask that the following factual statement be read and appended to the proceedings:

Concerning my critical remarks on the policy of the Central Committee toward the Borotbisty, Comrade Lenin indicated that my remarks displayed a lack of understanding of the national policy in Ukraine. Comrade Lenin based his argument on facts dating from December 1919 to March 1920. In view of this, I should like to stress the fact that in my criticism I had in mind a different period, that from March to August 1919 [the pre-Denikin period of Soviet rule in Ukraine]. I pointed out that at that time there was within the Communist Party (Bolshevik) of Ukraine a strong current in favor of merger with the Borotbisty, although the entire party expressed itself at the Third Congress (March 1919) against admission of the Borotbisty to Soviet institutions in Ukraine. The Central Committee [of the RCP(b)] did not support the trend which favored merger, although at that time this was the only correct [solution], and, notwithstanding the decision of the authoritative representation of the Ukrainian Communist organizations, proposed that the Central Committee of the CPU [(Bolshevik)] should bring Borotbisty into the Ukrainian Council of People's Commissars, which was, of course, carried out. I am deeply convinced that by doing this the Central Committee of the RCP[(b)] strengthened the Borotbisty and to a certain degree aided the marked growth of Borotbist influence among the masses of the urban proletariat after Denikin's expulsion. I repeat that in my speech I did not refer to the Central Committee's policy toward the Borotbisty during the last period, while Comrade Lenin spoke only of this period. Therefore his conclusions are based on an obvious misunderstanding, clear to all."[43]

The difference between Lenin and the CP(b)U lay in the fact the CP(b)U, if not subjected to pressure by Moscow, would have been willing to accept the Borotbisty in the pre-Denikin period rather than vie with them for influence among the masses, while the Central Committee of the Russian Communist Party (Bolshevik), even after the Denikin period, refused them entry in the CP(b)U, suggesting that they first be tested in the Soviet administrative system. But this, Hubnov believed, had merely helped to enhance Borotbist prestige among the masses.

It should also be pointed out that Bubnov, in contrast with Ravich-Cherkassky, spoke of the growth of Borotbist influence among the urban proletariat *after* Denikin's downfall. Indeed, this growth caused the greatest alarm among the Bolsheviks, while they could still tolerate Borotbist publications in Ukrainian, the appearance of the Borotbist daily *Krasnoye znamya* in Russian infuriated them, since this action indicated that the Russified proletariat of the Ukrainian cities might be prepared to follow the Borotbisty rather than the Bolsheviks, thereby seriously endangering their hegemony.

The emigre Ukrainian left Socialists were correct when they claimed that

> the entry of the Borotbisty into the CP(b)U was not a consequence of the inner convictions of the Borotbisty. . . .After having demanded an independent Ukrainian republic for so long, . . . they could hardly have changed their convictions in a few weeks. External circumstances proved stronger; the Borotbisty had to comply with Moscow's demands, if they did not want to be deprived of the opportunity of carrying on their work among the Ukrainian masses. The Ukrainian Communist Party (the former Independent Social Democrats) remained true to its platform, persisting in the creation of a party independent of Russian Communists which would be a section of the Third International and not a branch of the Russian Communist Party.[44]

Yet another reason for the dissolution of the UCP(b) is offered by the Borotbist Todos Taran, who joined the CP(b)U. Polish intervention in Ukraine in the spring of 1920, he considered, accounted for the fact that Blakytny, Hrynko and Shumsky "agreed unconditionally to the liquidation of their party and its merger with the CP(b)U."[45]

After it had absorbed the UCP(b), the CP(b)U did not direct its energy toward the consummation of a sovereign Soviet Ukraine, a goal which had been proclaimed in the Communist International's reply to the Borotbisty. The best evidence in support of this view was the continued existence of another Soviet-oriented Ukrainian party, the *Ukapisty*. Demanding a sovereign Soviet Ukraine, the *Ukapisty* were not forced to join the CP(b)U until 1925. The struggle for a sovereign Ukrainian S.S.R. was decided in the negative not by the internal development of Ukrainian political life but by the external pressure of administrative organization.

9 The Borotbisty in the CP(b)U

A. The CP(b)U and the UCP(b) Compared

To weigh properly the political strength of the Borotbisty at the time of their merger with the CP(b)U in April 1920, it will be useful to analyze the numerical strength of the respective parties. No exact membership figures are available for either party at the time of amalgamation, but it is possible to arrive at an approximation.

1 Composition of the CP(b)U

Mykola Skrypnyk, a representative of the CP(b)U, declared at the First Congress of the Communist International in March 1919 that the CP(b)U numbered approximately 30,000 members.[1] However, the influence of the CP(b)U over the masses markedly decreased during the second period of Soviet rule in Ukraine (February-August 1919), nor was the party very active in the underground during the Denikin period (August-December 1919). It can therefore be assumed that the number of members in the CP(b)U in the spring of 1920 was somewhat below the 30,000 figure, perhaps, between 20,000 and 25,000.

The leadership of the CP(b)U consisted of "old Bolsheviks,' for the most part factory workers, intellectuals and white collar workers. Among the factory workers were G.I. Petrovsky (who had been a Bolshevik member of the Fourth State Duma), Vlas Chubar and Dmytro Lebid' — all metallurgical workers from Katerynoslav — and Yakiv N. Drobnis, a weaver and war refugee from Poland. Intellectuals in the party included Khristian Rakovsky, a doctor; Volodymyr Zatonsky, docent at the Kyiv Polytechnic Institute; Aleksandr Shlikhter, an economist; Dmytro Manuilsky, a journalist who had spent much time in France; and Skrypnyk, an economist. Among the white collar worker members of the party were Stanislav Kossior and Eduard Kviring.

The thirteen-man Central Committee of the CP(b)U, created by the directive of the Central Committee of the Russian Communist Party (Bolshevik) of April 7, 1920, included eleven Bolsheviks: Artyom (pseudonym of Fyodor A. Sergeyev, a polytechnic student), Pyotr A. Zalutski (a factory worker), Sergei K. Minin (a journalist and writer, political officer of the Red Army)—all sent from Russia; Petrovsky, Rakovsky, Chubar, Manuilsky, Kossior, and Zatonsky—all "old Bolsheviks"; Yakov Yakovlev (pseudonym of Epshtein, a student from Katerynoslav); and Feliks Kon, a journalist and literary critic and a former Menshevik.[2]

The "old Bolsheviks" represented a small minority of the party, a relatively small number of persons placed in key positions in the larger cities. In many provincial capitals there were no more than two or three of them, the rest of the party consisting of workers, students and members of the petty bourgeoisie. In Poltava, for instance, where a Bolshevik group had existed before the Revolution, the "old Bolshevik" Drobnis was chairman of the party's Provincial Revolutionary Committee.[3] His deputy was Oleksiiv, a Poltava printer. The intellectuals Smetanych, chairman of the Provincial Revolutionary Tribunal, Orlovsky, chief of the finance department, and Pylypenko, the son of a local man of wealth, also belonged to the Bolshevik old guard. The secretary of the party's provincial committee was a young Russian, later replaced by Yerman, an energetic Byelorussian student. Glebov, a young journalist sent from Russia, edited the provincial party newspaper. The provincial food commissar was a worker sent from Russia, possibly an "old Bolshevik." If there were other "old Bolsheviks," they held no prominent positions; the rest of the party was made up of workers, petty bourgeoisie and intellectuals. Similar conditions prevailed in other provincial capitals, except in industrial areas where the majority of the party were factory workers.

At the district level, the Bolshevik organization in the non-industrial town of Kobeliaky, Poltava Province, can serve as an example of party composition. Two native "old Bolsheviks" who had gone to work in large cities before the Revolution headed the party organization. There were several workers from the Donets Basin and Kkaterynoslav, a few local peasants who had become Bolsheviks while in the Red Army, and several intellectuals and white collar workers. The great majority of the party's members, however, were students of bourgeois extraction who set the tone of the whole party organization. Petty bourgeois not only in social origin but in their way of life and thinking, they were indifferent, sometimes even hostile, to the Ukrainian liberation movement. They spoke only Russian. In Kobeliaky District the party had no organizational network throughout the volosts. In three or four of the fifteen volosts there were small Bolshevik groups of three to five persons; in some communities there were Bolshevik sympathizers. All told, the district organization, including members and candidates, had not more than fifty members. In addition there were several dozen members of the Bolshevik youth organization, chiefly in the town of Kobeliaky.

There is no doubt that the provincial organizations of the CP(b)U had many sincere and ardent revolutionaries, yet the milieu in which they worked and which often dominated them was that of the careerist and the philistine bourgeoisie (*meshchanstvo*). Members of the bourgeoisie joined the party for their own advantage. They served those who wielded political power within the party; they were the secretaries, the deputies, the assistants. In the early 1920's these philistines became a real threat to the Communist Party. They were openly criticized but continued to prosper. They have been brilliantly satirized by the Ukrainian writer Mykola Khvylovy in his short stories *Ivan Ivanovych* and *Revizor* [The Inspector General].

In Ukraine, where the Soviet regime was sustained by military occupation, Communist philistinism was even more wide-spread than in Russia. Surrounded by a sea of careerists, fanatical Bolsheviks often succumbed to material temptation.[4] In this respect the Borotbisty were diametrically opposed to the Bolsheviks. As members of an opposition party, they had not developed the philistine spirit.

2. Composition of the UCP(b)

The most salient characteristic of the Borotbist Central Committee was its cult of revolutionary romanticism, the heritage of the populist tradition. Literature and art played the predominant role in the propagation of this cult. Almost every member of the Borotbist Central Committee and many of the party's rank and file members had a poem, short story or novel to their credit. On the other hand, the party had no room for scientists. Unlike the Marxist parties, whose leaders were primarily economists or sociologists, the UCP(b) had not a single economist who could speak for the party. Borotbisty like Slipansky and Bilash became prominent as economists only after they entered the CP(b)U. Even a man like Poloz, with the temperament of a scientist and considerable talent, was unable to develop into an economist or sociologist.

Unofficial estimates put total membership of the UCP(b) in 1920 at 15,000. Skrypnyk, speaking at the Twelfth Congress of the Russian Communist Party (Bolshevik) in April 1923, stated that 4,000 Borotbisty had joined the CP(b)U.[5] G.I. Petrovsky, in an address before the Sixth All-Ukrainian Conference of the CP(b)U in November 1921, stated that

> On the basis of materials in the possession of the Central Committee, I can say that there were 554 Borotbisty among the responsible [party] workers. However, it was impossible to ascertain how many Borotbisty joined the party.[6]

In the city of Poltava the UCP(b) consisted mainly of student intellectuals and railroad workers. The organization was headed by Musindzon, a railroad worker, Vasyl' Lazorsky, a medical student, Mykola Khrystovy, a student and editor of the local party paper *Borotbyst*, and Hordiy Kotsyuba, a student, co-editor of *Borotbyst* and a writer.

In Kobeliaky District the Borotbist organization comprised approximately twenty-five persons from the town of Kobeliaky plus as many more from the surrounding villages. Like the Bolsheviks, the Borotbisty were well organized only in the provincial and district towns. In the volosts there were only very small party groups. In Kustolovo volost of Kobeliaky District, for example, there existed a party group of ten people. This compared with a Bolshevik group of five in the small neighboring town of Novyi Sendzhary.

Although the author was very well acquainted with the Borotbist organization in Kobeliaky District, it is difficult to present exact figures because membership was in a constant state of flux.

After the Denikin period the district organization existed only about two months inasmuch as the process of dissolution began in March 1920. In spite of attracting new sympathizers, the party failed to enroll many new members in this short period of time. In the town of Kobeliaky, however, as much as twenty per cent of the membership was new. In the entire district there were no more than fifty party members. If the Borotbist organization in Kobeliaky can be regarded as typical of other parts of the country, the approximately one hundred districts in Ukraine would have contained about 5,000 Borotbisty. It is possible that the party was stronger in Right Bank Ukraine, but on the other hand it was undoubtedly weaker in the industrial centers. Even if membership in the Borotbist youth organization is reckoned at several thousand, the total figure would still not reach 15,000.

In Kobeliaky District only about twenty of the fifty Borotbisty joined the CP(b)U. In general, Borotbisty who refused to join either did not wish to join (this was true mostly peasants), were not recommended by the Borotbist committee, or were not acceptable to the Bolshevik committee. Special committees consisting of representatives of both were formed to supervise the admission of Borotbisty to the CP(b)U. As a rule, Borotbisty recommended by their party were willingly accepted. Such members were active politically, mostly intellectuals and familiar with local conditions. But above all Ukraine was not a foreign land to them, as it was to the Russian Bolsheviks. Such people were badly needed by the CP(b)U.

In accordance with the April 7 directive from Moscow, two former Borotbisty were given posts in the Central Committee and two were assigned to each provincial and district committee of the CP(b)U. Blakytny and Shumsky became members of the new thirteen-man Central Committee. Blakytny was made deputy chairman of the Central Committee and was placed in charge of party work in the villages. Shumsky was elected to the party's Politburo and Orgburo at the plenary session of the Central Committee of April 15, 1920.[7] Petrovsky, Rakovsky, Yakovlev, and Kossior were the other members elected to the Politburo; Yakovlev and Kossior were also elected to the Orgburo. Soon afterward, however, Shumsky was sent to Poltava as chairman of the provincial executive committee, and with the conclusion of the Treaty of Riga on March 18, 1921 he became the first Soviet Ukrainian envoy to Poland. Both posts were highly responsible, but because Shumsky was the only Borotbist on the Ukrainian Politburo his removal from that body was hardly accidental.[8] He was replaced by Feliks Kon.

Because the UCP(b) had at most 5,000 members and because not all members joined the CP(b)U, Skrypnyk's figure of 4,000 Borotbisty entering the CP(b)U can be accepted as approximately correct. If Petrovsky's figure of 554 former Borotbisty among responsible party workers is accepted, it can be concluded that with few exceptions the entire Borotbist elite merged with the Bolsheviks.

B. A Letter From a Ukrainian SR Emigre

In addition to the Ukrainian emigre opinions presented in Chapter 8 on the dissolution of the UCP(b), it will be of interest to examine here a letter from a Ukrainian SR emigre, written in reply to a fellow SR who had become a Bolshevik, Their disagreements are indicative of the basic divergences within the Ukrainian liberation movement. The Bolshevik, initiating the correspondence, had charged that the other had "sold himself to the international bourgeoisie." In answer, the emigre' SR wrote as follows:

> You will not venture to speak of me as your antithesis. . . . And history will agree with you. It will record: K., an elementary school teacher, of peasant origin, a Ukrainian SR, later a Ukrainian Communist-Bolshevik; H., an elementary school teacher, of peasant origin, a Ukrainian SR. Both fought for the victory of the toiling people, for their government, for a "soviet system," for Ukraine, for a free world. Why then did they quarrel? Why did one become a "Janissary," the other take refuge among the "liberators"? Because they were the victims of nature and of circumstance. It was nature that endowed them with a different degree of understanding of the truth and conditions of life. One was caught unawares by Bolsheviks, who turned him into a "Janissary," while the other was lucky enough to escape from their clutches and found himself among the "liberators." It could have been the other way around. What would history do with us? And precisely what history do you have in mind? Of the future? If so, allow me to recall some facts of history: Mazepa's uprising and his manifesto about the struggle against Moscow, against its tyranny, against the abolition of an autonomous Ukraine, against the coercion of education and book printing, against coercion by Muscovite garrisons, etc. Some of the Ukrainian forces and the entire *Zaporozhskaya Sech'* followed Maz-

epa. But a manifesto issued by the Muscovite Tsar read: "Whither are the Orthodox going? You are being led to Catholicism by your [Cossack] elders and the gentry who exploit you. Down with Mazepa and the elders! Long live freedom and the Orthodox faith! Down with the oppressors! The Tsar defends the people against the gentry," etc.

History records that the people did not follow Mazepa. . . . The people, the toiling class, and all those who thought alike (if they thought at all) were deceived. "Freedom, the Orthodox faith, the Tsar, and Russia," soon led to *serfdom*, the abolition of all autonomy, dissolution of the *Sech'*, expropriation of the land from the peasants, the whip and the rod, abolition of education and the fundamentals of science, the proscription of the language of the people, the abolition of their name and dignity, and above all *the abolition of all opportunities for development*.

History therefore now says: if only the fools had not followed Moscow, had not trusted in Orthodoxy, freedom and other "Muscovite blandishments," but had risen as one man, then. . . at least we would now have school books in Ukrainian . . . and we would not learn only upon reaching maturity that you and I are Ukrainians and that we are not free. We would have our own schools, science, a Ukrainian literature, technology, and culture; the Ukrainian peasants would be better educated, and Ukrainian cities would be more Ukrainian. . . .

Whom does history blame for 1709? Muscovite history blames Mazepa and his followers; Ukrainian bourgeois history blames Moscow; and Ukrainian labor history blames both Moscow and Mazepa and his followers. It blames the latter not for having revolted against Moscow but for the failure of the revolt. . . [and] because by his policy Mazepa did not gain the sympathy of the toiling people. .

Now when you are fighting in Ukraine for schools, literature and in general for "Ukrainization," looking back into history, you must often tell yourself: it would be better if Ukraine had been Ukrainized earlier, so that now a soviet, working people's republic could be built; it would be better if all the school books had been written earlier, so that now social revolution could be advanced and the Ukrainian ruling classes sent to the devil. It would be better if the cities had been Ukrainized, so that the Ukrainian proletariat and peasantry could take part in the Soviets and the government would be Ukrainian, elected by you Ukrainian Communists and not appointed by Moscow. Upon reflection, you will come to the conclusion that it would have been better had our forefathers not believed in Moscow's "liberation ideology" but had risen as one man. There would be no serfdom, there would be a Ukrainian state and culture, and there would now be a Ukrainian social revolution, not Muscovite oppression in Ukraine.

Such is the judgment of history upon our ancestors!. . .

I sincerely believe, Comrade, that your conscience will not be altogether at rest if you leave our dispute to the judgment of history. Well, are you absolutely sure that all truth is on your side? I feel that you cannot say this. And in reality you would be right [to hesitate]. . . .

You (the Ukrainian "Janissaries") feel that you are a small minority ruled by an inflexible cruel power, which has forced you to capitulate. You had no other choice. Therefore you are doing your small task in attempting to "Ukrainize" something. You work industriously, honestly, to the point of exhaustion. You are terribly afraid lest you offend your superiors....

As an honest man and revolutionary you well know that if there were a Ukrainian Communist government in Ukraine, you would have no worries about Ukrainization. It would advance like the raging sea; it would flood all life. There would be Ukrainian schools. Books would be published by the million. You would have everything at home, and above all we would not be in emigration, but would be helping you, the Ukrainian Communists.... Tens of thousands of revolutionary, socialist, and democratic members of the intelligentsia would support your government, as a Ukrainian government.... There would be no "Janissaries" and no "liberators," and we would not have to communicate with you secretly. I would not be "selling" Ukraine to the capitalists abroad, and you would not be "selling" it at home. That is what a Ukrainian Ukraine would mean. It is from this situation that the "national problem" emerges.

But you speak of a "class struggle"! How can there be a class struggle between people of the same class? Logically, this is impossible.

We value the great sacrifice of those comrades who have collaborated superficially with the occupation government.... We say: let these comrades work there as best they may... but let them keep within the bounds of decency. ... Do cultural work with your own hands, strengthen life, preserve the benefits of the revolution—all this is heroic. Do not, however, do anything disgraceful, do not oppress the people.... Do not be the moral serfs of the present masters of Ukraine.... That is all we ask of you....

We are working in the cultural sphere and in this way we directly support those who are fighting for Ukrainian culture in Ukraine. Our activity disturbs the peace of the occupiers. We published *Nova Ukraina* [New Ukraine!, and in reply they issued *Chervony shlyakh* [Red Path], We founded the Ukrainian Agricultural Academy [in Podebrady, Czechoslovakia], and they renamed the Agricultural Institute in Kharkiv the Ukrainian Agricultural Academy. We announced a broad program of Ukrainian cultural work, and they answered us with a "policy of Ukrainization." All this has been done to divert the attention of the Ukrainian masses in Ukraine from us and to show that the problem of Ukrainian culture will be solved by *them*, the Bolsheviks....

Inexorable history has placed the same task before you and before us, Ukrainian revolutionaries, and we shall, each on his own ground, work according to his ability. So we are not angry with you and do not condemn you, since we value your work; but if "the immoderately devoted" begin to label us as fools, lacking the generosity of silence and modesty, then we shall reply with such words as "Janissary" in order to restrain them from utter baseness....

We remain silent; perhaps this is necessary for their Ukrainian work. If this will be useful for Ukraine, . . . then scold us! Say that we are "selling" Ukraine to West European imperialist capitalism; say that we have made a pact "with the landlords and capitalists," etc. Say anything. ... If you really bring liberation to Ukraine, ..., then, drowning in the sea of life, like those shipwrecked, we will bless the sun of a freed Ukraine with our last breath.[9]

While it is true that the Ukrainian emigration in the 1920's had some influence on the introduction of the Bolshevik policy of Ukrainization, it would be incorrect to portray Ukrainization as merely a product of competition with the Emigres. Similar policies aimed at stimulating native cultures were introduced in other non-Russian Soviet republics. A major factor contributing to this policy was the temporary liberalization of the Soviet system during the period of the New Economic Policy (NEP).

C. Borotbism Versus Philistinism in the CP(b)U

Cultural life and the formulation of the national problem in Ukraine were distinctly affected by the presence of a considerable number of Borotbisty in the CP(b)U. The 554 ex-Borotbist "responsible workers" were active in all provinces of life. Shumsky and Blakytny fought fiercely against Russifying influences in the national and cultural policies of the party. Other Borotbisty lent a strong Ukrainian coloring to party and government organizations and policies. To be sure, all this was not accomplished in a day. In the CP(b)U the Borotbisty waged both a hidden and at times an open struggle against the Bolshevik apparatchiki [functionaries]. The struggle was less intense in the agricultural areas where Bolshevik cadres were under stronger Ukrainian influence than in the industrial areas, particularly since the large cities in Ukraine where Ukrainians were a small minority had a colonial character, as Trotsky once shrewdly observed.[10]

Blakytny clashed openly with Grigorii Zinoviev during the Fourth All-Ukrainian Congress of Soviets, held in Kharkiv, May 18–21, 1920. At sessions of the CP(b)U delegation Zinoviev defended the centralist point of view in the national problem and more than once justified the Russification policy in Ukraine. He was influenced by the apparatchiki recruited from the petty bourgeoisie who persuaded Moscow that the Ukrainian national problem was synonymous with Petlyurism. Asked by a former Borotbist why state institutions in the Ukrainian capital bore the sign "R.S.F.S.R." and whether or not a similar designation would be used in a Soviet Germany, Zinoviev evasively replied that "the English workers' delegation which arrived recently in Moscow stated that the English workers had been won over to the R.S.F.S.R." Debate continued over Zinoviev's report on the form of the relationship between the Ukr.S.S.R. and the R.S.F.S.R. To Zinoviev's contention that whoever demands greater independence for Ukraine puts a finger in Petlyura's mouth (that is, is playing Petlyura's game), Blakytny replied that whoever subordinates Ukraine to Russia puts not only a finger but a hand, and a head too, in Petlyura's mouth. Zinoviev's resolution calling for federation was adopted.

The fact that Yuriy Lapchynsky's "Group of Federalists" was expelled from the CP(b)U at this time is evidence of the fact that no one in the party really believed in federation. Lapchinsky's group stood for a genuine federation of the Ukr.S.S.R. and the R.S.F.S.R. The Bolshevik journalist A. Verkhoturs'kyi described these events in the following words:

> The relationship between the two Soviet republics was predetermined by the objective conditions of our economic and political struggle in Ukraine. . . . Either the closest federal union with Soviet Russia and triumph for Soviet government in Ukraine, or independence and triumph for the most reactionary bourgeois government. . . . How clear this "either-or" was has been proved by the entry of the Borotbisty, recent advocates of independence, into the Communist Party [(Bolshevik)] of Ukraine. . . . The Congress unanimously and without debate accepted the law on federation.[11]

But the former Borotbisty had not renounced the idea of independence when they joined the CP(b)U. That they were not expected to do so may be seen from Lenin's "Letter to the Workers and Peasants of Ukraine."x However, to Verkhotursky, independence was synonymous with Petlyur-ism. His view was typical of the CP(b)U's position at that time.

During the sessions of the CP(b)U delegation Zinoviev defended the April 7 directive by the Russian Central Committee which had dissolved the Central Committee elected at the March conference of the CP(b)U. The directive had declared that the

---

x   See pp. 226–228

CP(b)U, plagued by "angry quarrels and recriminations," contained two currents. Although the party was not divided on any basic issue, nonetheless internal strife was leading to organizational weakness. Consequently, the Russian Central Committee had appointed a new Central Committee for the CP(b)U and ordered a purge of the "unprincipled and adventurous fellow-travelers, demagogic elements, semi-Makhnoists and opportunists."

> At a time when the best elements of the Ukrainian proletariat have endured countless sacrifices in the more than two years' heroic struggle, many philistine elements of the intelligentsia and semi-intelligentsia in the cities and small towns of Ukraine have managed to survive. These elements enter or leave the party depending on whether the party is in power or underground. This declassed, demoralized Ukrainian element rushes into every region retaken by the Soviet government and not directly under party control and attempts to seize leadership. . . . These philistine elements are hotbeds of intrigue, recrimination and squabbling. . . [and] should be expelled from the party.[12]

It was proposed that the CP(b)U reregister all members in its regional organizations. The directive announced that several responsible party workers were being transferred from Ukraine to Russia.[13]

It is clear that the former Borotbisty drew the attention of the Russian Central Committee to these philistine elements in the CP(b)U. Warnings must have come from Shumsky, Blakytny and perhaps Poloz, who was then the Ukrainian envoy in Moscow. The purge in the CP(b)U was primarily concerned with Right Bank Ukraine, where infiltration in the party by the local petty bourgeoisie was greatest. There also, lighting against Petlyura continued, and Ukrainians were most reluctant to join the CP(b)U. Zatonsky, Blakytny and Kon were put in charge of the purge in this area.[14] Blakytny was certain to see that Ukrainian revolutionaries would not be purged.

Later events showed how farcical the purge was. It was conducted from above in a purely bureaucratic fashion. The Ukrainian Central Committee and the purge commission relied not on the opinions of the party rank and file but on the *apparachiki*, who were interested only in saving themselves and their friends. In addition, the appointment of the new Ukrainian Central Committee in itself indicated that Moscow did not trust the rank and file members of the CP(b)U but preferred to seek support among the philistine Russian "colonizers" in Ukraine. Thus the Soviet government relied on the very elements which were supposed to be purged. As a result, the philistines not only remained in the party but strengthened their position.

During the Fifth All-Ukrainian Conference of the CP(b)U, held in Kharkiv November 17–22, 1920 Blakytny expressed himself strongly against the inconclusiveness of the purge In his supplementary report on "The Next Tasks of the Party.[15] In his pamphlet *The Communist Party of Ukraine and Ways to Strengthen It*, in which he quoted copiously from the April 7 directive of the Russian Central Committee, Blakytny sharply criticized the philistinism within the CP(b)U.[16] He attacked the anti-Ukrainian trend of the party which, in this respect, allied itself with the Russian Mensheviks and SR's and even with the monarchists. His protest reflected the views of many former Borotbisty and perhaps was the result of joint planning. Nevertheless, Blakytny's plea was unsuccessful. The bourgeois elements in the CP(b)U which had taken the earlier rebuke from the Russian Central Committee in silence were not prepared to allow this Ukrainian Communist, whom they regarded practically as a Petlyurist, to go unpunished. Soon afterward, Blakytny's influence within the CP(b)U was curtailed.

Zinoviev declared at the sessions of the CP(b)U delegation at the Fourth Congress of Soviets that the Bolshevik Party should be "a party of iron discipline and strict centralization, and with a military system at its core." In Ukraine, however, such a party could be sustained only by the philistines; in the Soviet Union, such a party paved the way for the establishment of Stalin's dictatorship, by which Zinoviev himself was to perish.

The victory of philistinism in the CP(b)U presaged the elimination of Borotbist influence. During the Sixth All-Ukrainian Conference of the CP(b)U, held November 9–13, 1921, not one former Borotbist, was elected to the presidium. Neither Blakytnyi nor Shumsky (then Ukrainian envoy in Poland) was re-elected to the

Central Committee. The former Borotbisty continued active in government, but they were now less prominent in the party. An attempt to view the national problem objectively had been made in a resolution approved by a party conference in the spring of 1921.[17] The resolution condemned the oppression of Ukrainian culture under tsarism and declared that no national oppression would be possible under the Soviet system. The resolution shows traces of Borotbist influence, but it went unheeded for several years, until a time when the policy of Ukrainization began to be put into effect.

D Shumskism

The final expression of the Borotbist spirit in the CP(b)U, which goes by the name of "Shumskism," remains to be considered. Strictly speaking Shumskism, or the nationalist deviation in the CP(b)U, dated from April 1920 when the Borotbisty joined the CP(b)U. This tendency, aiming at an independent Ukrainian communism, was tolerated within the CP(b)U until a new Ukrainian policy was initiated by the Russian Communist Party (Bolshevik) in 1925.

Kaganovich was sent from Moscow and assigned as secretary of the CP(b)U in May 1925 for the purpose of strengthening a policy of Ukrainization. With respect to the question of Ukrainization it would seem that there could be no real differences between Kaganovich and Shumsky; however, for reasons unknown to the author, Shumsky opposed Kaganovich's appointment. It was rumored that Shumsky, heading a "conspiracy" against Kaganovich, had proposed that Chubar be appointed party secretary, and that the former Borotbist Hrynko replace Chubar as Chairman of the Ukrainian Council of People's Commissars. Through his local lieutenant Andriy Khvylya, who informed against Shumsky, Kaganovich learned of the "conspiracy," and now used an old Bolshevik trick to deal with his opponents. He steered toward Ukrainization, thus depriving Shumsky of any basis for opposition. Using a typical Stalinist device, Kaganovich accused Shumsky of nationalist deviation, labelling it Shumskism; thereafter everything Shumsky had expressed openly in the CP(b)U was branded Shumskyism. Shumsky was removed from his post as People's Commissar of Education and transferred to Moscow as Chairman of the Trade Union of Education Workers; similarly Hrynko was "kicked upstairs," becoming Deputy Chairman of the State Planning Commission of the U.S.S.R. in Moscow. The other "conspirators" did not share Shumsky's views on the national problem and therefore presented no serious threat to Kaganovich. Many Borotbisty believed that Kaganovich had purposely compromised those Ukrainian Communists who were the staunchest defenders of Ukrainization. Kaganovich launched a similar campaign against the Ukrainian writer Mykola Khvyl'ovyi and the economist Mykhaylo Volobuyev.

In the opinion of the author it was Stalin rather than Kaganovich who directed this phase of Bolshevik policy in Ukraine and in other non-Russian republics. Stalin was willing to allow the rebirth of national cultures, but he was unwilling to entrust the direction of its development to native Communists lest they become popular in their own countries and perhaps later prove a threat to Moscow. Stalin trusted only his own *apparatchiki*, such as Kaganovich; Ukrainians could be used only as assistants. In order to justify the removal of Ukrainian Communists like Shumsky, Stalin had to ban as nationalist all ideas of independence, ideas which had been permissible during Lenin's lifetime. Khvylovy, for example, had been just as great a nationalist in 1923 as he was in 1926. Clearly, Ukrainization was a double process: de-Russification was carried out within the cultural field, yet at the same time political centralization hardened, with all independent or even federalist views condemned. Kaganovich's personal contribution to this policy perhaps lay in the fact that Shumskyism was equated with nationalist deviation. Stalin expressed his attitude toward Ukrainian communism in a letter dated April 26, 1926 "To Comrade Kaganovich and Other Members of the Central Committee of the CP(b)U," in which he attacked Khvyl'ovyi's ideology:

> Khvyl'ovyi's demand for the "*immediate* de-Russification of the proletariat" in Ukraine, his opinion that "Ukrainian poetry must get away from Russian literature and [its] style as quickly as possible," his assertion that "the ideas of the proletariat are known to us without Muscovite art," his enthusiasm for

> some sort of Messianic role for the "young" Ukrainian intelligentsia, and his ludicrous, non-Marxist attempt to divorce culture from politics—all this, and much besides, must... now sound more than strange from the mouth of a Ukrainian Communist. While the proletarians of Western Europe and their communist parties are full of sympathy for "Moscow," the citadel of the international revolutionary movement and of Leninism, while the proletarians of Western Europe joyfully turn toward the banner waving over Moscow, the Ukrainian Communist Khvylovy has nothing better to say to "Moscow" than to appeal to Ukrainian public men to get away "as quickly as possible" from "Moscow." And this is called internationalism! What can we say of other Ukrainian intellectuals who do not belong to the Communist camp, if Communists begin to talk, and not only talk, but write in our Soviet press in the language of Khvylovy?[18]

The condemnation of Shumsky and Shumskyism meant that Stalin's national policy was not a revolutionary cultural program but a tactical maneuver to safeguard the alliance of the Russified proletariat in the non-Russian republics with the native peasantry. Stalin was obviously afraid to de-Russify the Ukrainian proletariat. Lenin's description of Stalin as a "great power Derzhimorda" was, after all, quite correct.[19]

Defending himself against the surprise attack on his ideological position, Shumsky made the following plea before the Politburo of the Central Committee of the CP(b)U on May 12, 1926:

> I declare that I have obeyed no tradition other than the struggle for the class and national liberation of the working class in alliance with the peasantry. I have not strayed from that path during the entire span of my revolutionary activity which began in 1909. ... I do not, therefore, renounce anything from my past, since I consider that I fought as a Leninist Bolshevik should fight under the conditions of Ukrainian reality, although at that time I was not yet in Lenin's party. ... I have no intention of renouncing my past; on the contrary I am proud of my past; it contains nothing unworthy of a revolutionary Bolshevik. From the first days of the Revolution I have been and I am now a Ukrainian Bolshevik.[20]

Shumsky pleaded that in the contest between Ukrainian and Russian culture the Russians should be more tolerant toward Ukraine and avoid possible conflicts. Asked if he agreed with the views expounded in Ukrainian literature by Khvylovy, Shumsky replied that he did not agree with the aggressive form which that writer's ideas had assumed. Unfortunately, only excerpts of Shumsky's speech appear in Skrypnyk's address condemning Shumsky.

Skrypnyk quoted Shumsky as saying that "a thin film of Ukrainian Communists floats on the rapid stream of Ukrainian cultural regeneration.'[21] Shumsky apparently had demanded that the party take a more direct and intelligent interest in cultural development and asked that the trade unions be Ukrainized as soon as possible.

Kaganovich himself, in a letter dated June 4, 1926 written jointly with Chubar to members of the Politburo of the Central Committee of the CP(b)U, declared that

> Shumsky's behavior illustrates to a certain degree the complexities and difficulties in solving the tasks which face us. One must not confuse Shumsky's subjective motives with objective conditions in the country and reduce the whole matter to the notion that Shumsky, dissatisfied with his post, started a personal squabble. It is necessary to analyze the conditions which made it possible for him to raise this question in such acute form at this time.[22]

The whole Communist Party of Western Ukraine (CPWU), active in Ukrainian areas under Polish control, sided with Shumsky. Thus Shumskism became an international problem. In his speech "The Nationalist Deviation in the CPWU," delivered at the plenary session of the Central Committee of the CP(b)U on June 7, 1927, Skrypnyk declared:

> Failing to find support in Ukraine among the ranks of our party, Comrade Shumsky attempted to gain ground and support outside the bounds of our party, in the ranks of another Communist organization — the CPWU.
> Comrades, we heard the declaration of Comrade [Karlo] Maksymovych, member of the Politburo of the Central Committee of the CPWU, asserting that the Shumsky problem is not solely a problem for the CP(b)U and that his transfer from the soil of the Great Ukraine to the R.S.F.S.R. should be decided [in consultation] with them. He declared that [otherwise] this might lead to a misunderstanding....
> Then we had the declaration of Comrade Turyansky [another member of the Central Committee of the CPWU], who also protested at the meeting of the Polish-Baltic territorial secretariat of the Communist International on March 26, 1927.... Finally we have the opposition of the entire Central Committee of the CPWU, which expressed dissatisfaction with Comrade Shumsky's assignment and declared its belief that Comrade Shumsky's attitude was correct.[23]

Skrypnyk further accused Shumsky of being the cause of conflict between the CPWU and the CP(b)U, of describing the CP(b)U in

1920 as a party of "occupiers" and of directing the chauvinist policies of Khvylovy and his group. Despite Shumsky's removal to Moscow, the campaign against him continued for several years. On behalf of the Politburo of the Central Committee of the CP(b)U, Skrypnyk wrote that the economist Volobuyev's theory was merely the economic justification of Shumskism.[24] As late as mid-June 1929 Skrypnyk was compelled to denounce the "remnants of 'Shumskism' in the ranks of our party, which must be unmasked and fought."[25]

The attack on Shumsky and Shumskism was the first serious setback suffered by the Ukrainian Communists in their fight for the equality of the Ukr.S.S.R. with the R.S.F.S.R. Further blows came during the famine of 1933 when Stalin's emissary, Pavel P. Postyshev, not only purged Ukrainian nationalists but exiled or killed millions of Ukrainians. At that time most of the former Borotbisty were removed from party and administrative work; expelled from the CP(b)U, many were arrested and deported. Panas Lyubchenko and Andriy Khvylya, Stalin's faithful collaborators, survived until the Yezhov period (1937–1938). Today not a .single-former Borotbist remains at liberty in the U.S.S.R,, and it is doubtful that a single one is alive.

* * *

In conclusion it can be said that Ravich-Cherkassky's thesis of the multiple origin of the CP(b)U is contradicted by the history of *Borotbism*. Contrary to other revolutionary movements, Bolshevism was constructed from the top down. The Bolshevik Party was, and is today an elite which selects its members and is not elected by them. The struggle of this elite for power is dictated by the belief that only a party which is built from the top down will be sufficiently militant to realize the program of the dictatorship of the proletariat. On this premise the Bolshevik Party united with other revolutionary parties for the sole purpose of destroying them, after which their most valuable elements could be used for the benefit of the Party. This idea was clearly formulated in Lenin's speech before the Ninth Congress of the Russian Communist Party (Bolshevik), in which he boasted of having conquered the Borotbisty.[26]

In the 1930's compelled to change their policies by the growing demands of Russian nationalism, the Bolsheviks destroyed the last vestiges of Borotbist influence in Ukraine. Bolshevism changed its social character, but the Party remained faithful to the principle underlying its organization. In this respect Stalin proved to be the most apt pupil of Lenin.

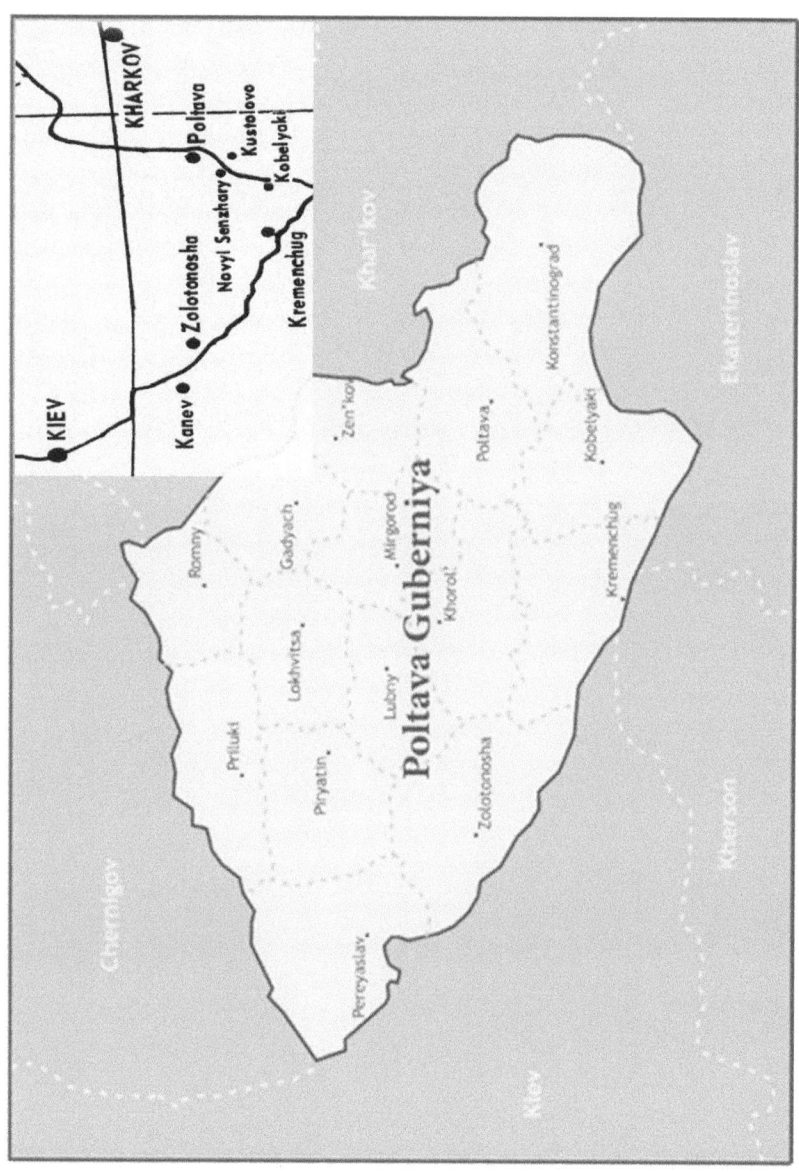

Appendix 1
Reminiscences of the Borotbist Organization in the District of Kobeliaky

During the years 1918–1920 I had the opportunity to observe at close quarters two party organizations of the Borotbisty: the volost center in the village of Kustolovo, Kobeliaky District, in the province of Poltava, and the district organization in the town of Kobeliaky itself. .In what follows I shall try to describe the activities of these two organizations and to sketch some of their individual members. My intention is to give an idea not only of the Borotbist leadership but of the Borotbist rank and file members as well.

During the time of the Hetmanate the democratically-minded zemstvos, which consisted of socialist supporters of the Ukrainian National Union, were actively engaged in cultural and educational work, establishing libraries and reading rooms in villages throughout the country.

In August 1918 Dalekyi, a lecturer and librarian about twenty years of age who had been appointed by the district zemstvo, arrived in the village of Drabinovka, Kustolovo volost, where he was put in charge of a library. He was also expected to give talks on popular topics to the villagers.

On his way to Drabinovka, Dalekyi had passed through Poltava, where he had attempted to contact the Borotbist center. For this purpose he had secured a pass with a UPSR stamp from the secretary of the volost committee to which he had belonged earlier. Similarly, another former member of the volost committee, who was then in touch with the Bolsheviks, tried to contact them in Poltava. Both he and Dalekyi knew that a Provincial Insurgent Committee (consisting of Borotbisty, *Borbisty*, Anarchists, and Bolsheviks) existed in Poltava—the so-called HAPKA. The police, however, had uncovered its meeting place, and Dalekyi almost fell into their hands while trying to locate it. With the help of a schoolboy he finally succeeded in contacting the Borotbist group, which met at a private house. Although the daughter was the only Borotbist member of the family, with a few precautions the house served as a meeting place for the entire HAPKA. It is little wonder that under such circumstances, typical also of other revolutionary groups, underground work had a somewhat amateurish air. Due only to the slack methods of the Hetmanite guards, mostly former tsarist policemen, were revolutionaries of all varieties able to survive.

When Dalekyi produced his UPSR pass one of the Borotbisty told him it was no longer valid, and Dalekyi therefore proceeded to Drabinovka on his own initiative without establishing any contact with the center. This state of affairs was typical of the Borotbist and other underground organizations of the period.

While still at school, Dalekyi had been an active member of am underground youth organization under the influence of Ukrainian SR's [Socialist Revolutionaries] and SD's [Social Democrats]. Subsequently, in the summer of 1917, Paleky became an active member of a UPSR volost committee. When the Hetman regime was established, the UPSR dissolved all volost organizations; only individual members of this particular organization continued to work, singly and at their own risk. One of them, connected with the Bolsheviks, brought to Dalekyi's village some Bolshevik literature which he had received from Russia. Another was personally in touch with Andriy Zalyvchy, a member of the Borotbist Central Committee, while yet another distributed all kinds of revolutionary pamphlets in the villages. These underground activities had been brought to the attention of the Hetmanite police. The danger of arrest caused Dalekyi to flee toward Drabinovka, which lay in a different district.

A group of revolutionary-minded young peasants was already In existence in Drabinovka. Although this group gravitated toward the UPSR (Borotbisty), only one of its members, the peasant B., kept in touch with the Borotbist center in the small town of Novyi Sendzhary. Dalekyi established contact with this revolutionary circle. Soon the library and reading room became the meeting place of the group. Dalekyi had brought with him proclamations of the Second All-Ukrainian Peasants' Congress of May 1918, which had been held illegally in Kyiv during the early period of the Hetmanate. These proclamations had, in fact, been composed by the Ukrainian Right SR's, but they were filled with revolutionary-sounding passages from among which the Drabinovka dissenters chose those which best suited their mood. Apart from the proclamations, the group had no other known revolutionary literature; yet it is possible that the peasant B. from time to time brought Borotba, the underground organ of the Borotbist Central Committee.

Of the members of the Drabinovka circle, only Dalekyi and B. had had some party training. B., who maintained contact with the Borotbist center in Novyi Sendzhary, was twenty-four years old, married, and the father of two children. His parents had very little land. He had completed the village school and was intelligent, politically mature and devoted to the party. In the summer of 1917, after being demobilized from the tsarist army, he had become an active but inconspicuous member of the UPSR. He had no need to hide, therefore, during the Hetmanate.

The others in the Drabinovka group were village youths, all of whom had served in the army but none of whom had much education or native intelligence.

The village of Drabinovka provided an ideal ground for revolutionary work, since on several occasions it had been subjected to punitive expeditions by the Hetmanite militia. The peasants supported the revolutionary group in many ways, but except for Dalekyi the local intelligentsia were hostile to revolutionary ideas. Some were sympathetic, it is true, to the former Central Rada, but they were not prepared to participate in any conspiracy against the Hetmanate. One of them, Ponomarenko, of peasant descent, was a lieutenant in the army and later became a prominent officer in the army of the Ukrainian People's Republic. As for the others, they were supporters of the old regime. Later they all became followers of the Ukrainian People's Republic and active anti-Bolsheviks. Many of them were sons of the local Orthodox clergy. One student, a son of a shopkeeper, held himself aloof and later followed Denikin.

In autumn 1918 rumors swept the revolutionary group in Drabinovka that an uprising against the Hetmanate was about to break out. One gloomy November morning the peasant B. brought the news that such an uprising had, in fact, already begun. The church bells in the village resounded as though for a fire alarm.

About a hundred peasants assembled in the village hall, a small turnout in proportion to the size of the village. Two speakers—Dalekyi and B.—addressed the crowd. The librarian delivered a fiery though rather vague speech. He spoke of the sufferings of the peasants and demanded that all the land be given to them. He said, furthermore—and quite without foundation in fact—that the entire Ukraine was up in arms and that a revolution had broken out in Germany. He exhorted his audience to rise in the name of land and freedom.

No more than a dozen young peasants responded to his call; the rest dispersed in silence. (This is worth keeping in mind, for when we read of such peasant uprisings in belles-lettres and poetry we invariably find them described as mass movements. The fact was that only a few peasants were prepared to act in open rebellion, although many others were sympathetic to the idea of rebellion.) The insurgents in Drabinovka at once requisitioned from some of the rich peasants two revolvers of the Bulldog and Smith-Wesson type and a couple of shotguns. There were no landowners in the village, although some peasants had up to 500 hectares of land (approximately 1,250 acres). The insurgents moved on to the volost center Kustolovo, seven kilometers away, which was supposed to be the center of the rebellion. Toward evening, rumor spread in the village that a punitive detachment of the German army was on its way to Drabinovka, but this proved to be a false alarm.

In Kustolovo the peasant rebellion had a more serious character. Scores of peasants took up arms, among them men of military experience. Leader of the Kustolovo insurgents was Oleksa Pyatenko (pseudonym of Herashchenko), a native of Novyi Sendzhary, who was then twenty-six years old. A government clerk by profession and an amateur actor in travelling repertory companies by choice, he was also a courageous and able military leader. The Kustolovo insurgents seized the volost building and killed the chief of police who had taken part in punitive expeditions against the peasants. From Kustolovo the insurgents moved on to the small town of Novyi Sendzhary, eight kilometers distant. On the way they fought their first skirmish, with the German guard of the large steam-operated mill. It soon became obvious that the rebellion would not spread to other villages in the neighborhood and that, isolated as they were, they would have to maneuver carefully while advancing in the direction of Poltava, until the time when mass uprisings, prompted by the Directory, should begin.

Following the uprising against the Hetmanate, a volost revolutionary committee was formed in Kustolovo and the Borotbist center became its nucleus. The center, consisting chiefly of underground workers and insurgents, was headed by Ivan Spivak, who also assumed the chairmanship of the revolutionary committee. Spivak, who came from a family of middle peasants, was twenty-six years old and a veteran of the navy. An able organizer, courageous and coolheaded like most ex-sailors, be was very leftist in his views, yet quite conscious of his Ukrainian nationality. On the national problem he had reservations toward the Bolshevik point of view.

Next came Stepan Derkach, a member of the committee, over twenty-five years of age, unmarried, and a farm hand. He was a fanatical revolutionary and internationalist who changed his name to Apfelblat to demonstrate his disregard of nationality. While he felt no particular aversion to the Bolsheviks, he remained loyal to the Borotbisty.

The man in charge of finances of the revolutionary committee was Ivan Spivak's older brother Yakiv, a married man of thirty with several children. Obviously a new convert to the revolutionary faith, he was less ardent than his brother. Both the Spivak brothers were strongly influenced by their younger step-brother Omelko, a student who headed the Borotbist organization in the district of Kobeliaky.

Then there was Mysan, a former sailor, the son of a wealthy peasant..During his service in the navy he had become a Bolshevik. He joined the Borotbisty because there was no Bolshevik organization in that volost.

Still another member of the revolutionary committee was the librarian, Dalekyi, already known from Drabinovka. Here he was in charge of the cultural section. By nature a fanatic and a dreamer, he attempted to reconcile the Ukrainian struggle for national liberation with international communism.

Others included S.H., a sister of one of the prominent Borotbisty, an intelligent peasant girl of about twenty-four; Ya., a poor peasant twenty-six years old, politically immature, formerly a soldier who, after the uprising, became a volost militiaman; and D., another former soldier who, after participating in the rebellion against the Hetmanate, joined the militia. The hitter two, though half-illiterate, were devoted revolutionaries, not mere soldiers but active workers.

In addition to these members, the volost revolutionary committee included several other peasants from neighboring villages. Among them were the peasant B. from Drabinovka, and Ya.S., the village blacksmith. S. was chairman of the volost council before the Hetman regime, and during the Hetmanate went into hiding in the steppes. Although the head of a large family and kind and honest, he was an alcoholic. Further to the right than most of the Borotbisty, he nonetheless chose to remain with the Borotbisty after the downfall of the Hetmanate, when the right and center Ukrainian SR's joined the Directory.

All those I have described and mentioned by name perished in the course of the Revolution.

During the period of the Directory, which in the province of Poltava lasted but a short time, the Borotbist party center in Kustolovo organized a council of peasants' deputies and established revolutionary rule. The system of government was based on the Soviet principle, although it was less harsh than that practiced by the Bolsheviks. Perhaps the fact that the government of the Directory was still functioning in the neighboring areas was responsible for this fact.

After the arrival of the Red Army in Kustolovo, a public meeting was held in the village at which time a sailor—the commander or commissar of the local Red Army unit—gave an address. Under the new regime, on orders from the Bolsheviks, the Borotbist revolutionary committee established a system of taxing rich peasants three thousand rubles or more for each homestead. These taxes were rather high; the salary of a village teacher in those days was, after all, only one hundred rubles a month. Peasants who could not raise the required amount were placed under arrest until relatives did so for them- Above all, taxation hurt the former members of the pro-Herman Union of Agricultural Owners (*Soyuz Kbliborobiv-Vlasnykiv*).

Other measures affecting the peasants were the division of land on large farms, mass propaganda in the villages and the separation of church from state. Registers of births, deaths and marriages were transferred from clerical to civilian authorities, and no religious instruction was to be offered in the schools. The peasants looked on the transfer of registers as a godless act and protested sharply. During a peasant meeting in Drabinovka, for instance, a member of the committee who spoke in favor of this measure barely escaped a beating from the enraged peasants.

The educational section of the revolutionary committee carried on intensive activity in the villages, founding *Prosvity* [Enlightenment societies] in seven out of the eight communities of the volost. These became young people's cultural centers. In general the'village intelligentsia of Kustolovo volost took no part in political life. Being more national-minded and opposed to the Bolshevik occupation, they participated, at most, in theatrical performances only. Dalekyi, of course, an active Borotbist, was an exception.

One morning in January 1919 the bodies of seven men who had been executed were found just outside Kustolovo. The Kobeliaky District Revolutionary Committee accused the volost committee of having carried out the execution and ordered an investigation. Of the seven, five had been rich peasants, former supporters of the Hetmanate, and two had been among P'yatenkos partisans. It was explained that the rich peasants had been executed for their participation in the Hetmanate punitive expeditions and the two partisans for looting. Their guards shot them as they were en route to the district town. The District Committee condemned the action of the local Borotbisty and ordered a trial. However, no severe action was taken against the offenders; the times were against it. Although terror occurred widely throughout the district, it was controlled by the Cheka, which existed only in district towns. Independent terrorist acts were therefore not condoned. The execution of the five rich peasants had been an act of revenge, while the shooting of the two partisans was intended to serve as an example of impartial revolutionary justice.

I turn now to a consideration of activities at the district Ievel. After the downfall of the Hetmanate, during the Directory, P'yatenko's unit was based in the town of Kobeliaky. The Bolshevik insurgent detachment under V. Upyr', which had revolted in one of the volosts of the district, was also .stationed in Kobeliaky. The two units remained in separate ramps, however, and to an extent even competed with each other. They formed military support for the Kobeliaky District

Revolutionary Committee, which consisted of Borotbisty, Bolsheviks and one *Borbist*. Since the District Revolutionary Committee did not recognize the Directory as its government, the town was often referred to as the "Kobeliaky Red Republic." There were several such districts-for instance, the one in Pereyaslav—in Ukraine in those days.

The delegation from Kobeliaky District to the Poltava Province Peasants' Congress, held in late December 1918, voted with the majority in favor of a soviet government and against the Directory. Because the delegates to the Congress had been molested by units of Ataman Bolbochan, they had sought help from the Soviet Red Army, which was slowly advancing from Kharkiv to Kyiv. Peasant congresses then had a singular air about them-red banners and yellow and blue banners together. At the end of sessions the peasants would sing both "The Testament" (*Zapovit*), to the words of a famous poem by Taras Shevchenko, and "Ukraine Is Not Yet Dead" (*Shche ne vmerla Ukraina*), both Ukrainian national anthems. Even later, under the Bolshevik regime, they continued to sing "The Testament" and frequently sang the other song, too, in spite of Bolshevik disapproval and the substitution for it of the 'Internationale."

The Borotbist insurgent unit led by P"yatenko and the Bolshevik unit of Upyr' and Klymenko harassed the forces of the Ukrainian People's Republic which were retreating from Poltava in the direction of Kremenchug to Kyiv. P'yatenko's partisans' on-one occasion cut off rail communications of the Petlyurist Ataman

Bolbochan at the station in Kobeliaky, despite the fact that the Borotbisty were not anxious to fight the Petlyurists. They regarded their conflict with the Petlyurists as a domestic quarrel, while they viewed the Red Army as a Russian occupation force. Among the Borotbisty these views were held mostly by the intelligentsia and only to a lesser degree by the peasants, who had little understanding of the value of a sovereign state. Many peasants, notably B., nonetheless realized the importance of a Ukrainian state.

An interesting incident took place in connection with P'yatenko's skirmish with Bolbochan's detachment at the railway station. A young officer, Chalyi, failed to engage Bolbochan's forces in battle and was subsequently accused by the Bolsheviks of indecision. One might have assumed that by this action he had been expressing his nationalist sympathies, were it not for the fact that a few months later Chalyi went over to the Bolsheviks and became one of their most dependable leaders.

In their action against the forces of the Ukrainian People's Republic, the Borotbisty first of all were guided by the desire to demonstrate their devotion to the cause of the proletarian revolution and thus to secure a place for their party in the soviet system. Second, they were incensed by the command of the Ukrainian Republican forces in Left Bank Ukraine wielded by the former Hetmanite colonel, Ataman Bolbochan, who was notorious for his severity toward the peasants. Rumors also circulated that he was in touch with the White Russian forces (rumors which were later substantiated); the reputation of the Ukrainian Republican army was thereby damaged.

When I visited the Borotbist provincial committee to see an old friend, after the Ukrainian Republican forces had withdrawn and a soviet government had been set up in Poltava, I witnessed the following characteristic scene. Into the committee room came a man whom I recognized as the recent loader of the anti-Hetmanate uprising and supporter of the Directory, Mysevra. I remembered the familiar figure—all Poltava knew him-with his Cossack tuft of hair displayed proudly on his shaved head. This Cossack style of haircut was used only by the most devoted officers of the Ukrainian People's Republic. On this particular day, the tuft was missing and

Mysevra had a guilty look about him. He began to talk with the fanatical Borotbist Roman Matyash, the actual leader of the peasant congress in Poltava which had been repressed by Bolbachan's forces. Their conversation was stormy. As far as I could make out, Mysevra had come to register as a member of the Borotbist party, or at least to file an application for admission. This suggested that he had been a former member of the UPSR, most likely belonging to the center.

He was finding it difficult to explain why he had not retreated with Petlyura's forces. He was not the only Petlyurist officer who had decided to break with the Ukrainian People's Republic. His action was hardly cowardly. On the contrary, much courage had been needed to come to Borotbist headquarters. In the course of the conversation, however, Matyash yelled at him, berating him as a Petlyurist and finally turning him out, repeating that there could be no cooperation between Borotbisty and Mysevra. This incident clearly illustrates how unpredictable was the attitude of leftist Ukrainians toward the Soviet government.

The Kobeliaky District Revolutionary Committee represented the flower of the Borotbist and Bolshevik forces of the district. The Bolsheviks held a slight majority; although their numerical strength in the district was smaller than that of the Borotbisty, they had a powerful ally in the Red Army. The Borotbisty were richer than the Bolsheviks in personalities. The Bolshevik chairman of the Revolutionary Committee was a young, inexperienced student, Aronsky. The only other prominent Bolshevik was Babchenko, a teacher by profession, an "old Bolshevik," head of the party's district organization. Since Kobeliaky District had no industry, neither Borotbisty nor Bolsheviks had any workers in their ranks. Both, however, had several peasant leaders, although the Borotbist leadership was predominantly in the hands of the intelligentsia.

The Borotbist district organization of Kobeliaky was impressive. It included the following men: Omel'ko Spivak, a twenty-two year old student, was the head of the Borotbist center in the district and a member of the District Revolutionary Committee. A fanatical revolutionary and a brilliant organizer, he would certainly have developed into a national Borotbist leader had he not perished six months later. He was inclined to rationalism and was a powerful influence on his two revolutionary brothers in Kustolovo.

Oleksa P'yatenko, the partisan leader, was a member of the District Revolutionary Committee.

Shevchenko, a married village teacher and former officer, age twenty-six years, was finance officer in the Revolutionary Committee. He was a taciturn, quiet man of moderate views, very much opposed to the Russian occupation and sympathetic to the Ukrainian People's Republic.

Holovnya, a twenty-five year old, unmarried medical student, was a typical 'eternal student,' and appeared bored with revolutionary work.. A former SR, he somehow developed into a communist.

S.O., an agricultural technician, more than thirty years of age and a bachelor, was a quiet, reticent idealist. He became the party treasurer.

Yosip Kraynyk, about twenty-eight years old and married, was a village teacher. He was elected deputy chairman of the educational section by the teachers' congress after the downhill of the Hetmanate. He had joined the Borotbisty in Kobeliaky, where he became chief of their educational section. (In general, educational affairs in the Soviet Ukraine were almost exclusively in the hands of the Borotbisty. Kraynyk was an able cultural organizer and a good orator, although he was not interested in politics as such. He later died of typhus at the front.

P ... tsya, about thirty years old, a former government clerk and wartime officer, was in charge of the legal section of the Revolutionary Committee and later of the Executive Committee. (After the establishment of Soviet control in a particular area a Revolutionary Committee was formed to administer the area until elections to the local congress of Soviets were held. The congress elected an Executive Committee which then re-placed the Revolutionary Committee.) During the Denikin occupation, P. . . tsya refused to leave with the other Borotbisty, choosing to remain with his family. This made him an object of suspicion in Borotbist circles, to which, however, he returned after Denikin's downfall.

The most interesting and outstanding figures in the Borotbist organization in Kobeliaky were a middle-aged couple, the Khmielevtsevs (a pseudonym), Nina a doctor and Illya an agronomist.. Both were about forty years of age, Russian Social Democrats who lived in Geneva as emigres. It was rumored that Nina had been the secretary of the Bolshevik Central Committee there. She knew the Geneva Bolsheviks, but only Lenin among them received her unqualified approval. The Khmelevtsevs arrived in Kobeliaky in 1917 where they became active as Social Democrats (Internationalists or Left Mensheviks). She worked in the district zemstvo.

In 1919 Nina converted Omel'ko Spivak, head of the Borotbist organization, to Marxism. Under her influence the Borotbist organization in Kobeliaky split away from its center, branding the latter's national policy as opportunist; it called itself the Ukrainian Communist Party (which I shall hereafter refer to as the Kobeliaky UCP or the Kobeliaky Communists). This event happened three months prior to the merger of the UPSR (Communists-Borotbisty) and the USDRP (Left Independents) to form the UCP (Borotbisty), and seven months before the USDRP (Independents) became the UCP (*Ukapisty*). The Kobeliaky UCP was, therefore, the first such Ukrainian Communist nucleus.

In Kobeliaky Nina Khmelevtsev, together with Omel'ko Spivak, established contact with the underground USDRP (Independents). A secret meeting was arranged in Poltava..They spoke for the Kobeliaky UCP; Avdiyenko and Didych, for the Independents. The Kobeliaky delegates proposed that the Independents come out into the open, adopt a communist program and, together with the Borotbisty, form a Ukrainian communist party. The ideology of this new party was to be based on Shakhray's book *The Current Situation*, which was often discussed at meetings of the Kobeliaky Communists presided over by Nina Khmelevtsev. The Kobeliaky Communists failed to persuade the Independents to leave the anti-Bolshevik underground. In principle the Independents agreed with the idea, but such a move, they argued, would be difficult to carry out in practice, for relations were strained; moreover Denikin's forces were already advancing from the south. They therefore deferred making this move until Denikin's downfall.

Then at their party congress, held in late January 1920 they adopted a communist program and a new name, Ukrainian Communist Party (*Ukapisty*). In consequence, from January to March of 1920 there were two communist parties in Ukraine in addition to the CP(b)U: the UCP (Borotbisty) and the UCP (*Ukapisty*). The latter was numerically weak, but it had some outstanding theorists and thinkers, and in this respect stood well above the Borotbisty.

The Kobeliaky Communists in 1919 were a stronger organization than other Borotbist organizations and persistently claimed leadership in the district. Although their history in the summer and fall of 1919 must be regarded as the story of a separate political group, they played an important part in the final phase of the Borotbisty's existence as a party. After the Denikin period, its leadership almost entirely extinguished, and in spite of its previous gravitation toward the USDRP (Independents), this group rejoined the Borotbisty.

At the Kobeliaky District Congress of Soviets, the Kobeliaky Communists won a majority of the seats, but could not obtain from the local Bolsheviks the posts of the local military, Cheka and food departments. Relations became so tense that a commission headed by two members of the Bolshevik Central Committee in Kyiv, one of them Ivan Kulyk, was sent down to curtail or at least neutralize the activities of the Kobeliaky Communists. However, it gained no concessions, and in fact Nina Khmelevtsev cleverly outmaneuvered Kulyk. The Bolsheviks, who nominally held supremacy in the area, had henceforth great difficulty in keeping the Kobeliaky Communists in line.

At the end of June, Kobeliaky District was stirred by the alarming news of Denikin's advance from the south. When the Volunteer Army occupied Katerynoslav and was approaching Poltava, the Kobeliaky Communists easily obtained the consent of the Bolsheviks to form a military unit which was called "The Regiment of the Kobeliaky District Executive Committee." This action was in accord with the Borotbist policy of forming a Ukrainian Red Army. P"yatenko, whom the Bolsheviks reluctantly recognized as the best partisan leader, was appointed commander of the Regiment, with

Shevchenko as his chief of staff. Dalekyi, the party's secretary, became the political commissar attached to the Regiment. Although many volunteers from the villages enrolled in the Regiment, the peasants in Kustolovo volost, called to a meeting on orders from the district authorities, listened silently to Dalekyi's exhortation to volunteer. Few responded. All the commanding posts were held by the Kobeliaky Communists, and although some of the company commanders were Bolsheviks, the latter did not even have a party center in the Regiment. This state of affairs was typical of the anti-Denikin fighting front. Most of the partisan units fighting in the Red Army on this front were Borotbisty; officially, of course, they served under a Bolshevik supreme command. Men of the Kobeliaky Regiment told of how a Bolshevik army instructor, dispatched to the Regiment to create a Bolshevik cell, was expelled by the partisans.

In its retreat northward the Kobeliaky Regiment was augmented by many men, some of whom brought their wives. The entire Borotbist organization in Kustolovo volost as well as non-party chairmen and workers of the village councils joined the regiment. In Zolotonosha District the regiment was joined by partisan forces led by Yakiv Ohiy, who had recently been an active Borotbist in Kobeliaky, and Kost' Matyash, a relative of the Poltava Borotbist leader Roman Matyash. In spite of this union it remained a partisan-type military formation; Ohiy retained autonomy over his own units, and his followers remained loyal to the Borotbist center and were not won over to the Kobeliaky UCP.

The Bolshevik front against Denikin was crumbling; large Red units were being encircled. The retreating Red armies, preoccupied more with the requisitioning and exporting of Ukrainian food and cattle than with the defense against Denikin, alienated many Ukrainians. Rumors persisted that the Bolsheviks were not concerned with the defense of Ukraine at all, that their southern headquarters, together with General Yegorov, had, in fact, a secret agreement with the Whites.

In view of the disquiet, the decision not to leave Ukraine but to continue guerilla warfare against Denikin, a plan which had originated in Pyatenko's headquarters and among the Kobeliaky Communists, gained great popularity. Dalekyi, who was at the front at that time, was ordered behind the enemy's lines to explore the feasibility of the plan. From his report it was clear that the plan was not workable; P"yatenko's forces continued their retreat, but across the Dnepr into Right Bank Ukraine rather than into Russia. Nina Khmelevtsev had advanced this idea. She contended that it was the duty of the Kobeliaky Communists to fight for an independent Ukrainian nation, even if that meant merging with the army of the Ukrainian People's Republic to withstand all foreign occupation. Only then could Ukrainian Communists strive to establish the dictatorship of the proletariat and a soviet form of government.

During the retreat, P"yatenko's forces grew into a small army, being reinforced by Ukrainians from the Bolshevik units who did not want to leave Ukraine. In the town of Zolotonosha, an entire Red Army division was disarmed and for the most part incorporated into P'yatenko's forces, which then numbered over ten thousand strong and became known as the "Headquarters of the Insurgent Armies of Left Bank Ukraine." In its ranks were some Jews and Russians who had lost contact with their former Bolshevik units. These men did not share the plan to join the army of the Ukrainian People's Republic. The military command of this large force was in the hands of the Kobeliaky Communists.

During the crossing of the Dnepr Nina Khmelevtsev and her husband were killed by unknown partisans. Deprived of their chief leader, the Kobeliaky Communists negotiated in Kanev District for a possible union with Ataman Zeleny on the basis of Ukrainian Communism. Zeleny was in touch with the USDRP (Independents), and this fact led to some hope for a possible merger of the two military forces. Under the pressure of Deni-kin's forces, however, P'yatenko's units had to retreat in the in the direction of the Ukrainian Republican Army. Thus, more by force of circumstances than by deliberate choice, P'yatenko's partisans joined the Third Galician Corps of this army and assumed the name of "The Poltava Insurgent Brigade." By that time, P'yatenko's forces had been decimated by Denikin.

The presence of the Poltava Insurgent Brigade in the army of the Ukrainian People's Republic was anomalous, to say the least.

Its composition—including Russians and Jews—and its Communist leadership aroused deep suspicion. The brigade was placed under the supervision of the army's counter intelligence; the Kobeliaky Communists and the Ohiy-Matyash Borotbisty had to resort to secret conferences. The red flags of P'yatenko's forces were replaced by the yellow and blue banners. The brigade's band, chiefly made up of Jewish musicians, gingerly played the Ukrainian national anthem during official ceremonies.

The position of the brigade soon grew critical. Dalekyi was sent to Kyiv, then occupied by Denikin's forces, to contact the Borotbist underground. However, in his meeting with the UPSR (Center) he failed to persuade them to accept the Communist platform. A representative of the Borotbist Central Committee in Kyiv, Lisovyk, visited the brigade and tried to persuade them to leave the Republican Army and to act as an independent partisan unit. Conditions for raids by such units were becoming more favorable.

In the end, the Poltava brigade lost the confidence of the Republican command. A large Red Army detachment led by Yakir was attempting to break through the Denikin lines from Odessa to the north. Orders were issued to engage it in battle when it made contact with the Republican Army, orders which applied no less to the Poltava Brigade, which duly engaged Yakir's spearhead. However, in the course of battle Bolshevik elements who had joined the brigade in Zolotonosha went over to Yakir's Red detachment, and the commander of the artillery battery, Shvarts, ordered the brigade guns to be fired at the Republican Army. This incident added to the discredit of the brigade. To make matters worse, the Republican Army was disintegrating. Typhus claimed thousands of victims; scores of brigade members fell sick. Last but not least, homesickness was an active factor. Everything culminated in the decision to break with the Republican Army. The majority of the partisans joined the Borotbisty Lisovyk, Ohiy and Kost' Matyash, who formed an independent partisan unit which in the history of the Civil War has become known as the "Ohiy-Matyash Partisan Unit."

The Kobeliaky Communists remained isolated. P'yatenko joined forces with the Anarchist Zinovyev, who held a position between the Denikin and Petlyura fronts in the forest near Kozyatyn.

Because P'yatenko wanted to operate on the Left Hank, Zinovyev arrested and destroyed most of the Kobeliakyans, among them Omelko Spivak, P'yatenko and Shevchenko. Many others of the original Kobeliaky organization died of typhus. Those who returned home after the downfall of Denikin became the nucleus of a new Borotbist organization in Kobeliaky District.

The Kobeliaky Communists who survived the events of 1919 were Dalekyi, S.O., Holovnya, Derkach, Mysan, B., a peasant H, (also from Drabinovka), and several others. Dalekyi now headed the new Borotbist District Committee, which published the newspaper *Kobelyats'ky Borotbyst*. Under Dalekyi's able leadership this committee undertook wide activities and enjoyed greater popularity than the local committee of the CP(b)U. Its membership was not large, amounting to no more than fifty. The town of Kobeliaky itself had only about twenty-five members and candidates of the UCP(b).

Because the Borotbisty in Kobeliaky were stronger than the Bolsheviks, they were invited to join the District Revolutionary Committee (S.O. was the representative chosen), and were put in charge of cultural activities (in the person of Lymar). They also received seats in the departments of the District Executive Committee: land-S.O.; education-Lymar; economic council—Batyr; health-Holovnya; and justice— P...tsya.

There was sharp rivalry between the Borotbisty and the Bolsheviks for influence over the masses. The Bolsheviks accused the Borotbisty of hiding their counterrevolutionary attitude under a soviet cloak. During the district peasant congress, called soon after the downfall of Denikin, at which the Borotbisty had a large majority, they were severely attacked by the Bolsheviks. A critical moment came when the resolution calling for the compulsory contribution of food by the peasants was put to a vote. Dalekyi spoke in favor of the resolution, but he made it clear that by supporting this Bolshevik measure the Ukrainian peasants had not relinquished their hope of establishing a Ukrainian soviet government of their own. The resolution passed with little opposition.

In March 1920 the Borotbist party voted to merge with the CP(b)U. The Kobeliaky Borotbisty went along not because they felt that they could exist peacefully with the Bolsheviks, but because they hoped that thereby they would swamp the Bolsheviks. Events soon showed them their mistake.

When the Bolsheviks won over some old tsarist generals, headed by Brusilov, to support the Red Army in the war against Russia's "historic enemy" the Poles, a group of former Borotbisty within the local CP(b)U objected to the new Bolshevik slogans which had dropped to second place the defense of the revolution against counter revolution. Representatives of this group—Dalekyi and Batyr's brother, a metallurgical worker and secretary of the Bolshevik organization—established contact with Yuriy Lapchynsky's "Federalists" within the CP(b)U during the Fourth All-Ukrainian Congress of Soviets in Kharkiv. There Dalekyi also contacted representatives of the *Ukapisty*, who were at that time publishing the newspaper *Chervony prapor* [Red Banner].

Under the impact of these talks Dalekyi's group in Kobeliaky entered into a close relationship with the *Ukapist* Central Committee. Dalekyi also sent a declaration to the Poltava Province Committee of the CP(b)U, stating that his group was withdrawing from the party. The declaration, signed by twenty-four members, stated that since the CP(b)U was fighting for the preservation of the Russian state, the Ukrainian Communists would betray the Revolution and the Ukrainian people if they remained in the party. Furthermore, the declaration went on, the group was going to join the *Ukapist* party. The signatories included all the leaders of the District Committee, Ohiy too, as well as some Bolsheviks and five Jewish members of the CP(b)U.

After this action the Bolshevik headquarters in Kobeliaky stood empty. It was locked up and the key sent to the representative of the Poltava Province Committee of the CP(b)U. As this event attracted considerable attention, Lenin was obliged to mention "the Kobeliaky Communists" in his address before the Tenth Congress of the Russian Communist Party (Bolshevik) in March 1921.

Appendix 2
Biographical Sketches of Individual Borotbisty

The following abbreviations have been used (in addition to those for political parties, expansions for which will be found in the text):

fnu:	first name unknown.
pseud.:	pseudonym.
BSE:	*Bolshaya sovetskaya entsiklopediya* [Large Soviet Encyclopedia], Moscow, 1st ed.
LE:	*Literaturnaya entsiklopediya* [Literary Encyclopedia], Moscow, 19291939.
Leytes:	Leytes, O. and M. Yashek, *Desyat' rokiv ukrainskoi literatury* (19171927) [Ten Years of Ukrainian Literature, 19171927], ed. by Serhiy Pylypenko, Kharkiv, 1928, Vol. I (*Biobibliohrafichyny* [Biobibliography]).
MSB:	*Malaya sovetskaya entsiklopediya* [Small Soviet Encyclopedia], Moscow, edition indicated.

The sources listed are in addition to the author's own knowledge.

BARON, see Lashkevych.

BLAKYTNY, Vasyl' M. (*pseud*, of Ellansky), b. January 10, 1895, into the family of the parish priest in the village of Kozly, Chernihiv Province. After graduating from a theological seminary, B. attended the Commercial Institute in Kyiv. While still a student he took an active part in revolutionary life, later joining the Kyiv organization of Ukrainian SR's. In the period 19111917 B. was in charge of the revolutionary youth movement. During the Revolution he was active in the UPSR in Chernihiv Province. At the Fourth Congress of the UPSR (May 1918) he was elected *in absentia* to the Borotbist controlled Central Committee. Imprisoned for several months under the Hetmanate, he later worked in the UPSR (Borotbisty) organizations in Odessa, Nikolayev and Poltava. In Poltava he led the uprising against the Hetmanate. During this; time B. was editor of *Borotba*. After the merger of the UCP(b) with the CP(b)U, he became a member of the latter's new Central Committee (chosen April 7, 1920) and sat on the Revolutionary Military Council of the Twelfth Army. B. was later entrusted with' the direction of CP(b)U party work in the villages. In 1920 B. became a member of the Central Executive committee of the Ukr.S.S.R. and later of the U.S.S.R. He was also chairman of the Ukrainian State Publishing House and editor of *Visti Vseukrainskoho Tsentralnoho Vykonavchoho Komitetu* [News of the All-Ukrainian Central Executive Committee] from 1920 to 1925. Under his editorship, *Visti* enjoyed great popularity not only in the Ukraine but also among Ukrainians abroad. In spite of his delicate constitution, B. Had the tenacity and endurance required for political work. He was a good diplomat and orator, a devoted underground worker and a Ukrainian patriot. It was his idea that the publication date of *Visti* should be reckoned from the year of the Revolution. B. was also founder in 1922 and spiritual leader of the literary organization *Hart* [Tempering]. As a poet he wrote under the pen name Ellan]. One of his collections of verse is entitled *Udary molota i sertsya* [Strokes of Hammer and Heart]. Some of his satires appeared under the name Valer Pronoza. He was awarded the order of the Red Labor Banner. B. died of a heart ailment on December, 1925. In the mid1930's B. was declared a Ukrainian nationalist: his works were banned and his statue in Kharkiv Was removed in 1933.

Sources: BSE, 1927, Vol. VI, cols. 472473; MSE, 1st ed., 1931, Vol. X, cols. 252253.

CHABAY, fnu, educated in the field of agriculture, in the 1920's was secretary of the Poltava District Committee of the CP(b)U, and later deputy director of the organization section of the Central Committee of the CP(b)U, engaged in electing cadres of leaders, primarily for the provinces.

DEMYANOVSKY, *see* Lazorsky.

DIHTYAR, *fnu* (variant spelling Dehtyar), b. in Kobeliaky District, Poltava Province, became a member of the Borotbist Central Committee when his party, the USDRP (Left Independents), merged with the UPSR (Borotbisty Communists).

ELLANSKY, *see* Blakytny.

HNYDA, *see* Lisovyk.

HONCHARENKO, *see* Taran.

HRYNKO, Hryhoriy F., b. 1890. After completing the gymnasium he studied at the University of Moscow. The *Large Soviet Encyclopedia*, first edition, states that H. took part in SR revolutionary activity "while still a sixteen year old schoolboy," but this is doubtful. When H. became a member of the board of the People's Commissariat of Education of the Ukr.S.S.R. in 1919, he at first owed allegiance to no party; moreover, it must be borne in mind that the material on his life was published at a time when it was desirable to stress one's revolutionary past and play down one's education. In 1913 he was expelled from the university for participation in a student strike and was compelled to serve in the army as a private. During World War I he served at the front and was commissioned.

It is known that in 1917 H. was teaching in a gymnasium in Kharkiv. H., a good orator, was the best educated and perhaps the ablest of all the Borotbisty. In 1919, while in the Commissariat of Education, he joined the UCP(b), rising rapidly to the highest levels of the party. H. differed from most of the Borotbisty in that he was not a revolutionary dreamer. Having joined the party rather late, he was more easily attracted to Bolshevism. Without party training or tradition, H. was often regarded by the Borotbisty as a careerist, although he was generally respected for his integrity. During the Denikin occupation, H. did not go underground but, together with Kovaliv, was sent to Moscow by the Borotbist Central Committee to negotiate for admission to the Communist International. With the third period of Soviet rule in the Ukraine H. became the Borotbist delegate on the All Ukrainian Revolutionary Committee.

Later and until 1923 he was appointed Commissar of Education of the Ukr.S.S.R., as such directing a celebrated school reform. In 1923 H. was appointed Chairman of the State Planning Commission of the Ukr.S.S.R. and became Deputy Chairman of the Council of Peoples Commissars of the Ukr.S.S.R. In the years 19261929 he worked in Moscow as Deputy Chairman of the State Planning Commission of the U.S.S.R., where he was named head of a special committee to prepare the First Five Year Plan (see Grinko, G.F. [i.e., Hryn'ko H.F.], *The Five-year of the Soviet Union*, New York, 1930). In late 1929 he was appointed Deputy People's Commissar of Agriculture of the U.S.S.R. and in 1930 (1931?) People's Commissar of Finance of the U.S.S.R., in which post he helped to stabilize the Soviet financial system. While a convinced Communist himself, H. often spoke ironically of Stalin, a fact which was probably responsible for his downfall. He was executed following the trial of the so-called "right deviation" (Bukharin, Rykov, *et al.*) in March 1938.

Sources: *BSE*, 1930, Vol. XIX, col. 397; *MSE*, 2nd rd., 2nd ed 1935, Vol. Ill, col. 509.

HUKOVYCH, *fnu,* became a member of the Borotbist Central Committee when his party, the USDRP (Left Independents), merged with the UPSR (Borotbisty Communists). H was a journalist by profession.

KALYUZHNY, Naum (*pseud,* of Shaytelman), of Jewish origin, b. in Mirgorod, Poltava Province. A journalist by profession, he took an active part in the Ukrainian SR movement. About ten years older than most of the Borotbist leaders, he was not a regular member of the Central Committee, although he performed the duties of such a member. In the CP(b)U, K. edited *Selyanska bidnota* [Village Poor], an official newspaper of the CP(b)U. He was later put in charge of the propaganda train which carried Grigorii Petrovsky, Chairman of the All Ukrainian Executive Committee, across the country. In the 1920's K., as head of the Ukrainian section, worked as a counsellor in the Soviet embassy in Prague. He was arrested and disappeared in the 1930's.

KHRYSTOVY, Mykola F., b. ca. 1895, the son of wealthy peasants in Poltava Province. His education was not completed. His brother was leader of an anti Bolshevik uprising in 1920 in Poltava Province. In the CP(b)U, Kh. was in charge of the arts section of the People's Commissariat of Education of the Ukr.S.S.R. An editor and cultural worker, he helped to Ukrainize the opera and the theater. He was arrested and after Skrypnyk's downfall (July 1933) was deported to the district of Vologda.

KHVYLYA, Andriy (*pseud.*), b. 1898, probably of German origin, in the province of Khotin, studied in the secondary agricultural school in Poltava during World War I, participating in the socialist *Yunatska Spilka* [Youth Union], through which he joined the UPSR. He began his work in the CP(b)U as chairman of the Sumy District Executive Committee. He later entered the Kharkiv Agricultural Institute, where he became the party secretary. When Lazar Kaganovich was appointed secretary of the CP(b)U in 1925, Kh. became his lieutenant in uncovering "deviationists" within the party. Given free access to the headquarters of the party's Propaganda and Agitation Section by Shumsky, Kh. disclosed the latter's "conspiracy" against Kaganovich, an action for which he was made deputy to M. Popov, Chief of the Propaganda and Agitation Section. He became a member of the Central Committee and, following Shumsky's downfall (ca. 1927), chief of the Party's new Cultural Propaganda Section. After Skrypnyk's suicide (July 7, 1933) he became deputy to People's Commissar of Education of the Ukr.S.S.R. Volodymyr P. Zatonsky took an active part in the campaign against "Ukrainian nationalism on the cultural front." In a series of articles Kh on orders from Moscow, advanced the idea of the "brotherly propinquity of the Ukrainian and Russian languages," an idea which has guided Soviet linguistic policy in the Ukraine up to the present.

Kh., who was disliked by most of the former Borotbisty, was a typical Soviet careerist, the best example of which was his chief Kaganovich. It was rumored that before the Revolution he had been a tsarist agent provocateur who betrays members of the *Yunatska Spilka* [Youth Union] to the police.

In 1937 Kh. was arrested on charges of Ukrainian nationalism. It was said that he succeeded in gaining a personal audience with Stalin, who confronted him with Panas Lyubchenko, the chairman of the Soviet Ukrainian government. Soon afterward Kh. was shot.

Sources: Leytes, pp. 534535.

KORYAK, Volodymyr D. (*pseud*), b. 1889 of Jewish origin into a white collar family, in Slovyansk, Donets Basin. K. never completed the gymnasium and was self-taught. K. joined the Kharkiv group of the UPSR; in 1915 he was arrested and exiled to Turgai Territory. Released in 1917, K. was imprisoned during the Hetmanate and in the Denikin period. As a member of the CP(b)U, K. worked in the People's Commissariat of Education of the Ukr.S.S.R. (1919–1925) and in the Ukrainian State Publishing House (1925–1931?). He was one the founders of the literary organization *Hart* | Tempering] in 1923 and in January 1927 of *Vseukrainska Spilka Proletarskykh Pys'mennykiv* [All-Ukrainian Association of Proletarian Writers], abbreviated VUSPP. The author of a history of Ukrainian literature from a Marxist viewpoint, K. was also a lecturer in Ukrainian literature at the Kharkiv Institute of Education and the Artyom Communist University. In the 1930's K. became the Party's chief literary critic against Khvylyovism. He was deported during the Yezhov period (1937–1938).

Sources: *LE*, 1931, Vol. V, cols. 499–500; Leytes, p. 243.

KOTKO, see Lyubchenko, Mykola.

KOTSYUBA, Hordiy M., b. 1892 into a peasant family in the village of Kostov, near Valid, Kharkiv Province. A Borotbist who never joined the CP(b)U, K. began publishing as a professional writer in 1919. The author of several highly artistic novels, he belonged to the literary organizations *Pervshykh khorobrykh* [The First Brave], *Hart* [Tempering] and *Vilna Akademiya Proletarskoi Literatury* [Free Academy of Proletarian Literature], abbreviated VAPLITE. K. disappeared in the period 1933–1937.

Sources: *LE*, 1931, Vol. V, col. 526; Leytes, p. 258.

KOVALIV, Levko, a vivid figure among the Borotbist elite, was first active in the SR student organization in Kyiv during World War I. Perhaps the loss of his wife (who was executed by the Denikin counter-intelligence together with Mykhaylychenko and the poet Vasyl Chumak) influenced K.'s further political career. After the dissolution of the UCP(b), rather than enter the CP(b)U he forsook politics altogether. A brilliant mathematician, chemist, and chess player, K. was also an artist. A striking example of his talent as a painter is his design for the cover of Mykhaylychenko's *Blue Novel*. Vyacheslav Lashkevych (q.v.) once characterized K. as "a man with the mind of a genius, one who should write down his thoughts at once."[y] K. perished in the 1930's.

KOVALIVA, Klyavdiya, nee Yakovleva, the wife of Levko Kovaliv (*q.v.*), was executed by the Denikin counter intelligence in the period November December 1919.

LASHKEVYCH, Vyacheslav (*pseuds.*, Baron and Marchenko), b. into the family of a village teacher, in the village of Marchenka, Poltava District, Poltava Province. L. withdrew from the Borotbist Central Committee in 1919 to join the CP(b)U.

LAZORSKY, Vasyl (*pseud*, of Demyanovsky), b. 1895 into a family of the intelligentsia in the city of Poltava. A medical student with the mind of a theorist, L. was one of the leaders of the Borotbist organization in Poltava Province. Poor health limited his activity. In the CP(b)U he was one of the leaders of the trade union of agricultural workers on an all-Ukrainian scale. L. disappeared in the period 19331937.

LEBEDYNETS, Mykhaylo, a member of the Borotbist Central Committee, appeared in 1921 as chief procurator in the "trial" of the Central Committee of the UPSR (Center) in Kharkiv.

---

y   In conversation with the author.

LISOVYK, Oleksander (*pseud*, of Hnyda), b. 1895 or 1896, from a peasant family in Poltava Province. He completed the lower industrial arts school in Poltava. During World War I, L was active in the socialist *Yunatska Spilka* [Youth Union], in 1917 as a member of the Poltava organization of the UPSR, he held leftist views. In 1918 he participated in the uprisings against the Germans and the Hetmanate. In 1919 as a Borotbist, L headed the Poltava Province department of education. During the period he was appointed emissary for the Borotbist Central Committee to the Borotbist Ohiy-Matyash partisan unit. After joining the CP(b)U, L. headed the Artyomovsk District Executive Committee in the Donets Basin and was a member of the presidium of the Central Executive Committee both in the Ukr.S.S.R. and in the U.S.S.R. In the early 1930's he became the director of the Chief Administration of Automotive Transportation of the Ukr.S.S.R. Despite his great abilities as an organizer and administrator, L. failed to reach higher posts in the CP(b)U due to his Borotbist past. His opponents exploited his weakness for women. He was liquidated in the early 1930's.

LYTVYNENKO, Mykola, a member of the Borotbist Central Committee, was People's Commissar of Finance of the Ukr.S.S.R. in the spring of 1919. He probably died during the Denikin occupation.

LYUBCHENKO, Mykola, b. February 29, 1896 in the city of Kyiv. His father was a local civil servant. L. graduated from the gymnasium but did not complete his studies in the philological department of the University of Kyiv. L. was a well-known feuilletonist (his first work appeared in 1911) and the author of several books under the pen name of Kost' Kotko. He was an editor of the following newspapers: *Borotba* (1919), *Chervona pravda* [Red Path], *Visti VseUkraInskoho Tsentralnoho Vykonavchoho Komitetu* [News of the All-Ukrainian Central Executive Committee], *Kiyevskii proletarii* [Kyivan Proletarian] (1920), and *Kommunist* (1924–1927).

Sources: Leytes, p. 252.

LYUBCHENKO, Panas Petrovych, b. 1895 or 1896, of peasant origin in Kyiv Province. After completing a premedical course, he matriculated in the medical school at Kyiv University, which he completed after the Revolution. L. Was a representative of the UPSR in the Central Rada in 1917, and was elected to the Central Committee of the UPSR at the party's Third Congress. A product of Borotbist party schooling, he belonged to the younger generation of the Borotbist elite. His lack of education in the humanities placed him at a disadvantage in the highest Borotbist circles. It is possible that L. was at one time a member of the Borotbist Central Committee; he represented the Borotbist Central Committee in the unity negotiations with the center group of the UPSR during the Directory. As a Borotbist, he worked in the underground against the Hetmanate and the Denikin regime. During the Congress of Volost Executive Committees in Kyiv in June L delivered a brilliant speech criticizing Bolshevik food policy in the Ukraine. It was largely due to L.'s plea that half the delegates to the Congress voted for the Borotbist resolution. A good orator and organizer, L. was a born politician, cool and resourceful. Together with Poloz, he opposed the dissolution of the party at the last congress of the UCP(b) in March 1920.

L's first post in the CP(b)U was as chairman of the Chernihiv Province Executive Committee. During the NEP period he became the first chairman of the all-Ukrainian agricultural cooperative union *Silsky Hospodar* [Farmer]. He was later chairman of the Kyiv District Executive Committee, People's Committee of Agriculture of the Ukr.S.S.R., one of the secretaries of the Central Committee of the CP(b)U, Deputy Chairman of the Council of People's Commissars of the Ukr.S.S.R. and beginning in 1933 a member of the Politburo of the CP(b)U ,and Chairman of the Council of People's Commissars of the Ukr.S.S. R. It was said that before Vlas Ya. Chubar's removal as Chairman, Stalin called him to Moscow and inquired how collection was proceeding in Ukraine. When Chubar insisted that the quotas set for state grain deliveries could not be fulfilled, he was replaced by L., who agreed with Stalin that this could be done. In assuming the chairmanship of the Ukrainian government, L. became morally responsible for the famine of 1933. Ironically, his part in bringing about the famine later provided the basis for his own condemnation. L. was the only former Borotbist elected, as a candidate, to the Central Committee of the CPSU(b) at the Seventeenth Party Congress in 1934. Unlike all the other Borotbist leaders, L. in time decided to follow Stalin despite his former principles. But his Borotbist past led to his downfall during the Yezhov period. While expecting arrest, L., together with his wife (nee Marynych), a sociologist, committed suicide on August 30, 1937, (*Pravda*, Moscow, September 2, 1937).

MARCHENKO, *see* Lashkevych.

MATYASH, Kostyantyn (Kost'), b. ca. 1895, in Konstantinograd District, Poltava Province, a Borotbist partisan leader during the Denikin period.[z] In the CP(b)U, M. became head of the militia in Poltava Province and later director of the hogbreeding trust in Poltava. He was executed in the 1930's.

MATYASH, Roman, b. ca. 1895, in Konstantinograd District, Poltava Province, a surgeon's assistant by profession, was the leader of the Borotbist organization in Poltava Province during the Hetmanate in 1918 and the Denikin period in 1919. A typical party functionary and a fanatic, he dominated the peasant congress in Poltava Province during the Directory. He was killed in a railway accident during the Denikin period.'[aa]

MUSULBAS, M., probably of German origin, was a born party worker and a fanatic, modest but persevering in carrying out party tasks. The earliest information on his activity dates from the time when he was already in the CP(b)U. He began work as an instructor in the organization section of the Central Committee. He became secretary of the Odessa District Committee and later directed the rural section of the party. Arrested in 1937, M. was accused of recruiting party members for a counterrevolutionary organization and was executed.

---

z   See Appendix I,
aa   See Appendix I,

MYKHAYLYCH, see Mykhaylychenko.

MYKHAYLYCHENKO, Hnat (*pseud*. Ihnatiy Mykhaylych), b. September 27, 1892, of peasant origin, in Miropolye, Kursk Province. In 1907 he entered a school for medical assistants in Kursk; by 1909 he was a student of the agricultural school in Derkachi, near Kharkiv, where he became active in an underground SR circle. M.'s association with the radical Ukrainian SR's in the province of Kharkiv gave rise to his sympathies for left socialism. Expelled from school for revolutionary activity, he later entered Shanyavsky University in Moscow. M. was conscripted into the army during World War I, but deserted and took part in Kharkiv revolutionary circles until his arrest and exile to Siberia. Upon returning from exile in 1917, M. became one of the ideologists and leaders of the UPSR in Kharkiv. In the summer of 1919 he went to Galicia to contact Ukrainian revolutionary organizations. He was executed in Kyiv by the Denikin counterintelligence, December 3, 1919.

M. was a writer of considerable promise. His works include *Blakytny roman* [Blue Novel], written in the symbolist tradition and several lyrical plays, published in the almanacs *Chervony vinok*, [Red Wreath] and' *Muzahet* [Musagetes] and the literary journal *Mystetstvo* [Art].

Sources: Leytes, pp. 323324.

NATALKA, wife of Naum Slyvenko, the most famous woman in the Borotbist movement, was a modest student, capable and methodical. Unlike most of the wives of the Borotbisty, N.remained active politically after having borne a child. She became an instructor in the Central Committee of the CP(b)U, but disappeared during the period 1933–1937.

OHIY, Yakiv, b. ca. 1890, in Poltava District, Poltava Province a semi-literate farm hand, acquired his education in various party courses. He was a Borotbist partisan leader of uprisings against the Germans and later against Denikin. In CP(b)U he headed district committees in Poltava Province and was later Deputy People's Commissar of Agriculture of the

Ukr.S.S.R. An able administrator and extremely popular with the peasants, O. was executed during the collectivization drive.

OZERSKY, Yuriy (*pseud*, of Zebnytsky), b. ca. 1896, son of a priest. His education was in the fields of history and philosophy. In the CP(b)U he worked as a member of the managing board of the People's Commissariat of Education of the Ukr.S.S.R., and as Deputy Chief of the Agitation and Propaganda Section of the Central Committee of the CP(b)U. Later he headed the Political Education Section in the Commissariat of Education. O. disappeared in the 1930's after Skrypnyk's downfall (July 1933).

PANCHENKO, Mykhaylo Yu., b. ca. 1888, in the city of Poltava, somewhat older than most of the other members of the Borotbist Central Committee, was graduated from a university before the Revolution. For a short time in 1919 he was People's Commissar of Education of the Ukr.S.S.R. A convinced SR, P. refused to join the CP(b)U. Later he worked as an editor, writer and film scenarist (e.g., the film *Taras Shevchenko*). P. disappeared along with other members of the Borotbist Central Committee in the 1930's.

PANKIV, *fnu*, b. ca. 1894, in Galicia, was taken prisoner by the Russians during World War I. A professional painter and writer, he was the leader of the USDRP (Left Independents). Together with Hukovych and Dihtyar, he became a member of the Borotbist Central Committee. Because of serious illness which interrupted his political career, P. was unable to accept the high posts proffered him by the CP(b)U. He died before World War II.

POLOTSKY, Oleksander, perhaps of Asiatic origin, was older than most of the other members of the Borotbist Central Committee. After joining the CP(b)U, he worked in various Soviet trade delegations abroad. He disappeared before Skrypnyk's downfall (July 1933).

POLOZ, Mykhaylo, b. in 1889 or 1890, probably into a landowner's family. While a student he was conscripted into the army and eventually became an officer. In 1917, as a member of the Central Rada, P. was one of the Ukrainian delegation to the Brest Litovsk peace conference. A thinker and theorist, P. made an important contribution to the UPSR, especially in its pre-Communist period. He represented the SR tradition and, together with Panas Lyubchenko, opposed the Borotbist merger with the CP(b)U. In the spring of 1919 P. became Chairman of the Supreme Economic Council of the Ukr.S.S.R. After joining the CP(b)U in 1920, he was for several years envoy of the Ukr.S.S.R. in Moscow. It was rumored that he owed this appointment to the intervention Lenin, who valued his counsel on policy toward the Ukrainian peasant. He was later People's Commissar of Finance of the Ukr.S.S.R. and a member of the Central Committee of the CP(b)U. On July 8, 1933, the day after Skrypnyk's suicide, P. was arrested. He was last seen on the Solovetsky Islands forced labor camp in June 1934.

PROFESOR, see Prykhodko.

PRONOZA, see Blakytny.

PRYKHODKO, Antin (*pseud*. Professor), of peasant origin, was a student when the Revolution broke out. An outstanding organizer, he became a member of the Borotbist Central Committee. P. was a professor—a modest, quiet and contemplative man. Perhaps because of these qualities he found it difficult to accept Marxism wholeheartedly. As a member of the CP(b)U, he never advanced beyond the post of Deputy People's Commissar (Education and Justice), although in these positions he played a prominent part in enrolling Ukrainian, support for the Soviet regime. He was liquidated with the other members of the Borotbist Central Committee In the 1930's.

SAKHNIVSKA, see Vovchyk.

SAMUTIN, Fedir, b. 1899, in Pereyaslavl District, Poltava Province, was head of the Borotbist district organization in the town of

Pereyaslavl. In the CP(b)U he headed the Poltava District Executive Committee. S. was chief of the agitation and propaganda section of the Odessa District Committee, and later of the Vinnitsa Province Committee. He disappeared in the period 19331937.

SHAYTELMAN, *see* Kalyuzhny.

SHPOL, *see* Yalovy.

SHUMSKY, Oleksander Ya., came in all probability from a priest's family in Volyn' Province. He probably received his education in Moscow. In debates with his opponents in the CP(b)U he claimed that his revolutionary career began in 1909. Perhaps the only member of the Borotbist Central Committee without literary ambitions, he was a practical man, not a romanticist, a fact which brought him little popularity in the party. He was regarded as Blakytnyi's intellectual inferior. As an example of Sh.'s exemplary behavior, there is a story that, while holding the post of people's commissar, for some offense he was assigned by the Central Committee of the CP(b)U to serve as a private in the Red Army, and there diligently carried out the orders of young officers. In 1919, during the second period of Soviet rule in the Ukraine. Sh. was appointed People's Commissar of Education of the Ukr.S.S.R., to succeed the Borotbist Mykhaylo Panchenko. He immediately initiated a campaign against Russification, preparing a draft decree to encourage Ukrainian culture.[bb]

Together with Blakytny, Sh. was the initiator of the merger of the UCP(b) with the CP(b)U. Fearing that his party would be crushed by the Bolsheviks, he hoped that the Borotbisty could continue working for their ideals within the CP(b)U. Sh. became the most prominent Borotbist in the CP(b)U. He occupied the following party and government posts: member of the Politburo and Orgburo of the Central Committee, member of the delegation of the CP(b)U to the Communist International, People's Commissar of Internal Affairs of the Ukr.S.S.K. (1920), Chairman of the Poltava Province Executive Committee and the Province Committee of the CP(b)U

---

bb   See Appendix 4

(1920), Ukrainian envoy to Poland (1921-1923), Chief of the Agitation and Propaganda Section of the Central Committee of the CP(b)U (1923-1925), and People's Commissar of Education (1925-1927). During the years 1925-1927, Sh. carried out a policy of Ukrainization, which was continued by his successor Mykola O. Skrypnyk. In this period he became the opponent of Lazar M. Kaganovich, then Secretary of the Central Committee of the CP(b)U, and, as a result, was transferred to Moscow, where he became Chairman of the Trade Union of Education Workers. Accused of deviating from the party line, Sh. was dismissed from the latter post and appointed Dean of the Institute of National Economy in Leningrad. He was arrested in 1933, during the purges in Ukraine conducted by Pavel Postyshev. It was rumored that he was shot while trying to cross the Finnish border. He was last seen on Popov Island in the Solovetsky Islands forced labor camp in June 1934. Because Sh. had been in opposition to the CP(b)U as early as 1925, his name was excluded from the first edition of the *Large Soviet Encyclopedia*, which included some material on the Borotbisty Hryn'ko and Blakytny.

SLIPANSKY, *fnu*, b. ca. 1897, probably in the town of Skvira, Kyiv Province, a Borotbist active at the district level, S. completed *Vseukrainsha Assotsiatsiya Markso-Leninskykh Institutiv* [All-Ukrainian Association of Marx-Lenin Institutes], abbreviated VUAMLIN, becoming a graduate student (*aspirant*) in the 1920's. He soon demonstrated his talent as an agricultural economist and became head of the Ukrainian Academy of Agricultural Sciences. S. disappeared in the Yezhov period (1937-1938).

SLYVENKO, Natalka, *see* Natalka.

TARAN, Todos' (*pseud*, of Honcharenko), b. 1896 into a prosperous peasant family in Poltava Province. His education in mathematical physics remained unfinished. He joined the Borotbisty as a member of the USDRP (Left Independents). In the CP(b)U, T. worked as assistant editor of the government newspaper *Visti Vseukraihskoho Tsentralnoho Vykonavchoho Komitetu* [News of the All-Ukrainian

Central Executive Committee]. In 1926, when the main organ of the Central Committee of the CP(b)U, *Komunist*, began to be published in Ukrainian, T. became its virtual editor. In the 1930's he became a member of the Central Committee of the CP(b)U. He disappeared during the Yezhov period.

TARANENKO, Korniy, b. ca. 1895, in Kremenchuk District, Poltava Province, a graduate of a commercial institute, headed the Borotbist faction at the Toilers' Congress in January 1919. Later in 1919 he became Deputy Chairman and then Chairman of the Supreme Council of National Economy of the Ukr.S.S.R. After joining the CP(b)U, T. became director of the All Union Sugar Trust in Moscow. The most prominent economist of the Borotbisty, T. disappeared in the 1930's

TRYLISKY, Oleksa, received an education in agronomy before the Revolution. A good administrator, he became chairman of the Odessa District Executive Committee at the end of the 1920's and later Deputy People's Commissar of Agriculture of the Ukr.S.S.R. Arrested while chairman of the Vinnitsa Province Executive Committee, T. was executed in the period 1936–1937.

VOVCHYK, Lida (*pseud,* of Sakhnivs'ka), b. ca. 1898, in the town of Lokhvitsa, Poltava Province, was the daughter of a priest. V. was the wife of Blakytny (*q.v.*). She disappeared in the period 1933–1937.

VOYTSEKHIVSKY, Yu., b.ca. 1895, was educated at a university. As head of the Borotbist Revolutionary Committee of Right Bank Ukraine in late 1919 he attempted to form a Borotbist Red Army, together with Ataman Volokh. In the CP(b)U, V. at various times occupied the posts of

Chairman of the Kyiv District Executive Committee, Chairman of the Ukrainian State Publishing House, and Secretary of the Ukrainian Central Executive Committee. He disappeared with other Borotbisty in the 1930's.

YAKOVLEV, *fnu*, brother of Klyavdiya Kovaliva (*q.v.*), became in the spring of 1919 deputy to the Latvian Latsis, chief of the Cheka in Ukraine.^{cc} It was said that he saved Ukrainians from execution. In the CP(b)U in 1920 Ya. became deputy to the People's Commissar for Foreign Affairs of the Ukr.S.S.R., Khristian Rakovsky. With the help of the former chief of the Cheka, Felix Dzerzhinsky, Ya. secured a post in the textile industry in Moscow. There is no information available about his subsequent fate.

YAKOVLEVA, see Kovaliva.

YALOVYI, Mykhaylo (pen name under the Soviet regime, Yul'yan Shpol), b. 1891, the son of well to do peasants in Konstantinograd District, Poltava Province. His medical studies unfinished, Ya. became an editor and literary critic. In 1920 he edited the newspaper *Selyanska bidnota* [Village Poor]. A close friend of Mykola Khvylovy and his group, Ya. Was one of the leaders and first president of the literary organization *Vilna Akademiya Proletars'koi Literatury* [Free Academy of Proletarian Literature], abbreviated VAPLITE, in 1926-1927. He was the author of the novel *Zoloti lysenyata* [The Golden Little Foxes] and many articles in the field of literature. Arrested in the 1930's, Ya. later died in a forced camp.

ZALYVCHY, Andriy, b. 1897 into a poor peasant family in the village of Misky-Milny, Oposhnya volost, Poltava Province. As a young boy he was taken under the wing of the landowner and banker Rubinshtein, who had an estate near Oposhnya. Rubinshtein sent Z., who already showed promise, to the gymnasium in Kharkiv, where he became a gold medallist. Later Z. studied law at the University of Kharkiv, but in 1915, before completing his studies, he was arrested as a Ukrainian SR and deported to Turgai Territory in Central Asia. In 1917 he returned to Ukraine and devoted himself to party work. Together with Mykhaylychenko, Z. was initiator of the so-called "Left Bank current" in the UPSR,

---

cc   See note 47, p. 397

which became the seedbed of the Borotbist party. A dynamic personality, Z. became one of the driving forces of the party. Lisovyk (*q.v.*) once said that he "set the tone in the Central Committee." Z. perished in the uprising against the Hetmanate in Chernihiv, December 13, 1918. A small collection of his impressionist short stories was published posthumously. Before the Revolution of 1917 Z. translated some of the poetry of Horace into Ukrainian.

Sources: Leytes, p. 181.

ZEBNYTSKY, *see* Ozersky.

ZINA (*pseud.*), b. 1898, a medical student, was active in the underground during the Denikin period and later became a district social worker. She disappeared in the period 1933–1937.

Appendix 3
Platform of the Central Committee of the Ukrainian Party of Socialist Revolutionaries: The Present State of Affairs and Party Tactics (approved by Central Committee on June 3, 1918[dd])

I. In appraising the present state of affairs, the Central Committee of the Ukrainian Party of Socialist Revolutionaries affirms the following:

1. The Revolution in the Ukraine is today deep in crisis anddecay. The bourgeoisie (the landowners and industrial-capitalists) in the Ukraine, united with petty bourgeois circles (the kulak-proprietors) and supported by the international bourgeoisie (German, Russian, Polish, and other) and relying on the forces of Germanimperialism, led a counterrevolutionary offensive which ended in the so-called coup in April of this year.

2. The counter-revolution, with the proxies of the international bourgeoisie the Hetman and his government--brought to naught all the gains of a year of the Ukrainian revolution. The great conquest of the national movement in Ukraine--the Ukrainian People's Republic with national-personal autonomy--has been destroyed. Having abolished all political and civil liberties, won by the revolution and having destroyed all organizations of the toiling people, the reactionaries have established a monarchist state, that has trampled all socio-economic reforms, above all the greatest of them--the socialization of land and labour legislation.

II. Considering the breadth and character that the revolutionary movement in Ukraine assumed, which is more significant than a year of the masses' revolutionary education, on the one hand and, on the other, considering the inevitability of a revolutionary reso-

---

dd   "Platforma Tsentral'noho Komitetu Ukrai'ns'koi' Parttii 'Sotsiyalistiv-Revolyutsioneriv (rozuminnya suchasnoho mentu i taktyka partii')," *Borotba*, No. 1, August 1918, reprinted in Khrystyuk, op. cit,. Vol. IV, pp. 91–94. Italics in the original.

lution of the burden of the universal storm by international democracy, The Central Committee of the UPSR *considers the present reaction in Ukraine as a temporary decline of the revolution*, the reasons of which are:

1. The absence of strong organizations at the centre and, mainly, locally, which alone might provide the support for the revolutionary movement and, at the right moment, repel the counterrevolution;

2. The one-sided national policy of the Ukrainian Central Rada, from which Ukrainian democracy from the very beginning demanded answers to a whole series of social questions, whose concretization and complete resolution could alone provide the basis for uniting all Ukrainian toiling people around their leading organs and, conversely, the delay of which, together with an exclusively national policy, elicited distrust in the masses and a Bolshevik movement as a reaction to the prevailing situation;

3. *The destructive Bolshevik attack of Ukraine*, which broke and demoralized the working classes of society, which, with its misunderstanding of the national question and its centralism produced chauvinism in the popular masses, created the basis for national separatism and sovereignty and their pact with German military force, which in liquidating the attack, inevitably also destroyed or liquidated the organizations of revolutionary democracy in Ukraine;

4. The flexible and uncertain internal policy of the Mala Rada and its government, the Council of People's Ministers, which wavered between the petty bourgeois and labouring classes of society, allowing the accelerated organization of reaction, distancing itself more and more from revolutionary democracy and not giving it the opportunity to organize itself, under the considerable influence and pressure that the international and especially the German imperialist bourgeoisie exerted on the Ukrainian government:

5. The impermissible and criminal, from the point of view of international socialism, union of the Ukrainian government with the German military discredited the Central Rada in the eyes of much of the labouring classes, compromised the very idea of the national liberation movement and the Ukrainian socialist parties,

demoralized Ukrainian democracy, objectively led to the liquidation of all the revolution's gains, opened a wide field in Ukraine for the activity of international reaction, which, in the person of the German bourgeoisie, supported by the bayonets of the Austro-German army in Ukraine and taking advantage of the absence of the [Ukrainian Peoples] Republic's military force and the lack of strong democratic organizations, openly assisted the bourgeoisie in its struggle against land reform and other social reforms, pursuing its own aims, namely:

a) the transformation of Ukraine into its colony;

b) taking back all concessions, made in the Brest treaty under the pressure of military circumstances on the eastern front and from a desire to take quick advantage of the political circumstances in Russia to weaken its imperialist rival;

c) the creation in Ukraine of a fictitious autonomous government that would obediently carry out all instructions from Berlin toward political and social levelling with the metropolis; dissatisfaction with the liberal-democratic policy of the Ukrainian Central Rada and a fear that the convening of the Ukrainian Constituent Assembly might change this policy in the direction of revolutionary democracy;

d) a desire to prevent revolutionary actions of the German working classes, to cover them with the military, `liberating' and economic victories of the German state, in order to keep them firmly in the grip of the imperialist, militarist bourgeoisie;

6. The absence of support for the revolutionary movement in Ukraine on the part of international democracy, which, disunited since the war and the destruction of the II International, was unable to give a proper, organized reply to the united actions of the black international against the red.

III. Noting that the revolutionary movement in Ukraine was forced to deviate and enter this phase of decline by the unsound policy of the revolution's previous administrative organs, by the destruction of democratic organizations, and mainly by the direct intervention in the course of events by previously outside agents, by the lack of international democratic organizations, separated by artificial state borders and by war, and by the lack of solidarity actions on their part, The Central Committee of the UPSR thinks that the struggle of working people with the present reaction for their national and socio-economic liberation can be fully successful only when that struggle is based on class conscious and politically conscious democratic organizations in Ukraine and is carried on in full contact with democrats of other countries, especially of the Central European states, with which Ukraine is linked historically--when the democrats of those states support the revolutionary movement in Ukraine with a readiness to wage an open struggle with their own bourgeoisies.

The Ukrainian revolution, being not only a political-national, but a profoundly social revolution, which from the very beginning strove to transform itself into an international revolution, and took up as its political slogan an unlimited federation of republics (which in the case of Ukraine was to realize by means of a resolution of the Ukrainian Constituent Assembly), was forced by unfavourable circumstances to remain within a national framework and was thereby nearly finished. Now the introduction into it of an element of internationalism pushes it inexorably onto this path, the path of renewing the struggle to realize its slogans--to build a socialist international, to liquidate the universal war into which the Ukrainian state is now being drawn, *to convene the Ukrainian Constituent Assembly,* the struggle for land and freedom, for federation.

Defending the party's old position, and realizing *that the slogan of independence as an end in its self is only a weapon in the hands of the reactionary bourgeoisie,* the Central Committee of the Ukrainian Party of Socialist Revolutionaries believes that the aspirations to have a state, necessarily connected with imperialist tendencies, weaken the class struggle of the workers and inevitably comes into conflict with it. Therefore the independence of the state cannot be the necessary slogan of the toiling people in its struggle, but only a tactical means of attaining world-wide federation.

IV. 1. On the basis of all the above, the Central Committee of the USPR will, in the revolutionary struggle for the liberation of the Ukrainian toiling people, *co-ordinate its actions with the actions of international revolutionary democracy,* entering into the closest relations especially with the socialist parties of Germany, Austro-Hungary, Great Russia, Poland and other neighboring states, unswervingly maintain class tactics, based on the revolutionary organizations of the toiling people of Ukraine, without which no struggle or uprising can have any positive results and which will be strong only when they are organized under common slogans, realizable by a single tactic.

2. In view of the fact that an imperialist, enlightened despotism can also be a threat to the revolution, if the German bureaucracy makes calculated political and even social concessions to Ukrainian democracy in its eastern policy in order to mitigate the revolutionary energy of the toiling masses, the Central Committee of the UPSR opposes such compromises, is uncompromising toward the reactionary bourgeois Hetmanate government and, with the present policy, opposes all opportunism and the entry of democratic elements into the Hetmanate government.

3. Considering the fact that the premature actions of individual villages and townships result only in their defeat at the hands of reactionary military forces and their loss of faith in the revolution, disorganize and demoralize the masses, cause a useless and even harmful waste of revolutionary forces, the Central Committee of the UPSR deter the peasantry from such unorganized actions.

4. Standing for international socialism and the common interests of the workers of all nations and countries and not recognizing as a method of class struggle the path of war and the creation of military fronts, which inevitably disunites and destroys the forces of democracy itself, and *condemning the armed invasion of Ukraine by the (Moscow) Bolsheviks*, The Ukrainian Party of Socialist-Revolutionaries will struggle against demagogic slogans, calculated only to inflame national antagonisms, slogans that call exclusively for a military uprising and armed struggle against the German army in Ukraine, and will appeal for a struggle on the domestic class front.

5. Because the Austro-German cannot long be maintained in a series of punitive expeditions and repressions of popular revolutions, because the loss of its imperialists illusions will inevitably bring rebellion within it, and with it rebellion within the Central

Powers themselves, the Ukrainian Party of Socialist-Revolutionaries will carry on propaganda and organization toward this end among the foreign troops in Ukraine.

6. *Aiming at a revolution that will guarantee all the demands of the Ukrainian toiling people, the UPSR will,* on the one hand, carry on continual and active agitation and fight to disorganize reaction, its government, its military and political-social support centrally and locally, gathering together partisan units that will actively defend the idea of socializing the land, will guard freedom, not allowing imperialist reaction to obscure class consciousness with apparent benefits (those indicated); on the other hand, it will at the same time carry on propaganda, preparations and organization of revolutionary centres of peasants and workers (land committees, factory and railroad committees, councils of workers and peasants deputies, revolutionary committees) in order to seize power overthrow the reactionary government and seize power for democracy with the slogan of a revolutionary uprising with continuous and simultaneous solidarity action locally and at the centre together with an organized strike.

7. *Taking into consideration the fact, as long as the socialist parties figure only as an organized minority and until international socialist democracy creates a single organized unit, a complete social revolution cannot be carried out, there cannot be a socialist revolution and the dictatorship of toiling democracy in separate countries, the Central Committee of the UPSR considers that the transfer of power to the toiling masses as represented by the councils of workers' and peasants' deputies is possible only for in brief periods of revolutionary ferment--insofar as the revolution is created by the toiling people and supported by its organizations, insofar as the gains of the revolutionary movement are safe and reaction is not victorious,--at the same time the transfer of formal power to local self-governments, elected on the basis of a five-member formula must be prepared and to the parliament at the centre, the first of which must be the Ukrainian Constituent Assembly.*

8. Cognizant of the fact that the ground for revolutionary work and mood among the toiling masses are favourable, and that realizing that the slogan of the Ukrainian Constituent Assembly is today the slogan that revolutionizes the masses, the Central Committee of the UPSR considers it necessary for the Ukrainian Constituent

Assembly to convene and open as soon as possible, to express its attitude toward the contemporary events, to address a challenge and protest to democrats of the whole world, a call to revolutionary struggle against international reaction and the Hetmanate government, an appeal for the unity of all Ukrainian democrats in their struggle for land and freedom."

Appendix 4
Draft Decree on Encouraging the Development of Culture of the Ukrainian People[ee]

Explanatory Note to the Decree

In the course of the development of the world revolution the Soviet government of Ukraine has become, by force of circumstances, a source of supply for Soviet Russia and the bridge which links the latter with the outbreaks [i.e., centers] of European revolution. To strike at this bridge and destroy it is the aim of counterrevolution. Establishment of this bridge has more and more become an [urgent] necessity for the motive forces of the all-Russian [Rossiiskaya] Revolution.

Hence the intermittance and complexity of the development of the revolution in Ukraine; hence its involvement by attendant factors, external forces and blows. During the fierce reaction of the Hetmanate and the time of the mighty surge of the proletarian revolution, leadership was in the hands of external forces, in large measure alien to the basic conditions of life of the Ukrainian people and to the natural course of their revolutionary development.

This circumstance, this constant pressure of external forces, entangles manifestations of the social struggle with those of the national struggle, disproportionately aggravates the manner in which the already complex national question is raised and gives vitality to the nationalist movement originating among the bourgeoisie and the bourgeois intelligentsia.

At the same time the proposition which conditions us to regard Ukraine merely as a convenient ground for the development and maneuvering of the military forces of the socialist revolution, on the one hand, does not provide an opportunity to exhaust and

---

ee "Proyekt dekreta o sodeistvii razvitiyu kul'tury ukrainskovo naroda," in K razreshetiiyu natsional'novo voprosa [Toward a Solution of the National Question], 2nd enlarged ed., Kyiv, *Borotba*, 1920, pp. 15-20.

enroll in the struggle all reserves of the local social forces and, on the other hand, impedes a formulation, in all its fullness, of the question— of limitless importance—concerning the development of the culture of the Ukrainian people.

Constrained by centuries of national and social oppression, without schools in their native language, deprived of an intelligentsia, and reduced to inertia resulting from the Russification of all state and public institutions throughout the land, the Ukrainian proletariat and peasantry are faced either with the nationalist tendencies of the bourgeois intelligentsia or with the actual domination of the Great Russian language and culture in all the vast apparatus of the Soviet government in Ukraine.

The one threatens, through the nationalist poison, to obscure the purity of the class consciousness of the working masses; the other does not provide or create the conditions for the natural development of national forms of culture and their use as an important weapon in the struggle for international unification of the toiling masses.

Formal recognition of the equal rights of languages and cultures, a policy of neutrality [in these matters], offers no solution to these socio-political and cultural conflicts.

The century-old process of systematic and planned "Russification" [*obrusitelstvo*] brought about a state of affairs in which the Ukrainian nation, once literate almost to a man [sic], by 1898 had a literate population of only 13.5 per cent; the cities were transformed from centers for the crystallization of cultural attainment into coercive seats of an alien culture; the school became, as Ushinski[ff] aptly remarked, the only place in the village where the spoken language was not understood. The entire state technical apparatus, all leaders and agents of the government for decades were trained automatically and without exception to eliminate all Ukrainian forces from administrative life. There developed a serious inertia which is reflected with rare eloquence in the figures for the ratio of the [total]

---

ff   Probably Konstantin D Ushinski (1824–1970), a prominent Russian educator. – Ed.

population to the secondary schools in Ukraine: Ukrainians, 77.1 per cent[gg] of the population, have 121 schools; Russians, 12.6 per cent of the population, have 950 schools; in other words, the quota of secondary schools for the entire native population is 10.8 per cent, while the quota for the Russian population is 84.7 per cent.

Text of the Decree

The victorious movement and lasting success of the communist revolution, which is paving the way for the construction of new social relationships and which is enrolling in this construction vast masses of the proletariat and peasantry, depend in large measure on the fullness, clarity, firmness, and sharpness of the class consciousness among these masses of revolutionary builders, on the constancy of their consciousness in the face of enormous ideological dangers resulting from the social system which is being overthrown.

The clarity and constancy of class consciousness, its depth and strength, are directly linked with the general cultural level of the working class, with the degree to which the working class, as a whole and among its individual members, is enrolled in active and independent creative work in the culture of mankind. But the growth of culture, especially at its outset, is unthinkable outside of national forms, outside the natural and free development of the national element of a given people; therefore, the paths of the Communist International lie not on the plane of disregard and oppression of national forms, particularly among backward nationalities, but in the necessity of raising their cultural development to the level of the more progressive nationalities and of merging them at the heights of international unity of all toilers.

Whoever sincerely desires the growth of consciousness and international unification of the working masses can only want and strive for the most rapid development of the national forms of culture among those peoples who, like the Ukrainian people, have

---

gg Cf.figure of 71.1 per cent in Appendix 5,

been held in a state of national stagnation and oppression by the harsh rule of capitalist society.

In the extraordinarily complex circumstances of the development of the socialist revolution in Ukraine, special attention must be devoted to projecting a true policy with regard to the development of national cultures, in order thereby to disarm those social groups who, through their naive or Jesuitical guardianship of national culture, conceal social aims which are alien and hostile to the working class and who regard the development of national forms not as a road to international unification of the toilers, but as a means of realizing their own imperialist desires.

On these ground's, in supplementing and elaborating upon the corresponding articles [of the Constitution] of the Provisional Workers' and Peasants' Government, the Central Executive Committee directs the People's Commissariat of Education, as the organ responsible for cultural and educational work in the Republic, systematically and in a planned manner to pursue a policy of encouraging in every way the development of Ukrainian culture in all branches of national life. It is therefore essential:

1. In education outside the schools, as the most important field of educational activity, during the trying period of the socialist revolution, to carry on systematic work in widening the limits and deepening the basis of class consciousness, utilizing for this purpose all facts and impulses flowing from the national element which is native and close to the people.

2. In social education (the pre-school and school system) for theUkrainian population in schools and other educational institutions, to carry on instruction in the native Ukrainian language.

Note 1. For the non-Ukrainian population schools will be founded with instruction in the language of that nationality for which the school is opened.

Note 2. Determination of the language of instruction in educational institutions will be made by the People's Commissariat of Education through its organs.

3. In the realization of this task, to organize on a broad basis the training of a suitable cadre of professionals [*rabotniki*] and the publication of appropriate literature and teaching materials.

4. In the organization of higher institutions of learning, tirelessly to pursue the constantly growing need and demand for the suitably trained Ukrainian professional in all walks of life, the professional able with his creative initiative to enter this life and enrich the spontaneous growth of national culture.

5. Into the unplanned and chaotic growth of the Ukrainian book market, to bring organization and system, which will lead to the broad development and dissemination of both original works of Ukrainian national literature and translated literature in all problems and branches of learning.

6.In the field of art, to develop, discover and record the resultsof all branches of national art work in national forms, by organizing appropriate institutions and [taking] proper steps.

* * *

The pamphlet in which the above draft decree was published presented the following commentary relative to the decree:[hh]

People's Commissar of Education Comrade Shumsky presented the above draft decree for consideration to the Commissariat's managing board, which took it up on August 2, 1919. As a contribution to the history of attempts to solve the so-called "national problem," it is worth while to recall the debates which arose in the board in connection with this draft decree. The basic idea of the decree was that the aspirations of backward nations for rebirth is not a regressive phenomenon as it has been regarded by orthodox Marxists and representatives of the [Russian] C[ommunist] P[arty] in Ukraine. Because of this, up to our own day many unsuccessful steps have been taken in education policy, all of one stamp—fear of expressing one's mind on the "national problem." And the problem is still being set aside somewhere. But we have at last decided to place this problem on the agenda and give it a communist base. From the capitalist system we have inherited a national oppression, which has provoked a series of aspirations for creative work. Yet not only are we failing to satisfy these aspirations; we are turning

---

hh   Ibid, pp. 114–115

them into weapons in the hands of our enemies. We must control these aspirations and give them a class character. On the basis of all this, Comrade Shumsky regarded as imperative the immediate publication of a decree, by which the Central Executive Committee would order the People's Commissariat of Education systematically and in a planned manner to pursue a policy which would most contribute to an all-round development of the culture of the Ukrainian people in all branches of national life.

During the board's discussion of the draft, there were heated debates which in the main came to the conclusion that publication of the decree, in the opinion of its opponents, was quite unnecessary. On the contrary [they thought], the draft might inflame the passions of the nationalists at a time when it would be more appropriate to pour cold water over their heads. Practically speaking, why should the Central Executive Committee issue orders to the People's Commissariat of Education, as if all were not well there? The publication of a decree covering the defense of one national culture [they believed] would be useless since the problem of the culture of other nationalities had not been raised. Solution of the language problem, which by the decree was to be entrusted to the organ of the People's Commissariat of Education (note 2, point 2 of the decree), was, in the opinion of its opponents (members of the board—Comrades Hopner, Demba, Dehtyarev, Nazarov, and Deputy People's Commissar [of Education] Salko), a matter only for the local proletariat through [the channels of] soviet deputies and executive committees.

In reply, Comrade Shumsky again affirmed that the decree aimed at eliminating the political factor from the "national problem," making it purely an issue of culture, and that therefore there was no danger here of arousing passions. With regard to Ukrainian culture, hidden sabotage had often been observed, but this would be impossible after publication of such a decree, because it would then be sabotage n gainst the government. The language problem could not be left to (lie village or local executive committee; as teachers we must oppose this and not follow such a "democratic" path. The decree aimed at raising the cultural level of the masses and increasing the number of class professionals, but this would remain impossible as long as teachers were labelled "Petlyurists."

We would never remove the [label] so long as we expressed no clear opinion on the problem of national culture and so long as numerous cadres of teachers remained unorganized and unused. Comrade Shumsky considered the decree perfectly acceptable in principle and in practice and regarded it as a great mistake of the Communist Party, which is in power, that up to this time it had not issued such a decree. Such a decree would establish the equal rights of cultures in practice, not on paper, would eliminate the hegemony of Russian culture and would provide broad opportunities for the development of Ukrainian culture. Such was the point of view of the Communists-Borotbisty.

Comrade Shumsky's ideas were supported by board members Comrades Hrynko and Mizernytsky. Members of the Commission of Fifty under the Central Executive Committee, who also regarded publication of the decree as imperative, participated in the discussion of the draft. They cited several examples of how disregard for Ukrainian culture by local authorities had harmed the general political work of the [Ukrainian] Soviet Republic.

Comrade Beskrovnyi, a member of the Commission recently returned from a trip to the provinces, expressed the belief that the bemoaning which could be sensed in the draft decree had foundation in fact, especially in Right Bank [Ukraine].

Upon conclusion of the debates the board voted against the decree five (Communists-Bolsheviks) to three (Communists-Borotbisty).

Thus deprived of an opportunity to offer the draft to the Central Executive Committee on behalf of the Commissariat of Education, Comrade Shumsky introduced it on August 7 on his own behalf, as People's Commissar of Education.

The draft was to be examined in the Central Executive Committee, but the military events of August 1919 made this impossible. It could not be placed on the agenda of the meeting of the Central Executive Committee before the Soviet government's evacuation from Kyiv.

Appendix 5
Memorandum of the Ukrainian Communist Party (Borotbisty) to the Executive Committee of the Third Communist International[ii]

In the course of the development of the world revolution the Soviet government of Ukraine has become, by force of circumstances, a source of supply for Soviet Russia, which is hated by the entire capitalist world, and more importantly, the bridge which links it with the approaching dawn of the European revolution.

To strike at this source, this bridge, and to destroy it—this is the aim of the Russian and world-wide counterrevolution.

To endeavor again and again to re-build it—this is the urgent necessity for the motive forces of the all-Russian [*Rosiyska*] Revolution.

Hence the intermittence and extraordinary complexity of the revolutionary movement in Ukraine; hence its involvement, fraught with consequences, by attendant factors and external forces and blows.

During the fierce reaction of the Hetmanate and at the time of both outbreaks of the proletarian revolution, leadership was in the hands of external forces, in large measure alien to the basic conditions of life of the Ukrainian people and to the natural course of their revolutionary movement.

This circumstance, this constant pressure of external forces, greatly entangles the already extraordinarily complex interrelations of socio-economic and national-political phenomena in Ukraine; it conditions us to regard Ukraine rather as the object now of reactionary blows, now of revolutionary counteractions, than as the subject of a genuine and organic revolutionary development, and thereby does not provide an opportunity to exhaust, enroll in

---

ii Memorandum Ukrainkoi Komunistychnoi Partii (Borotbystiv) do Vykonavchoho Komitetu III-bo Komunistychnoho Internatsionalu, Kyiv, Borotba, 1920, pp. 7–22.

the struggle and utilize all reserves of the local social forces capable of fighting for a communist reorganization of society.

Moreover, this constant pressure of external forces, in large measure remote from a true understanding of the interrelations of local socio-economic and national-political phenomena, not only has impeded the course of class differentiation, not only has ignored or neutralized those socio-economic categories which by duty should be active on the side of the Soviet government; through a series of numerous tactical errors, inevitable in the circumstances, it has driven them into the camp of active counterrevolution.

The serious, though doubtless temporary, failure of the attempt, for a second time, to organize a Soviet government in Ukraine was due largely to these circumstances; therefore, a precise and profoundly realistic study of this experience is the most urgent task of those who claim leadership of the communist revolution in Ukraine and, in turn, of those who issue the general directives of the responsible leaders of the Third International.

A study of this experience [and] an analysis and appraisal of the tactical considerations which it has prompted [are] easiest of all to conduct along two lines, the socio-economic and the national-political, which are, to be sure, quite inseparable in the single stream of life.

I

In the socio-economic sphere, Ukraine represents at once a peculiar and largely independent national-economic organism with a specific economic life and a rather complex system of social relations.

In Ukraine, which is an agricultural country not only at present but in the perspective of the further growth of its productive forces, the proletariat makes up no more than 15 per cent of the total toiling population in the process of socio-economic development; its ranks are divided on the one hand into an industrial proletariat, which is in large measure organized (by the very nature of its life), and on the other hand into an agricultural proletariat, which is widely scattered and little organized. The next social force in order of natural affinity for the aims of the socialist revolution in Ukraine is the scattered, semi-proletarianized poor peasantry, which forms about 30 per cent of the total population. Next comes the fairly compact mass of the so-called middle peasantry, of considerable importance in the total agricultural production of Ukraine, with the deep-rooted psychology of the proprietor and landowner. This class represents 45 per cent of the total population.

This ratio of the toiling social elements in Ukraine lends a peculiar, specifically agrarian color to the whole development of the socialist revolution and is the inevitable result of the economic structure of Ukraine, where the major part of all industry is connected with the land and engaged in the processing of agricultural products. The mass production of raw materials. — primarily agricultural, with a minimum of processing— is the dominant characteristic of the economy of Ukraine. Thus only a very insignificant part of the Ukrainian proletariat is concentrated in great industrial centers such as the Donets-Kryvyi Rih area, the northern part of Chernihiv Province and several large cities. The over-whelming majority of the proletarian forces is employed and scattered throughout various types of enterprises connected with the, processing of agricultural products and, to a rather large extent, borders unconsciously on the next social category, the village semi-proletariat. This latter group (the village semi-proletariat) obtains the main share of its livelihood not from its own individual farms (in complete shell-like isolation), but from its labor on large intricately organized estates, on which the division of Iabor is highly developed and which are being transformed into real Agricultural factories. Here the semi-proletarian elements of the village feel the profoundly organizing influence of a developed capitalistic enterprise and a large labor collective.

In addition, it is noteworthy that on the one hand the isolation of the urban industrial proletariat and on the other hand the unawareness of the transition of the agricultural proletariat and semi-proletariat of the village are strengthened to a significant degree by the peculiar and enduring national, cultural and customary mode of rural life, which is quite different from the tenor of life of the thin stratum of the Russified, urban industrial proletariat.

In the purely agrarian region of Ukraine, which in contrast to Great Russia did not experience the commune system, the economic differentiation of the village is well-advanced; in turn, the only remaining task is the ideological clarification and organizational consolidation of this differentiation.

In this process, of special significance is the fact that the average size of land allotment per person throughout the entire Ukraine amounts to only 1.75 desyatins (Kyiv Province, 1.2; Podol'ye Province, 1.2; Volyn' Province, 1.7; Chernihiv Province, 2.0; Poltava Province, 1.5; Kharkiv Province, 2.9; Katerynoslav Province, and Kherson Province, 2.3). Therefore, with respect to the amount of land owned, that category which we call the middle peasantry is very close to the poor peasantry and maintains itself, on a par with the middle peasantry only by virtue of the relatively high level of agricultural cultivation.

Thus in Ukraine the proletarian forces, which are the natural agents of the communist revolution, represent about 45 per cent [of the total local population], including the village semi-proletariat which is under the collective organizational arrangement in large agricultural enterprises. Only these forces, consonant with the eeconomic structure of the country, have a grouping and concentration different from that in the majority of European countries, particularly in Great Russia.

From the outset of the revolutionary movement this fact has set before the leading groups of the proletariat the challenging and extraordinarily complex task of the immediate enrollment of the village proletariat and semi-proletariat in active communist work. The complete disregard of this task is the basic cause of the latest defeat of the Soviet government in Ukraine.

The organized consolidation of communist achievements in Ukraine which are being accomplished through the violence of the Revolution (probably unlike [the situation] anywhere else) will be possible only if there is no turning away from this task, and if the leading forces of the communist revolution exert all their efforts toward its execution. However, the fulfillment of this task can be envisaged only if the leadership over this process is in the hands of those communist forces which are organically linked with the sum total of the socio-economic conditions and the potentialities of Ukraine.

Only with the enrollment of all local communist forces in creative work is it possible to conceive of the establishment of a proletarian state apparatus, which is alive to complex reality and which is, through the correct basic communist line, capable of embodying all the necessary latitude which was so brilliantly elaborated upon by the leader [i.e., Lenin] of the Russian faction of international communism at the Eighth Congress of the [Russian Communist] Party.

II

Along with all the socio-economic complexity of the situation, the aggravation of national-political conditions adds further complication. The complexity and acuteness of these and similar conditions have had at times a highly pernicious influence on the development of the proletarian revolution, which has depended far more upon the constant (persistent) intrusion, in the course of this development, of external forces, alien to the sum total of local conditions.

Consonant with the peculiar socio-economic structure, there has developed in the course of history an extraordinarily enduring, national cultural setting which is original in its very foundations.

An independent language, with all its imagery and fancy which help in understanding the world, the richly developed and strikingly characteristic song, the customs and folkways which are peculiar and sharply different from those of Great Russia and which reflect precisely the nature of economic conditions—in short the totality of the national cultural experience proved capable of withstanding century-long oppression by the Russifying landowning and bourgeois state machine. During this oppression, the totality of the cultural-national experience, in its own way, was preserved compact and alive only in the social depths, in the Ukrainian proletariat, in the heart of the Ukrainian proletariat and semi-proletariat, in the heart of those social groups which are the bearers of the communist revolution.

Powerless to break the constancy of the cultural-national feeling of the Ukrainian proletariat and peasantry, the state machine succeeded in checking this cultural growth, and transformed the cities from centers for the crystallization of cultural attainment in the country into culturally-isolated islands and coercive seats of an alien culture, artificially implanted and therefore parasitic.

There developed a serious national-political inertia which is reflected rather sharply even in the figures for the ratio of the [total] population to the secondary schools in Ukraine: Ukrainians, 71.1[jj] per cent of the population, have 121 schools; Great Russians, 12.6 per cent of the population, 950 schools; that is, the quota of secondary schools for the entire native population is 10,8 per cent, while the quota for the thin stratum of the Great Russian population is 84.7 per cent. In other words, the nationalities and the schools are in inverse ratio.

It follows that prior to the socialist revolution in Ukraine were such that the Ukrainian proletariat and semi-proletariat, which are now the motive forces of the communist revolution, were faced either with the nationalist tendencies of the Ukrainian bourgeoisie and bourgeois intelligentsia or with the actual domination of the Great Russian language and culture and with the inertia resulting from Russification in the entire governmental apparatus in Ukraine. The one threatens and frequently succeeds in obscuring the purity of the class consciousness of the working masses through the nationalist opiate; the other does not provide or create the conditions for the growth of the extraordinarily enduring forms of culture which are peculiar to the Ukrainian proletariat and semi-proletariat and for their use as a powerful factor in the struggle for international unity of the working class.

The government which attempts to control the course of the proletarian revolution in Ukraine and sets as its task the enrollment of ever broader ranks of the proletarian' and semi-proletarian masses in communist construction is in this sense a pledge of success; in connection with the development of national forms of culture, such a government should adopt a strong position, a policy

---

jj   Cf figure of 77.1 per cent in Appendix 4, p. 323

commensurate with all the complexity of the socio-political situation in Ukraine and with the importance of cultural-educational work, unthinkable when based on the previous standards of alien national forms. During the communist revolution the national question is a question of tactics. However, simply to take into account the persistence of the national cultural experience of the Ukrainian proletariat and semi-proletariat is sufficient to [compel us to] search for suitably easier ways of drawing them into the orbit of international communism not on the plane of hopeless and perilous attempts of further de-nationalization, but in the large perspective of the natural, organic survival of national forms and their victory at the heights of international unity of the working class of all countries and nations. Therefore, in the sphere of national culture, a broad and planned policy of encouraging the development of proletarian culture in national forms, which are native and close to the Ukrainian proletariat and peasantry, will be not an impediment but an active factor in the communist revolution.

This policy, incontestably imperative in view of the growth of the cultural level of the toiling masses of Ukraine without which the development of their class consciousness would be impossible, is likewise dictated by the pressing need to disarm counterrevolutionary enemies, who so obtrusively and at times so successfully attempt to substitute the national struggle for the social task of the working class. In this sense, it is extremely significant that the national slogan, which was raised by all the anti-Soviet uprisings, was successful in just those insurgent regions (Kyiv, Poltava and Chernihiv Provinces) where the poor peasants participated, while, conversely, the slogan scarcely figured in the purely kulak uprisings of Kherson Province.

It is altogether natural that the carrying out of this tactical line, perhaps to a greater degree than in the field of socio-economic phenomena, demands the establishment of a proletarian governmental apparatus which is extremely sensitive to the phenomena of local reality and which is capable of avoiding both a relapse into the old inertia resulting from Russification and the mistakes on the side of Ukrainian chauvinism. But the establishment of such an apparatus without the fullest enrollment in this work of all local forces and those close to them would be a hopeless task.

The striking peculiarity of the socio-economic and national-cultural structure of Ukraine clearly raises the political side of the question concerning the necessity of establishing Ukraine as a separate Soviet Republic, as an independent member of the growing world-wide federation of Soviet Republics. The sum total of the specific conditions and peculiarities of the construction of economic life and the grouping of social forces which determines the course and themes for the development of the social revolution must with inevitable finality find its state-political achievement in all spheres of life, for only under such conditions is there a possibility for the maximum use of all the real forces and conditions of the country in the interests of the dictatorship of the proletariat as the best planned organization for the growth of the productive forces. Each tactical mistake in this sphere, every interference or pressure by an outside force discordant with local conditions, complicates the work of further differentiation, [and] interrupts the ideological clarification and the organizational consolidation of already defined class groups—in other words, temporarily substitutes the national for the social struggle.

IV [sic]

A simple analysis of the socio-economic structure and the national-political situation in Ukraine clearly reveals all the peculiarity of the grouping and development of the local motive forces of the revolution in general and of the proletarian forces in particular. These peculiarities determine the unique lot of Ukrainian socio-political parties.

In the pre-revolutionary period the comparatively weak concentration of the village proletariat and semi-proletariat, the low and artificially maintained level of cultural development, together with the exploitation of their forces by the centralizing state machine inevitably impeded the organizational-ideological, consolidation of the spontaneous revolutionary impulses of the proletarian and semi-proletarian masses and caused the increasing penetration of active revolutionary elements into Russian revolutionary parties.

The inevitable development of Ukrainian socialist parties and appearance on the scene of active leadership over the revolutionary movement was delayed. Despite all of this, from the outset of the all-Russian Revolution, the leadership over this movement in Ukraine speedily passed into the hands of Ukrainian parties, and the period of conciliatory socialism transpired under the badge not of Russian but of Ukrainian SR's and SD's, mirroring all the specific peculiarities of the local socio-economic structure and the ideological climate.

A similar delay, caused by the peculiar nature of the grouping and development of the motive forces of the proletarian revolution in Ukraine and by the whole international situation seriously reflected therein, has occurred with the growth of the Ukrainian Communist Party as the center for the enrollment of the local social forces which are bringing about the communist revolution.

The disunity of the agricultural and the small urban proletariat, the proximity of a large part of the latter to the Great Russian proletariat, the alien — in large-measure occupational — character of the establishment of Soviet government in Ukraine for a second time with all its inevitable tactical errors, and, finally, the dangerous period of bourgeois-landowner reaction failed to create favorable conditions for the enrollment of large numbers of the Ukrainian proletariat and semi-proletariat in active communist construction.

Moreover, these conditions in large part extinguished the enormous charges of potential and actual revolutionary energy contained in the circles of the village proletariat and semi-proletariat. These very circumstances retarded the already complex and difficult process of the formation and organizational-ideological crystallization of the communist party, which is growing organically out of the sum total of socio-economic and cultural conditions of Ukraine.

Nevertheless, from the outset of the proletarian revolution in Russia the tendency to create a local communist party has been quite clear, and the center of its crystallization plainly in evidence. Furthermore, with the prolonged interruption in the development of the revolution in Ukraine, at all major junctures of this development the organizational-ideological center of the Ukrainian Communist Party has appeared with ever increasing activity as a section of international communism and has fought in the ranks of the Third International for the establishment of the dictatorship of the proletariat.

The peculiarity of the socio-economic structure of Ukraine is also evident from the fact that the organizational nucleus of the Ukrainian Communist Party, which after a certain inevitable delay is now linked organically with the masses of the agricultural proletariat (the overwhelming majority of Ukrainian proletarian forces), was formed within the ranks of the disintegrating party of Ukrainian SR's. This party's sphere of interest was the agricultural proletariat and semi-proletariat until the outbreak of the communist revolution.

A second creative force of the Ukrainian Communist Party again consonant with the peculiar nature of the socio-economic groupings and the national cultural peculiarities of Ukraine is the "Left Independent" wing of the Ukrainian Social Democratic Workers' Party.

The reason for the existence of this "wing" lies on the one hand in the persistence of the national cultural experience among a certain (firm) section of the Ukrainian proletariat, including the industrial proletariat, and on the other hand in the disregard on the part of the all-Russian revolutionary Social Democracy for the acuteness and complexity of the national question in Ukraine.

This protracted crystallization of communist forces, growing organically out of the whole mass of the socio-economic structure and national-cultural conditions of Ukraine, a process which by the end of the second proletarian revolution in Ukraine had reached a measure of finality in the formation of the Ukrainian Communist Party (Borotbisty), clearly outlines both the perspectives of the further development of the communist revolution and the nature of the relations between the two communist centers of Ukraine.

The natural delay on the part of the overwhelming majority of the Ukrainian proletariat and semi-proletariat in entering organized participation in the communist revolution and communist construction, the historically formed bond between a large number of an important segment of the urban industrial proletariat of Ukraine and the Great Russian proletariat, the urgent need to broaden the basis of the revolution during the extremely difficult struggle against world counterrevolution, at the same time, the old inertia—not easily overcome—of the centralizing state machine have created the historically inevitable characteristics of the largely occupation type construction of the Soviet government in Ukraine and at the same time, the historically inevitable, temporary organization of the Russian Communist Party in Ukraine, which in fact has been and is the Communist Party (Bolshevik) of Ukraine.

These historically inevitable characteristics of the enrollment of Ukraine, under occupation, in the orbit of the communist revolution and the occupation-type construction of its Soviet government have hastened and at the same time profoundly complicated the development of the communist revolution in Ukraine and the communist center, which is growing organically out of the totality of the socio-economic and cultural national structure of Ukraine.

However, this process has been going on in silence; the broad ranks of the Ukrainian proletariat and semi-proletariat are drawing their own conclusions based on the experience of the revolution which has developed through the establishment of the Ukrainian Communist Party (Borotbisty), the organically emerging center for the enrollment and organizational-ideological unification of communist forces of Ukraine.

To what extent this center is inevitably the organic consequence of the sum total of the peculiarities of the socio-economic structure of Ukraine is evident from the fact that, having emerged from the ranks of the nationalist Ukrainian socialist parties, it has become at the same time the center which is uniting and more and more is enrolling wide proletarian circles of all nationalities living in the territory of Ukraine. This proves that the distinction—artificially created by tsarism—between the industrial and agricultural proletariat of Ukraine is rapidly disappearing. This very tendency serves as the pledge that in the further course of the communist revolution the mighty surge toward active creative work by the broadest proletarian and semi-proletarian masses of Ukraine will lead inevitably to the fusion of all proletarian forces into a single type, cultural in its deepest foundations and determined by the totality of the development of the productive forces of Ukraine, which will display a certain internal unity with all the variety of their social peculiarities.

The international situation and the extreme intensity of the struggle between world revolution and world counterrevolution demand both the speediest entry of the Ukrainian proletarians into the ranks of active fighters for the communist revolution and the speediest reconstruction of the Ukrainian Soviet Republic.

This reconstruction, consonant with all the experience of the past period of the revolution, should and will be undertaken by the single Ukrainian communist center which in the course of the development of the revolution has grown out of the total conglomeration of the socio-economic and cultural-national forces, conditions and potentialities of Ukraine.

Kyiv, August 28, 1919

C[entral] C[ommittee] of the Ukrainian Communist Party (Borotbisty).

SPECIAL SUPPLEMENT
Soviet Responses to Maistrenko's Borotbism

For over sixty years the Communist rulers of the Soviet Union proclaimed they had solved the national question in the USSR.[1] The narrative of the "building of socialism and the achievement of factual equality between nations" was communicated throughout Soviet society and internationally.[2] It was therefore particularly awkward for the Kremlin when the credentials of the Communist Party to having achieved a resolution of the nationalities problem were challenged by socialist critics such as Ivan Maistrenko. Such dissent within the Soviet Union was subject to various levels of repression, this was combined with an ongoing information war of *dezinformatsiya* to counter critics at home and abroad, Maistrenko's *Borotbism* became a target of the Kremlin information war.

For decades many historians had viewed the revolution in Ukraine as part and parcel of the Russian Revolution, a view mirroring to some degree Soviet historiography. The publication in 1954 of *Borotbism A Chapter in the History of Ukrainian Communism* provided not only one of the first significant accounts of the Ukrainian Revolution in English, but also addressed a parallel deficiency of the pivotal role of Ukrainian socialism. At this time study of such currents as the Borotbisty remained marginal in the USSR, official Soviet history of the revolution had crystallized during the ascendancy of Stalinism. Molded by 'Marxism-Leninism', history was encaged within the parameters of *partiinost* and served as a source of legitimacy for the system. As an increasing number of studies appeared in the west which challenged Soviet and Western orthodoxy on Ukrainian history, Soviet historiography sought to counter them.

Simultainous with the publication of Maistrenko's *Borotbism*, a work appeared in the Ukrainian SSR by Andriy Likholat which continued the Stalinist approach to the UCP(Borotbisty). In *The defeat of the nationalist counterrevolution in Ukraine* (1917–1922) Likholat writes that:

Having lost any influence among the working masses, the petty-bourgeois nationalist parties were forced to disguise their anti-people nature by false statements about changing their programmatic position. Inside each of these parties formed "left" factions and currents, which declared themselves supporters of the Bolsheviks and Soviet power. These factions soon took shape in independent parties, which in some cases, in order to deceive the masses, acquired communist names. The Borotbisty group, which emerged from the party of Ukrainian "left" SRs in May 1918, in March 1919, adopted the name "Socialist-Revolutionaries-Communists."[3]

The Soviet approach to the the Borotbisty was also being shaped by more current concerns. The Tito-Stalin split was only a few years earlier, Maistrenko and the Vpered group had good relations with Milovan Djilas and Yugoslav communists. Djilas highlighted the fate of Ukraine and predicted a growing impetus towards independence by the national Communist bureaucracy in East Europe.[4] The first reference to Maistrenko's *Borotbism* was in a subsequent work by Oleksandr Slutsky, *On the Third Congress of the CP(b)U*, in which he writes:

> The struggle of the Borotbisty against Soviet power and the Communist Party in 1919–1920 and in the current stage is a matter of fervent approval by bourgeois historians. They see it as an affinity with the notorious "national communism". In particular, the contemporary American magazine Ukrainian Quarterly tries to reclaim *Borotbism* as the first statement of "national communism". In the preface to the book of the bourgeois nationalist I. Maistrenko *Borotbism*, published in 1954 in the United States with the aim of promoting *Borotbism* it is stated: "*Borotbism*, though rooted in Ukrainian soil and character, has parallels in recent history ... The theory and practice of national communism was first developed in Ukraine ".[5]

With a number of reviews appearing in scholarly journals and Maistrenko's work established as a key source to an emerging generaton of interested scholars, a refutation of Maistrenko was required.[6] This was published in the official *Ukrainian Historical Journal* in the Ukrainian SSR, in a lengthy review by R. G. Symonenko entitled "Against Bourgeois Nationalist Misrepresentations of the History of Ukraine".[7]

Symonenko considered the decision of the Research Program on the USSR to publish *Borotbism* part of a new approach by "Ukrainian bourgeois nationalists", this was not only to show that in 1917–1920 it was Ukrainian socialist parties who enjoyed popular support not the Bolsheviks, but an effort by "the Ukrainian emigre nationalist counter-revolution to breathe life into the theory and practice of modern "national communism", a program for a Ukrainian Titoism. Something the Kremlin could not tolerate.[8]

Symonenko's review of *Borotbism* was in the orthodox vain of the official Soviet history. This presented the Russian Bolsheviks in the leading role of the revolutionary process during 1917-1920, the UPSR and USDRP characterized as "petty-bourgeois parties" who attempted to retard the socialist revolution. The importance of the national question is minimized and written of pejoratively. Symonenko claims the scholarly sources of *Borotbism* to be weak because Maistrenko cites the works of leaders of Ukrainian socialist parties such as Khrystiuk, Vynnychenko, Shapoval and Fadenko. Of course it is not noted that Maistrenko could not access archives in Soviet Ukraine for fear of his life.[9]

Symonenko could not make this claim with regard to Maistrenko's chapter of "Reminiscences of the Borotbist Organization in Kobelyaky". Here the author resorts to traditional Stalinist falsification. Asserting Maistrenko revealed a "distrust of the true Revolutionary creativity of Ukrainian workers," evidenced in the "constant hostility of the Borotbisty to Soviet power in Ukraine, their close cooperation with the enemies of the Ukrainian people", including the Petlyurist Ataman Bolbochan. Soviet readers of the time were in no position to read *Borotbism*, as such they could not know Symonenko referenced a page which stated the opposite, that the Borotbisty insurgents were attacking the conservative commander Bolbochan.[10] Similar untruths are continued with the ridiculous claim of the Borotbisty/Maistrenko's "support of the White Poles against Soviet Ukraine", whilst simultaneously stating he was associated with the Federalist Opposition inside the CP(b)U.

Symonenko makes the traditional charge against Maistrenko that he sought to "divide the unity in the revolutionary struggle of the Russian and Ukrainian workers, in the revolutionary process for the liberation of both great peoples".[11] Most "outrageous" in his view is Maistrenko's conclusion that those Ukrainian socialist parties who became dependent on Russian parties had lost their freedom of action especially in the national liberation of Ukraine.[12]

To habitually label all critics as "bourgeois nationalists" was difficult if there was no Ukrainian bourgeoisie at the time of the revolution, something Ukrainian socialists saw as Ukraine being 'bourgeoisless". Maistrenko is accused by Symonenko of guilt of association with these ideas of classlessness of the Ukrainian nation, the "the cornerstone of the writings of bourgeois falsifiers of history". This accusation of falsehood is also levelled at the credential of the left-wing of the UPSR and USDRP in 1917–1918.

Symonenko considered the planned "coup" of the left-wing of the Ukrainian Socialist Revolutionaries but a quarrel over the premiership and composition of the General Secretariat of the UNR. Following its failure it is claimed the "unity of the Socialist Revolutionaries and the Social Democrats, the "Left" and the "Right" was quickly restored."[13] This dishonest conclusion is drawn from Maistrenko's consideration that antagonism in Ukrainian political life was not as deeply ingrained as in Russia, due to there being few Ukrainian landlords and capitalists.[14] This according to Symonenko links Maistrenko not only with the ideas of Hrushevsky but the leading Marxist historian's in Soviet Ukraine in the 1920's, Matvyi Yavorsky and Moysey Ravych-Cherkassky who presented the CP(b)U as having dual roots in both Russian and Ukrainian socialist parties. This was viewed as heresy and they suffered official disapproval under Stalin and perished in the purges.[15]

Such works of historians of the 1920's generation are cited in *Borotbism*, it is also the generation that was disfavoured by official Soviet historiography. The writings of those who participated in the revolution were viewed as not fully scholarly, due to their personal experience it was claimed made them unable to correctly evaluate events.[16] What is not stated is these Ukrainian historians were victims of the ascendant Stalinist system at this time. Maistrenko's participation in the events he writes of afforded him even less credence in the eyes of official Soviet history.

Symonenko considers the account of Vynnychenko of the fall in 1919 of the Directory being due to the peasants mobilising against them, as evidence of the "the absurdity of talking about the export of Soviet power from Russia to Ukraine". This is also considered evidence of a lack of influence and size of the Borotbisty, whilst on the other hand the purportedly weak Borotbisty it is claimed had the capacity to mobilise an array of commanders and forces against the Ukrainian Soviet government.[17]

Symonenko claims that Maistrenko in his own book reveals this betrayal by the Borotbisty by colluding with amongst others Ataman Hyrhoryiv in his uprising against the Bolsheviks under the slogan "Soviets without Communists".[18] Conveniently Symonenko did not inform readers that an entire section of Maistrenko's book is entitled "Joint Action Against Hyrhoryiv" or that the Bolsheviks by this time had brought the Borotbisty into the government.[19]

Symonenko is forced to concede that the Borotbisty efforts to form a Ukrainian Red Army left a significant part of the masses pondering why two forces with the same programme for soviet power—should fight amongst themselves when facing the threat of Denikin. Interestingly Symonenko also points to the hostility between the Borotbisty and left-wing of the USDRP, the Nezalezhnyky as a factor in their failure.[20] According to Symonenko the reasons underpinning the very existence of the Borotbisty was not a genuine radicalism of the mass membership of the UPSR but a fear that the Ukrainian socialists would undermine the national revolution by driving the masses into the Bolshevik camp. [21]

From claims of the Borotbisty being a grand conspiracy Maistrenko is then condemned for falsification of history by his failure to inform readers of the fate of the Borotbisty: "He did not want to inform the reader about the great work that the communists did, re-educating those who came from the UKP(b), who resolutely broke with their Borotbisty past and sought to work honestly to contribute to socialist construction in Ukraine."[22]

Symonenko's demand for honesty did not allow him to reference to the actual fate of the Borotbisty who remained in the CP(b)U. That Pavel Postyshev, Stalin's personal representative in Ukraine in a report to the Plenum of the Central Committee of the CP(b)U said the Borotbisty and former *Ukapisty* who joined the CP(b)U, "not only failed to dissolve in our Bolshevik melting pot and become Bolsheviks, but they actually came to the CP(b)U keeping intact their own position and continuously conducted counter-revolutionary and perfidious activities aimed at undermining the

Party and Soviet rule".[23] Based on confessions obtained an "All-Ukrainian Borotbist Center" was concocted in order to justify the terror against the remaining Borotbisty.[24]

In 1938 the paper *Bilshovyk Ukrainy* charged the Borotbisty of being agents of Ukrainian nationalism and imperialism, the split in the UPSR being a "Jesuit manoeuvre of the Ukrainian nationalist counter-revolution".[25] Maistrenko's friend Hryhory Kostiuk wrote in his study of *Stalinist Rule in the Ukraine* that the "Soviet perversion of Borotbist history and ideology shows that *Borotbism* (Ukrainian Communism) was deeply rooted in Ukraine and that it had continued to represent a vital force in the politics of the country until 1938."[26]

The response to Maistrenko's *Borotbism* appeared to confirm that twenty years later it remained a matter of concern to the Soviet authorities. In the 1970's the increased study of Ukrainian communism in the West was perceived by the party leadership in the Ukrainian SSR as propaganda for a Ukrainian "national communism", steps were taken to counteract such a threat.[27]

An official pamphlet was published in 1971 as a critique of the Borotbisty in Soviet Ukraine, and then in 1975 a book in English by Inessa Zenushkina, *Soviet Nationalities Policy and Bourgeois Historians*.[28] This was published in response to growing concern at the changing approach towards Ukrainian history in American publications, problems previously restricted to "Ukrainian bourgeois nationalist emigres" being now reflected in the works of leading scholars.[29] In ritualist form Maistrenko was branded a "bourgeois nationalist" who "was formerly active in the petty-bourgeois Borotba party then in existence in Ukraine and belonged to its most anti-Soviet wing."[30] Readers were referred to Symonenko's earlier "detailed critical analysis".

Yet the years of *dezinformatsiya* and repression did not fully destroy the memory of the Borotbisty in Ukraine. This can be seen in the echoes amongst the dissident movement of intellectuals and youth of the 1960's. In his internationaly recognised book issued in 1965 *Internationalism or Russification* by the Marxist dissident Ivan Dzyuba, it was noted how Lenin's appeal for unity with the Borotbisty was "later violated, and in particular the Borotbist Communists, who met with a positive attitude from him, were removed from the leadership of Soviet Ukraine and later exterminated almost to a man."[31]

Maistrenko's *Borotbism* which was originally written in Ukrainian remains unpublished in Ukraine, when it finally is published he shall at last have the final word against his Stalinist detractors.

CHRISTOPHER FORD

Bibliography

Items followed by numbers enclosed in brackets are listed in Juriy Lawrynenko, *Ukrainian Communism and Soviet Russian Policy Toward the Ukraine: An Annotated Bibliography 1917–1953*, New York, Research Program on the U.S.S.R., 1953. Roman numerals denote the major divisions of the Lawrynenko bibliography; arabic numerals, main entries within a particular division.

Starred items have been introduced by the editor.

A. General Works

Antonov-Ovseyenko, V[ladimir] A., *Zapiski o grazhdanskoi voine* [Notes on the Civil War], Moscow, 1932, Vol. III. [III-130]

Bakunin, Mikhail, *Gosudarstvennost' i anarkhiya* [Statehood and Anarchy], Petersburg [sic]-Moscow, 1922.

Bessedovsky, Grigoty, *Revelations of a Soviet Diplomat*, London, 1931. [cf. 1–4]

*Bunyan, James, and H.H. Fisher, *The Bolshevik Revolution 1917–1918: Documents and Materials*, Stanford, 1934.

•Chamberlin, William H., *The Russian Revolution 1917–1921*, 2 vols., New York, 1935.

Denikin, General A[nton] I., *Ocherki russkoi smuty* [sketches of Russian Turmoil], Berlin, [1926] Vol. V.

Die deutsche Okkupation der Ukraine: Geheimdokumente, Strasbourg, 1937. [III-235]

Doroshenko, D[mytro I.], *Z istorii'ukrains'koipolity chnof dumky za chasiv svitovof viyny* [On the History of Ukrainian Political Thought During the World War], Prague, 1936. [II-5]

Fedenko, Panas, *Ukratns'kyi hromads'kyi ruhh u XX stolitti* [The Ukrainian Social Movement in the Twentieth Century], Podebrady, Czechoslovakia, 1934. [Il-lfl] Short title: *Hromads'kyi rukh*.

*Heifetz, Elias, *The Slaughter of the Jews in the Ukraine in 1919*, New York, 1921.

"Hrushevsky, Michael, *A History of Ukraine*, New Haven, 1941.

Istoriya KP(b)U v materialakh i dokumentakh: khrestomatiya, 1917–1920 rr. [History of the CP(b)U in Materials and Documents: An Anthology, 1917–1920], ed. by S. Barannyk, Kh. Mishkis and H. Slobods'kyi, [Kyiv] 1934, Vol. II. [v-32] „ Short title: *Istoriya KP(b)U, Krazresheniyu natsional'novo voprosa* [Toward a Solution of the National Question], 2nd enlarged ed., Kyiv, 1920. [III-354]

Khrystyuk, Pavlo, *Zamitky i materiialy do istoriï ukraïns'koï revoliutsiï 1917–1920 rr.* (Ukrains'ka Revolyutsiya: rozvidky y materiyaly) [Notes and Materials on the History of the Ukrainian Revolution, 1917-1920 (The Ukrainian Revolution: Notes and Materials)], 4 vols., Vienna, 1921–1922. [Ill-41]

Kin, D., *Denikinshchina* [The Denikin Era], Leningrad, [l927 or 1928]. [II-250]

Kovaliv, Levko, *Do chleniv Ukrainskoi Komunistychnoi' Partii (borotbystiv)* [To Members of the Ukrainian Communist Party (Borotbisty)], Kyiv, "Borotba," 1920.

Kubanin, M., *Makhnovshchina: krest'yanskoye dvizheniye v stepnoi Ukraine v gody grazhdanskoi voiny* [Makhnoism: A Peasant Movement in the Ukrainian Steppes During the Civil War], Leningrad, 1927. [III-327]

Lebid', D[mytro], *Itogi i uroki tryokh let anarhho-makhnovshchiny* [The Results and Lessons of Three Years of Anarcho-Makhnoism], Kharkiv, 1921. [IH-328]

Lypynsky, Vyacheslav K., *Lysty do brativ-khliborobiv: pro ideyu i orhanizatsiyu ukraï'ns'koho monarkhizmu* [Letters to Brother Agriculturists: The Concept and Organization of Ukrainian Monarchism], Vienna, 1926. [I-26]

Makhno, Nester, *Pod udarami kontrrevolyutsii, apreliyun' 1918 g.* [Under the Blows of Counterrevolution, April-June 1918], Paris, 1936. [III-332]

Mazepa, I[saak], *Pidstavy nashoho vidrodzhennya* [Foundations of Our Regeneration], [Munich?] 1946, Vol. I. Short title: *Pidstavy*.

——— ,*Ukraina v ohni i hurt revolyutsii', 1917–1921 r.* [The Ukraine in the Fire and Storm of Revolution, 1917–192l], 2nd ed., [Munich] 1950–1951, Vols. I-II. [III-49] Short title: *Ukraina*.

Memorandum Ukrainskoi Komunistychnoi Partii (borotbystiv) do Vykonavchoho Komitetu Ill-ho Komunistychnoho Internatsionalu [Memorandum of the Ukrainian Communist Party (Borotbisty) to the Executive Committee of the Third Communist International], Kyiv, 1920. [III-374]

Mikhnovsky Mykola, *Samostiyna Ukraina* [An Independent Ukraine], Lviv, 1900; new ed., n.p. , 1948. [II-74]

Milyukov, P[avel N.], *Rossiya na perelome: bolshevistskii period russkoi revolyutsii* [Russia in Crisis: The Bolshevik Period of the Russian Revolution], Paris, 19–27, Vol. II.

BIBLIOGRAPHY 351

Mykhaylo, N., *Moskofily, narodovtsi i konsolidatsiya* [Moscophiles, Populists and Consolidation], Lviv, 1898.

Petrovsky D., *Revolyutsiya i kontrrevolyutsiya na Ukraine* [Revolution and Counterrevolution in the Ukraine], Moscow, 1920. [cf. V-91]

Proyekt rezolyutsii o politike partii [Draft Resolution on Party Policy], "Group of Federalists," February 1920. Excerpts in Shrah, pp. 30-31.

Radykaly iradyhalizm [Radicals and Radicalism], Lviv, 1896. (Khlopska biblioteka [Peasant Library], Vol. IV.)

Rafes, M[oisei] G., *Dva goda revolyutsii na Ukraine: evolyutsiya i raskol "Bunda"* [Two Years of Revolution in the Ukraine: Evolution and Split Within the Bund], Moscow, 1920. [III-74]

Ravich-Cherkassky, M[oisei], *Istoriya Kommunisticheskoi Partii (bolshevikov) Ukrainy* [History of the Communist Party (Bolshevik) of the Ukraine], Kharkiv, 1923- [V-18]

*Reshetar, John S., Jr. *The Ukrainian Revolution, 1917-1920: A Study in Nationalism.* Princeton, 1952. [III-80]

Sadovsky, V[alentyn], *Natsional'na polityka Sovyetiv na Ukraini* [Soviet National Policy in Ukraine], Warsaw, 1937. (*Pratsi Ukrainskoho Naukovoho Instytuiu* [Works of the Ukrainian Scientific Institute], Vol. XXIX.) fc-45]

Shakray, Vasyl' M., and Serhiy Mazlakh, *Do khvyli: shcho diyet'sya na Ukraini i z Ukrainoyu* [The Current Situation: What Is Happening in and to the Ukraine], Saratov, 1919. [lll-9l] Short title: *Do khvyli.* A typescript copy was used.

Shapoval, Mykyta, "Miy shlyakh: konspekt spomyniv do 1927" [My Path: A Synopsis of Recollections up to 1927], manuscript. Short title:"Miy shlyakh." For published form, see article by Mandryka.

Skrypnyk, Mykola O., *Dzherela taprychyny rozlamu v KPZU* [Origins and Reasons for the Split in the CPWU], Kharkiv, 1928. [VriI-66] Short title: *Dzherela.*, - *Statti y promovy* [Articles and Speeches], Kharkiv, 1929, Vol. II, Part I. [V-2l]

Trotsky, Leon, *Stalin: An Appraisal of the Man and His Influence*, ed. and tr. by Charles Malamuth, New York-London, 1941.

Tyutyunnyk, Yu[rko], *Zymovyi pokhid 1919-1920 rr.* [The Winter Campaign of 1919-1920], Kolomyya-Kyiv, 1923.

Vsesoyuznaya Kommunisticheskaya Partiya (bol'shevikov) v feza-lyutsiyakh i resheniyakh s"yezdov, konferentsii i plenumov TsK (1898-. . .) [Resolutions and Decisions of Congresses, Conferences and Plenary Sessions of the Central Committee of the Communist Party of the Soviet Union (Bolshevik), 1898-. . .], 4th ed., Moscow, 1932, Vol. I; 6th ed., 1941, Vol. I. [IX-46]

Vynnychenko V[olodymyr K], *Vidrodzhennya natsii* [The Rebirth of a Nation], 3 parts, Kyiv-Vienna, 1920. [IIII-115]

Zaslavski, D[avid I.], M.P, *Drahomanov: kritiko-biograficheskii ocherk* [M.P. Drahomanov: A Critico Hiographical Sketch], Kyiv, 1924.

His M.P. Drahomanov: *k isforii uhrainskovo natsionalizma* [M.P. Drahomanov: Toward » History of Ukrainian Nationalism], Moscow, 1934,is a revised edition. [Il-117]

*Zaliznyak, Mykola, *Samostiyna Ukraina- ne sotsiyalistychne haslo?* [An Independent Ukraine: Is It Not a Socialist Slogan?], n.p. , UPSR, 1915. [II-115]

Zatonsky, Volodymyr, *Othrytoye pis'mo k TsK UKP(b)* [An Open Letter to the Central 'Committee of the UCP(b)]. Probable title of a pamphlet published in the period December 1919-January 1920.

B. Congresses and Conferences

1. Communist International

(1st) *Pervyi kongress Kominterna, marta 1919 g.: protokoly kongressov Kommunisticheskovo Internatsional a* [First Congress of the Comintern, March 1919: Proceedings of the Congresses of the Communist International], ed. by Ye. Korotki, B. Kun and O. Pyatnitski, Moscow, 1933-

2. CP(b)U

(6th) *Byulleten' VI Vseukrainskoi konferentsii Kommunisticheskoi Partii (bol'shevikov) Ukrainy (9–13 noyabrya 1921 g.)* [Bulletin of the Sixth All-Ukrainian Conference of the CP(b)U, November 9-13, 1921], Kharkiv, 1921. [V-17l]

3. RSDRP(b) and RCP(b)

*(7th) *Sed'maya. [Aprel'skaya] Vserossiiskaya i Petrogradskaya Obshchegorodskaya Konferentsii RSDRP(b)* [Seventh (April) Ail-Russian and Petrograd All-City Conferences of the RSDRP(b)], Moscow, 1934.

(8th) *VIII s'yezd Rossiiskoi Kommunisticheskoi Partii (bolshevikov): stenograficheskii otchot, Moskva, 18–23 marta 1919 goda* [Eighth Congress of the Russian Communist Party (Bolshevik): Verbatim Report, Moscow, March 18-23, 1919], Moscow 1919-

(8th) *Vos'moi Vserossiishii s"yezd Rossiiskoi Kommunisticheshoi Partii (bol'shevikov):protoholy zasedanii i rezolyutsii* [Eighth All-Russian Congress of the Russian Communist Party (Bolshevik): Proceedings of Sessions, and Resolutions], [Kazan'] 1919- [IX-143]

(9th) *Devyatyi s"yezd Rossiiskoi Kommunisticheskoi Partii (bol'shevikov): stenograficheskii otchot (29 marta 4 aprelya 1920 g.)* [Ninth Congress of the Russian Communist Party (Bolshevik): Verbatim Report (March 29- April 4, 1920)], Moscow, 1920. [IX-142]

(10th) *Desyatyi s"yezd Rossiiskoi Kommunisticheshoi Partii: stenograficheskii otchot, 8–16 marta 1921 g.* [Tenth Congress of the Russian Communist Party: Verbatim Report, March 8–16, 192I], Moscow, 1921. [IX-184]

(12th) *Dvenadtsatyi s"yezd Rossiiskoi Kommunisticheskoi Partii (bol'shevikov): stenograficheskii otchot 17–25 aprelya 1923 g.* [Twelfth Congress of the All-Russian Communist Party (Bolshevik): Verbatim Report, April 17–25, 1923], Moscow, 1923- [IX-186]

C. Articles

Anulov, F., "Soyuznyi desant na Ukraine: vospominaniya i dokumenty" [The Allied Landing in the Ukraine: Memoirs and Documents], *Letopis' revolyutsii* [Annals of the Revolution], Kharkiv, 1923, No. 5, pp. 167–211: 1924, Nos. 1(6), pp. 5–75; 2(7), pp. 5–38. [m-227]

Blakytnyi, Vasyl' M., "Komunistychna partiya Ukraihy i shlyakhy 'ii zmitsnennya" [The Communist Party of the Ukraine and Ways to Strengthen It], Kommunist, Kharkiv, November 17, 19, 1920. [III-344; X-68]

*Blakytnyi Vasyl' M., "Tezy i spivdopovid' v pytanni 'Cherhovi zavdannya partii' na V Vseukrains'kiy konferentsii' KP(b)U" [Theses and Supplementary Report on the Question "The Next Tasks of the Party" at the Fifth All-Ukrainian Conference of the CP(b)U]. [III-346]

Butsenko, A[fanasiy], "O raskole USDRP, 1917–1918" [Concerning the Split in the USDRP, 1917–1918], *Letopis' revolyutsii* [Annals of the Revolution], Kharkiv, No. 4, 1923, pp. 121–122. [IV-2]

Chechel', Myk[ola], "Chomu prypynyv svoye istnurannya revolyu-tsiynoradyans'kyi bl'ok?" [why Did the Revolutionary-Soviet Bloc Cease to Exist?], *Boritesya-poborete!* [Fight and Conquer!], Vienna, October 1920, No. 2, pp. 50–56. [III-403]

Doroshenko Volodymyr, "The Life of Mykhaylo Drahomanov," *The Annals of the Ukrainian Academy of Arts and Sciences in the U.S.*, New York, Vol. II, Spring 1952, No. 1(3) (*Mykhaylo Drahomanov: A Symposium and Selected Writings*), pp. 6–22.

Fedenko, P[anas], "Naddnipryanshchyna vid 1914 r." [Russian Ukraine After 1914], *Ukrainska zahal'na entsyklopediya* [Ukrainian General Encyclopedia], Lviv, 1934, Vol. Ill, cols. 630–641. Short title: "Naddnipryanshchyna."

Hrushevs'kyi, Mykhaylo, "Mizh Moskvoyu y Varshavoyu" [Between Moscow and Warsaw], *Boritesya-poborete!* [Fight and Conquer!], Vienna, October 1920, No. 2, pp. 1-18. [Ill-408] Short title: "Mizh Moskvoyu y Varshavoyu."

Hryhoryi'v, Nykyfor, [An Open Letter to Pavlo Khrystyuk], *Vilna spilka* [Free Union], Lviv, No. 1, October 1921, pp. 114-120.

"KP(b)U i denikinshchina: k pyatiletiyu vosstanovleniya Sovvlasti na Ukraine" [The CP(b)U and the Denikin Era: The Fifth Anniversary of the Restoration of Soviet Power in the Ukraine], *Letopis' revolyutsii* [Annals of the Revolution], Kharkiv, January-February 1925, No. 1(10), pp. 5-68. [V-59] Short title: "KP(b)U i denikinshchina."

Khvylya, A[ndriy], "Borotbisty," *Bolshaya sovetskaya entsiklopediya* [Large Soviet Encyclopedia], Moscow, 1927, Vol. VII, cols. 193-194. [cf. IH-349]

Kommunist, Kharkiv, May 20, 1920, No. 1; June 10, No. 2; March-

D. Letters, Speeches, Draft Projects, Resolutions

"K rabochim i krest'yanam Ukrainy" [To the Workers and Peasants of the Ukraine], dated December 14, 1919, *Kommunisticheskii internatsional* [Communist International], Petfograd, November-December 1919, Nos. 7-8, cols. 1121-1126; also in "KP(b)U i denikinshchina," pp. 62-65-

"K vsem partiinym organizatsiyam K.P.(b)U." [To All Party Organizations of the CP(b)U], December 15, 1919, by the Central Committee of the CP(b)U, in "KP(b)U i denikinshchina," pp. 57-58; also in *Istoriya KP(b)U*, pp. 541-542.

"Kommunisticheskii Internatsional ob Ukrainskikh partiyakh" [The Communist International on Ukrainian Parties],-dated Petrograd, January 5, 1920, *Kommunisticheskii internal sional* [Communist International], Petrograd, November-December 1919, Nos. 7-8, cols. 1125-1126; also in *Istoriya KP(b)U*, pp. 638-639-

"Komunistychnyi Internatsional vidmovlyaye borot'bystam v pryinyatti'ikh do svo'ikh lav: postanova Vykonkomu Kominternu" [The Communist International Refuses to Accept the Borotbisty into Its Ranks: Resolution of the Executive Committee of the Comintern], in *Istoriya KP(b)U*, pp. 639-640. [IH-357]

Lenin, Vladimir I., [Letter to Trotsky, December 1922], *Sotsialisticheshii vestnik* [Socialist Courier], Berlin, December 17, 1923, Nos. 23-24 (69-70), p. 14.

———, [Our Attitude Toward the Borotbisty], in Wolfe, pp. 177-178.

———, *Sochineniya* [Works], 2nd ed., Moscow, 1932, Vol. XXIV: "Proyekt programmy R.K.P.(b.)" [Draft Program of the RCP(b)], pp. 87-108.

"Zaklyuchitel'noye slovo po dokladu o partiinoi programme 19 marta" [Concluding Remarks on the Report of the Party Program of March 19], pp. 148-156.

———, *Sochineniya*, 4th ed., Moscow, 1946, Vol. VI; 1948, Vol. XIX; 1950, Vol. XXX.

———, *Stat'i i recbi ob Ukraine* [Articles and Speeches on Ukraine], ed. by Nikolai N. Popov, Kyiv, 1936. [IX-23]

"Pis'mo k rabochim i krest'yanam Ukrainy po pobodu pobedy nad Denikinym" [Letter to the Workers and Peasants of the Ukraine Concerning the Victory over Denikin], pp. 339-343- [III-363; IX-9I]

"Rezolyutsiya Ts.K. R.K.P.(b) o sovetskoi vlasti na Ukraine" [Resolution of the Central Committee of the RCP(b) on Soviet Power in the Ukraine], of November 29, 1919, pp. 331-333. IIX-12I]

"Zaklyuchitel'noye slovo na [VIII] vserossiiskoi konferentsii RKP(b) po voprosu o sovetskoi vlasti na Ukraine, 3 dekabrya 1919 g." [Concluding Remarks at the (Eighth) All-Russian Conference of the RCP(b) Concernijttg the Soviet Power in the Ukraine, December 3, 1919], pp. 334-335-[III-363]

"Zamechaniya na proyekt postanovleniya ispolkoma kominternapo voprosu o 'borot'bistakh' 22 fevralya 1920 g." [Remarks on a Draft Resolution of the Comintern Executive Committee on the "Borotbisty," February 22, 19201, p. 344. [ill-367]

"Ob otnoshenii k melko-burzhuaznym partiyam" [On the Attitude (of the CP(b)U) Toward Petty Bourgeois Parties], March 1919, in Rafes, p. 163-

"Obrashcheniye glavnokomanduyushchavo k naseleniyu Malorossii" [Appeal from the Commander-in-Chief to the Population of Little Russia], in Denikin, Vol. V, pp. 142-143.

"Ob"yedineniye kommunistov na Ukraine" [The Amalgamation of Communists in the Ukraine], *Kommunisticheskii internatsional* [Communist International], Petrograd, [May] 1920, No. 9, cols. 1655-1656. [III-378]

"Plyatforma Tsentral'noho Komitetu Ukraihs'koi'Partii'Sotsiyalistiv-Revolyutsioneriv (rozuminnya suchasnoho mentu i taktyka partif)" [Platform of the Central Committee of the Ukrainian Party of Socialist Revolutionaries: The Present State of Affairs and Party Tactics], approved June 3, 1918, in Khrystyuk, Vol. IV, pp. 91-94.

"Proyekt prohramy partii' U.S.R., pryinyatoi Kyivskoyu hrupoyu ukrains'kykh sotsiyalistiv-revolyutsioneriv" [Draft Party Program of the Ukrainian Socialist Revolutionaries, Endorsed by the Kyiv Group of the Ukrainian Socialist Revolutionaries], in Zhyvotko, p. 131.

"Proyekt Prohramy RUP" [Draft Program of the RUP], in Fedenko, *Hromads'kyi rukh*, p. 12.

Skrypnyk, Mykola O., "Natsionalistychnyi ukhyl v KPZU" [The Nationalist Deviation in the CPWU], speech of June 7, 1927 in the Central Committee of the CP(b)U, in Skrypnyk, *Dzherela*, pp. 3–77.

Stalin, J.V., "Tovarishchu Kaganovichu i drugim chlenam TsK KP(b)U" [To Comrade Kaganovich and Other Members of the Central Committee of the CP(b)U], *Sochineniya* [works], Moscow, 1948, Vol. VIII, pp. 149–154. [iX-p. 33l]

"V Ispolnitel'nyi Komitet III Kommunisticheskovo Internalsionala" [To the Executive Committee of the Third Communist International], from the UCP(b), dated August 1919, in *Kommunisticheskii internatsional* [Communist International], Petrograd, November–December 1919, Nos. 7–8, cols. 1111–1112. [IH-399]

"Vsem organizatsiyam kommunisticheskoi partii Ukrainy" [To All Organizations of the Communist Party of the Ukraine], directive of the RCP(b) dated Moscow, April 7, 1920, in Ravich-Cherkassky, pp. 235–238; also in *Istoriya* KP(b)U, pp. 555–557.

"Vseukrainskii Revolyutsionny Komitet k rabochim i krestyanam Ukrainy" [The All-Ukrainian Revolutionary Committee to the Workers and Peasants of the Ukraine], December 1919. in "KP(b)U i denikinshchina," pp. 58–62; also in *Istoriya* KP(b)U, pp. 551–553-

"Vystupleniye borotbistov vo Vseukrainskii Revkom" [Entry of the Borotbisty into the All-Ukrainian Revolutionary Committee], dated Moscow, December 17, 1919, in "KP(b)U i denikinshchina," pp. 67–68. [III-400]

Index of Names

Appendix 1 and persons mentioned in Appendixes 2-4 have been indexed.

An asterisk preceding a name indicates that a biographical sketch of that person can be found in Appendix 2.

*

*Blakytnyi, Vasyl' M. (pseud, of Ellans'kyi, Brat and Pronozn) 186, 189, 268, 308, 353
*Hukovych 207, 209, 242, 306
*Kotsyuba, Hordiy M 221, 243, 260
*Kovaliv, Levko 121, 123, 135, 136, 148, 234, 235, 248, 297, 301, 350
*Lazorsky, Vasyl' (pseud, of Demyanovs'ky) 260, 296
*Lytvynenko, Mykola (Kost Kotko, pen name) 184, 186, 198
*Lyubchenko, Panas Petrovych 81, 135, 167, 174, 192, 248, 273, 300, 307
*Matyash, Kostyantyn (Kost') 236, 244
*Matyash, Roman 172, 286, 290
*Mykhaylychenko, Hnat (Ihnatiy Mykhaylych, pseud.) 135, 136, 139, 148, 163, 174, 183, 186, 187, 192, 216, 301, 305, 311
*Ohiy, Yakiv 219, 220, 244, 290, 292, 294, 302
*Panchenko 130, 198, 248, 308
*Pankiv 207, 209
*Poloz, Mykhaylo 122, 130, 135, 136, 139, 168, 176, 198, 238, 241, 244, 248, 260, 267, 303
*Taran, Todos' (pseud, of Honchatenko) 219, 254, 297
*Taranenko, Korniy 177, 192
*Yakovlev 182, 198, 258, 261
*Zalyvchyi, Andriy 122

A

Aleksandriya 221
Alexander II 108
Anhel 169, 221
Antonovych, Dmytro 108, 109
Apostalovo 186
Artyom, Fyodor A. (pseud, of Sergeyev) 187, 258, 300
Astrov, N.I, 215
Aussem, Vladimir Kh. 187, 188, 189
Avdiyenko, M. 79, 288
Averin 189

B

Bakunin, Mikhail 102, 112, 349
Bashtanka (Poltavka) 221
Batyr 293, 294
Bilash 260
Bolbochan, Col. Peter (Ataman) 10, 169, 171, 172, 185, 186,

187, 189, 190, 198, 199, 213,
221, 222, 236, 239, 284, 285,
291, 310, 343, 345
Brusilov, Gen. 294
Bubnov, Andrei 226, 252, 253,
254
Butsenko, Afanasiy 353

C

Chechel, Mykola 136, 148, 149,
353
Chekhovs'kyi, Volodymyr M.
136, 148, 149, 353
Chicherin Georgii V 187, 190
Chubar, Vlas Ya 257, 258, 269,
272, 303
Chuhay, Viktor 122
Chumak, Vasyl' 156, 216, 301

D

Dalekyi (Maistrenko) 74, 277,
278, 279, 280, 281, 283, 290,
292, 293, 294
Denikin, Gen. Anton 9, 20, 21,
67, 75, 76, 77, 164, 179, 190,
199, 200, 205, 209, 213, 214,
215, 216, 218, 219, 220, 221,
222, 223, 225, 227, 228, 230,
231, 232, 234, 236, 242, 246,
253, 254, 257, 261, 279, 287,
288, 289, 290, 291, 292, 293,
297, 300, 301, 302, 303, 304,
305, 312, 345, 349, 350, 354,
355
Derkach, Stepan 281, 293
Doroshenko, Dmytro 102, 103,
349, 353
Drabinovka 75, 278, 279, 280

Drahomanov, Mykhaylo 7, 101,
102, 104, 108, 109, 110, 111,
113, 117, 118, 153, 352, 353
Drobnis, Yakiv 226, 257, 258
Dybenko 187
Dzerzhinsky, Felix 311

E

Eichhorn, Gen 156

F

Fedenko, Panas 114, 169, 349,
353, 356

G

Glebov 258

H

Herzen, Alexander 102
Hindenburg, Gen 137
Holubovych, Vsevolod 60, 136,
139, 140, 149, 151
Hrushevsky, Mykhailo 36, 63,
136, 174, 251, 344, 349

K

Kaledin 56
Kerensky, Alexander 40, 133
Khrystyuk, Pavlo 120, 121, 122,
123, 126, 129, 133, 134, 137,
140, 145, 148, 153, 168, 174,
183, 193, 195, 197, 200, 251,
313, 350, 354, 355
Khvist, Vasyl' 120
Kibalchich, D. 102
Kin, D. 216, 219, 220, 350
Klunnyi 192
Klymenko 220, 284

Kolchak, Admiral 199, 217, 234, 236
Kolosov 219, 221, 222
Kolyachenko, K 218
Kon, Feliks 258, 262, 267
Korzh, K 148
Kossior, Stanislav 232, 234, 257, 258, 261
Kostryuchenko, Hryhoryiy 216
Kovalevsky, Mykola 121, 123
Kovenko 139, 171
Kraynyk, Yosip 287
Kubanin, M. 197, 350
Kulyk, Ivan 289
Kun, Bela 66, 352
Kviring, Eduard 250, 257

L

Lapchynsky, Yuriy 38, 78, 80, 266, 294
Lavrov, Peter 108
Lazarev, Ye 119
Lebid, Dmytro Z 257, 350
Lenin, Vladimir I 10, 23, 47, 52, 55, 59, 65, 67, 69, 70, 112, 133, 156, 182, 190, 191, 208, 210, 212, 213, 226, 227, 228, 232, 236, 242, 249, 252, 253, 266, 270, 271, 273, 274, 288, 294, 307, 309, 333, 347, 354
  attitude toward the Borotbisty, 212
  use of the term 226
Lizogub, D. 102
Lukashevych, Vasyl' 101
Luxemburg, Rosa 181
Lypynskyi, Vyacheslav K 106
Lyzohub, Fedir A. 163

M

Makarenko, Andriy 167
Makhno, Ataman Nester 10, 98, 167, 169, 179, 197, 199, 236, 350
Maksymovych, Karlo 272
Manuilsky, Dmytro Z 212, 226, 232, 234, 247, 257, 258
Martos, Borys 39, 45, 126, 133
Marx, Karl 70, 110, 117, 309
Mashenko, H. 218
Matena-Bohayevych 168
Maynes, R. 218
Mazepa, Isaak 103
Mazurenko, Viktor 175
Mazurkevych 173, 174
Mikhnovsky, Mykola I. 105, 112, 350
Minin, Sergei. K 258
Mirbach, Count 156
Mizernytsky 327
Modzhyuk (pseud, of Mykhaylychenko?) 135, 136, 139, 148, 163, 174, 183, 186, 187, 192, 216, 301, 305, 311
Moriyevich, V. 102
Mstislavski, Sergei D. (pseud of Maslovski) 216
Mysan 281, 293

N

Nemolovsky, I. 238, 240
Neronovych, Yevhen 57, 211

O

Okhrymovych, Yu. 136, 149

Oleksander *(pseud,* of Hynda) 24, 104, 111, 119, 122, 135, 136, 168, 302, 306, 308
Osadchy, M. 126

P

Petrenko 188, 189
Petrovsky, D. 198
Petrovsky, Grigorii I 298
Popov, M. 299
Porsh, Mykola 34, 41, 45, 55, 113
Postyshev, Pavel P. 83, 273, 309, 345
Prokopovych, V. 121
Pyatakov, Georgii L 43, 181, 182, 184, 187, 192, 193, 232, 247
Pyatenko, Ataman Oleksa (pseud. of Herashchenko) 168, 221, 280, 290
Pylypenko, Serhiy 196, 258, 295

R

Rafes, Moisei G. 61, 168, 176, 177, 178, 184, 194, 198, 209, 351, 355
Rakovsky, Khristian 66, 67, 187, 188, 190, 191, 192, 194, 207, 214, 232, 234, 237, 253, 257, 258, 261, 311
Ravich-Cherkasski, Moisei 209
Romanovs 243
Rubinshtein 311
Ryabtsev 141

S

Sadovsky, Valentyn 231, 233, 351

Saltan, M. 136, 149, 151
Serdyuk 48, 170, 220
Sevryuk, Oleksander 136, 151
Shadyliv, O. 174
Shakhray, Vasyl' 32, 41, 46, 57, 58, 63, 78, 94, 107, 137, 180, 211, 288
Shapoval, Mykyta, Yu 118, 119, 120, 123, 124, 135, 139, 140, 145, 151, 175, 343, 351
Shavryn 220
Shemet, Serhiy 106
Shepel 169
Shevchenko, Taras 48, 75, 284, 287, 290, 293, 306
Shlikhter, Aleksandr G. 193, 257
Shrah, Mykola 122, 136, 148, 149, 151, 351
Shumsky, Oleksander Ya 24, 135, 139, 172, 174, 183, 198, 238, 241, 244, 248, 251, 254, 261, 265, 267, 268, 269, 270, 271, 272, 273, 299, 325, 326, 327
Shvarts 292
Skoropadsky, Hetman Pavlo 23, 62, 75, 88, 143, 168, 169
Skrypnyk, Mykola O. 57, 81, 107, 257, 260, 262, 271, 272, 299, 306, 307, 309, 351, 356
Skyrta 220
Slyvenko, Naum 305
Smetanych 258
Spivak, Ivan 281
Stalin, Joseph V 16, 23, 60, 82, 83, 84, 89, 90, 92, 181, 212, 232, 268, 270, 271, 273, 274, 298, 300, 303, 342, 344, 345, 351, 356
Stefanovich, Ya 102

Steshenko, Ivan 109, 110
Sverdlov, Yakov 190

T

Terletsky, Ye 233
Tkachenko, Mykhaylo S. 45, 130
Trotsky, Lev D 10, 37, 48, 49, 190, 212, 241, 265, 351, 354

Y

Ya 102, 135, 282, 303, 308, 311
Yakir 292
Yakovleva, Barbara 156
Yanko 175
Yefremov, Serhiy O. 120, 121
Yegorov, Gen 290
Yerman 258
Yevshan 120
Yudenich, Gen 236

Yurvyn 221

Z

Zaliznyak, Mykola 118, 120
Zaliznyak, Volodymyr 123, 149
Zalutski, Pyotr A. 258
Zaslavski, David I 104, 352
Zatonsky, Volodymyr P. 181, 225, 232, 235, 247, 257, 258, 267, 299, 352
Zeleny, Ataman 169, 179, 197, 291
Zhelyabov, Andrei I 102
Zhupanov 221
Zhyvodko, Arkadiy 119
Ziber, Mykola I 110
Zinoviev, Georgii Ye. (pseud. of Radomysl'ski) 77, 248, 265, 266, 268
Znamenka 187, 189, 190
Zvenigorod 167

Index of Subjects

A

Agriculture 133, 192, 298, 303, 305, 310
  agricultural associations 127, 128, 131
  nationalization of the land 112, 121
  socialization of the land 59, 125, 146, 199
  state farms 226, 230
  Ukrainian Land Reserve, see also Famine 125, 127

All-Russian Congress of Soviets, Seventh 246

All-Russian Constituent Assembly 39, 51, 125, 131, 133, 134

All-Russian Soviet of Peasants' Deputies 126

All-Russian Teachers' Union, see Teachers' Union 227

All-Ukrainian Congress of Soviets of Workers', Peasants' and Soldiers' Deputies (Kharkov) 187
  First 138

All-Ukrainian Congress of Volost Executive Committees 200, 207

All-Ukrainian Council of Peasants' Deputies 126, 130, 173
  Second Session 130, 132
  Third Session 132, 133, 134, 137

All-Ukrainian Military Congress 50, 131
  Third 131

All-Ukrainian Peasants' Congress 125
  First 125, 127
  Second, see also All-Ukrainian Council of Peasants' Deputies 8, 143, 278

All-Ukrainian Workers' Congress 127, 144
  First 127
  Second 8, 144

Anarchists 99, 153, 156, 169, 277
  Ukrainian, see also Makhno 98

Armenian unity party (117

August Conference of Emissaries
  Congresses Fifth (of the UPSR) (Kharkiv, Mar. 6–8) 195
  Congresses First (of the UPSR) (August 1919) 8, 123, 124, 125, 127
  Congresses Second (of the UPSR) (March 1920) 8, 128

Austria-Hungary, see also Central Powers 49, 59, 138, 140, 141, 155, 318

B

Berliner Tageblatt 163

Bor'bisty (Ukrainian Party of Left Socialist Revolutionaries) [Ukrains'ka Parity a livykh Sotsiyalistiv-Revolyutsioneriv] 98

Borotbist Central Committee 121, 122, 173, 198, 214, 216, 217, 234, 238, 248, 259, 278, 279, 292, 297, 298, 301, 302, 303, 306, 307, 308

Borotbist Conferences and Congresses
Kharkiv Province (July 14–15, 1918) 9, 42, 56, 149, 160, 300, 332

Borotbyst (Poltava city organ), 243, 260, 293

Brest-Litovsk, Treaty of 154, 156

Brotherhood of Saints Cyril and Methodius 117

C

Cadets (Constitutional Democrats) 144, 151, 186, 188

Central Bureau of Trade Unions (Kiev), 170

Central Executive Committee 57, 63, 197, 198, 302, 310, 324, 326, 327
All-Russian 246
Ukrainian 79, 296, 302, 310

Central Powers, see also Austria-Hungary, German government 49, 59, 138, 140, 141, 318

Cheka 198, 283, 289, 311

Chernihiv (city) 51, 52, 120, 122, 161, 168, 169, 173, 174, 182, 217, 242, 295, 303, 312, 331, 332, 335

Chervony prapor (Red Banner) 294

Chervony shlyakh (Red Path) 264

Comintern, see International, Third 242, 244, 248, 249, 250, 352, 354, 355

Commission of Fifty 327

Communist Bund, see Jewish Communist Party 99

Communist Party (Bolshevik) of the Ukraine, see CP(b)U 353, 356

Communist Party of Western Ukraine, see CPWU 89, 272

Congress of Soviets of the Donets and Kryvyi Rih (Krivoi Rog) Regions 138

Cossacks 26, 49, 50, 58, 60, 61, 74, 82, 104, 236, 239, 263, 285
Don 49, 50, 56, 131, 217

Council of People's Commissars 48, 50, 56, 137, 138, 140, 181, 198, 303

Council of Workers' and Peasants' Defense, Ukrainian, 199

CP(b)U (Communist Party (Bolshevik) of the Ukraine) [Komunistychna Partiya (bil'shovykiv) Ukrainy] 9, 10, 11, 69, 77, 78, 80, 81, 82, 83, 97, 98, 99, 195, 196, 197, 209, 211, 215, 220, 221, 222, 223, 225, 231, 234, 235, 238, 241, 242, 243, 244, 246, 248, 249, 250, 251, 252, 253, 254, 257, 259, 260, 261, 262, 265, 266, 267, 268, 269, 270, 271, 272, 273, 289, 293, 294, 296, 298, 299, 300, 301, 302, 303, 304, 305, 306, 307, 308, 309, 310, 311, 342, 343, 344, 345, 350, 352, 353, 354, 355, 356
Taganrog Conference (Apr. 1918) 250

CPWU (Communist Party of Western Ukraine) [Komunistychna Partiya Zakhidno'i Ukrainy] 90, 272, 351, 356

Culture, Ukrainian
the Ukrainian National Union 157

D

Directory 9, 63, 64, 151, 164, 167, 168, 169, 170, 171, 172, 173, 174, 175, 176, 177, 178, 179, 181, 183, 184, 185, 186, 188, 191, 192, 193, 206, 209, 225, 281, 282, 284, 285, 303, 304, 345

E

Executive Committee of, see also All-Ukrainian Peasants' Congress 173, 192, 205, 214, 242, 244, 245, 246, 247, 248, 249, 250, 329, 350, 354, 356

G

Galicia 22, 24, 26, 89, 104, 105, 109, 110, 305, 306
Georgian Party of Socialist Federalists 117
German government 158
Great Britain (see also Entente power) 199, 215
Group of Federalists 266, 351

H

Habsburgs 26
Haslo (Watchword), organ of the RUP 112, 113
Haydamak brigade 237
Hromada (Community) 101, 102, 108, 109, 110
Hungary 65, 66, 193, 317

I

Independents, see Ukrainian Party of Independents Socialists, USDRP (Independents), USDRP (Left Independents) 63, 66, 126, 152, 169, 177, 181, 191, 199, 207, 208, 209, 288, 289, 291
Insurgent Armies of Left Bank Ukraine 291
International
  Communist International 11, 205, 208, 214, 234, 235, 243, 244, 245, 246, 247, 248, 250, 251, 254, 257, 272, 297, 308, 323, 329, 350, 352, 354, 355, 356
  Second 154, 246
  Second Third (Comintern) Communist International 16, 91, 121, 129, 154, 208, 214, 217, 244, 245, 246, 247, 315, 354, 356, 368
  Third (Comintern) 206, 207, 210, 244, 250, 254, 330, 338
Ireland 70

J

Jewish Bund 61, 184
Jewish Communist Party 99
Jewish National Autonomy 69
July days 128

K

Kherson 186, 189, 190, 220, 332, 335
Kiyevskoye ekho (Kievan Echo) 218
Kobeliaky (district) 10, 277
Kobeliaky Communists 288, 289, 290, 291, 292, 293, 294
Kyiv (district) 9, 17, 30, 31, 32, 33, 37, 39, 42, 43, 44, 47, 48, 49, 50, 51, 53, 54, 55, 57, 58, 59, 60, 61, 62, 64, 74, 75, 76, 82, 85, 86, 87, 88, 89, 90, 109, 110, 111, 119, 120, 121, 123,

125, 127, 128, 130, 131, 133,
134, 136, 138, 139, 141, 143,
144, 145, 151, 153, 154, 161,
163, 167, 168, 170, 171, 172,
173, 174, 176, 177, 178, 183,
185, 188, 192, 194, 195, 200,
205, 207, 211, 215, 216, 217,
218, 219, 220, 221, 222, 239,
242, 257, 278, 284, 289, 292,
295, 301, 302, 303, 305, 309,
310, 321, 327, 329, 332, 335,
340, 350, 351, 352, 355, 356

Kyiv Polytechnic Institute 257

Kyiv University 110, 303

L

Left Bank Ukraine, see also
Kharkiv and Poltava
Provinces 98, 184, 214, 221,
238, 242, 285

Left Independents, see USDRP
98, 205, 207, 208, 209, 210,
288, 297, 298, 306, 309

Left USDRP (Left Ukrainian
Social Democratic Workers'
Party) 211

M

Mensheviks, see RSDRP 11, 37,
38, 40, 41, 42, 43, 46, 51, 52,
53, 55, 56, 60, 101, 104, 105,
114, 144, 161, 199, 268, 288,
352

Military Revolutionary
Committees
in the city of Aleksandrovsk 187
South-Western Front 50
Ukrainian Military
Revolutionary Committee in
Kyiv 167

Monarchism, Ukrainian 350

Moscow (city) 15, 16, 21, 23, 26,
65, 77, 90, 121, 125, 126, 136,
144, 156, 176, 179, 181, 190,
192, 193, 212, 213, 214, 225,
234, 235, 238, 241, 242, 251,
252, 253, 254, 261, 262, 263,
265, 267, 268, 269, 270, 271,
273, 295, 297, 299, 303, 305,
307, 308, 309, 310, 311, 317,
349, 351, 352, 353, 354, 355,
356

N

Nationalism
Russian 368

New Economic Policy 80, 265

Nova Chortoriya 237

Nova Ukraina (New Ukraine),
264

P

Paris Peace Conference 178

Petrograd 15, 40, 41, 43, 46, 47,
48, 49, 50, 57, 59, 121, 127,
128, 130, 131, 132, 133, 136,
137, 144, 151, 156, 180, 236,
244, 245, 352, 354, 355, 356

Poland 155, 257, 262, 268, 309,
317

Politburo 213, 261, 271, 272,
273, 303, 308
Ukrainian 262

Poltava Insurgent Brigade 291

Poltava Province Executive
Committee 221, 308

Poltava Province Peasants'
Congress (Dec. 1918) 284

Proletarskaya pravda (Proletarian
Pravda) 242

Prosvity (Enlightenment
societies), 283

Provisional Government
(Petrograd) 15, 36, 37, 38, 40,
41, 43, 45, 46, 47, 48, 49, 50,
57, 59, 121, 125, 127, 128, 130,
131, 132, 133, 136, 137, 144,
151, 156, 180, 236, 244, 245,
352, 354, 355, 356

Provisional Organizational
Committee of the Central
Faction 149

R

RCP(b) (Russian Communist
Party (Bolshevik) 11, 16, 65,
69, 156, 191, 198, 200, 209,
211, 225, 226, 228, 229, 233,
243, 251, 252, 253, 254, 258,
260, 269, 274, 294, 339, 352,
353, 355, 356

Revolutionary Committees 238

Revolutionary Communists 99

Revolutionary Ukrainian Party,
See also RUP 7, 101, 103, 105,
106, 111, 112, 113, 114, 115,
118, 119, 356

Right Bank Ukraine 29, 129,
221, 222, 238, 239, 240, 241,
261, 267, 291, 310

Robitnycha hazeta (Workers'
Gazette) USDRP organ 144,
243

Robitnycha hazeta-proletar
(Workers' Gazette-
Proletarian) 243

Rostov-on-Don 163

RSDRP (Russian Social
Democratic Workers' Party)
[Rossiiskaya Sotsial-
Demokraticheskaya
Rabochaya Partiya] 11, 38,
41, 46, 51, 52, 53, 55, 56, 60,
101, 104, 105, 114, 199, 352

RSDRP(b) Bolsheviks 11, 46, 52,
53, 55, 56, 60, 352

Russian Communist Party
(Bolshevik), see RCP(b) 16,
65, 69, 156, 191, 198, 200, 209,
211, 225, 226, 228, 229, 233,
243, 251, 252, 253, 254, 258,
260, 269, 274, 294, 339, 352,
353

Russian Empire 25, 26, 27, 34,
47, 69, 102, 104, 108, 110, 115,
129, 134, 368

Russian Left SR's (Russian Party
of Left Socialist
Revolutionaries) 108, 139,
140, 153, 156, 161, 162, 163

Russian Red Army 64, 181, 233,
234, 235, 247

Russian Right SR's (Russian
Party of Right Socialist
Revolutionaries) 156, 161,
227

Russian Social Democratic
Workers' Party, see RSDRP
11, 38, 41, 46, 51, 52, 53, 55,
56, 60, 101, 104, 105, 114, 199,
352

Russian SR's (Russian Party of
Socialist Revolutionaries) 40,
43, 52, 56, 106, 118, 123, 125,
128, 129, 133, 156, 226

Russified 28, 29, 31, 39, 106, 151,
179, 211, 254, 271

S

Slovyansk 84, 85, 86, 90, 300

Socialism, see also Marxism,
Social Democracy 7, 69, 78,
109, 110, 117, 120, 159, 208,
218, 250, 288, 307, 341

Society of Ukrainian
    Progressives (TUP), see also
    UPSF 39, 105, 124, 146
Society of United Slavs 101
Southern Society 101
Soviet platform 17, 210, 227,
    237, 251
Soviet Russia 13, 59, 63, 77, 139,
    161, 171, 178, 186, 192, 193,
    205, 214, 230, 232, 239, 245,
    246, 247, 266, 321, 329, 349
Soyuz Khliborobiv-Vlasnykiv
    (Union of Agricultural
    Owners) 283
Soyuz Vyzvolennya Ukra'iny,
    see 115
Spilka (Ukrainian Social
    Democratic Union)
    [Ukrainska Sotsiyal-
    Demokratychna Spilka] 7,
    39, 103, 105, 111, 114, 115,
    122, 125, 243, 299, 300, 302
State Duma
    Fourth 257
    Second 114, 120

T

Taganrog 163, 250
Taganrog Conference 250
Taurida 60, 186
Trade Union of Education
    Workers, U.S.S.R. 270, 309
Trudova respublika (Toilers'
    Republic) 174

U

Ukapisty (Ukrainian Communist
    Party) [Ukrains'ka
    Komunistychna Partiya] 25,
    78, 83, 98, 107, 115, 209, 211,
    221, 255, 288, 289, 294, 346

Ukrainian Constituent
    Assembly 52, 128, 137, 155,
    315, 318
Ukrainian Democratic Agrarian
    Party 106, 151
Ukrainian Democratic Party
    105
Ukrainian military academy
    242
Ukrainian National Union
    (Ukrainskyi Natsional'nyi
    Soyuz) 153, 158, 167, 168,
    175, 176, 206, 277
Ukrainian Party of Left Socialist
    Revolutionaries, see Bor'bisty
    98
Ukrainian Party of Socialist
    Revolutionaries, see UPSR 8,
    10, 15, 19, 36, 51, 74, 75, 97,
    106, 117, 119, 120, 123, 147,
    195, 196, 205, 313, 316, 355
Ukrainian People's Defense
    (Ukrains'ka Narodna
    Oborona, UNO) 119
Ukrainian People's Party
    (Ukra'ins'ka Narodna
    Partiya) 105, 112
Ukrainian People's Republic
    (Ukrains'ka Narodna
    Respublika, UNR) 44, 48, 57,
    58, 59, 61, 64, 65, 106, 123,
    132, 133, 138, 139, 143, 144,
    151, 167, 178, 190, 199, 200,
    205, 214, 236, 237, 238, 239,
    240, 243, 249, 279, 284, 285,
    286, 287, 291, 313
Ukrainian Radical Democratic
    Party 105
Ukrainian Radical Party 105,
    109

INDEX OF SUBJECTS 369

Ukrainian Red Army (Bolshevik) 10, 185, 192, 199, 233, 234, 235, 239, 289, 345
Ukrainian Social Democratic Union, see *Spilka* 103, 114
Ukrainian Social Democratic Workers' Party [Ukrainska Sotsiyal-Demokratychna Robitnycha Partiya], see USDRP 36, 39, 40, 41, 43, 46, 49, 50, 53, 55, 57, 58, 60, 63, 66, 78, 80, 98, 101, 106, 111, 113, 114, 115, 117, 124, 127, 131, 139, 140, 144, 146, 167, 168, 171, 173, 175, 176, 177, 178, 191, 199, 205, 207, 208, 210, 231, 243, 288, 289, 291, 297, 298, 306, 309, 338, 343, 344, 345, 353, 368
Ukrainian Socialist Committee (Ukrainska Sotsiyalistychna Komitet), pre-1917 122
Ukrainization 68, 80, 81, 82, 107, 126, 132, 180, 183, 210, 263, 264, 265, 269, 270, 309

Ukrainophiles 102, 108, 111, 112

W

War Communism 63, 192
Western Europe 28, 271
White Guards, see Russian Volunteer Army 75, 76, 171, 218
Whites 76, 141, 171, 219, 221, 223, 290
World War I 104, 115, 120, 297, 299, 301, 302, 305, 306

Y

Yekaterinoslav (Katerynoslav) 30, 31, 46, 48, 51, 55, 58, 60, 63, 167, 173, 182, 183, 190, 221, 242, 250, 257, 258, 289, 332
Yelisavetgrad (Kirovograd) 31, 220

Notes

1. V.Vynnychenko, *Rozlad i pohodzhennia*, cited in Ivan L.Rudnytsky, *Essays in Modern Ukrainian History*, Edmonton, 1987, p. 419.
2. Borotbisty is the plural form of Borotbist derived from the name of their party newspaper *Borotba* meaning struggle.
3. Micro histories of the UPSR and Borotbisty are included in: Andrzej Rudzienski, Ukrainian Problem—Past and Present, From Czarism to Stalinism, *New International*, Vol.14 No.5, July 1948. Mace, James, *Communism and the Dilemmas of National Liberation*, Harvard, 1983, Reshetar, John, *The Ukrainian Revolution, 1917–1920: A Study in Nationalism*, New York, 1972, Borys, Jurij, *The Sovietization of Ukraine, 1917–1923*, Edmonton, 1980. There is no specific history of the USDRP, though in addition to the above two important unpublished studies which address this party and the wider Ukrainian socialist movement are: Boshyk, George.Y., *The Rise of Ukrainian Political Parties in Russia 1900–1907: With Special Reference to Social Democracy*, PhD Theses, St.Anthonys College Oxford, 1981, Bojcun, Marko, *The Working Class and the National Question in Ukraine*, 1880–1920, York University, Toronto, 1985.
4. The Borotbisty of the revolutionary period should not be confused with the small neo-Stalinist sect Ob'yednannia "Borot'ba" (Union of Struggle) formed in Ukraine in 2011. See: http://avtonomia.net/2014/03/03/statement-left-anarchist-organizations-borotba-organization/
5. Procyk, Anna, *Russian Nationalism and Ukraine, The Nationality Policy of the Volunteer Army during the Civil War*, CIUS, Edmonton, 1995, p. 49, and Prince Alexander Wolkonsky, *The Ukraine Question The Historic Truth Versus Separatist Propaganda*, Rome, Ditta E Armani, 1920.
6. See Michael Pszyk, 'Novorossiya's' Right-wing Friends', Ukraine Solidarity Campaign, <https://ukrainesolidaritycampaign.org/2017/07/28/novorossiyas-right-wing-friends/>. [Accessed 2 April 2018]
7. See Michael Pszyk, Novorossiya's' Leftist Friends', Ukraine Solidarity Campaign, <https://ukrainesolidaritycampaign.org/2017/07/28/novorossiyas-leftist-friends/>. [Accessed 2 April 2018].
8. It is true the claim to be waging an anti-fascists struggle has been utilized to secure willing support from the neo-Stalinist left and others, simultaneously the Russian Empire nationalism and even Tsarist goals of the Russian forces in East Ukraine are undisguised. This Russian aggression of 2014 directed towards Eastern Ukraine presents many similarities to the aggression directed towards Western Ukraine in 1914.
9. An appalling example this is the work of the British Stalinist Andrew Murray, *The Empire and Ukraine*, Manifesto Press, London 2015. In contrast even to Soviet historians Murray makes no reference at all to a Ukrainian Revolution in 1917, or to it creating an autonomous Ukraine and the Ukrainian Peoples Republic. History for Murray conveniently begins in 1918 with the German sponsored Hetmanate. *Ibid. Empire and Ukraine* P. 49–50.

10	On these ideas of Maistrenko and his comrades of the URDP see: Chris Ford, 'Socialism, Stalinism and National Liberation: Coming to Terms with a Changed World, The Ideas of the URDP (Vpered Group) in the Post-War Era', *Debatte*: Journal of Contemporary Central and Eastern Europe, Volume 14, , 2006 - Issue 2, pp. 119–143.
11	See, Andor, Laszlo and Summers, Martin, *Market Failure A Guide to the East European 'Economic Miracle'*, London 1998, and Haynes, Mike, *Russia Class and Power 1917–2000*, London 2002.
12	Russia's Near-Abroad policy has been structured under the supervision of the Ministry of Foreign Affairs and its specialized agency, *Rossotrudnichestvo* (the Federal Agency for the Commonwealth of Independent States, Compatriots Living Abroad, and International Humanitarian Cooperation. See: Marlene Laruelle, The "Russian World", Russia's Soft Power and Geopolitical Imagination, Center on Global Interests, Washington, 2015
13	Babenko,A (Ivan Maistrenko), 'Stalinizm, suchasna forma rosiys'koho imperializmu., *Vpered*, no.7–8 (19–20), Munich, 1951.
14	Kremlin backing for European reactionary forces can been seen in such examples as support for the French National Front, Forza Italia, Silvio Berlusconi's party in Italy, the Austrian Freedom Party, the Catholic-monarchist Carlist movement in Spain, the Hungarian Jobbik party, the Greek Golden Dawn party and the Bulgarian Ataka party, through to the British National Party (BNP) and the German Zuerst journal.
15	Eight of its Ukraine's oblasts were targeted as winnable by Kremlin strategists. Almost simultaneously with the developments in Crimea, rallies broke out in Kharkiv, Odesa, Luhansk, Donetsk, Kherson, Dnipro, Zaporizhia, Mykolayiv and many smaller towns. These saw pro-Kremlin rallies, Russian flags, attempts to seize the Security Bureau of Ukraine or police premises and proclaim People's Republics—in some places more successfully than in others. However, the proxy forces did not gain the mass support that the organizers presumed, and they often had to bring in 'guest protesters' from Russia to try to turn the tide.
16	Ihor Losiev, 2 June 2016, 'The Battle for Historical Memory', <http://ukrainianweek.com/History/166557> [accessed 2 April 2018].
17	Seventy scholars of Ukraine based in Western Europe, North America and Ukraine condemned these laws. The legislation has drawn criticism from other institutions ranging from the United States Holocaust Museum to the OSCE. The Provisions of the institute are available on-line at: <http://www.memory.gov.ua/page/polozhennya-pro-ukrainskii-institut-natsionalnoi-pamyati> [Accessed 2 April 2018].
18	In this model the 'Ukrainian State', (the Hetmanate) of Pavlo Skoropadsky installed by the Kaisers Germany, is placed on a par with the Ukrainian Peoples Republic it overthrew. This state was itself guilty of crimes later Communists and Nazis are today condemned by the law of Ukraine for committing.
19	Viatrovych makes no differentiation between the Stalinist era and the revolutionary period. See Volodymyr Viatrovych, '"Decommunization" and Academic Discussion',<https://krytyka.com/en/solutions/opinions/decommunization-and-academic-discussion.> [Accessed 2 April 2018].

20 Andreas Umland, 'The Ukrainian government's Memory Institute against the West',<http://www.neweasterneurope.eu/articles-and-commentary/2284-the-ukrainian-government-s-memory-institute-against-the-west>. [Accessed 2 April 2018].
21 A Babenko, 'Ukrayins'ka natsional'na revolyutsiya i natsionalistychna reaktsiya', *Vpered*, Munich, No.3. (12), 1950.
22 These competing conceptions of Ukraine are not present in the official state narrative. This model of "historical memory" is reinforced by four memory laws including 'On the Legal Status and Honoring the Memory of Fighters for Ukraine's Independence in the Twentieth Century'. See <http://www.memory.gov.ua/laws/law-ukraine-legal-status-and-honoring-memory-fighters-ukraines-independence-twentieth-century.> [Accessed 2 April 2018].
23 The editors protested that the leading political circles of the emigration were blocking Vynnychenko from reaching the émigré community. It was highlighted how the old Russian writer and white emigre Aleksandr Kuprin had returned to Moscow to a heroic welcome, yet they failed to respect the only Ukrainian author whose drama was known in all European theatres and leader of the first Independent Ukrainian State. V. Vynnychenko, 'Rozlad i pohodzhennia,Vidpovid moim prykhylnykam i neprykhylnykam' , *Nasha Borotba*, Geneva, 1948,
24 *Ibid*, Rozlad i pohodzhennia, p. 6
25 *Ibid*, Rozlad i pohodzhennia, p. 6
26 UHVR - abbreviation of the Ukrainian Supreme Liberation Council the commanding center of the Ukrainian Insurgent Army in the 1940's. Vynnychenko warned Stalinist communism, sooner or later, will be eliminated and Ukrainian politicians needed to consider what order should replace it, answering the question what should Ukraine be? Rozlad i pohodzhennia, *Ibid*, p. 19
27 *Ibid*, Rozlad i pohodzhennia, p. 7
28 *Ibid*, Rozlad i pohodzhennia, p. 8
29 George Barr Carson, 'Reviews', *American Slavic and East European Review*, Vol.15, No.3 (Oct., 1956), p. 425.
30 Levynsky, Volodomyr, *L'internatonale socialiste et les peuples opprimes*, Prague, 1920, Rosdolsky, Roman, *Engels and the 'Non historic' Peoples: the National Question in the Revolution of 1848*, Glasgow, 1987.
31 Marx, Karl *Secret Diplomatic History of the Eighteenth Century*, Lawrence and Wishart, London, 1969, p. 118–121. (Proof Copy).
32 Volobuyev was an economist and government official heading a branch of the Commissariat of Education. His articles 'On the Problem of the Ukrainian Economy' were published in *Bilshovyk Ukrainy* January 30th and February 16th, 1928. Though an ethnic Russian he was a spokesman for the Ukrainian communists and defender of Ukraine's right to control its economy. Volobuyev showed how central control and continued Russian chauvinism perpetuated the exploitation of Ukraine within the USSR. He was attacked by the Stalinist authorities. M. Volobuyev, 'Do problemy ukrainskoyi ekonomiky', in *Dokumenty ukrainskoho komunizmy*, Ivan Maistrenko Ed, New York, 1962, 132–230.
33 *Ibid, Dokumenty ukrainskoho komunizmy* , p. 185–186

34	Kononenko, Konstantyn, *Ukraine and Russia: A History of the Economic Relations Between Ukraine and Russia* (1654–1917). Milwaukee: Marquette University Press, 1958, p. 108.
35	The national composition of the nascent capitalist class in 1832 reveals the composition of factory owners as: Russian 44.6 %, Ukrainian 28.7, Jewish 17.4 %, Foreign 3.6 %, Other 5.7 %. The Composition of merchants as: Russian, 52.6% Ukrainian, 28.7 %, Jewish, 17.4 % Foreign 1.9 %, Other 2.4 %. *Ibid*, Volobuyev, *Dokumenty ukrainskoho komunizmy*, p. 154.
36	Bohdan, Krawchenko, *Social Change And National Consciousness In Twentieth-Century Ukraine,* Oxford, p. 39–44
37	Krawchenko, Bohdan, *Encyclopedia of Ukraine*, vol. 5 (1993), Toronto, p. 718–720
38	There were more Ukrainian workers located in Right-Bank and Left-Bank Ukraine than in the Southern Steppe, where the mining and steel industry was congregated with cities such as Katerynoslav and Kryvyi Rih, whilst provinces of Kyiv, Poltava, Volhynia and Podhillia became central to the food industry. Bohdan Krawchenko, The Social Structure of the Ukraine in 1917, *Harvard Ukrainian Studies*, Vol. 14, No. 1/2 (June 1990), pp. 97–112, p. 110
39	Friedgut, Theodore H., *Iuzovka and Revolution*, Princeton, 1989, Vol,I: 208.
40	Richtysky, Andriy, 'Memorandum Ukrainskoi Kumunistichnoi Partii Kongresovi III Komunistychnoho Internationalu', *Nova Doba*, no.4, 1920 in *Dokumenty Ukrainskoho Komunizmu*, New York, 1962 p. 45–66, Bojcun, 'Approaches to the Study of the Ukrainian Revolution', *Journal of Ukrainian Studies* Vol. 24: 1 (summer 1999), Friedgut, *Ibid*, p. 208–144.
41	Richtysky, Andriy, 'Memorandum Ukrainskoi Kumunistichnoi Partii Kongresovi III Komunistychnoho Internationalu', *Nova Doba*, no.4, 1920 in *Dokumenty Ukrainskoho Komunizmu*, New York, 1962 p. 45–66, Bojcun, 'Approaches to the Study of the Ukrainian Revolution', *Journal of Ukrainian Studies* Vol. 24: 1 (summer 1999), *Ibid,* Friedgut, p. 208–144.
42	*Ibid*. Friedgut, Theodore H., *Iuzovka and Revolution,* Princeton, 1989, Vol,II, p. 144
43	Magocsi, Paul , *A History of Ukraine*, Toronto, 1996, p. 331
44	Borys, Jurij, *The Sovietization of Ukraine*, CIUS, Edmonton, 1980, p. 65
45	Verstiuk, Vladyslav , 'Conceptual Issues in Studying the Ukrainian Revolution', *Journal of Ukrainian Studies*, Vol.24, No.1, Summer 1999, p. 14
46	Guthier, Steven L. 'Ukrainian Cities during the Revolution and the Interwar Era', in ivan L. Rudnytsky (ed.), *Rethinking Ukrainian History* (Edmonton, 1981), p. 157.
47	In 1840 the Russian government stripped Kyiv of municipal autonomy and encouraged Russian students, troops and merchants to settle there. The majority Ukrainian composition of Kyiv was completely reversed by 1897. Other urban centers had an even larger Russian presence and were more tightly controlled. Odessa the largest city of Ukraine before 1917 was founded by decree of Empress Catherine as a military and commercial outpost. Ukrainians represented 9.4% of Odessa in 1897, composing the poorer strata working in quarries, mines and unskilled labor. Luhansk was founded by the Tsar, to produce iron for the military, similarly with a small Ukrainian populace.
48	*Ibid*, Borys, p. 66

49	Krawchenko, Bohdan, 'The Social Structure of the Ukraine in 1917', *Harvard Ukrainian Studies*, Vol. 14, No. 1/2 (June 1990), p .99
50	*Ibid*, Krawchenko, p. 100
51	*Ibid*, Krawchenko, p. 101
52	Skorovstanskii, V, [Vasyl Shakhray] *Revoliutsiia na Ukraini*, Saratov, 1918, p. 7
53	Ibid, Skorovstanskii, *Revoliutsiia na Ukraini*, Saratov, 1918, p. 7–8.
54	Verstiuk, Vladyslav, 'Conceptual Issues in Studying the History of the Ukrainian Revolution', *Journal of Ukrainian Studies*, Vol. 24, no. 1, 1999, p. 14. Weinstein, H.R, 'Land Hunger and Nationalism in the Ukraine 1905–1917', *The Journal of Economic History*, Vo.2, No.1,May 1942, p. 24.
55	E.H.Carr considered Ukraine had a far greater differentiation, see *Socialism in One Country 1924–1926*, 2 vols. London, 1970, Vol.1: 257–58.
56	Soviet literature often exaggerated the size and role of the wealthy strata, one history published in the Ukrainain SSR presented it as "one quarter of the peasant population", *A History of Ukraine*, Ed. Yurki Kondufor, Kyiv, 1986, p. 119.
57	Bohdan Krawchenko notes: The average peasant farm in the Ukraine in 1917 was approximately 7.7 hectares. The landholding of the Ukrainian peasant was actually larger than that of his French, Belgian, or Danish counterpart. But whereas the latter could earn a comfortable living on such a farm, the former could not because of a shortage of draught animals and implements primitive agricultural techniques, and cultural backwardness. Lack of intelligent state policies promoting infrastructures in agriculture credit facilities, grain elevators, agricultural schools, etc.) compounded the difficulties. Operating at a subsistence level (it was estimated that 5.5 hectares were needed to make ends meet), under the Ukraine's climatic conditions, the peasant could expect to experience pangs of hunger every two or three years when the harvest was poor. *Ibid*, Krawchenko *The Social Structure of the Ukraine in 1917*, p. 107
58	*Ibid*, Krawchenko, p. 106–107
59	*Ibid*, Weinstein, Land Hunger and Nationalism, p. 29.
60	Due to the anti-semitic restrictions of the Pale of Settlement, three out of four of these petty traders was Jewish, economic grievances easily turning to anti-Semitic channels. *Ibid*, Weinstein, Land Hunger and Nationalism, p. 30.
61	Holubnychy, 'Agrarian Revolution in Ukraine', *Soviet Regional Economics: Selected Works of Vsevolod Holubnychy*, Alberta, 1982, p. 4
62	*Ibid*, Holubnychy, p. 6.
63	Bojcun, Marko, *The Working Class and the National Question in Ukraine, 1880–1920*, (Graduate Program in Political Science, York University, Toronto Ontario 1985, p. 71
64	Porsh, Mykola, *Avtonomiy Ukrainy*, Kyiv, 1907, p. 131.
65	Goldelman, Solomon, *Jewish National Autonomy in Ukraine 1917–1920*, Chicago, 1968, Moses, Silberfarb, *The Jewish Ministry and Jewish National Autonomy in Ukraine 1918/19*, New York, 1993.
66	'Declaration of the Provisional Government', 'The Kerensky Provisional Government and the Ukrainian Central Rada', Walter Dushnyk, *Ukrainian Quarterly*, Summer 1967, Vol XXIII, No.2, New York. p. 25

67 Hamrets'ky, Yu, 'Stavlennya Rad robitnychykh i soldats'kykh deputativ Ukrayiny u period dvovladdya do pytan' natsional'no-vyzvol'noho rukhu, *Ukrayinsky istorychny zhurnal*, 1966, № 7, p. 12
68 Prymak, Thomas M, *Mykhailo Hrushevsky, The Politics of National Culture*, Toronto, 1987, 127–128.
69 *Ibid*, Hamrets'ky, p. 4
70 Trotsky, Leon, *History of the Russian Revolution*, Vol.III, London, 1967, p. 47–49.
71 *Ibid*, Hamrets'ky, p. 13
72 *Robitnycha hazeta*, Tsentral'nyy orhan Ukrayins'koyi Sotsial-Demokratychnoyi Robitnychoyi Partiyi, Kyiv, no.33, 11 May 1917,
73 Lapchinsky, Yurii , Z pershykh dniv vseukrainskoyi vlady, *Letopis revoliutsiyi*, 1927, No. 5–6, p. 56. Cited in *'The "Ukrainian Problem" and how Stalin tried to solve it,'* James E Mace, (unpublished manuscript.)
74 Vynnychenko, Volodymyr, *Vidrodzhennia natsii, Kyiv-Vienna*, Tom.1, p. 102.
75 Raya Dunayevskaya identified a similar problem in the anti-colonial revolutions after 1945: 'The greatest obstacle to the further development of these national liberation movements comes from the intellectual bureaucracy which has emerged to 'lead' them. In the same manner the greatest obstacle in the way of the working class overcoming capitalism comes from the Labor bureaucracy that leads it', Raya Dunayevskaya, *Nationalism, Communism, Marxist Humanism and the Afro-Asian Revolutions*. Cambridge, 1961, p15.
76 *Ibid*, Yu.Hamrets'ky, p. 7
77 *Chervony Prapor*, Orhan Orhanizatsiynoho Komitetu Fraktsiyi U.S.D.R.P, Kyiv, 22 January 1919.
78 Vynnychenko believed they had taken Marx's theory of the development of capitalism in an ideal context, recalling the comparably large size of the French peasantry at the time of the Paris Commune. *Ibid, Vidrodzhennia natsii*, p. 91.
79 The conference of the Ukrainian Social Democrats held on 4–5 April 1917, considered it 'as the very first and urgent present objective of the Ukrainian proletariat and the entire country', *Robitnycha Hazeta*, 7 April 1917.
80 Lenin wrote: "Their radicalism stands higher than that of the workers and soldiers councils...the conflicts the Ukrainians are having with the Government, and especially those of Ukrainian soldiers, grow fiercer all the time." Cited in Bojcun, *Ibid*, p. 270.
81 The principle resolutions adopted by the Fourth Congress of the USDRP was drafted by Mykola Porsh, the congress itself was influenced not only by the traditional left leaders but the new generation of militants such as Neronovych and Richytsky. The report and resolutions of the congress were published in *Robitnycha Hazeta*, 1, 3, 5 and 7 October 1917.
82 Porsh complained that: 'At first the Central Rada was a bloc of parties united around the slogan of autonomy and federation. When our party entered the Rada, it replaced its class orientation with a national one. Some of our comrades said quite plainly that until we achieve the goal of unity there can be no class struggle in the Central Rada ... As far as I am concerned, Ukrainian Social Democrats had no right compromising on class interests in deference to general, national ones'. *Robitnycha Hazeta*, 4 October 1917.

83	These problems of the revolution were highlighted in the writings of the leading Ukrainian Bolsheviks Vasyl Shakhray and Serhii Mazlakh and in a series of books in 1918-1919. See: Vasyl Skorovstansky, [Shakhrai]. *Revoliutsiia na Ukraine*, 2nd ed.Saratov, 1918, and Shakhray i Maslakh. *Do khvyli: Shcho diiet'sia na Ukraý˜ni i z Ukrainoiu*, Saratov, 1919. The latter is also in an English edition, Vasyl Shakhrai, and Serhii Maslakh. *On the Current Situation in the Ukraine*, ed. PeterJ. Potichnyj, (University of Michigan Press, 1970.) This became key texts of the pro- independence currents of Ukrainian communism during the revolution.
84	*Ibid*, Krawchenko *The Social Structure of the Ukraine in 1917*, p. 111.
85	There is no complete study of the Ukrainian question in these debates. Works which cover this period include: V. Levynsky, *L'internatonale socialiste et les peuples opprimes*, Vienna, 1920, A. Karpenko, 'Lenin's Theory of The National Question And Its Contradictions', *META*, 2 No. 3-4, 1979, M. Yurkevich, 'A Forerunner of National Communism: Lev Yurkevych (1885-1918), *Journal of Ukrainian Studies*. 7:1, spring 1982, Lev Rybalka (Yurkevych) 'Rosiiski marksysty i ukrainskyi rukh', *Dzvin* 7-8. 1913.
86	It included representatives of the Councils of Workers' and Soldiers' Deputies of Kyiv, Kharkiv, Katerynoslav and Odessa. *Robitnycha Hazeta*, no.169, 27 October 1917.
87	In effect, this new body formed what the majority of workers, peasants and soldiers had been striving for, a socialist coalition based upon the popular revolutionary organizations. It was the refusal of the Menshevik and Russian SR. leadership to meet this demand, which had persuaded the majority of Bolsheviks in organizing the overthrow of the discredited bourgeois-socialist coalition Provisional Government. The Mensheviks and right-SRs, along with the Bund, sabotaged the Committee for the Defense of the Revolution in Kyiv. They pushed a motion through the Mala Rada, condemning the Bolshevik/Left SR seizure of power in Petrograd. Ukrainian socialist parties delegates on the committee went along with this, not out of support for the ousted Provisional Government, but because the Menshevik and Bund delegates on the Central Rada, happened to be Russian and Jewish minority representatives, whom the Ukrainians were anxious to keep on board. In practice, the Central Rada was prepared to acknowledge the Soviet government in Russia, but not its designs upon Ukraine.
88	Wade, Rex A. *Red Guards and Workers Militias in the Russian Revolution*, Stanford, , 1984, p. 261-262.
89	Pidhainy, Alexander, The Kievan Organization of the RSDRP(Bolsheviks), , MA Thesis, University of New Brunswick,1967, p. 79
90	*Ibid*, Shakhray p. 70
91	Holubnychy, Vsevolod, `The 1917 Agrarian Revolution in the Ukraine', *Soviet Regional Economics: Selected Works of Vselovod Holubnychy*, Edmonton:, 1982. P.43. On the ground it peasants were not examining nuances of the Lenin's *Decree on the Land* and the Third *Universal* – private property on the land had been abolished and given over to the land committees, which they controlled. They did not intend to relinquish the gains of their revolution, but to those who understood the retreat it fuelled distrust of leadership of the UNR.
92	Kreizel, *Iz istorii profdvizheniya g. Kharkova v 1917 godu*, Kharkiv, 1921.

93	Shukman, Harold, *The Blackwell encyclopedia of the Russian Revolution*, New York, 1988, P. 23
94	*Ibid*, Skorovstanskii, *Revoliutsiia na Ukraini*, 74.
95	Bojcun, Marko,'Approaches to the Study of the Ukrainian Revolution 1917–21', *Journal of Ukrainian Studies*, Vol 24:1 (1999).
96	*Robitnycha Hazeta*, November 3, 1917.
97	The Kyiv Bolshevik Yevgenia Bosh records that the Third Universal was welcomed by 'a significant number of soviets in Ukraine'. *Ibid*, Bojcun, *Working Class and the National Question*, p. 306. Similarly Shakhray, a Poltava Bolshevik, records the 'Proclamation of the Ukrainian Republic was met with huge demonstrations all over Ukraine. A significant part of the Soviets also welcomed it.' *Ibid*, Skorovstanskii, *Revoliutsiia na Ukraini*, p. 74.
98	In their campaign for the re-election of the Rada through a congress of soviets, the Bolsheviks did not seek unity with like minded Ukrainian socialists, nor secure support from the soviets which had already backed such a congress. Instead it was called by the RSDRP Kyiv Committee. See, Prymak, Thomas M , 'The First All-Ukrainian Congress of Soviets and its Antecedents', *Journal of Ukrainian Studies*, No.6, Spring (1979).
99	Pavlo Khrystyuk, *Zamitku i materialy do istoriyi ukrayinskoyi revolyutsiyi 1917–1920*, New York, 1969, Vol, p. 36–49.
100	This was also reflected inside the Central Rada with the establishment of a Secretariat of Internationality Affairs with key commissars for Jewish and Polish affairs. Goldelman, Solomon I, *Jewish national autonomy in Ukraine 1917–1920*, Chicago, 1968.
101	Zdorov, Andriy,Ukrayins'ky Zhovten'. Robitn'o-Selyans'ka Revolyutsiya V Ukrayini (Lystopad 1917–Lyutyy 1918), Odesa, p. 63
102	*Ibid*, p. 70–71
103	The issue of repression against workers' organizations (prohibition and arrests of Soviets, factory and mine committees, strikes, trade unions etc.) in the part of Donbass occupied by Kaledin, this was raised in negotiations between the General Secretariat and the Don government by Secretary General of Labor M. Porsch following complaints that came from the workers.
104	*Ibid*, pg 72.
105	Guthier, Steven L, 'Popular Base of Ukrainian Nationalism', *Slavic Review* Vol. 38, No. 1, 1979, p. 36.
106	Borys, Jurij , *Sovietization of Ukraine, Edmonton*, 1980, p. 170.
107	*Ibid*, Guthier, *Popular Base*, p. 42.
108	https://www.marxists.org/archive/lenin/works/1919/dec/16.htm
109	*Ibid*, Murray, pg 54
110	Radkey summed up that: 'In the face of such a clear-cut demonstration of strength, it is simply not possible to contend that the Ukrainian movement was a weak and artificial thing, concocted by a group of hyper-nationalistic intellectuals...' Radkey, Oliver Henry, *Elections to the Russia Constituent Assembly*, Harvard, 1950, p. 30.
111	Zenushkina, I, *Soviet Nationalities Policy and Bourgeois Historians, The Formation of the Soviet Multinational State (1917–1922) in Contemporary American Historiography*, Moscow,1975, p. 147.

112	Volodymyr Vynnychenko,, *Vidrodzhennia Natsii*, Kiev-Vienna, 1920, Tom. I, p. 219.
113	*Robitnycha Hazeta* 177, November 5, 1917
114	Forty soviets from Ukraine attended the Second All Russia Congress of Soviets and endorsed the Bolshevik the seizure of power. Velychenko, Stephen *Painting Imperialism and Nationalism Red: The Ukrainian Marxist Critique of Russian Communist Rule in Ukraine, 1918–1925,*. Toronto, 2015. p. 25
115	*Ibid,* Zhdorov p. 139
116	*Ibid,* Zdorov, p. 145. At that time, most of the Kyiv garrison had already become Ukrainianize. In particular, in November 1917, 36,680 voters of the garrison participated in the elections to the All-Russian Constituent Assembly, of which more than 19,000 were in the Ukrainianized units. The overall distribution of votes in the Kyiv garrison was as follows: for the USDRP-UPSR bloc - 46.4%, for the Bolsheviks - 37%, for Russian Socialists - 7.1% 48.
117	Medvedyev, Y, 'Z Kharkova do Kyyeva y nazad', *Litopys revolyutsiyi* Kharkiv, 1928, (28). P.241–244
118	*Ibid* p. 242
119	As relations deteriorated the USDRP blamed the Bolsheviks for deepening a divisive wave of national feelings by 'struggling against the Central Rada, which the Ukrainian people rightfully regard as the expression of their interests. So we can note that the Bolshevik party, which is to all appearances the most revolutionary and democratic, has by its tactics caused a total rupture between the Russian and Ukrainian democracies and the obfuscation of contradictions among the Ukrainian people in a wave of nationalism', *Robitnycha Hazeta*, 5 December 1917.
120	An appeal to the Ukrainians on 8 December 1917 by the leading organs of soviet power in Russia, including the Central Executive Committee, demanded the 'immediate re-election of the Rada' with the proviso: 'Let the Ukrainians predominate in these soviets'. However when the Council of Peoples Commissars declared a war on the Central Rada behind the back of the CEC it did not receive unanimous or uncritical endorsement for its action. Ed. John Keep *The Debate on Soviet Power, Minutes of the All-Russian Central Executive Committee of Soviets*, Oxford, 1979, p. 195–223.
121	Lenin, V. I, 'Manifesto To The Ukrainian People, With An Ultimatum To The Ukrainian Rada', https://www.marxists.org/archive/lenin/works/1917/dec/03.htm [Accessed 5 April 2018].
122	Wade, Rex, 'Ukrainian Nationalism and 'Soviet Power': Kharkiv, 1917', in *Ukrainian Past, Ukrainian Present*, Bohdan Krawchenko (ed), Basingstoke, 1993, pp 70–83.
123	*Літопис революції* (Харків), 1927, №5–6, 'Маніфест до всіх робітників, селян та салдатів України', <https://vpered.wordpress.com/2017/12/18/kharkiw-manifest/> [Accessed 8 April 2018].
124	Shakhrai, Vasyl, [V. Skorovstansky], *Revoliutsiia na Ukraine*, 2nd ed. (Saratov 1918), p. 110-11.
125	Radkey, Oliver, *The Elections to the Russian Constituent Assembly of 1917*, Harvard, 1950, p. 21
126	*Ibid,* Zdorov, p. 214–215

127 Vynnychenko also tried in vain to convince his USDRP comrades to take over completely and form a Ukrainian radical left government and seek peace with Soviet Russia. V, Vynnycneko, *Vidrodzhennia Natsii*, Kiev-Vienna, 1920, Tom. II, p. 220-22.
128 Grasiozi, *Bol'sheviki i krest'yany na Ukraine*, 1918-1919, p. 43.
129 V.Vynnychenko, *Vidrodzhennia Natsii*, Kiev-Vienna, 1920, Tom. I, p. 219.
130 We exerted valiant efforts in order to stop that `invasion`, as we used to call it, to win over our soldier masses, which were inert towards us, to our side. But they displayed no wish to fight against the Bolsheviks even in Kyiv, fraternizing with them and taking their part. The Ukrainian Government could not rely on any of the units quartered in Kyiv; it had no reliable unit even for its own protection.' *Ibid*, Vynnychenko, Tom.II, p. 216.
131 *Ibid*, Holubnychy, p. 47
132 Medvedev, Roy, *Let History Judge*, New York, 1972, p. 16.
133 *Ibid*,Borys, *Sovietization of Ukraine*, p. 190
134 Bojcun unpublished, The Fall of the Rada. 2018.
135 M Rafes, *Dva roku revolyutsiyi v Ukrayini. Evolyutsiya ta rozkol Bundy*, Moscow, 1920. p. 81-82
136 Tsentral'noho Derzhavnoho Arkhivu,(Kyiv) TsDAVO, f. 1326, op. 1, spr. 7, ark. 84.
137 On 9 March 1918 Colonel von Stolzenberg told his High Command: 'It is very doubtful whether this government, composed as it is exclusively of left opportunists, will be able to establish a firm authority' Oleh, Fedyshyn, *Germany's Drive to the East and the Ukrainian Revolution, 1917-1918*, New Brunswick, 1971, p. 96.
138 Ibid, Vynnychenko, Tom. 3, op. cit., p. 24.
139 'Ukrainian History: Deja Vue', *Ukrayinska Pravda*, Kyiv, October 11, 2005.
140 Hunczak, Taras, 'The Ukraine under Hetman Pavlo Skoropadsky,' The Ukraine, 1917-1921, A Study in Revolution, p. 71.
141 In a telegram from German Ambassador to Ukraine, Baron Mumm, to the German Foreign Office, dated 30 April 1918, *Ibid*, Fedyshyn, pg. 184.
142 There was also a shift in working class opinion on the national question, with significant support for an independent Ukraine. This was confirmed by the Second All-Ukrainian Workers Congress on 13 May 1918; despite a non-Ukrainian majority it agreed to a united struggle with the peasantry for an independent Ukrainian Peoples Republic, sentiments further expressed at the All-Ukrainian Conference of Trade Unions, again largely non-Ukrainian in composition, See, *Ibid*, Krawchenko, *Social Change*, p. 74.
143 Mace, James, *Communism and the Dilemmas of National Liberation, National Communism in Soviet Ukraine, 1918-1933*, Harvard, 1983, p. 59.
144 Amongst others this is the assessment of George Luckyj in his foreword to *Borotbism* in the 1954 edition.
145 Vynnychenko writes the Directory "did not even give the population a chance to catch its breath and see at least some difference between itself and the Hetmanshchyna", Ibid, Vynnychenko, *Vidrodzhennnia Natsii*, Tom.III, p. 145.
146 Ibidn, Bojcun, *Working Class and the National Question*, p. 393.

147 Mazepa,I, *Ukraina v ohni I buri revolutsii 1917-1921*, Tom.I, p. 28, Adams, Arthur, *The Bolsheviks In The Ukraine The Second Campaign*, 1918-1919, New Haven 1963, p. 120-123,
148 *Ibid,* Adams, p. 93
149 Ibid, Richtysky, 'Memorandum Ukrainskoi Kumunistichnoi', *Nova Doba.*
150 Draper, Hal, *Socialism From Below*, Almeda, , 2001, p. 1-33.
151 It is important to note that contrary to cold-war historiography and its descendants, Bolshevism was far from a monolith. We find within Bolshevism, with its popular base of support, both 'souls of socialism' so to speak.
152 *Ibid,* Maistrenko, *Borotbism,* p. 102.
153 Cited in, Krawchenko, Bohdan, *The National Renaissance and the Working Class in Ukraine During the 1920s,* paper delivered to the Colloque International, Paris, November 1982. (unpublished)
154 Silnycky, F, 'Lenin i Borotbisy', *Novy Zhournal,* no.118, 1975, p. 230-231, cited in Zbigniew Kowalewski, *International Marxist Review,* Vo.4. no.2, 1989.
155 Key texts are, *Christian Rakovsky, Selected Writings on Opposition in the USSR 1923-30,* ed. Gus Fagan, London, 1980, Pierre Broué: *Rakovsky, Cahiers Léon Trotsky,* no.17-18. L'Institut Léon Trotsky, 1984. Neither of them engage critically with the policy of Rakovsky in Ukraine in 1919.
156 Rakovsky, Beznadezhnoe delo, *Izvestiia,* no.2, (554) January 3,1919.
157 According to Balabanoff, first Secretary of the Communist International and a friend of Rakovsky's sent to assist him in Kiev, "the Bolsheviks had set up an independent republic in the Ukraine. In actuality that section of it in which Soviet rule was established was completely dominated by the Moscow regime". Balabanoff, Angelica, *My Life as a Rebel,* London 1938, p. 234.
158 This rejection flew in the face of earlier instructions of Lenin to Rakovsky that the non-Bolsheviks soviet parties be involved.
159 Babenko, A, *Bolshevist Bonapartism*, Nasha Borotba, Geneva, 1948, p. 6.
160 On 17 April 1919, Red Army commander on the Ukrainian front Antonov-Ovseyenko raised demands similar to Vynnychenko and the Ukrainian left. Under order to go on the offensive westwards he was hindered because "land and national policy in Ukraine cuts at the roots of the military leadership to overcome these disintegrating influences". He proposed a new policy where the "Nezalezhnik SD's and Ukrainian SRs" were included in the government and "to compel foreigners 'Great Russians' to adjust themselves with greatest tact towards the local population" and "to halt the plundering of Ukraine's bread and coal", *Ibid,* Adams, , p. 266.
161 Tokes, Rudolf, *Bela Kun and the Hungarian Soviet Republic,* Stanford: Hoover. 1967, pg,202. Vynnychenko concluded if the plan had been accepted the Soviet governments in Hungary and Bavaria could have been saved.
162 On the attitude of the Volunteer Army towards the Ukrainian question see, Procyk, Anna, *Russian Nationalism and Ukraine: The Nationality Policy of the Volunteer Army during the Civil War,* Edmonton, 1995.
163 A Volunteer army spy reported on the mood in threatened Petrograd: "The worker elements, at least a large section of them, are still Bolshevik inclined. Like some other democratic elements, they see the regime although bad as their own...Psychologically, they identify the present with equality and Soviet power and the Whites with the old regime and its scorn of the masses."

	Figes, Orlando, *A People's Tragedy, The Russian Revolution 1891–1924*, Pimlico, 1996, p. 675.
164	*Ibid*,Maistrenko, *Borotbism*, p. 196.
165	*Ibid*, Bojcun, Journal of Ukrainian Studies, p. 37.
166	Kostiuk, Hryhory, *Stalinist Rule in Ukraine*, New York, 1960, p. 39.
167	This is how Ievhen Hirchak a comrade of Skrypnyk described Ukrainization, Dmytryshyn, Basil, *Moscow & the Ukraine, 1918–1953: A Study of Russian Bolshevik Nationality Policy*, New York, 1956, p. 71.
168	Whilst some figures like Khvylovyi openly admired Trotsky, the Left Opposition failed to develop a united anti-Stalinist bloc with this radical current in Ukraine. The ideas of some prominent figures in the Left Opposition such as V.Vaganian were a continuation of the left-communist views, and Zinoviev in 1927 attacked the policy of Ukrainization as "Petliurovshchina". Only in September 1927 did the Left Opposition advocate a more "conscientious" program of *korenizatsiia*. Kostiuk considered that it was only in the Gulag that the activists of the opposition currents united when it was already too late.
169	Ibid, Krawchenko, *The National Renaissance and the Working Class*.
170	This speech was not published in the Collected Works of Lenin but was reported in the press at the time. See Serbyn, Roman,, 'Lenin et la question Ukrainienne en 1914: Le discourse separatiste de Zurich', *Pluriel-debat'*, no. 25, 1981.
171	Marx, Karl, - 'Marx to Ludwig Kugelmann', London, 29 November 1869, *Marx and Engels Collected Works*, Volume 43, Moscow, p. 389.

NOTES TO BIOGRAPHICAL NOTE

172	Ivan Maistrenko, *Istoriya moho pokolinnya spohady uchasnyka revolyutsiynykh podiy v Ukrayini*, Edmonton, 1985, p. 6
173	Education at the time was conducted in Russian, and this caused great difficulty for Ukrainian children like Maistrenko and his brothers and sisters.Ibid, Maistrenko, *Istoriya moho pokolinnya*, p. 3
174	Ibid, Maistrenko, *Istoriya moho pokolinnya*, p. 1–2.
175	Ibid, Maistrenko, *Istoriya moho pokolinnya*, p. 15
176	Ibid, Maistrenko, *Istoriya moho pokolinnya*, p. 24
177	Ibid, Maistrenko, *Istoriya moho pokolinnya*, p. 19–20
178	Ibid, Maistrenko, *Istoriya moho pokolinnya*, p. 33.
179	Ivan Maistrenko, *Borotbism A Chapter in the History of the Ukrainian Revolution*, Stuttgart, 2007, pg.226-231, Ibid, Maistrenko, *Istoriya moho pokolinnya*, p. 34
180	Ibid, *Borotbism*, p. 233.
181	Ibid,*Borotbism,* p. 231
182	Ibid,*Borotbism,* p. 239
183	Ibid, *Borotbism*, p. 240
184	Ibid, Maistrenko, *Istoriya moho pokolinnya*, p. 19–20
185	Ibid, Maistrenko, *Istoriya moho pokolinnya*, p. 86–87
186	Ibid, Maistrenko, *Istoriya moho pokolinnya*, p. 101
187	Ibid, Maistrenko, *Istoriya moho pokolinnya*, p. 111–112
188	Yurenko O.P, 'Ivan Maystrenko: zhyttya naukova i publitsystychna spadshchyna', Ukrayins'kyy istorychnyy zhurnal, Kyiv, 1999, No.6, p. 13
189	Ibid, Yurenko p. 13

190	Ibid, Maistrenko, *Istoriya moho pokolinnya*, p. 136
191	Ibid, Maistrenko, *Istoriya moho pokolinnya*, p. 136
192	Ibid, Maistrenko, *Istoriya moho pokolinnya*, p. 136
193	Ibid, Maistrenko, *Istoriya moho pokolinnya*, pg. 137, Yury Lapchynsky resigned from the CP(b)U and joined the new Ukrainian Communist Party formed by the left-wing of the USDRP. See 'Fehler! Nur Hauptdokument**Comrade G. Lapchynsky's letter to the editors of *Chervony Prapor*', in Chervony Prapor July 11, 1920.
194	Maistrenko, *Istoriya moho pokolinnya*, p. 146–147
195	Maistrenko, *Istoriya moho pokolinnya*, p. 147.
196	Maistrenko, *Istoriya moho pokolinnya*, p. 160
197	Maistrenko, *Istoriya moho pokolinnya*, p. 159
198	Maistrenko, *Istoriya moho pokolinnya*, p. 170–171
199	Maistrenko, *Istoriya moho pokolinnya*, p. 167
200	Maistrenko, *Istoriya moho pokolinnya*, p. 168
201	Maistrenko, *Istoriya moho pokolinnya*, p. 169
202	Maistrenko, *Istoriya moho pokolinnya*, p. 172–173
203	Maistrenko, *Istoriya moho pokolinnya*, p. 154
204	Maistrenko, *Istoriya moho pokolinnya*, p. 195
205	Maistrenko, *Istoriya moho pokolinnya*, p. 222–224
206	Maistrenko, *Istoriya moho pokolinnya*, p. 231.
207	Maistrenko, *Istoriya moho pokolinnya*, p. 221–222.
208	Maistrenko, *Istoriya moho pokolinnya*, p. 222.
209	Yurenko O.P, 'Ivan Maystrenko: zhyttya naukova i publitsystychna spadshchyna', Ukrayins'kyy istorychnyy zhurnal, Kyiv, 1999, No.6, p. 116
210	Ibid Yurenko, p116
211	Maistrenko, *Istoriya moho pokolinnya*, p. 251
212	Maistrenko, *Istoriya moho pokolinnya*, p. 254
213	Maistrenko, *Istoriya moho pokolinnya*, p. 254
214	Maistrenko, *Istoriya moho pokolinnya*, p. 254
215	Maistrenko, *Istoriya moho pokolinnya*, p. 254
216	Maistrenko, *Istoriya moho pokolinnya*, p. 254
217	Maistrenko, *Istoriya moho pokolinnya*, p 259
218	Maistrenko, *Istoriya moho pokolinnya*, p 260
219	Maistrenko, *Istoriya moho pokolinnya*, 262–326
220	Maistrenko, *Istoriya moho pokolinnya*, p. 255
221	Maistrenko, *Istoriya moho pokolinnya*, p. 255
222	Yurenko O.P, 'Ivan Maystrenko: zhyttya naukova i publitsystychna spadshchyna', Ukrayins'kyy istorychnyy zhurnal, Kyiv, 1999, No.6, p. 117
223	Maistrenko, *Istoriya moho pokolinnya*, p. 325
224	Maistrenko, *Istoriya moho pokolinnya*, p. 331
225	Maistrenko, *Istoriya moho pokolinnya*, p. 328
226	Maistrenko, *Istoriya moho pokolinnya*, p. 328
227	Maistrenko, *Istoriya moho pokolinnya*, p. 328
228	Maistrenko, *Istoriya moho pokolinnya*, p. 330
229	Maistrenko, *Istoriya moho pokolinnya*, p. 334
230	Maistrenko, *Istoriya moho pokolinnya*, p. 335
231	Maistrenko, *Istoriya moho pokolinnya*, p. 336

232	Maistrenko, *Istoriya moho pokolinnya*, p. 337
233	Maistrenko, *Istoriya moho pokolinnya*, p. 339
234	Maistrenko, *Istoriya moho pokolinnya*, p. 339
235	Maistrenko, *Istoriya moho pokolinnya*, p. 340
236	Maistrenko, *Istoriya moho pokolinnya*, p. 341
237	Maistrenko, *Istoriya moho pokolinnya*, p. 341
238	Maistrenko, *Istoriya moho pokolinnya*, p. 345
239	Maistrenko, *Istoriya moho pokolinnya*, p. 349
240	Maistrenko, *Istoriya moho pokolinnya*, p. 350
241	Maistrenko, *Istoriya moho pokolinnya*, p. 351
242	Maistrenko, *Istoriya moho pokolinnya*, p. 352
243	Maistrenko, *Istoriya moho pokolinnya*, p. 355
244	Maistrenko, *Istoriya moho pokolinnya*, p. 355
245	Maistrenko, *Istoriya moho pokolinnya*, p. 356
246	Maistrenko, *Istoriya moho pokolinnya*, p. 359
247	Maistrenko, *Istoriya moho pokolinnya*, p. 360
248	Maistrenko, *Istoriya moho pokolinnya*, p. 363
249	A Babenko [Ivan Maistrenko], 'Is an Underground Possible in Russia? Experiences and Problems of the Resistance Movement', *The New International*, December 1949,pg.240
250	Maistrenko, *Istoriya moho pokolinnya*, p. 364
251	Maistrenko, *Istoriya moho pokolinnya*, p. 365
252	Maistrenko, *Istoriya moho pokolinnya*, p. 366
253	Maistrenko, *Istoriya moho pokolinnya*, p. 370
254	Maistrenko, *Istoriya moho pokolinnya*, p. 367
255	Maistrenko, *Istoriya moho pokolinnya*, p. 368
256	Maistrenko, *Istoriya moho pokolinnya*, p. 374
257	Maistrenko, *Istoriya moho pokolinnya*, p. 374
258	As relayed to the author by Levko Maystrenko
259	*Vpered*, Ukrainian Review for Workers, Munich, No.3, 1949
260	V. Vynnychenko, 'Rozlad i pohodzhennia,Vidpovid moim prykhylnykam i neprykhylnykam' , *Nasha Borotba,* Geneva, 1948
261	A Babenko, *Bolshevist Bonapartism*, Babenko, A, (Maistrenko) Nasha Borotba, Geneva, 1948, p. 9.
262	Babenko, *Bolshevist Bonapartism*, p. 13.
263	*Vpered*, Ukrainian Review for Workers, Munich, 1949, No.2
264	*Meta*, A Left Wing Discussion Journal, Volume.2, No.1, Summer 1978, p. 3.
265	Ibid, *Meta*
266	Maistrenko, *Istoriya moho pokolinnya*, , p. x-xi

NOTES TO CHAPTER ONE

1. The Southern Society was the more radical wing of the oppositionist movement of enlightened Russian nobles, mainly military officers, which culminated in the Decembrist uprising of 1825- Under the extremist Pavel Pestel the Southern Society favored a centralist republic, patterned after Jacobin France. The Society of United Slavs, which had its strength mainly among the lower-ranked army officers, eventually amalgamated with the Southern Society. Its ethical program, which emphasized the liberty of the individual and brotherly

love, was more clearly formulated than its constitutional program, which called for an ill-defined federated republic of all Slavic peoples. For the most detailed treatment in English of the DeCem-brist uprising, see Mazour, Anatole G., The First Russian Revolution, 1825: The Decembrist Movement, Its Origins, Development, and Significance, Berkeley, 1937.

The word narod can be translated as "nation," "people" or "the peasantry." In this instance "the peasantry" is meant. It was Peter Lavrov (1823-1900) who provided the theoretical basis for the movement known as narodnichestvo [populism].

The RSDRP, the first Marxist party in Russia, was founded in Minsk in 1898 and held its Second Congress in Brussels and London in 1903.

The Little Russian Society, which shared the ideas of the Decembrists, existed in the early 1820's and advocated an independent Ukraine.

The Brotherhood of SS. Cyril and Methodius was organized in Kiev in 1846 by the poet Taras Shevchenko and a group of his friends. Under the influence of the ideas of the Society of United Slavs and western European romanticism, it advocated the abolition of serfdom, political liberty and a federation of Slavic republics. Although it was suppressed in 1847, its influence was fundamental in the subsequent Ukrainian movement.

The Hromada was an underground cultural society founded in Kiev in the 1850's. Following a relaxation of the official ban on Ukrainian books, it became in the early 1870's a center of educational and cultural, but not political, activity.

Drahomanov (1841-1895) was born into a small landowning family in Poltava. Brought up on the ideas of the Decembrists (his uncle was a member of the Society of United Slavs), he became a scholar of ancient history. Drahomanov's interest in Ukrainian political life developed through a study of Ukrainian folklore and a comparative

study of the evolution of western political institutions (see Doro-shenko, Volodymyr, "The Life of Mykhaylo Drahomanov," The Annals of the Ukrainian Academy of Arts and Sciences in the U.S., New York, Vol. II, Spring 1952, No. 1(3), pp. 6-22. This issue of The Annals was entitled Mykhaylo Drahomanov: A Symposium and Selected Writings (hereafter cited as Symposium). See also pp. 12-13, below. For a discussion of the RUP and the USDRP, see pp. 15-21.-Ed.

2 Vasylenko-Polons'ka, N., "Ukrai'na v druhiy polovyni XIX–napochatku XX st." [The Ukraine in the Second Half of the Nineteenth and the Beginning of the Twentieth Century], Entsyklopediya uhrainoznavstva [Encyclopedia of Ukrainian Knowledge], Munich-New York, 1949, Part II, p. 474.

3 Bakunin, Mikhail, Gosudarstvennost' i anarkhiya [Statehood and Anarchy], Petersburg[sic]-Moscow, 1922, pp. 53, 89.

4 Doroshenko, D[mytro I.], Z istorit ukrai'ns'koi' politychnotdumky za chasiv svitovoi' viyny [On the History of Ukrainian Political Thought During the World War], Prague, 1936, p. 17.

5 Mazepa, I[saak], Pidstavy nashoho vidrodzhennya [Foundations of Our Regeneration], [Munich?] 1946, Vol. I, p. 139. (Here after cited as Pidstavy.)

6 Doroshenko, op. cit., p. 10.

7 Mazepa, Pidstavy, p. 146.

8	Ibid., p. 143.
9	Doroshenko, op. cit., p. 12.
10	Quoted in Mazepa, Pidstavy, p. 147
11	Doroshenko, op. cit., p. 15
12	Vasylenko-Polons'ka, op. cit., p. 472.
13	Zaslavski, D[avid I.], M.P. Dragomanov: kritiko-biograficheshii ocherk [M.P. Drahomanov: A Critico-Biographical Sketch],Kiev, 1924, p. 94. [Zaslavski's M.P. Dragomanov: k istorii uhrainskovo natsionalizma (M.P. Drahomanov: Toward a History of Ukrainian Nationalism), Moscow, 1934, is a revised edition in which he "corrected" his "mistakes." The Zaporozhskaya Sech', literally "the fortress below the rapids," was established by Cossacks on the islands in the lower Dnepr River in the early part of the sixteenth century and existed until its break-up under Catherine II in 1785. The influx of Ukrainian serfs and peasants fleeing from their Polish and Lithuanian landlords in the North and West and of Russian serfs and peasants fleeing from Russian masters in the North and East provided a continual source of replenishment for the Zaporozh'ye Cossacks in this frontier no man's land contested by Poland, Muscovy, Turkey, and the Crimean Tatars. – Ed.]
14	Quoted in Fedenko, Panas, Ukraihskyi hromads'hyi rukh u XX stolitti [The Ukrainian Social Movement in the Twentieth Century], Podebrady, Czechoslovakia, 1934, p. 8. (Hereafter cited as Hromads'kyi rukh.) [Naddnipryans'ka Ukrai'na included all Ukrainian territory within the pre-1917 borders of the Russian Empire, and was used to distinguish this area from Ukrainian territory, primarily Galicia, within the Austro-Hungarian Empire. – Ed.]
15	Radykaly i radykalizm [Radicals and Radicalism], Lvov, 1896, p. 12 (Khlops'ha biblioteka [Peasant Library], Vol. IV).
16	Ibid
17	Doroshenko, op. cit., p. 21.
18	Ibid., p. 9.
19	Lypnys'kyi, Vyacheslav K., Lysty do brativ-hhliborobiv: pro ideyu i orhanizatsiyu uhrai'ns'koho monarkhizmu [Letters to Brother Agriculturists: The Concept and Organization of Ukrainian Monarchism], Vienna, 1926
20	This curious move by a Ukrainian socialist party was related to the author by two members of the USDRP, the party workers Dmytro Shabala and Nykyfor Lobada, the latter a member of the Central Committee of the USDRP
21	Zaslavski, op. cit., p. 82
22	Mazepa, Pidstavy, p. 139
23	Robitnycha hazeta [Workers' Gazette], Kyiv, 1918, No. 335
24	Stakhiv, Matviy, "Drahomanov's Impact on Ukrainian Politics," Symposium, p. 59.
25	Radykaly i radykalizm, op. cit., p. 18
26	Mykhaylo, N., Moskofily, narodovtsi i konsolidatsiya [Mosco-philes, Populists and Consolidation], Lvov, 1898, p. 6. [Bohdan Khmel'nyts'kyi, Hetman of the Zaporozhye Cossacks in the middle of the sixteenth century, attempted to maintain a sovereign Cossack Ukraine by military and diplomatic maneuverings with the Polish king, the Muscovite tsar and the Crimean khan. In 1654, he signed the Treaty of Peteyaslavl with Russia, a treaty which has been vari= ously interpreted as a contract between equals, an outright annexation

on the part of Moscow, and a federation with Russia allowing for Ukrainian autonomy. — Ed.]
27 Robitnycha hazeta, op. cit.
28 Quoted in Fedenko, Hromads'kyi rukh, p. 8.
29 Vsesoyuznaya Kommunisticheskaya Partiya (bol'shevikov) v rezolyutsiyakh i resheniyakh s"yezdov, konferentsii i plenumov TsK (1898-...) [Resolutions and Decisions of Congresses, Conferences and Plenary Sessions of the Central Committee of the Communist Party of the Soviet Union (Bolshevik), 1898-...], 4th ed., Moscow, 1932, Vol. I, pp. 238-240, 6th ed., 1941, Vol. I, pp. 210-211. [in 1903 in his "O-manifeste armyanskikh Sotsial-Demokratov" (On the Manifesto of the Armenian Social Democrats), Lenin affirmed "the right of self-determination for every nationality" within the Russian state (see Lenin, V.I., Sochineniya [Works], 4th ed., Moscow, 1946, Vol. VI, pp. 291-294). In 1913 in point four of "Tezisy po natsional'nomu voprosu" (Theses on the National Question), Lenin stated: "The recognition by Social Democracy of the right of all nationalities to self-determination in no way means that Social Democracy refuses to evaluate the expediency of state separation... in each particular case. On the contrary, it is precisely an independent evaluation which Social Democracy must give, taking into account both the conditions of development of capitalism and the oppression of the proletarians of various nations by the united bourgeoisie of all nationalities, and also the common tasks of democracy, in the first place the interests of the class struggle of the proletariat for socialism" (ibid., 1948, Vol. XIX, p. 214).-Ed.]
30 As Vynnychenko aptly stated at the First All-Ukrainian Congress of Councils on December 4 (17), 1917 in Kyiv, protesting the ultimatum of the Russian Bolsheviks in Petrograd to the Ukrainian Central Rada in Kyiv (see p. 51), for the Bolsheviks to recognize the Ukraine and at the same time send an ultimatum was the equivalent of — was in fact the logical sequel to — Lenin's position in 1906 of simultaneously asserting the right of the Ukraine to succession and opposing the establishment of Ukrainian schools as a threat to working class unity (Khrystyuk, Pavlo, *Zamitky i materiyaly do istorii ukrainskoi revolyutsii 1917-1920 rr.* [Notes and Materials on the History of the Ukrainian Revolution, 1917-1920 (The Ukrainian Revolution: Notes and Materials)], Vienna, 1921, Vol.11, p. 71).
31 Mikhnovs'kyi, Mykola, Samostiya Ukraina [An Independent Ukraine], Lviv, 1900; the quoted material is cited from a new ed., n.p., 1948, pp. 29-30.
32 The material from Haslo is quoted in Fedenko, Hromads'ky rukh, p. 12.
33 Quoted in ibid.
34 Mazepa, Pidstavy, pp. 149-150. Italics in the original
35 [For full text of the charter, see Ravich-Cherkasski, M[oisei], Istoriya Kommunistickeskoi Partii (bol'shevikov) Ukrainy [History of the Communist Party (Bolshevik) of the Ukraine], Kharkov, 1923, p. 190.—Ed. Material on the Spilha, in Fedenko, Hromads'kyi rukh, pp. 32-33.] For a brief, but vivid sketch of the evolution of Ukrainian prerevolutionary political life by Mykyta Shapoval, one of the oldest and most prominent of the Ukrainian SR's, see "Narodnytstvo v Ukr. vyzvol'nomu rukhovi (Promova t. M. Yu. Shapovala na konferentsii' UPSR. 9-10 lypnya 1928 r. v Prazi.)" [Populism in the Ukrainian Liberation Movement (Comrade M.Yu. Shapoval's Speech at the UPSR

	Conference in Prague, July 9–10, 1928)], Vil'tta spilka [Free Union], Prague-Lvov, No. 3, 1927–1929, pp. 95–98. (Hereafter cited as Shapoval, "Narodnytstvo."
36	Quoted in Fedenko, *Hromads'kyi rukh*, p. 33
37	Doroshenko, op. cit., p. 21.
38	Fedenko, Hromads'kyi rukh, p. 34. Italics in the original.
39	"Do tovaryshiv z Ukrai'ns'koiSotsiyal-Demokratychnoi'Spilky ta Ukrai'ns'koi' Sotsiyal-Demokratychnoi' Robitnychoi' Partii'."

NOTES TO CHAPTER TWO

1. Zhyvotko, Ark[adiy], "Do istorif ukr. partii' sotslyalistiv-revolyutsioneriv" [On the History of the Ukrainian Party of Socialist Revolutionaries]. *Vil'na spilka* [Free Union], Prague-Lvov, No. 3, 1927–1929, p. 128.
2. See e.g., Zaliznyak, Mykola, *Samostiyna Ukraina – ne sotsiyalistychne haslo?* [An Independent Ukraine: Is It Not A Socialist Slogan?], n.p. , UPSR, 1915.-Ed.
3. Shapoval, 'Narodnytstvo," *op. cit.*, p. 100.
4. Ibid
5. Shapoval, Mykyta, "Miy shlyakh: konspekt spomyniv do 1927 roku" [My Path: A Synopsis of Recollections up to 1927], manuscript. (Hereafter cited as Shapoval, "Miy shlyakh.") The material was presented in somewhat different form by Mandryka, M., "Z zhyttya M. Shapovala" [From the Life of M. Shapoval], Vil'na spilka, op. cit., pp. 8–14.
6. Lazarev, Ye., *Zemlya i volya*, St. Petersburg, 1906. Lazarev, born in 1855 of peasant origin, was twice exiled to eastern Siberia for spreading propaganda among soldiers and peasants. Later one of the founders of the Russian SR party, he helped George Kiennan gather material for his *Siberia and the Exile System*, New York, 1891 (see Laserson, Max M., *The American Impact on Russia – Diplomatic and Ideological-1784–1917*, New York, 1950, pp. 306–312). Lazarev spent the years 1891–1893 in America, returned to Russia in 1917, but emigrated to Czechoslovakia in 1919. A brief biography is available in *Deyateli revolyutsionnovo dvizheniya v Rossii: bibliograficheskii slovar'* [Figures of the Revolutionary Movement in Russia: Biobibliographical Dictionary], Moscow, 1930, Vol. II, cols. 737–740.-Ed.
7. Shapoval, *"Miy shlyakh," op. cit.*
8. *Zhyvotko, op. cit.,* p. 128.
9. Ibid
10. Ibid p. 129–130
11. Khrystyuk, *op. cit.*, Vol. I, p. 35- This opinion is shared by Vasylenko-Polons'ka, op. cit., p. 475-
12. Shapoval, "Narodnytstvo," *op. cit.,* pp. 100–101.
13. Zhyvotko, *op. cit.,* p. 131; Khrystyuk, *op. cit.,* Vol. I, pp. 35, 125, note 10.
14. "Proyekt prohramy partii U.S.R., pryinyatoi Kyivskoyu hrupoyu ukraihs'kykh sotsialistiv-revolyutsioneriv," in Zhyvotko, op. cit., p. 131.
15. Khrystyuk, *op. cit.,* Vol. I, p. 125, note 10
16. Zhyvotko, *op. cit.,* p. 131

NOTES TO CHAPTER THREE

1. Khrystyuk, op. cit., Vol. I., p. 26, note 1.

2	Vynnychenko, V[olodymyr], *Vidrodzhennya natsii* [The Rebirth of a Nation], Kiev-Vienna, 1920, Part I, p. 251. [The Ukrainian Central Rada (Ukraihs'ka Tsentral'na Rada) was first formed March 3 (17), 1917 by the Society of Ukrainian Progressives, later renamed the Ukrainian Party of Socialist Federalists. On April 4-9 (17-21), the Rada convened an All-Ukrainian National Congress, comprising delegates from various professional bodies, the town councils, the zemstvos, and the peasant cooperatives. Drawing on the delegates to the various congresses of peasants', workers' and soldiers' deputies being held at this time, the Rada was gradually enlarged to about 800 members. In mid-June (old style), the Rada established a cabinet, the General Secretariat. In effect the Rada became a provisional Ukrainian parliament. For a detailed treatment of its role in 1917, see Reshetar, John S., Jr. *The Ukrainian Revolution, 1917-1920: A Study in Nationalism*, Princeton, 1952, pp. 47-142,-Ed.]
3	Shapoval, "Narodnytstvo," *op. cit.*, pp. 112-114; see Khrystyuk, *op. cit.*, Vol. II, pp. 116-119.
4	Ibid, Vol. I, pp. 35, 36.
5	Ibid
6	Ibid, pp. 36-37
7	Ibid, pp. 37, 24-25- According to Khrystyuk, the peasant union was an institution whose form had been worked out during the Revolution of 1905
8	Ibid, p. 65 and note 1. [The close organizational ties between the Peasant Union and the First All-Ukrainian Peasants' Congress can be seen from the fact that the Congress elected not only its own interim body the All-Ukrainian Council of Peasants' Deputies, but also the Central Executive Committee of the Peasant Union (ibid, p. 128, note 20). Ed.
9	*Ibid, pp.* 65-67 and note 1, p. 67, including the text of the resolution.
10	Such was the attitude taken by the First Session of the All-Ukrainian Council of Peasants' Deputies, June 22 (July 5), 1917 (ibid. p. 45, note 2).-Ed.
11	Ibid., p. 100.
12	Ibid. p. 101.
13	Ibid., p. 102
14	Ibid, 102,103 note 1.
15	Text of resolution in ibid., p. 108.
16	Texs in ibid, pp. 108-109. Italics in the original
17	Ibid, p. 139, note 34. The other members were Saltan, Okhrymovych, Sevryuk, Isayevych, Khrystyuk, Lyzanivsky, Chechel', Iolonsky, Shleychenko, Bazyak, Shrah, Kovalevs'kyl, Korzh, Kovalenko, and Puhach.
18	Ibid., p. 110
19	Ibid, Vol.II, p. 24
20	Ibid, p. 25. Italics in the original
21	Ibid, p. 25-26
22	Ibid, p. 26. Italics in the original
23	Ibid, p. 26, note 1.
24	Ibid
25	A First Military Congress had met on April 5 (18) with delegates representing one million Ukrainian soldiers; in May a second congress of delegates, representing 1,736,000 soldiers, convened despite a ban by the Petrograd minister of war (Hrushevsky, Michael, A History of Ukraine, New Haven, 1941,

pp. 524–525). Following a Congress of Soldiers' and Peasants' Deputies, which convened in Kiev, June 2–10 (15–23), the Rada issued its First Universal [Manifesto] on June 10, proclaiming autonomy for the Ukraine (ibid, p. 525); text in Vynnychenko, op. cit., Parti, pp. 219–224.-'Ed.

26 Shapoval, "Narodnytstvo," op. cit., p. 194. [According to Khrystyuk, op. cit., Vol. II, p. 39, note 1, there were 3,000 delegates, two-thirds of whom supported the UPSR. — Ed.]

27 Khrystyuk, ibid, pp. 39, note 1, and 46, 47, 48. Italics in the original.

28 Ibid, pp. 195, note 13, and 194, note 12. [One month later at its Third Congress, the UPSR adopted a similar military program (see p. 50 below),-Ed.

29 One desyatin equals 2.70 acres. Texts of the Third Universal and the supplementary explanation on land reform, in ibid,, pp. 51–53, 58–59. [Also in Vynnychenko, op. cit., Part II, pp. 74–80; English translations available in Bunyan, James, and H.H. Fisher, The Bolshevik Revolution 1917-1918: Documents and Materials, Stanford, 1934, pp. 439–441, and in Chamberlin, William H., The Russian Revolution 1917–1921, New York, 1935, Vol. II, pp. 479–482. The Second Universal had been issued July 3 (16), (text in Vynnychenko, op. cit., Part I, pp. 279–282) in response to the Provisional Government's declaration to the Rada of July 2 (15), which nominated the General Secretariat as the "supreme authority for the administration of local affairs in the Ukraine" (text in ibid., pp. 282–284, and English translation in Chamberlin, op. cit., Vol. I, pp. 454–455).— Ed.]

30 Khrystyuk, op. cit., Vol. II, pp. 62–63, 59, and 195, note 15; Fedenko, Hromads'ky rukh, p. 79; the assessment by Lenin wasmade in his closing address to the All-Russian Conference of the Russian Communist Party (RCP), December 3, 1919, Lenin, V.I.,Stat'i i rechi ob Ukraine [Articles and Speeches on the Ukraine], Moscow, 1936, p. 336. (Hereafter cited as Stat'i i i rechi.) [See also Radkey, Oliver H., The Election to the All-Russian Constituent Assembly of 1917, Cambridge, Harvard University Press, 1950.— Ed.] The elections to the Ukrainian Constituent Assembly, held December 27 (January 9), indicated the increased strength of the Ukrainian parties, especially the UPSR. "In those areas where elections were held, [they] gained more than 70 per cent of all the votes" (Mazepa, I[saak], Ukraiha v ohni i hurt revolyutsii', 1917–1921 r. [The Ukraine in the Fire and Storm of Revolution, 1917-1921], 2nd ed., [Munich] Prometey, 1950, Vol. I, p. 34: hereafter cited as Ukraiha. However, due to the war between the Rada and the Russian Bolsheviks, which had begun December 12 (25), elections were not held throughout the entire country.

31 Khrystyuk, op. cit., Vol. II, p. 63.
32 Ibid, pp. 64, 61
33 Ibid., 62
34 Ibid., 196, note 16
35 Ibid., p. 65 Italics in the original
36 Ibid
37 Ibid., pp. 66–67. Italics in the original
38 Shapoval, "Narodnytstvo," op. cit., p. 105.
39 In the ultimatum the Russian Bolsheviks accused the Rada of "carrying on a two-faced bourgeois policy. . . by disorganizing the front. . . disarming the

Soviet troops in the Ukraine [and]... supporting the Cadet-Kaledin conspiracy.... in refusing to let through troops against Kaledin" (Izvestiya, December 6(19), 1917; English trans, in Chamberlin, op, tit., Vol. I, pp. 486-488). Italics in the original. — Ed.
40   Khrystyuk, op. pit., Vol. II, pp. 69-71.
41   Ibid., p. 73
42   Ibid., p. 84
43   Ibid., p. 74
44   Text in ibid, pp. 102-106, and in Vynnychenko, op. cit. Part II, pp. 244-252.
45   Shapoval, "Narodnytstvo," op. cit., p. 125.
46   Vynnychenko, op. cit,, Part II, pp. 220-221. Italics in the original.
47   It will be recalled that it was during this period that the Central Powers were negotiating the Treaty of Brest-Litovsk. The Central Rada signed the treaty on February 9, 1918. — Ed.
48   Khrystyuk, op. cit., Vol. II, pp. 134-140.
49   Shakhray, Vasyl' M., and Serhiy Mazlakh, Do khvyli: shcho diyet'sya net Uhraihi i z Ukraihoyu [The Current Situation: What Is Happening in and to the Ukraine], Saratov, 1919- (Hereafter cited as Shakhray, Do khvyli.) The material in the text is quoted from Chapter 18, "Ukraihs'ka Komunistychna Partiya (bol'shevykiv)" [Ukrainian Communist Party (Bolsheviks)], of the typescript

NOTES TO CHAPTER FOUR
1   Materials on the Second Peasants' Congress are taken from Khrystyuk, op. cit., Vol. Ill, pp. 14-15.
2   Materials on the Second Workers' Congress are taken from ibid., pp. 16-17.
3   Ibid., p. 17. [The Fifth Congress of the USDRP was held in Kyiv in mid-May. — Ed.]
4   Materials on the Fourth Congress are taken from ibid., pp. 19-23. In preparing this section the author has made extensive use of Khrystyuk.
5   Shapoval, "Narodnytstvo," *op. cit.,* pp. 107-108.
6   According to Shapoval, ibid., the New Central Committee consisted of Mykhaylychenko, Prykhodko, Blakytny, Mykhaylo Poloz, iiud Oleksander Shumsky. Neither Khrystyuk or Shapoval gives the complete composition of the Committee.
7   Khrystyuk, *op. cit., Vol.* Ill, pp. 23-24.
8   Ibid., p. 24
9   Although the Borot'bisty officially retained the name "UPSR" until March 1919, their party will hereafter be referred to as the "UPSR (Borot'bisty)" to distinguish it from the UPSR (Center), which emerged as a separate party in January 1919.
10 Extreme hostility between the right wing (Mykola Zaliznyak and Mykola Kovalevsky in Vienna) and the center (Shapoval and Hryhoryiv in Prague) become apparent only in emigration. The situation was further complicated by the so-called "returners," a group headed by Professor Hrushevsky which went back to the U.S.S.R. in 1924. The right wing in emigration soon disintegrated, while the center formed a strong group, especially active in the Ukrainian Sociological Institute in Prague, until the death of Shapoval in 1932.

11 See the declaration of General Groener in Die deutsche Okkupa-iion der Ukraine: Geheimdokumente, Strasbourg, 1937, p. 84.
12 Khrustyuk, op. cit., Vol. Ill, p. 106.
13 Vynnychenko, op. cit., Part III, pp. 72-74
14 Khrystyuk, op. cit., Vol. Ill, pp. 87-90.
15 Ibid., p. 95, note 1
16 "Uhodovtsi," Borotba, No. 1, August 1918, quoted in Khrystyuk, op. cit., Vol. III, p. 96.
17 "Ukrainsky Natsionalny Soyuz," Borotba, No. 2, October 1918J quoted in Khrystyuk, op. cit., Vol. Ill, pp. 96-97. Italics in the original.
18 Quoted in ibid. pp. 97-98. Italics in the original.
19 Ibid., pp. 98-99
20 Materials on the August Conference are taken from ibid., pp. 99-101. [Whenever forced to operate underground, the Borotbisty reterred to an underground party agent as an "emisar." — Ed.J
21 From the resolution quoted in ibid., p. 104.
22 Ibid., pp. 101-102, 107, 108. [The Don government was under the control of General Krasnov, the anti-Bolshevik Ataman of the Don Cossacks. — Ed.]
23 Mazepa, Ukraina, Vol. I, p. 58.

NOTES TO CHAPTER FIVE
1   Makhno, like most of the semi-literate Ukrainian workers, was at first ashamed to use the Ukrainian language, regarding it as a "peasant" language. However, his view changed markedly in the course of the Revolution. In his memoirs he describes the first time he heard Ukrainian spoken by someone other than a peasant. On a train from Moscow to the Ukraine in 1918, Makhno found that the Ukrainian conductors demanded that he make his inquiries in Ukrainian. "I was struck by the request," he writes, "but there was nothing I could do.... I was forced to speak... in such broken Ukrainian that I was ashamed.... The incident made me think" (Makhno, Nestor, Pod udarami kontrrevolyutsii, aprel'-iyun' 1918 g. [Under the Blows of Counterrevolution, April-June 1918], Paris, 1936, p. 153) — Later, Makhno frequently used the Ukrainian language in his propaganda, referring to Ukrainian history and literature. For example, the December 7, 1919 issue of Shlyakh do voli [Road to Freedom], the daily organ of Makhno's followers in Katerynoslav, carried his proclamation "To All the Toiling People of the Ukraine" (Do vs'oho pratsyuyuchoho lyudu Ukrainy) and used as a motto Ivan Franko's poem "The Last Judgment" (Strashnyi sud). His use of the Galician Franko's text was indicative of the fact that he had already risen above the masses in his understanding of the national problem.
2   Khrystyuk, op. cit., Vol. Ill, pp. 130-131.
3   Vynnychenko, op. cit., Part III, p. 114
4   Khrystyuk, op. cit., 1922, Vol. IV, p. 8 note.
5   Shulhyn, Oleksander, "Doha het'manshchyny" [Era of the Hetmanate], Entsyklopediya ukrai'noznavstva, Part II, p. 517; see also Khrystyuk, op. cit., Vol. HI, pp. 140-141.

6	Ibid., Vol. IV, p. 8, note 1. [Fastov, variant spelling Khvastov, about 30 miles southwest of Kyiv. Poloz was probably referring to Petlyura's tendency to assume the role of military dictator. — Ed]
7	Khrystyuk, op. cit., Vol. Ill, pp. 140-141.
8	Rafes, M[oisei] G., Dva goda revolyutsii na Ukraine: evolyutsiya i raskol "Bunda" [Two Years of Revolution in the Ukraine: Evolution and Split Within the Bund], Moscow, 1920, p. 127.
9	Literally, Sich Riflemen.-Tr.
10	Fedenko, [Panas], "Naddnipryanshchyna vid 1914 r." [Russian Ukraine After 1914], Ukrainska zahal'na entsyklopediya [Ukrainian General Encyclopedia], Lviv, 1934, Vol. Ill, col. 635. (Hereafter cited as "Naddnipryanshchyna.") Ataman Hryhoryiv is not be be confused with Nykyfor Hryhoryiv, a leader of the center of the UPSR.
11	There is no doubt that the use of the yellow and blue colors by the Hetman regime discredited this flag, which had been symbolic of Ukrainian independence.
12	Vynnychenko, op. cit., Part III, p. 124. Because of the feminine suiffix "a" the peasants believed Petlyura was a woman.
13	It should be observed that Petlyura's forces halted outside Kyiv until the German forces had evacuated the city. — Ed.
14	Rafes, op. cit., pp. 116-117.
15	Vynnychenko, op. cit., Part III, pp. 183-242 passim.
16	Khrystyuk, op. cit., Vol. IV, p. 11.
17	Vynnychenko, op. cit., Part III, pp. 244-245.
18	Khrystyuk, op. cit., Vol. IV, p. 11
19	Rafes, op. cit., p. 145.
20	Mazepa, Ukraina, Vol. I, pp. 74-76, 84.
21	Vynnychenko, op. cit., Part III, p. 204
22	Materials on the peasant congresses are taken from Khrystyuk, op cit., Vol. IV, pp. 45-47.
23	Ibid., p. 48. Italics in the original
24	Materials on unity negotiations are taken from ibid., pp. 7-8, note 1, p. 12.
25	Fedenko, "Naddnipryanshchyna," op, cit., cols. 635-636.
26	Ibid.; cf. Khrystyuk, op. cit., Vol. IV, pp. 69-73.
27	Fedenko, "Naddnipryanshchyna," op. cit., col. 636.
28	Quoted in Mazepa, Ukraina, Vol. I, p. 80.
29	Shynkar' had reached Kyiv, wounded by Bolbochan's men who had attempted to kill him (Khrystyuk, op. cit., Vol. IV, p. 12).
30	Rafes, *op. cit.,* p. 113-114. Italics in the original. U.
31	Ibid., p. 120. V2.
32	Ibid., p. 122
33	Ibid., p. 129
34	Ibid., pp. 134-143 *passim.*
35	Materials on the Toilers' Congress are taken from *ibid.*, pp. 143- 151. Mazepa, *Ukraina*, Vol. I, pp. 75-93, and Khrystyuk, *op. cit.*, Vol. IV, pp. 57, 61-63
36	Not to be confused with Georgii Ye. Zinovyev, a Russian Bolshevik. — Ed.
37	Anulov, F., "Soyuznyi desant na Ukraine: vospominaniya i dokumenty" [The Allied Landing in the Ukraine: Memoirs and Documents], *Letopis' revolyutsii*

[Annals of the Revolution], Kharkiv, 1923, No. 5, pp. 167-211; 1924, Nos. 1(6), pp. 5-75; 2(7), pp. 5-38.
38   Text of declaration in Khrystyuk, *op. cit.*. Vol. IV, pp. 66-67.
39   *Ibid.*, Vol. Ill, p. 123.
40   This was particularly evident in the policy of the Union of Industry, Commerce, Finance, and Agriculture (*Soyuz Promyshletmosti, Torgovli, Finansov i Selskovo Khozyaistva* shortened to *Protofis*), which demanded, among other things, closer economic ties with Russia.

NOTES TO CHAPTER SIX

1   Antonov-Ovseyenko, V[ladimir] A., *Zapishi o grazhdanskoivoine* [Notes on the Civil War], Moscow, 1932, Vol. Ill, p. 11. My italics.—I.M.[Maistrenko]
2   Ibid., p. 14.
3   Vasyl' Shakhray was the first to point out the harmfulness, from the viewpoint of Bolshevik self-interest, of the anti-Ukrainian policy of the Bolshevik organization in Ukraine. In his *Do hhvyli* he termed this the "Katerynoslav point of view," since it was first apparent in the Katerynoslav branch of the Bolshevik party.
4   Pyatakov's extreme leftist views on the national question were evident as early as the April Conference of the RSDRP(b) in 1917 (see Sed'maya [Aprel'skaya] Vserossiiskaya i Petrogradskaya Obshchegorodskaya Konferentsii RSDRP(b) [Seventh (April) All-Russian and Petrograd All-City Conferences of the RSDRP(b)], Moscow, 1934, pp. 269-271). For his stand in opposition to Lenin in March 1919» see Vos'moi Vserossiiskii s"yezd Rossiiskoi Kammunisticheskoi Partii (bol'shevikov): protokoly zasedanii I rezolyutsii [Eighth All-Russian Congress of the Russian Communist Party (Bolshevik): Proceedings of Sessions and Resolutions], [Kazan'], 1919, Pp. 56-57.-Ed.
5   Quoted in Antonov-Ovseyenko, op. cit., p. 12.
6   See e.g., Lenin's "Punkt programmy v oblasti natsional'nikhotnoshenii" [Plank on National Relations in the Program], of his "Proyekt programmy R.K.P.(b.)" [Draft Program of the RCP(b)], inLenin, Sochineniya, 2nd ed., 1932, Vol. XXIV, p. 96; also note 29,p. 25.
7   Khvylya, A[ndriy], "Borotbisty," Bol'shaya sovetskaya entsiklopediya [Large Soviet Encyclopedia], Moscow, 1927, Vol. VII, col. 193-
8   Khrystyuk, op. cit., Vol. IV, pp. 75-76
9   Rubach, M. A., "K istorii grazhdanskoi voiny na Ukraine: perekhod Grigor'yeva k sovetskoi vlasti" [On the History of the Civil War in Ukraine: Hryhoryi'v's Shift of Allegiance to the Soviet Power], *Letopis' revolyutsii*, 1924, No. 3(8), p. 175. To say that "the Borotbisty wavered between the Directory and the Bolsheviks" obscures the issue. They agreed with the Directory in demanding an independent Ukraine, but differed with it on social problems.
10 Rafes, op. cit., pp. 154-155.
11 Rubach, op. cit., p. 180.
12 The following materials cited in the text relative to the telephone and wire negotiations between Hryhoryi'v and the Red Army command are taken from ibid., pp. 178-185. Evidently the material was in the personal archives of Rakovsky.

13	Not Vynnychenko, but Semen Mazurenko and Mykhaylo Poloz wrnt to Moscow.
14	This was not so. The Kharkiv government consisted entirely of Bolsheviks. [The composition of the government was as follows: Chairman and People's Commissar of Foreign Affairs—Rakovsky; Council of National Economy of Ukraine—Pyatakov, Kviring and Kukhimovich; People's Commissariat of War—Pidvoys'kyi and Mezhlouk; People's Commissar of Soviet Propaganda—Artyom; People's Commissariat of Internal Affairs—Avdiyenko and Voroshilov; People's Commissar of National Education—'Zatons'kyi; People's Commissar of Agriculture—Kalegayev; People's Commissar of Justice—Khmelnytsky; People's Commissariat of Food Supplies—Shlikhter and Mubnov; People's Commissar of Justice—Zemyt; People's Commissar of Mines—Zharko; Head of Supreme Socialist Inspection and People's Commissar of Control of the Republic—Skrypnyk; Commander-in-Chief of the Army of the Ukr.S.S.R.—Antonov-Ovseyenko; Head of the Revolutionary Military Council—Antonov-Ovseyenko; members of the government—Yu. Kotsyubynsky and Shchadenko (from the government's proclamation dated Kharkiv, January 28, 1919 reprinted in Khrystyuk, np. cit., Vol. IV, pp. 80–81).- Ed.]
15	Aussem no doubt was purposely misinformed, for Blakytny knew more about the center than other Borotbisty. Engaged in a diplomatic game, Blakytny remained silent.
16	This is the Borotbist proclamation which Rafes refers to as "the declaration of the Council of Chief Revolutionary Emissaries" (see p. 117). Unfortunately, it has not been possible to find a copy of it. Ibid., p. 78.
17	Ibid., pp. 78,
18	Ibid,134. [Cf. Chamberlin, op. cit., Vol. II, pp. 166, 214.—Ed.] Hryhoryiv's raid inspired the Soviet Ukrainian Yuriy Yanovs'kyi's novel Chotyry shabli [Four Sabres], published in 1930.
19	Rakovsky made two men out of Ellansky, one of whose pseudonyms was Blakytny. Marchenko was the other Borotbist negotiator in Kharkiv.
20	"Zaklyuchitel'noye slovo po dokladu o partinoi programme 19 marta" [Concluding Remarks on the Report of the Party Program of March 19], in Lenin, Sochineniya, 2nd ed., 1932, Vol. XXIV, p. 154.
21	Khrystyuk, op. cit., Vol. IV, p. 81. Several representatives of the Jewish pro-Soviet parties were appointed as well as the Ukrainian SD Independents Yu. Mazurenko (Foreign Affairs), Drahomyretsky (Education) and M. Avdiyenko (Internal Affairs).
22	ibid., pp. 78–79, note 1. One pood equals 36.11 Ibs. The proclamation exhorted "every factory, committee, trade union,local soviet, and party cell to send their active workers on this task...Every worker chosen means an additional piece of bread, sugar and meat for the hungry." (Italics in the original.)
23	Ibid, pp. 130–131.
24	Quoted in ibid, pp. 79–80, note.
25	Shlikhter, A[leksandr G.]; "Bor'ba za khleb na Ukraine v 1919 godu" [The Struggle for Grain in Ukraine in 1919], Litopys revolyutsii', March-April 1928, No. 2(29), p. 135.

26   The emergence of Bela Kun's Soviet Hungary whetted the appetite of Moscow, whose leaders were still easily persuaded that every flicker on the western horizon was a sign of imminent world proletarian revolution. To establish territorial contact with Soviet Russia, Bela Kun offered Vynnychenko his services as mediator in the Russo-Ukrainian war. [The Directory's envoy in Budapest initiated the negotiations (Reshetar, op. cit,, pp. 278–279).-Ed.] "However," notes Vynnychenko, "negotiations came to naught. The barrier could not be overcome, and Hungary... [lost] its communist government in several months" (Vynnycheako, op. cit., Part III, p. 321). Vynnychenko argues that the ultra-left Pyatakov regime fostered Russian imperialism rather than the interests of proletarian world revolution. In fact, it ruined Moscow's chance of launching a revolutionary offensive along the Danube valley; such a move could have been under taken only after a compromise settlement with Ukraine.

27   Khrystyuk, op. cit., Vol. IV, p. 130, note 2.

28   Quoted in ibid., p. 173.

29   Quoted in ibid., pp. 172–173, note 2.

30   In Kyiv the Ukrainian Workers' Club in Lukyanivka was converted into a Russian theater, while Red Army troops occupied the premises of the Ukrainian People's University (ibid., p. 90).

31   The shifting position of the USDRP (Independents) clearly illustrates the devastating effects of Bolshevik policy in this period. After the downfall of the Hetmanate, this Marxist and working class Ukrainian party accepted a soviet platform and, together with the Borotbisty, opposed the pro-Directory majority at the Toilers' Congress in late January (see pp. 100–101). It was this party which engineered the uprising of Ataman Zeleny's Dnepr divisions against the Directory (ibid, pp. 76–77). Together with the Bolsheviks and the Borotbisty, the Independents signed the proclamation of the Kyiv City Council which announced the expulsion of the Directory from Kyiv and welcomed the entry of "Red Soviet battalions led by the Workers' and Peasants' Government of Ukraine" on February 4, 1919 (ibid., p. 81). Yet by the end of March the USDRP (Independents), supported by the now separate party the UPSR (Center), directed an uprising against the Bolshevik-controlled Soviet government (ibid., p. 131). In the face of Denikin's advance from the south, the Independents called off their uprising against the Bolsheviks, July 18–19, 1919 (ibid., p. 134). By early 1920 the Independents had become the Ukrainian Communist Party (UCP), which finally merged with the Bolsheviks in 1925.

32   As Khrystyuk notes, this statement must be understood in exactly the opposite sense.

33   Ibid, p. 89, note.

34   Ibid Italics in the original.

35   Ibid.

36   Khvylya, op. cit.* col. 193; cf. Khrystyuk, op. cit., pp. 129–130, who indicates that the party name was changed to "Ukrainian Party of Socialist Revolutionaries (Communists)." The omission of the term "Borotbisty" may have been due to haste or carelessness; in any event by the time that Khrystyuk was writing, the "Borotbist" part of the title had receded to secondary importance.

37	The author knew both Lashkevych and Pylypenko; the former joined the CP(b)U probably before the Fifth Congress of the Borotbisty.
38	Rafes, op. cit., p. 162.
39	"*Stednyaki,*" a term used to distinguish those peasants who could be classified as neither kulaks nor poor peasants. In the absence of specific figures for land ownership in given regions, the term tended to become arbitrary. — Ed.
40	"Ob otnoshenii k melka-burzhuaznym partiyam," in ibid., p. 163 — Italics in the original.
41	Ibid
42	Khrystyuk, op. cit., Vol. IV, p. 89, note
43	Kubanin, M., Makhnovshchina: krest'yanskoye dvizheniye v stepnoi Ukraine v gody grazhdanskoi winy [Makhnoism:, A Peasant Movement in the Ukrainian Steppes During the Civil War], Leningrad, 1927, p. 5.
44	Ibid., p. 73.
45	Rafes, op. cit., p. 163.
46	Poloz was Chairman of the Supreme Council of National Economy, not deputy chairman, as indicated by Kubanin (Kubabin, op. cit.,p. 124).
47	Yakovlev, a pilot during World War I and the son of a wealthy merchant who was an extreme monarchist, was "a man of extreme cruelty" (Bessedovsky, Grigory, Revelations of a Soviet Diplomat, London, 1931, pp. 11–14 passim). Several thousand killings in the Odessa area in the winter of 1919, evidently Yakovlev's responsibility, were probably his main recommendation for his post in the Cheka. [Yakovlev is not to be confused with the Bolshevik Yakov Epshtein, whose pseudonym was Yakovlev. — Ed.]
48	Rafes, op. cit., p. 164
49	Petrovsky, D., Revolyutsiya i kontrrevolyutsiya na Ukraine [Revolution and Counterrevolution in Ukraine], Moscow, 1920, p. 37.
50	Fedenko, Hromads'kyi ruhh, p. 115, and Shlikhter, op, cit.,p. 106, both citing Rakovsky, Khristian G., Bor'ba za osvobozhdeniya derevni [The Struggle for the Liberation of the Countryside], Kharkiv, 1920.
51	See Chamberlin (op. cit., Vol. II, p. 217), who indicates that the immediate occasion for Hryhoryivs revolt was the Bolshevik issuance of "definite orders to march on Romania." — Ed.
52	Bor'bisty who opposed the Russian Bolshevik regime. Rafes writes: "From the party of Russian SR's there split off a group of Left SR's who by the time of the Hetman coup were united under the name "Ukrainian Party of Left SR's-Internationalists'. The party's active opposition to Soviet rule led to its repression in April 1919 and a further split into 'activists,' who went underground, and 'pacifists' (Borotbisty) [sic for Bor'bisty], who obtained control of Bor'ba, the central organ in Kyiv" (Rafes, op. cit., p. 11).
53	Probably the USDRP (Independents). The term "activist" was not current either in the contemporary press or at the various congresses, although it may have been used in governmental circles. The author vaguely recollects that the term was applied to Ukrainian SR's and SD Independents who resisted the Bolshevik regime in the underground.
54	Kubanin, op. cit., pp. 48–74 passim.
55	Quoted in Mazepa, Ukraina, 1951, Vol. II, pp. 28–29. Soviet propaganda linked Hryhoryi'v with Denikin and Kolchak.

56 See Chamberlin, op. cit., Vol. II, pp. 217-218, 233-234.-Ed.
57 "When Hryhoryiv was leading his uprising in the district of Yelisavetgrad, the bands of the Borotbist Shchohryn and the SR Klymenko entered Uman'" (Lebid", D[mytro], hogi i uroki tryokh let anarkho-makhnovshchiny [The Results and Lessons of Three Years of Anarcho-Makhnoism], Kharkiv, 1921, p. 19. Shchohryn is also mentioned in Rakovsky, op. cit., p. 4.
58 The author participated in the congress.
59 Khrystyuk, op. cit., Vol. IV, p. 82.

NOTES TO CHAPTER SEVEN
1 The absence of the word "Borot'bisty" from the old name of the party reflects their attempt to strip the term of its SR connotations.
2 "V Ispolnitel'nyi Komitet III Kommunisticheskovo Internatsionala" [To the Executive Committee of the Third Communist International]. Kommunisticheskii Internatsional [Communist International], Petrograd, November-December 1919, Nos. 7-8, cols. 1111-1112; also in Memorandum Ukraihs'koi' Komunistychnoi' Partii'(borot'bystiv) do Vykonavchoho Komitetu HI-ho Komunistychnoho Internatsionalu [Memorandum of the Ukrainian Communist Party (Borotbisty) to the Executive Committee of the Third Communist International], Kyiv,1920, pp. 3-6.
3 The CP(b)U made no secret, of the fact that it relied on the Red Army to subdue the Ukraine. Viewing these events retrospectively, the editors of Letopis1 revolyutsii declared that little attention was paid to underground activity, "since the fate of the Ukraine was being, decided by the Red Army and was closely linked with the all-Russian struggle against Denikin" (editorial preface to the article" KP(b)U i denikinshchina: k pyatiletiyu vosstanovleniya Sovvlastina Ukraine" [The CP(b)U and the Denikin Era: The Fifth Anniversary of the Restoration of Soviet Power in the Ukraine], Letopis' revolyutsii, January-February 1925, No. 1(10), pp. 7-8). Of the 35,000 members of the CP(b)U, by September 20,000 had joined the Red Army, which had evacuated in the face of the Denikin offensive (ibid., p. 6).
4 The first and largest left wing group which withdrew from the USDRP to accept the Soviet platform did so in the fall of 1917 in protest against the USDRP's attitude toward the October (old style) coup in Petrograd. Known as the "Left USDRP" until merging with the Bolsheviks, this group included such prominent leaders as Neronovych, Vrublevs'kyi, Petro Slyn'ko, Pavlo Popov, Halya Tymofiivna, Kryvorotchenko, Kas'yanenko, and Afanasiy Butsenko. According to Butsenko, it comprised about 225 members of the USDRP, almost 90 per cent of whom were workers (Butsenko,A[fanasiy], "O raskole USDRP, 1917-1918" [Concerning the Split in the USDRP, 1917-1918], Letopis' revolyutsii, 1923, No. 4, p. 121). Butsenko claims that in Poltava the old USDRP ceased to exist by the end of 1917.

A second, more serious split within the USDRP occurred early in 1919. A new left opposition, although not so extreme as the "Left USDRP," appeared at the beginning of 1918. At the Sixth Congress of the USDRP in January 1919, this opposition formed an Independent faction, which accepted the platform of soviet government (see f. 98), a socialist republic and independence for the

Ukraine. In March 1919, the Independent faction formed a separate party, the USDRP (Independents) (see Khrystyuk, op. cit., Vol. IV, p. 131, note).

5   "Zamechaniya na proyekt postanovleniya ispolkoma kominterna po voprosu o 'borot'bistakh' 22 fevralya 1920 g." [Remarks on a Resolution of the Comintern Executive Committee on the "Borot'bisty," February 22, 1920], in Lenin, Stat'i i rechi, p. 344.

6   Rafes, op. cit., p. 11. Rafes incorrectly writes of the merger between the Borot'bistry and the Left Independents as having occurred in July. Like many other contemporaries writing on the Denikin period, Rafes refers to the UCP(b) as the- "Ukapisty" and the CP(b)U as the CPU. The label "Ukapisty" eventually became the attribute of the USDRP (Independents) when they formed a separate party, the Ukrainian Communist Party, in late January 1920.

7   Ravich-Cherkassky, op. cit., pp. 143-144. Italics in the original

8   Quoted in *ibid.*, p. 144.

9   "Zaklyuchitel'noye slovo na [VHI] vserossiiskoi konferentsii RKP(b) po voprosu o sovetskoi vlasti na Ukraine, 3 dekabrya 1919g." [Concluding Remarks at the (Eighth) All-Russian Conference of the RCP(b) Concerning the Soviet Power in the Ukraine, December 3, 1919], Lenin, *Stat'i i rechi*, pp. 334-355.

10   The translation of the resolution is based on that of Bertram D.Wolfe, from his article "The Influence of Early Military Decisions upon the National Structure of the Soviet Union," *The American Slavic and East European Review*, Vol. IX, No. 3, October 1950, pp. 177-178. Used here by permission of the Columbia University Press

11   Ibid., p. 178

12   In *Kommunisticheskii internalsional*, op, cit., col. 1112.

13   "Obrashcheniye glavnokomanduyushchavo k naseleniyu Malo-rossii," reprinted in Denikin, General A[nton] I., *Ocherki russkoi smuty* [Sketches of Russian Turmoil], Berlin [1926], Vol. V, pp. 142- 143

14   Milyukov, P[avel N.], *Rossiya na perelome: bol'shevistskii russkoi revolyutsii* [Russia in Crisis: The Bolshevik Period of the Russian Revolution], Paris, 1927, Vol. II, p. 205, quoting Sokolov, K. M., *Pravleniye Generala Denikina: iz vospominanii* [The Government of General Denikin: From Reminiscences], Sofia, 1921.

15   Lapchyns'kyi, H. [Yuriy], "Gomel'skoye soveshchaniye: vospominaniya" [The Gomel' Conference: Recollections], *Letopis' revolyutsii*. December 1926, No. 6(21), p. 37.

16   Editorial preface to the article "KP(b)U i *denikinshchina*. ...," op. cit,, pp. 7-8.

17   Kin, D., *Denikinshchina*, [The Denikin Era], Leningrad [1927 or 1928], pp. 174-175.

18   Mstislavski, S[ergei] D., "Zanyatiye Kiyeva bol'shevikami" [The Occupation of Kiev by the Bolsheviks], *Byloye* [Past], Leningrad, 1925, No. 2(30), p. 181.

19   *Ibid.*, p. 176.

20   *Ibid.*, pp. 176-177.

21   Reprinted in *ibid.*, p. 178.

22   Reprinted in *ibid.*, pp. 178-179.

23   Ibid., p. 179.

24   Ibid. For reprinting the order from Borot'ba, the editorial board of *Kiyevskoye ekho* was arrested and sentenced (ibid., pp. 179-180).

25 Zheleznyak's report of January 12, 1920 to the Central Committee of the CP(b)U, quoted in Kin, op. cit., p. 194. The present author recalls that in Poltava a Petlyurist woman student worked with the Borot'bist underground until the arrival of the Red Army in December when she removed to territory controlled by the Ukrainian People's Republic.
26 *Ibid.*, p. 199.
27 The Red Army occupied Kharkov on December 12, and Kyiv on December 16 (Chamberlin, *op. cit.*, Vol. II, p. 281). — Ed.
28 Quoted in Kin, op. cit., pp. 210–211. [See the instruction of November 9 from the Rear Echelon Bureau to Bolshevik district committees and party workers in Chamberlin, op. cit., Vol. II, pp. 278–279.-Ed.]
29 Kin, op. cit., pp. 208–213 passim
30 *Ibid.*, p. 178.
31 *Ibid.* pp. 193, 214.
32 Ravich-Cherkassky, op. cit., pp. 145–146
33 The author can recall that the Borotbist partisan leader Chukhlib was quietly murdered by local Bolsheviks in Konstantinograd, Pol-ruva Province
34 It has been suggested that had Denikin temporized with Petlyura, his summer drive on Moscow might have succeeded (Chamberlin, op, cit., Vol. II, p. 259).-Ed.

NOTES TO CHAPTER EIGHT

1 *Desyatyi s"yezd Rossiiskoi Kommunisticheskoi Partii: stenograficheskii otchot, 8–16 marta 1921 g.* [Tenth Congress of the Russian Communist Party: Verbatim Report, March 8–16, 1921], Moscow, 1921, p. 110.
2 See note 9, p. 159.
3 "Pis'mo k rabochim i krest'yanam Ukrainy po povodu pobedy nad Denikinym," in Lenin, *Stafi i rechi*, p. 342. Italics in the original.
4 VIII s"yezd Rossiiskoi Kommunisticheskoi Partii (bol'shevikov): stenograficbeskii otcbot, Moskva, 18–23 marta 1919 goda [Eighth Congress of the Russian Communist Party (Bolshevik): Verbatim Report, Moscow, March 18–23, 1919], Moscow, 1919, p. 92
5 "Pis'mo k rabochim i krest'yanam Ukrainy po povodu pobedy nad Denikinym," in Lenin, Stat'i i rechi, p. 343.
6 "Rezolyutsiya Ts.K. R.K.P.(b) o sovetskoi vlasti na Ukraine," reprinted in Ravich-Cherkassky, op. pit,,-pp. 226–228; also in *Letopis' revolyutsii* January-February 1925, No. 1(10), pp. 65–67; Lenin, Sochineniya, 2nd ed., 1932, Vol. XXIV, pp. 552–554, 4th ed., 1950, Vol. XXX, pp. 142–144; Lenin, Stafii recbi. pp. 331–333. Italics in the origina
7 Sadovsky, V[alentyn], Natsional'na polityka Sovyetiv na Ukraini [Soviet National Policy in Ukraine], Warsaw, 1937 (Pratsi Ukrai'tts'koho Naukovoho Instytutu [Works of the Ukrainian Scientific Institute], Vol. XXIX), p. 37.
8 "K vsem partiinym organizatsiyam K.P.(b)U.,M *Letopis' revolyutsii,* January-February 1925, No. 1(10), p. 58 (published in a special edition of *Byulleten' Sekretariata TsK KP(b)U* [bulletin of the Secretariat of the Central Committee of the CIJ(b)U], December 15, 1919); also as "Do vsikh komitetiv komunistychnoi'partii' (bil'shovykiv) Ukrainy" [To All Committees of the Communist Party (Bolshevik) of Ukraine], *Istoriya KP(b)U v materialakh i dokumentahh:*

hhrestomatiya, 1917-1920 rr. [History of the CP(b)U in Materials and Documents: An Anthology, 1917-1920], ed. by S. Barannyk, Kh. Mishkis and H. Slobods'kyi, [Kyiv], 1934, Vol. II, pp. 541-542. (Hereafter cited as *Istoriya KP(b)U.)*

9   An editorial note in ibid., p. 542, indicates that the Committee was formed on December 11 as a temporary organ of power.

10 The editorial note in *ibid*, lists as members of the Committee those men mentioned in the text. However, it should be noted that Mstislavski (op. cit., p. 194) lists Rakovsky in place of Petrovsky and himself in place of Terlets'kyi; Ravich-Cherkassky *(op. cit,,* p. 139) lists Petrovsky as Chairman, Rakovsky as one of the Bolshevik members and VI. Kachynsky in place of Terletsky. That Rakovsky had been purged as a Trotskyite in 1926-1927 and was allowed to return from exile in Siberia only in 1934 (later to stand trial in 1938) could account for the omission of his name by the editors of Istoriya KP(b)U. To the best recollection of the present author however, Rakovsky was not a member of the Committee. Concerning the discrepancies over the Borbist member of the Committee, it is most likely that the Borbisty had several alternates. Kachynsky, known personally by the author, eventually became Commissar of Agriculture of the Ukr.S.S. R.; Mstislavski was probably the first to drop out.

11 Of Bolshevik favors to the Bor'bisty Hrushevs'kyi wrote: "On arrival in a district, the Russian Red Army dissolved the existing revolutionary committee organized by the Ukrainian Communists [i.e., Borotbisty] and formed a new one consisting of representatives of the Red Army. Later the new revolutionary committees were replaced by people appointed by provincial revolutionary committees, almost entirely Bolsheviks. Only in a few cases did the Borotbisty succeed in securing a seat on these new district committees, in localities where the Bolsheviks recognized the actual influence of the Borotbisty over the people .... However, the Russian Left SR's [Borbisty] were given seats everywhere, if they could provide a candidate. Thus it often happened that revolutionary committees consisting of three members were entirely Bolshevik, while on five-man committees the Bolsheviks held not less than three seats" (Hrushevsky, Mykhaylo, "Mizh Moskvpyu y Varshavoyu" [Between Moscow and Warsaw], Boritesya-poborete! [Fight and Conquer!], Vienna, October 1920, No. 2, p. 8. (Hereafter cited as "Mizh Moskvoyu y Varshavoyu.")

12 Vseukrainskii Revolyutsionnyi Komitet k rabochim i krest'yanam Ukrainy" [The All-Ukrainian Revolutionary Committee to the Workers and Peasants of Ukraine], Letopis' revolyutsii, January-February 1925, No. 1(10), pp. 58-62 (published in Izvestiya Khar'kovskovo Voyenno-Revolyutsionnovo Komiteta [News of the Kharkiv Military-Revolutionary Committee], December 26, 1919, No. 10); also in Istoriya KP(b)U, pp. 551-553- In a similar vein was the Third International's appeal "K rabochim i krest'yanam Ukrainy" [To the Workers and Peasants of Ukraine], dated December 14 and signed by Zinovyev, in Kommunisticheskii internatsional, November-December 1919, Nos. 7-8, cols. 1121-1126; also in Letopis' revolyutsii. January-February 1925, No. 1(10), pp. 62-65.

13 H. "Vystupleniye borot'bistov vo Vseukrainskii Revkom" [Entry of the Borotbisty into the All-Ukrainian Revolutionary Committee], Letopis revolyutsii, January-February 1925, No. 1(10), pp. 67-68 (published in Izvestiya

	Khar'kovskovo Voyenno-Revolyutsionnovo Komiteta, December 30, 1919, No. 13).
14	Kovaliv, Levko, Do chleniv Ukrainskoi Komunistychnoi Partii' (borotbystiv) [To Members of the Ukrainian Communist Party (Borotbisty)], Kyiv, "Borot'ba," 1920.
15	The probable title of the pamphlet, which was not available at te time of writing the present study, is Otkrytoye pis'mo k TsK UKP(b) [An Open Letter to the Central Committee of the UCP(b)].
16	Quoted in Kin, op. cit., p. 197.
17	Mazepa, *Ukraina*, Vol. I, p. 163.
18	"Haydamak," a Turkish word originally meaning "raider" or "brigand," applied in the eighteenth century to Ukrainian peasants in anti-Polish revolts, but here simply the name of military units whose soldiers were thus called Haydamaky. — EA
19	Ibid., 1951, Vol. II, pp. 47, 156–159 passim. Seized from the state treasury of the Ukrainian People's Republic were 2,500,000 Ukrainian karbovantsi and 30,000 tsarist silver rubles. At that time the face value of the Ukrainian harbovanets equaled the tsarist ruble.
20	Tyutyunnyk, Yu[rko], Zymovyi pohhid 1919-1920 rr. [The Winter Campaign of 1919-1920], Kolomyya-Kyiv, 1923, p. 23.
21	Mazepa, *Ukraina*, Vol. II, p. 174.
22	The following five quotations are taken from Tyutyunnyk, op. cit., pp. 20, 40–41 passim.
23	The Borotbisty were pledged by the Moscow agreement not to form a separate Ukrainian army. It was this agreement and doubts as to its possibilities which made the Borot'bist leaders so cautious, not, as Tyutyunnyk thought, their fear of ruining their chances of advancement in Moscow
24	The "Winter Campaign" was the name given to a large raid by the army of the Ukrainian People's Republic into the Soviet Ukraine in 1920.
25	Mazepa, *Ukraina*, Vol. II, pp. 174, 225–226.
26	Savytsky's letter and the subsequent material on the Volokh incident are in Tyutyunnyk, *op. cit.*, pp. 42–43, 44, 45. All italics in the original.
27	Pro-Soviet sympathies also penetrated the Ukrainian Galician Army under the influence of the Volokh incident and probably of Borot'bist propaganda. After nine months of unsuccessful battle against Poland, the Galician Army joined with the army of the Ukrainian People's Republic in fighting Denikin and the Bolsheviks. A Revolutionary Committee formed within the Galician Army signed an agreement with the pro-Soviet Podol'ye Province Revolutionary Committee to the effect that the army would be used "only against Poland and other invading states, until [Ukraine] is freed of enemy occupation and a socialist soviet government is firmly established" (Mazepa, Uhraina, Vol. II, pp. 174-183 passim). The army became the "Red Ukrainian Galician Army." Split up among Russian divisions, it refused, however, to fight against the Polish-Ukrainian army under Pilsudsky and Petlyura in their drive on Kyiv in April-May 1920. Part of the Red Galician Army surrendered to the Poles; the remainder was disarmed and shot by the Red Army (Tyutyunnyk,op. cit., p. 66).

The shift of allegiance of the Galician Army had a similar effect on Ukrainian SR's of the UPSR (Center) around the Ukrainian People's Army. Pro-Soviet elements in the Volyn' Division were allowed to send a delegation to the Russian 44th Division. Although received with great ceremony, it did not get to see the Borotbisty or Volokh; in the end "even those elements who had previously believed that the Russians would make no further 'mistakes' realized that the Russians. . . would destroy the Ukrainian army, even if it were ultrared." The general feeling in the army was well expressed by Panas Fedenko, the army's political adviser, in a letter to the commander of the Kyiv division, dated January 15, 1920:

"There is no doubt that the Borotbisty will wage war against the Bolsheviks; if not now, then later. That is why all kinds of elements, not at all Communist, are gathering around them now. First of all, they will be fighting the Bolsheviks over a Ukrainian army. If an armed force for the Ukrainian nation can be preserved, were it under Beelzebub himself not to mention the Borotbisty, then it should be preserved. The question is: are the Borotbisty sufficiently determined to do it. Since the state of our army and the [military] situation are such as to make partisan warfare unsuccessful, it is quite legitimate to find a way to save the army.... To help the Borotbisty organize a separate Ukrainian red army may be the way" (ibid., pp. 54-60 passim; italics in the original).

28 Quoted in Tyutyunnyk, op. cit., pp. 84-87 passim. 29-passim.
29 Ravich-Cherkassky, op. cit., pp. 146-148
30 Material from Proyekt rezolyutsii o politike partii is taken from Shrah, Myk[ola], "Slova y dila sotsiyalistiv v natsional'niy spravi" [Words and Deeds of Socialists on the National Question], Boritesya-Boborete!, October 1920, No. 2, pp. 30-31. Shrah does not mention the fact that the opposition was known as the "Group of Federalists" and was led by the old Bolshevik Yuriy Lapchynsky, who was at that time expelled from the CP(b)U. However, Shrah does quote a passage from "Proyekt deklaratsii pro ob"yednannya Radyanskykh respublik" [Draft Declaration on Unification of the Soviet Republics], a resolution by the UCP(b) in which the advocates of union with the CP(b)U are referred to as Soviet "touring actors." Unfortunately it has not been possible to find a copy of the text of this resolution.
31 Ravich-Cherkassky, op. cit., p. 148.
32 "Kommunisticheskii Internatsional ob Ukrainskikh partiyakh" | The Communist International on Ukrainian Parties], Kommunist, Kharkiv, January 30, 1920, No. 24; also in Kommunisticheskii internatsional, November-December 1919, Nos. 7-8, cols. 1125-1126; reprinted in Istoriya KP(b)U, pp. 638-639.
33 Komunistychnyi Internatsional vidmovlyaye borot'bystam v pryinyatti 'ikh do svo'ikh lav: postanova Vykonkomu Kominternu" | The Communist International Refuses to Accept the Borotbisty into Us Ranks: Resolution of the Executive Committee of the Comintern], Kommunist, Kharkiv, February 29, 1920, No. 50; reprinted in Istoriya KP(b)U, pp. 639-640. Italics in the original.
34 "Ob"yedineniye kommunistov na Ukraine" [The Amalgamation of Communists in Ukraine], Kommunisticheskii internatsional, [May] 1920, No. 9, cols. 1655-1656.

35   This was the basis of Tyutyunnyk's charge that "in social policy the Borotbisty never opposed Moscow" (Tyutyunnyk, op. cit., p. 82).
36   See note 5, p. 159.
37   This despite Lenin's insistence that the Borotbisty be accused not of nationalism but of bourgeois counterrevolution. — J.M.
38   Held April 1918, preliminary to the organization of the CP(b)U. -Ed.
39   Ravich-Cherkassky, *op. cit.*, pp. 148–149- Italics in the original.
40   Hrushevs'kyi, "Mizh Moskvoyu y Varshavoyu," op, cii,
41   Hryhoryi'v to Khrystyuk, in Vil'na spilka, No. 1, October 1921,pp. 114–120.
42   Devyatyi s"yezd Rossiiskoi Kommunisticbeshoi Partii (bol'shevikov): stenograftcheshii otchot (29 marta-4 aprelya 1920 g.) [Ninth Congress of the Russian Communist Party (Bolshevik): Verbatim Report (March 29–April 4, 1920)], Moscow, 1920, p. 77.
43   Ibid, pp. 114–115.
44   Chechel', Myk[ola], "Chomu prypynyv svoye istnuvannya revolyutsiynoradyansky bl'ok?" [Why Did the Revolutionary-Soviet Bloc Cease to Exist?], Boritesya-pobotete!, October 1920, No. 2, p. 54.
45   Taran, F., "Blakytnyi (Elansky) Vasyl' Mykhaylovych" [Vasyl Mykhaylovych Blakytnyi (Ellansky)], Chervony shlyakh [Red Path],Kharkiv, 1926, No. 2, p. 63.

NOTES TO CHAPTER NINE

1   *Pervyi kongress Kominterna*, mart 1919 g,: *protokoly kongreslov Kommunisticheskovo Internatsionala* [First Congress of the Comintern, March 1919: Proceedings of the Congresses of the Communist International], ed. by Ye. Korotki, B. Kun and O.Pyatnitski, Moscow, 1933, pp. 51–55.
2   *Kommunist,* Kharkiv, May 20, 1920S No. 1, pp. 1–27 passim. Cf. Ravich-Cherkasski, op. cit., p. 166; evidently "Petrov" is a typographical error for "Petrovski." The full text of the directive is in ibid,, pp. 235–238; also in *Istotiya KP(b)U,* pp. 555–557.
3   All material on the Borotbist and Bolshevik organizations in Poltava Province and Kobelyaki District is based on the personal knowledge of the author.
4   For example, the peasant V. Upyr', who was Bolshevik military commissar in Kobelyaki District in 1919, was a hardened Bolshevik who had helped to overthrow the Kereosky regime. At one time he led a partisan unit against the Hetmanate, yet taking fright at the withdrawal of the Ukrainian Bolsheviks during the Denikin occupation, he opened a store and sought the protection of thePhiliilistine element in the party.
5   Dvenadtsatyi s"yezd Rossiiskoi Kommunisticheskoi Partii (bol'shevikov): stenograficheshii otchot 17–25 aprelya 1923 g. [Twelfth Congress of the All-Russian Communist Party (Bolshevik): Verbatim Report, April 17–25, 1923], Moscow, 1923, pp. 454–468."Where are they now?" Skrypnyk asked at the Congress, and replied: "They have been dispersed!"
6   Byulletin' VI Vseukrainskoi konferentsii Kommunistichtakoi Partii (bol'shevikov) Ukrainy (9–13 noyabrya 1921 g.) [Bulletin of the Sixth All-Ukrainian Conference of the CP(b)U, November '"- 9–11, 192l], Kharkiv, 1921, p. 63. Petrovsky was speaking as head of the CP(b)U purge commission.

7	*Kommunist*, Kharkiv, May 20, 1920, No. 1, which commented in an editorial: "'The union with the Borotbisty has provided us with new workers both in the center and in local areas and has considerably strengthened our party. ... In most provinces union took place peacefully. In Poltava Province alone, due to misunderstandings'" after the [Fourth Party] Conference, amalgamation occurred only recently."
8	It should be noted that Shumsky was chief of the Agitation and Propaganda Section of the Central Committee of the CP(b)U for the period 1923-1925.-Ed.
9	Sh., H., "Tovarys'kyi lyst buvshoinu chlenovi UPSR, a teper KPbU" [Comradely Letter to a Former Member of the UPSR But Now of the CP(b)U], Vil'na spilka, No. 2, October 1923, pp. 210-219. Italics in the original.
10	Trotsky, Leon, *Stalin: An Appraisal of the Man and His Influence*, ed. and tr. by Charles Malamuth, New York-London, 1941, p. 264.
11	*Kommunist*, Kharkiv, June 10, 1920, No. 2, p. 25.
12	*Ibid*, May 20, 1920, No. 1.
13	*Ibid*.
14	*Ibid.*, June 10, 1920, No. 2, p. 27, which also gives the composition of the purge commission in Right Bank Ukraine.
15	Blakytnyi, Vasyl' M., "Tezy i spivdopovid' v pytanni 'Cherhovi zavdannya parti'i' na V Vseukraihsky konferentsii' KP(b)U" [Theses and Supplementary Report on the Question "The Next Tasks of the Party" at the Fifth All-Ukrainian Conference of the CP(b)U. *Istoriya KP(b)U*, pp. 636-637, reprinted a criticism of Blakytny's report by Ya. Yakovlev, published originally in Byulleten' V-oi Vseukrainshoi Konferentsii KP(b)U [Bulletin of the Fifth All-Ukrainian Conference of the CP(b)U], November 1920, No. 4, pp. 34-36.-E
16	Blakytnyi, Vasyl' M.,"Komunistychna partiya Ukrainy I shlyakhy 'ii' zmitsnennya"[The Communist Party of Ukraine and Ways to Strengthen It],
17	Published in the newspaper *Kommunist*, Kharkiv, November 17, 19, 1920.
18	Quoted in Skrypnyk, Mykola, "Natsionalistychnyi ukhyl v KPZU" [The Nationalist Deviation in the Communist Party of Western Ukraine], reprinted in his *Dzherela ta prychyny rozlamu v KPZU* [Origins and Reasons for the Split in the CPWU], Kharkiv, 1928, pp. 16-17. (Hereafter cited as *Dzherela*.) Part of the letter was published in Stalin, J.V., *Marksizm i natsional'no-holonial'nyi vopros* [Marxism and the National-Colonial Question], Moscow, 1934, pp. 172-173; a fuller text is published under the title "Tovarishchu Kaganovichu i drugim chlenam TsK KP(b)U" [To Comrade Kaganovich, and Other Members of the Central Committee of the CP(b)U], in Stalin, *Sochineniya* [Works], Moscow, 1948, Vol. III, pp. 149-154 (in which, incidentally, the editors claim that the letter is being published in full for the first time).
19	[The name of Derzhimorda, an officious and oppressive policeman in Gogol's play *The Inspector General*, has entered the Russian language as the synonym for official brutality.— Ed.] This description of Stalin, originally applied to Ordzhonikidze, was contained in a letter written by Lenin to Trotsky in December 1922 on the occasion of Stalin's attack on the Georgian Communist lender Budu Mdivani. The letter was printed in *Sotsialisticheskii vestnik* [Socialist Courier], Berlin, December 17, 1923, Nos. 23-24,(69-70), p. 14. In the Soviet Union it circulated clandestinely, together with Lenin's "'Testament," in the mimeographed edition ef the verbatim report of the plenary session of the

Central Committee of the Communist Party of the Soviet Union (Bolshevik) in 1926.
20 Quoted in Skrypnyk, Dzherela, pp. 13-14.
21 *Ibid*
22 Qouted in *ibid.*, p. 2
23 Ibid., pp. 5-6.
24 Skrypnyk, Mykola, "Lyst do tovarysha Lebedya" [Letter to Comrade Lebedya'], *Bilshovyk Ukrainy* [Ukrainian Bolshevik], Kharkiv, 1928, Nos. 9-10; reprinted in his *Statti y promovy* (Articles and Speeches], Kharkiv, 1929, Vol. II, Part I, pp. 302-314. Material on the Shumsky problem is available in *ibid.*,pp. 147-360; see also Skrypnyk, Mykola, "Khvylovyzm chy shumskyzm?" [Khvylyovism or Shumskism?] *Bilshovyk Ukrainy*, 1927, No. 2, pp. 26-39.
25 Skrypnyk, Mykola, "Dva sapoha--para" [two of a Kind], *Kommunist,* Kharkiv, June 16, 1929, No. 132.
26 See note 42, p. 202.

NOTES TO SPECIAL SUPPLEMENT

1 Alexander Zevelev, *How The National Question was Solved in the USSR*, Novosti Press Agency, Moscow 1977
2 Ibid, p. 35
3 A.V, Lykholat *Rozhrom Natsionalistychnoyi Kontrrevolyutsiyi V Ukrayini* (1917-1922 rr.) - K , Polityzdat Ukrayiny, 1954. Cited in Serhiy Hirik, Dzherela Doslidzhennya Ideynykh Zasad Ukrayins'koyi Komunistychnoyi Partiyi (Borot'bystiv) (1918-1920 Rr.), Dysertatsiya Na Zdobuttya Naukovoho Stupenya Kandydata Istorychnykh Nauk, Kyiv, 2015, P. 27
4 Milovan Djilas, *The New Class*, London, 1957, p. 156, 160.
5 O. Sluts'kyy, *Tretiy z"yizd KP(b)U* (K.: Politvydav URSR, 1958): 118, footnote.
6 For example, Russian Review, Vol.14, no.3(July 1955), p. 273, and American *Slavic and East European Review*, Vol.15, No.3, (October, 1956), pp. 425-426.
7 R. G. Symonenko, "Proty Burzhuaz Nonatsyunalistychnykh Fal'syfikatsiy Istoriyi Ukrayiny", *Ukrayinsky Istorychnyy Zhurnal*,No.3, 1958, p. 158-162.
8 Ibid, p. 158
9 Ibid, p. 159
10 Ibid, p. 159
11 Ibid p. 1568
12 Maistrenko *Borotbism,* p. 21, Symonenko, ibid, p. 158
13 Symonenko, ibid, p. 160
14 Maistrenko p. 55, Symonenko, ibid, p. 160
15 See Mace, p232-263, Symonenko, ibid, p. 160
16 Inessa Zenushkina, *Soviet Nationalities Policy and Bourgeois Historians*, Moscow, 1976, p. 15
17 Symonenko, ibid, p. 161
18 Symonenko, ibid, p. 161
19 Maistrenko, p. 126-127
20 Symonenko, ibid, p. 161
21 Symonenko, ibid, p. 161
22 Symonenko, ibid, p. 162
23 Hryhory Kostiuk, *Stalinist Rule in the Ukraine*, New York, 1960, p. 95-96

24	Ibid, p. 96–97.
25	Ibid, p. 98
26	Ibid, p. 98
27	This was expressed in a note by the secretary of the Central Committee of the Communist Party of Ukraine Valentin Malanchuk devoted to this topic, Ibid, Girik, p. 31
28	Ibid, Girik, p. 32–33
29	Ibid, Zenushkina, *Soviet Nationalities Policy*, p. 9
30	Ibid, Zenushkina, *Soviet Nationalities Policy*, p. 9
31	Ivan Dzyuba, *Internationalism or Russification*, New York, 1974, p. 57.

SOVIET AND POST-SOVIET POLITICS AND SOCIETY
Edited by Dr. Andreas Umland | ISSN 1614-3515

1 Андреас Умланд (ред.) | Воплощение Европейской конвенции по правам человека в России. Философские, юридические и эмпирические исследования | ISBN 3-89821-387-0
2 Christian Wipperfürth | Russland – ein vertrauenswürdiger Partner? Grundlagen, Hintergründe und Praxis gegenwärtiger russischer Außenpolitik | Mit einem Vorwort von Heinz Timmermann | ISBN 3-89821-401-X
3 Manja Hussner | Die Übernahme internationalen Rechts in die russische und deutsche Rechtsordnung. Eine vergleichende Analyse zur Völkerrechtsfreundlichkeit der Verfassungen der Russländischen Föderation und der Bundesrepublik Deutschland | Mit einem Vorwort von Rainer Arnold | ISBN 3-89821-438-9
4 Matthew Tejada | Bulgaria's Democratic Consolidation and the Kozloduy Nuclear Power Plant (KNPP). The Unattainability of Closure | With a foreword by Richard J. Crampton | ISBN 3-89821-439-7
5 Марк Григорьевич Меерович | Квадратные метры, определяющие сознание. Государственная жилищная политика в СССР. 1921 – 1941 гг | ISBN 3-89821-474-5
6 Andrei P. Tsygankov, Pavel A.Tsygankov (Eds.) | New Directions in Russian International Studies | ISBN 3-89821-422-2
7 Марк Григорьевич Меерович | Как власть народ к труду приучала. Жилище в СССР – средство управления людьми. 1917 – 1941 гг. | С предисловием Елены Осокиной | ISBN 3-89821-495-8
8 David J. Galbreath | Nation-Building and Minority Politics in Post-Socialist States. Interests, Influence and Identities in Estonia and Latvia | With a foreword by David J. Smith | ISBN 3-89821-467-2
9 Алексей Юрьевич Безугольный | Народы Кавказа в Вооруженных силах СССР в годы Великой Отечественной войны 1941-1945 гг. | С предисловием Николая Бугая | ISBN 3-89821-475-3
10 Вячеслав Лихачев и Владимир Прибыловский (ред.) | Русское Национальное Единство, 1990-2000. В 2-х томах | ISBN 3-89821-523-7
11 Николай Бугай (ред.) | Народы стран Балтии в условиях сталинизма (1940-е – 1950-е годы). Документированная история | ISBN 3-89821-525-3
12 Ingmar Bredies (Hrsg.) | Zur Anatomie der Orange Revolution in der Ukraine. Wechsel des Elitenregimes oder Triumph des Parlamentarismus?| ISBN 3-89821-524-5
13 Anastasia V. Mitrofanova | The Politicization of Russian Orthodoxy. Actors and Ideas | With a foreword by William C. Gay | ISBN 3-89821-481-8
14 Nathan D. Larson | Alexander Solzhenitsyn and the Russo-Jewish Question | ISBN 3-89821-483-4
15 Guido Houben | Kulturpolitik und Ethnizität. Staatliche Kunstförderung im Russland der neunziger Jahre | Mit einem Vorwort von Gert Weisskirchen | ISBN 3-89821-542-3
16 Leonid Luks | Der russische „Sonderweg"? Aufsätze zur neuesten Geschichte Russlands im europäischen Kontext | ISBN 3-89821-496-6
17 Евгений Мороз | История «Мёртвой воды» – от страшной сказки к большой политике. Политическое неоязычество в постсоветской России | ISBN 3-89821-551-2
18 Александр Верховский и Галина Кожевникова (ред.) | Этническая и религиозная интолерантность в российских СМИ. Результаты мониторинга 2001-2004 гг. | ISBN 3-89821-569-5
19 Christian Ganzer | Sowjetisches Erbe und ukrainische Nation. Das Museum der Geschichte des Zaporoger Kosakentums auf der Insel Chortycja | Mit einem Vorwort von Frank Golczewski | ISBN 3-89821-504-0
20 Эльза-Баир Гучинова | Помнить нельзя забыть. Антропология депортационной травмы калмыков | С предисловием Кэролайн Хамфри | ISBN 3-89821-506-7
21 Юлия Лидерман | Мотивы «проверки» и «испытания» в постсоветской культуре. Советское прошлое в российском кинематографе 1990-х годов | С предисловием Евгения Марголита | ISBN 3-89821-511-3
22 Tanya Lokshina, Ray Thomas, Mary Mayer (Eds.) | The Imposition of a Fake Political Settlement in the Northern Caucasus. The 2003 Chechen Presidential Election | ISBN 3-89821-436-2
23 Timothy McCajor Hall, Rosie Read (Eds.) | Changes in the Heart of Europe. Recent Ethnographies of Czechs, Slovaks, Roma, and Sorbs | With an afterword by Zdeněk Salzmann | ISBN 3-89821-606-3

24 *Christian Autengruber* | Die politischen Parteien in Bulgarien und Rumänien. Eine vergleichende Analyse seit Beginn der 90er Jahre | Mit einem Vorwort von Dorothée de Nève | ISBN 3-89821-476-1

25 *Annette Freyberg-Inan with Radu Cristescu* | The Ghosts in Our Classrooms, or: John Dewey Meets Ceauşescu. The Promise and the Failures of Civic Education in Romania | ISBN 3-89821-416-8

26 *John B. Dunlop* | The 2002 Dubrovka and 2004 Beslan Hostage Crises. A Critique of Russian Counter-Terrorism | With a foreword by Donald N. Jensen | ISBN 3-89821-608-X

27 *Peter Koller* | Das touristische Potenzial von Kam''janec'–Podil's'kyj. Eine fremdenverkehrsgeographische Untersuchung der Zukunftsperspektiven und Maßnahmenplanung zur Destinationsentwicklung des „ukrainischen Rothenburg" | Mit einem Vorwort von Kristiane Klemm | ISBN 3-89821-640-3

28 *Françoise Daucé, Elisabeth Sieca-Kozlowski (Eds.)* | Dedovshchina in the Post-Soviet Military. Hazing of Russian Army Conscripts in a Comparative Perspective | With a foreword by Dale Herspring | ISBN 3-89821-616-0

29 *Florian Strasser* | Zivilgesellschaftliche Einflüsse auf die Orange Revolution. Die gewaltlose Massenbewegung und die ukrainische Wahlkrise 2004 | Mit einem Vorwort von Egbert Jahn | ISBN 3-89821-648-9

30 *Rebecca S. Katz* | The Georgian Regime Crisis of 2003-2004. A Case Study in Post-Soviet Media Representation of Politics, Crime and Corruption | ISBN 3-89821-413-3

31 *Vladimir Kantor* | Willkür oder Freiheit. Beiträge zur russischen Geschichtsphilosophie | Ediert von Dagmar Herrmann sowie mit einem Vorwort versehen von Leonid Luks | ISBN 3-89821-589-X

32 *Laura A. Victoir* | The Russian Land Estate Today. A Case Study of Cultural Politics in Post-Soviet Russia | With a foreword by Priscilla Roosevelt | ISBN 3-89821-426-5

33 *Ivan Katchanovski* | Cleft Countries. Regional Political Divisions and Cultures in Post-Soviet Ukraine and Moldova| With a foreword by Francis Fukuyama | ISBN 3-89821-558-X

34 *Florian Mühlfried* | Postsowjetische Feiern. Das Georgische Bankett im Wandel | Mit einem Vorwort von Kevin Tuite | ISBN 3-89821-601-2

35 *Roger Griffin, Werner Loh, Andreas Umland (Eds.)* | Fascism Past and Present, West and East. An International Debate on Concepts and Cases in the Comparative Study of the Extreme Right | With an afterword by Walter Laqueur | ISBN 3-89821-674-8

36 *Sebastian Schlegel* | Der „Weiße Archipel". Sowjetische Atomstädte 1945-1991 | Mit einem Geleitwort von Thomas Bohn | ISBN 3-89821-679-9

37 *Vyacheslav Likhachev* | Political Anti-Semitism in Post-Soviet Russia. Actors and Ideas in 1991-2003 | Edited and translated from Russian by Eugene Veklerov | ISBN 3-89821-529-6

38 *Josette Baer (Ed.)* | Preparing Liberty in Central Europe. Political Texts from the Spring of Nations 1848 to the Spring of Prague 1968 | With a foreword by Zdeněk V. David | ISBN 3-89821-546-6

39 *Михаил Лукьянов* | Российский консерватизм и реформа, 1907-1914 | С предисловием Марка Д. Стейнберга | ISBN 3-89821-503-2

40 *Nicola Melloni* | Market Without Economy. The 1998 Russian Financial Crisis | With a foreword by Eiji Furukawa | ISBN 3-89821-407-9

41 *Dmitrij Chmelnizki* | Die Architektur Stalins | Bd. 1: Studien zu Ideologie und Stil | Bd. 2: Bilddokumentation | Mit einem Vorwort von Bruno Flierl | ISBN 3-89821-515-6

42 *Katja Yafimava* | Post-Soviet Russian-Belarussian Relationships. The Role of Gas Transit Pipelines | With a foreword by Jonathan P. Stern | ISBN 3-89821-655-1

43 *Boris Chavkin* | Verflechtungen der deutschen und russischen Zeitgeschichte. Aufsätze und Archivfunde zu den Beziehungen Deutschlands und der Sowjetunion von 1917 bis 1991 | Ediert von Markus Edlinger sowie mit einem Vorwort versehen von Leonid Luks | ISBN 3-89821-756-6

44 *Anastasija Grynenko in Zusammenarbeit mit Claudia Dathe* | Die Terminologie des Gerichtswesens der Ukraine und Deutschlands im Vergleich. Eine übersetzungswissenschaftliche Analyse juristischer Fachbegriffe im Deutschen, Ukrainischen und Russischen | Mit einem Vorwort von Ulrich Hartmann | ISBN 3-89821-691-8

45 *Anton Burkov* | The Impact of the European Convention on Human Rights on Russian Law. Legislation and Application in 1996-2006 | With a foreword by Françoise Hampson | ISBN 978-3-89821-639-5

46 *Stina Torjesen, Indra Overland (Eds.)* | International Election Observers in Post-Soviet Azerbaijan. Geopolitical Pawns or Agents of Change? | ISBN 978-3-89821-743-9

47 *Taras Kuzio* | Ukraine – Crimea – Russia. Triangle of Conflict | ISBN 978-3-89821-761-3

48 *Claudia Šabić* | "Ich erinnere mich nicht, aber L'viv!" Zur Funktion kultureller Faktoren für die Institutionalisierung und Entwicklung einer ukrainischen Region | Mit einem Vorwort von Melanie Tatur | ISBN 978-3-89821-752-1

49 *Marlies Bilz* | Tatarstan in der Transformation. Nationaler Diskurs und Politische Praxis 1988-1994 | Mit einem Vorwort von Frank Golczewski | ISBN 978-3-89821-722-4

50 *Марлен Ларюэль (ред.)* | Современные интерпретации русского национализма | ISBN 978-3-89821-795-8

51 *Sonja Schüler* | Die ethnische Dimension der Armut. Roma im postsozialistischen Rumänien | Mit einem Vorwort von Anton Sterbling | ISBN 978-3-89821-776-7

52 *Галина Кожевникова* | Радикальный национализм в России и противодействие ему. Сборник докладов Центра «Сова» за 2004-2007 гг. | С предисловием Александра Верховского | ISBN 978-3-89821-721-7

53 *Галина Кожевникова и Владимир Прибыловский* | Российская власть в биографиях I. Высшие должностные лица РФ в 2004 г. | ISBN 978-3-89821-796-5

54 *Галина Кожевникова и Владимир Прибыловский* | Российская власть в биографиях II. Члены Правительства РФ в 2004 г. | ISBN 978-3-89821-797-2

55 *Галина Кожевникова и Владимир Прибыловский* | Российская власть в биографиях III. Руководители федеральных служб и агентств РФ в 2004 г.| ISBN 978-3-89821-798-9

56 *Ileana Petroniu* | Privatisierung in Transformationsökonomien. Determinanten der Restrukturierungs-Bereitschaft am Beispiel Polens, Rumäniens und der Ukraine | Mit einem Vorwort von Rainer W. Schäfer | ISBN 978-3-89821-790-3

57 *Christian Wipperfürth* | Russland und seine GUS-Nachbarn. Hintergründe, aktuelle Entwicklungen und Konflikte in einer ressourcenreichen Region| ISBN 978-3-89821-801-6

58 *Togzhan Kassenova* | From Antagonism to Partnership. The Uneasy Path of the U.S.-Russian Cooperative Threat Reduction | With a foreword by Christoph Bluth | ISBN 978-3-89821-707-1

59 *Alexander Höllwerth* | Das sakrale eurasische Imperium des Aleksandr Dugin. Eine Diskursanalyse zum postsowjetischen russischen Rechtsextremismus | Mit einem Vorwort von Dirk Uffelmann | ISBN 978-3-89821-813-9

60 *Олег Рябов* | «Россия-Матушка». Национализм, гендер и война в России XX века | С предисловием Елены Гощило | ISBN 978-3-89821-487-2

61 *Ivan Maistrenko* | Borot'bism. A Chapter in the History of the Ukrainian Revolution | With a new Introduction by Chris Ford | Translated by George S. N. Luckyj with the assistance of Ivan L. Rudnytsky | Second, Revised and Expanded Edition ISBN 978-3-8382-1107-7

62 *Maryna Romanets* | Anamorphosic Texts and Reconfigured Visions. Improvised Traditions in Contemporary Ukrainian and Irish Literature | ISBN 978-3-89821-576-3

63 *Paul D'Anieri and Taras Kuzio (Eds.)* | Aspects of the Orange Revolution I. Democratization and Elections in Post-Communist Ukraine | ISBN 978-3-89821-698-2

64 *Bohdan Harasymiw in collaboration with Oleh S. Ilnytzkyj (Eds.)* | Aspects of the Orange Revolution II. Information and Manipulation Strategies in the 2004 Ukrainian Presidential Elections | ISBN 978-3-89821-699-9

65 *Ingmar Bredies, Andreas Umland and Valentin Yakushik (Eds.)* | Aspects of the Orange Revolution III. The Context and Dynamics of the 2004 Ukrainian Presidential Elections | ISBN 978-3-89821-803-0

66 *Ingmar Bredies, Andreas Umland and Valentin Yakushik (Eds.)* | Aspects of the Orange Revolution IV. Foreign Assistance and Civic Action in the 2004 Ukrainian Presidential Elections | ISBN 978-3-89821-808-5

67 *Ingmar Bredies, Andreas Umland and Valentin Yakushik (Eds.)* | Aspects of the Orange Revolution V. Institutional Observation Reports on the 2004 Ukrainian Presidential Elections | ISBN 978-3-89821-809-2

68 *Taras Kuzio (Ed.)* | Aspects of the Orange Revolution VI. Post-Communist Democratic Revolutions in Comparative Perspective | ISBN 978-3-89821-820-7

69 *Tim Bohse* | Autoritarismus statt Selbstverwaltung. Die Transformation der kommunalen Politik in der Stadt Kaliningrad 1990-2005 | Mit einem Geleitwort von Stefan Troebst | ISBN 978-3-89821-782-8

70 *David Rupp* | Die Rußländische Föderation und die russischsprachige Minderheit in Lettland. Eine Fallstudie zur Anwaltspolitik Moskaus gegenüber den russophonen Minderheiten im „Nahen Ausland" von 1991 bis 2002 | Mit einem Vorwort von Helmut Wagner | ISBN 978-3-89821-778-1

71 *Taras Kuzio* | Theoretical and Comparative Perspectives on Nationalism. New Directions in Cross-Cultural and Post-Communist Studies | With a foreword by Paul Robert Magocsi | ISBN 978-3-89821-815-3

72 *Christine Teichmann* | Die Hochschultransformation im heutigen Osteuropa. Kontinuität und Wandel bei der Entwicklung des postkommunistischen Universitätswesens | Mit einem Vorwort von Oskar Anweiler | ISBN 978-3-89821-842-9

73 *Julia Kusznir* | Der politische Einfluss von Wirtschaftseliten in russischen Regionen. Eine Analyse am Beispiel der Erdöl- und Erdgasindustrie, 1992-2005 | Mit einem Vorwort von Wolfgang Eichwede | ISBN 978-3-89821-821-4

74 *Alena Vysotskaya* | Russland, Belarus und die EU-Osterweiterung. Zur Minderheitenfrage und zum Problem der Freizügigkeit des Personenverkehrs | Mit einem Vorwort von Katljn Malfliet | ISBN 978-3-89821-822-1

75 *Heiko Pleines (Hrsg.)* | Corporate Governance in post-sozialistischen Volkswirtschaften | ISBN 978-3-89821-766-8

76 *Stefan Ihrig* | Wer sind die Moldawier? Rumänismus versus Moldowanismus in Historiographie und Schulbüchern der Republik Moldova, 1991-2006 | Mit einem Vorwort von Holm Sundhaussen | ISBN 978-3-89821-466-7

77 *Galina Kozhevnikova in collaboration with Alexander Verkhovsky and Eugene Veklerov* | Ultra-Nationalism and Hate Crimes in Contemporary Russia. The 2004-2006 Annual Reports of Moscow's SOVA Center | With a foreword by Stephen D. Shenfield | ISBN 978-3-89821-868-9

78 *Florian Küchler* | The Role of the European Union in Moldova's Transnistria Conflict | With a foreword by Christopher Hill | ISBN 978-3-89821-850-4

79 *Bernd Rechel* | The Long Way Back to Europe. Minority Protection in Bulgaria | With a foreword by Richard Crampton | ISBN 978-3-89821-863-4

80 *Peter W. Rodgers* | Nation, Region and History in Post-Communist Transitions. Identity Politics in Ukraine, 1991-2006 | With a foreword by Vera Tolz | ISBN 978-3-89821-903-7

81 *Stephanie Solywoda* | The Life and Work of Semen L. Frank. A Study of Russian Religious Philosophy | With a foreword by Philip Walters | ISBN 978-3-89821-457-5

82 *Vera Sokolova* | Cultural Politics of Ethnicity. Discourses on Roma in Communist Czechoslovakia | ISBN 978-3-89821-864-1

83 *Natalya Shevchik Ketenci* | Kazakhstani Enterprises in Transition. The Role of Historical Regional Development in Kazakhstan's Post-Soviet Economic Transformation | ISBN 978-3-89821-831-3

84 *Martin Malek, Anna Schor-Tschudnowskaja (Hgg.)* | Europa im Tschetschenienkrieg. Zwischen politischer Ohnmacht und Gleichgültigkeit | Mit einem Vorwort von Lipchan Basajewa | ISBN 978-3-89821-676-0

85 *Stefan Meister* | Das postsowjetische Universitätswesen zwischen nationalem und internationalem Wandel. Die Entwicklung der regionalen Hochschule in Russland als Gradmesser der Systemtransformation | Mit einem Vorwort von Joan DeBardeleben | ISBN 978-3-89821-891-7

86 *Konstantin Sheiko in collaboration with Stephen Brown* | Nationalist Imaginings of the Russian Past. Anatolii Fomenko and the Rise of Alternative History in Post-Communist Russia | With a foreword by Donald Ostrowski | ISBN 978-3-89821-915-0

87 *Sabine Jenni* | Wie stark ist das „Einige Russland"? Zur Parteibindung der Eliten und zum Wahlerfolg der Machtpartei im Dezember 2007 | Mit einem Vorwort von Klaus Armingeon | ISBN 978-3-89821-961-7

88 *Thomas Borén* | Meeting-Places of Transformation. Urban Identity, Spatial Representations and Local Politics in Post-Soviet St Petersburg | ISBN 978-3-89821-739-2

89 *Aygul Ashirova* | Stalinismus und Stalin-Kult in Zentralasien. Turkmenistan 1924-1953 | Mit einem Vorwort von Leonid Luks | ISBN 978-3-89821-987-7

90 *Leonid Luks* | Freiheit oder imperiale Größe? Essays zu einem russischen Dilemma | ISBN 978-3-8382-0011-8

91 *Christopher Gilley* | The 'Change of Signposts' in the Ukrainian Emigration. A Contribution to the History of Sovietophilism in the 1920s | With a foreword by Frank Golczewski | ISBN 978-3-89821-965-5

92 *Philipp Casula, Jeronim Perovic (Eds.)* | Identities and Politics During the Putin Presidency. The Discursive Foundations of Russia's Stability | With a foreword by Heiko Haumann | ISBN 978-3-8382-0015-6

93 *Marcel Viëtor* | Europa und die Frage nach seinen Grenzen im Osten. Zur Konstruktion ‚europäischer Identität' in Geschichte und Gegenwart | Mit einem Vorwort von Albrecht Lehmann | ISBN 978-3-8382-0045-3

94 *Ben Hellman, Andrei Rogachevskii* | Filming the Unfilmable. Casper Wrede's 'One Day in the Life of Ivan Denisovich' | Second, Revised and Expanded Edition | ISBN 978-3-8382-0044-6

95 *Eva Fuchslocher* | Vaterland, Sprache, Glaube. Orthodoxie und Nationsbildung am Beispiel Georgiens | Mit einem Vorwort von Christina von Braun | ISBN 978-3-89821-884-9

96 *Vladimir Kantor* | Das Westlertum und der Weg Russlands. Zur Entwicklung der russischen Literatur und Philosophie | Ediert von Dagmar Herrmann | Mit einem Beitrag von Nikolaus Lobkowicz | ISBN 978-3-8382-0102-3

97 *Kamran Musayev* | Die postsowjetische Transformation im Baltikum und Südkaukasus. Eine vergleichende Untersuchung der politischen Entwicklung Lettlands und Aserbaidschans 1985-2009 | Mit einem Vorwort von Leonid Luks | Ediert von Sandro Henschel | ISBN 978-3-8382-0103-0

98 *Tatiana Zhurzhenko* | Borderlands into Bordered Lands. Geopolitics of Identity in Post-Soviet Ukraine | With a foreword by Dieter Segert | ISBN 978-3-8382-0042-2

99 *Кирилл Галушко, Лидия Смола (ред.)* | Пределы падения – варианты украинского будущего. Аналитико-прогностические исследования | ISBN 978-3-8382-0148-1

100 *Michael Minkenberg (Ed.)* | Historical Legacies and the Radical Right in Post-Cold War Central and Eastern Europe | With an afterword by Sabrina P. Ramet | ISBN 978-3-8382-0124-5

101 *David-Emil Wickström* | Rocking St. Petersburg. Transcultural Flows and Identity Politics in the St. Petersburg Popular Music Scene | With a foreword by Yngvar B. Steinholt | Second, Revised and Expanded Edition | ISBN 978-3-8382-0100-9

102 *Eva Zabka* | Eine neue „Zeit der Wirren"? Der spät- und postsowjetische Systemwandel 1985-2000 im Spiegel russischer gesellschaftspolitischer Diskurse | Mit einem Vorwort von Margareta Mommsen | ISBN 978-3-8382-0161-0

103 *Ulrike Ziemer* | Ethnic Belonging, Gender and Cultural Practices. Youth Identitites in Contemporary Russia | With a foreword by Anoop Nayak | ISBN 978-3-8382-0152-8

104 *Ksenia Chepikova* | ‚Einiges Russland' - eine zweite KPdSU? Aspekte der Identitätskonstruktion einer postsowjetischen „Partei der Macht" | Mit einem Vorwort von Torsten Oppelland | ISBN 978-3-8382-0311-9

105 *Леонид Люкс* | Западничество или евразийство? Демократия или идеократия? Сборник статей об исторических дилеммах России | С предисловием Владимира Кантора | ISBN 978-3-8382-0211-2

106 *Anna Dost* | Das russische Verfassungsrecht auf dem Weg zum Föderalismus und zurück. Zum Konflikt von Rechtsnormen und -wirklichkeit in der Russländischen Föderation von 1991 bis 2009 | Mit einem Vorwort von Alexander Blankenagel | ISBN 978-3-8382-0292-1

107 *Philipp Herzog* | Sozialistische Völkerfreundschaft, nationaler Widerstand oder harmloser Zeitvertreib? Zur politischen Funktion der Volkskunst im sowjetischen Estland | Mit einem Vorwort von Andreas Kappeler | ISBN 978-3-8382-0216-7

108 *Marlène Laruelle (Ed.)* | Russian Nationalism, Foreign Policy, and Identity Debates in Putin's Russia. New Ideological Patterns after the Orange Revolution | ISBN 978-3-8382-0325-6

109 *Michail Logvinov* | Russlands Kampf gegen den internationalen Terrorismus. Eine kritische Bestandsaufnahme des Bekämpfungsansatzes | Mit einem Geleitwort von Hans-Henning Schröder und einem Vorwort von Eckhard Jesse | ISBN 978-3-8382-0329-4

110 *John B. Dunlop* | The Moscow Bombings of September 1999. Examinations of Russian Terrorist Attacks at the Onset of Vladimir Putin's Rule | Second, Revised and Expanded Edition | ISBN 978-3-8382-0388-1

111 *Андрей А. Ковалёв* | Свидетельство из-за кулис российской политики I. Можно ли делать добро из зла? (Воспоминания и размышления о последних советских и первых постсоветских годах) | With a foreword by Peter Reddaway | ISBN 978-3-8382-0302-7

112 *Андрей А. Ковалёв* | Свидетельство из-за кулис российской политики II. Угроза для себя и окружающих (Наблюдения и предостережения относительно происходящего после 2000 г.) | ISBN 978-3-8382-0303-4

113 *Bernd Kappenberg* | Zeichen setzen für Europa. Der Gebrauch europäischer lateinischer Sonderzeichen in der deutschen Öffentlichkeit | Mit einem Vorwort von Peter Schlobinski | ISBN 978-3-89821-749-1

114 *Ivo Mijnssen* | The Quest for an Ideal Youth in Putin's Russia I. Back to Our Future! History, Modernity, and Patriotism according to Nashi, 2005-2013 | With a foreword by Jeronim Perović | Second, Revised and Expanded Edition | ISBN 978-3-8382-0368-3

115 *Jussi Lassila* | The Quest for an Ideal Youth in Putin's Russia II. The Search for Distinctive Conformism in the Political Communication of Nashi, 2005-2009 | With a foreword by Kirill Postoutenko | Second, Revised and Expanded Edition | ISBN 978-3-8382-0415-4

116 *Valerio Trabandt* | Neue Nachbarn, gute Nachbarschaft? Die EU als internationaler Akteur am Beispiel ihrer Demokratieförderung in Belarus und der Ukraine 2004-2009 | Mit einem Vorwort von Jutta Joachim | ISBN 978-3-8382-0437-6

117 *Fabian Pfeiffer* | Estlands Außen- und Sicherheitspolitik I. Der estnische Atlantizismus nach der wiedererlangten Unabhängigkeit 1991-2004 | Mit einem Vorwort von Helmut Hubel | ISBN 978-3-8382-0127-6

118 *Jana Podßuweit* | Estlands Außen- und Sicherheitspolitik II. Handlungsoptionen eines Kleinstaates im Rahmen seiner EU-Mitgliedschaft (2004-2008) | Mit einem Vorwort von Helmut Hubel | ISBN 978-3-8382-0440-6

119 *Karin Pointner* | Estlands Außen- und Sicherheitspolitik III. Eine gedächtnispolitische Analyse estnischer Entwicklungskooperation 2006-2010 | Mit einem Vorwort von Karin Liebhart | ISBN 978-3-8382-0435-2

120 *Ruslana Vovk* | Die Offenheit der ukrainischen Verfassung für das Völkerrecht und die europäische Integration | Mit einem Vorwort von Alexander Blankenagel | ISBN 978-3-8382-0481-9

121 *Mykhaylo Banakh* | Die Relevanz der Zivilgesellschaft bei den postkommunistischen Transformationsprozessen in mittel- und osteuropäischen Ländern. Das Beispiel der spät- und postsowjetischen Ukraine 1986-2009 | Mit einem Vorwort von Gerhard Simon | ISBN 978-3-8382-0499-4

122 *Michael Moser* | Language Policy and the Discourse on Languages in Ukraine under President Viktor Yanukovych (25 February 2010–28 October 2012) | ISBN 978-3-8382-0497-0 (Paperback edition) | ISBN 978-3-8382-0507-6 (Hardcover edition)

123 *Nicole Krome* | Russischer Netzwerkkapitalismus Restrukturierungsprozesse in der Russischen Föderation am Beispiel des Luftfahrtunternehmens "Aviastar" | Mit einem Vorwort von Petra Stykow | ISBN 978-3-8382-0534-2

124 *David R. Marples* | 'Our Glorious Past'. Lukashenka's Belarus and the Great Patriotic War | ISBN 978-3-8382-0574-8 (Paperback edition) | ISBN 978-3-8382-0675-2 (Hardcover edition)

125 *Ulf Walther* | Russlands "neuer Adel". Die Macht des Geheimdienstes von Gorbatschow bis Putin | Mit einem Vorwort von Hans-Georg Wieck | ISBN 978-3-8382-0584-7

126 *Simon Geissbühler (Hrsg.)* | Kiew – Revolution 3.0. Der Euromaidan 2013/14 und die Zukunftsperspektiven der Ukraine | ISBN 978-3-8382-0581-6 (Paperback edition) | ISBN 978-3-8382-0681-3 (Hardcover edition)

127 *Andrey Makarychev* | Russia and the EU in a Multipolar World. Discourses, Identities, Norms | With a foreword by Klaus Segbers | ISBN 978-3-8382-0629-5

128 *Roland Scharff* | Kasachstan als postsowjetischer Wohlfahrtsstaat. Die Transformation des sozialen Schutzsystems | Mit einem Vorwort von Joachim Ahrens | ISBN 978-3-8382-0622-6

129 *Katja Grupp* | Bild Lücke Deutschland. Kaliningrader Studierende sprechen über Deutschland | Mit einem Vorwort von Martin Schulz | ISBN 978-3-8382-0552-6

130 *Konstantin Sheiko, Stephen Brown* | History as Therapy. Alternative History and Nationalist Imaginings in Russia, 1991-2014 | ISBN 978-3-8382-0665-3

131 *Elisa Kriza* | Alexander Solzhenitsyn: Cold War Icon, Gulag Author, Russian Nationalist? A Study of the Western Reception of his Literary Writings, Historical Interpretations, and Political Ideas | With a foreword by Andrei Rogatchevski | ISBN 978-3-8382-0589-2 (Paperback edition) | ISBN 978-3-8382-0690-5 (Hardcover edition)

132 *Serghei Golunov* | The Elephant in the Room. Corruption and Cheating in Russian Universities | ISBN 978-3-8382-0570-0

133 *Manja Hussner, Rainer Arnold (Hgg.)* | Verfassungsgerichtsbarkeit in Zentralasien I. Sammlung von Verfassungstexten | ISBN 978-3-8382-0595-3

134 *Nikolay Mitrokhin* | Die "Russische Partei". Die Bewegung der russischen Nationalisten in der UdSSR 1953-1985 | Aus dem Russischen übertragen von einem Übersetzerteam unter der Leitung von Larisa Schippel | ISBN 978-3-8382-0024-8

135 *Manja Hussner, Rainer Arnold (Hgg.)* | Verfassungsgerichtsbarkeit in Zentralasien II. Sammlung von Verfassungstexten | ISBN 978-3-8382-0597-7

136 *Manfred Zeller* | Das sowjetische Fieber. Fußballfans im poststalinistischen Vielvölkerreich | Mit einem Vorwort von Nikolaus Katzer | ISBN 978-3-8382-0757-5

137 *Kristin Schreiter* | Stellung und Entwicklungspotential zivilgesellschaftlicher Gruppen in Russland. Menschenrechtsorganisationen im Vergleich | ISBN 978-3-8382-0673-8

138 *David R. Marples, Frederick V. Mills (Eds.)* | Ukraine's Euromaidan. Analyses of a Civil Revolution | ISBN 978-3-8382-0660-8

139 *Bernd Kappenberg* | Setting Signs for Europe. Why Diacritics Matter for European Integration | With a foreword by Peter Schlobinski | ISBN 978-3-8382-0663-9

140 *René Lenz* | Internationalisierung, Kooperation und Transfer. Externe bildungspolitische Akteure in der Russischen Föderation | Mit einem Vorwort von Frank Ettrich | ISBN 978-3-8382-0751-3

141 *Juri Plusnin, Yana Zausaeva, Natalia Zhidkevich, Artemy Pozanenko* | Wandering Workers. Mores, Behavior, Way of Life, and Political Status of Domestic Russian Labor Migrants | Translated by Julia Kazantseva | ISBN 978-3-8382-0653-0

142 *David J. Smith (Eds.)* | Latvia – A Work in Progress? 100 Years of State- and Nation-Building | ISBN 978-3-8382-0648-6

143 *Инна Чувычкина (ред.)* | Экспортные нефте- и газопроводы на постсоветском пространстве. Анализ трубопроводной политики в свете теории международных отношений | ISBN 978-3-8382-0822-0

144 *Johann Zajaczkowski* | Russland – eine pragmatische Großmacht? Eine rollentheoretische Untersuchung russischer Außenpolitik am Beispiel der Zusammenarbeit mit den USA nach 9/11 und des Georgienkrieges von 2008 | Mit einem Vorwort von Siegfried Schieder | ISBN 978-3-8382-0837-4

145 *Boris Popivanov* | Changing Images of the Left in Bulgaria. The Challenge of Post-Communism in the Early 21st Century | ISBN 978-3-8382-0667-7

146 *Lenka Krátká* | A History of the Czechoslovak Ocean Shipping Company 1948-1989. How a Small, Landlocked Country Ran Maritime Business During the Cold War | ISBN 978-3-8382-0666-0

147 *Alexander Sergunin* | Explaining Russian Foreign Policy Behavior. Theory and Practice | ISBN 978-3-8382-0752-0

148 *Darya Malyutina* | Migrant Friendships in a Super-Diverse City. Russian-Speakers and their Social Relationships in London in the 21st Century | With a foreword by Claire Dwyer | ISBN 978-3-8382-0652-3

149 *Alexander Sergunin, Valery Konyshev* | Russia in the Arctic. Hard or Soft Power? | ISBN 978-3-8382-0753-7

150 *John J. Maresca* | Helsinki Revisited. A Key U.S. Negotiator's Memoirs on the Development of the CSCE into the OSCE | With a foreword by Hafiz Pashayev | ISBN 978-3-8382-0852-7

151 *Jardar Østbø* | The New Third Rome. Readings of a Russian Nationalist Myth | With a foreword by Pål Kolstø | ISBN 978-3-8382-0870-1

152 *Simon Kordonsky* | Socio-Economic Foundations of the Russian Post-Soviet Regime. The Resource-Based Economy and Estate-Based Social Structure of Contemporary Russia | With a foreword by Svetlana Barsukova | ISBN 978-3-8382-0775-9

153 *Duncan Leitch* | Assisting Reform in Post-Communist Ukraine 2000–2012. The Illusions of Donors and the Disillusion of Beneficiaries | With a foreword by Kataryna Wolczuk | ISBN 978-3-8382-0844-2

154 *Abel Polese* | Limits of a Post-Soviet State. How Informality Replaces, Renegotiates, and Reshapes Governance in Contemporary Ukraine | With a foreword by Colin Williams | ISBN 978-3-8382-0845-9

155 *Mikhail Suslov (Ed.)* | Digital Orthodoxy in the Post-Soviet World. The Russian Orthodox Church and Web 2.0 | With a foreword by Father Cyril Hovorun | ISBN 978-3-8382-0871-8

156 *Leonid Luks* | Zwei „Sonderwege"? Russisch-deutsche Parallelen und Kontraste (1917-2014). Vergleichende Essays | ISBN 978-3-8382-0823-7

157 *Vladimir V. Karacharovskiy, Ovsey I. Shkaratan, Gordey A. Yastrebov* | Towards a New Russian Work Culture. Can Western Companies and Expatriates Change Russian Society? | With a foreword by Elena N. Danilova | Translated by Julia Kazantseva | ISBN 978-3-8382-0902-9

158 *Edmund Griffiths* | Aleksandr Prokhanov and Post-Soviet Esotericism | ISBN 978-3-8382-0903-6

159 *Timm Beichelt, Susann Worschech (Eds.)* | Transnational Ukraine? Networks and Ties that Influence(d) Contemporary Ukraine | ISBN 978-3-8382-0944-9

160 *Mieste Hotopp-Riecke* | Die Tataren der Krim zwischen Assimilation und Selbstbehauptung. Der Aufbau des krimtatarischen Bildungswesens nach Deportation und Heimkehr (1990-2005) | Mit einem Vorwort von Swetlana Czerwonnaja | ISBN 978-3-89821-940-2

161 *Olga Bertelsen (Ed.)* | Revolution and War in Contemporary Ukraine. The Challenge of Change | ISBN 978-3-8382-1016-2

162 *Natalya Ryabinska* | Ukraine's Post-Communist Mass Media. Between Capture and Commercialization | With a foreword by Marta Dyczok | ISBN 978-3-8382-1011-7

163 *Alexandra Cotofana, James M. Nyce (Eds.)* | Religion and Magic in Socialist and Post-Socialist Contexts. Historic and Ethnographic Case Studies of Orthodoxy, Heterodoxy, and Alternative Spirituality | With a foreword by Patrick L. Michelson | ISBN 978-3-8382-0989-0

164 *Nozima Akhrarkhodjaeva* | The Instrumentalisation of Mass Media in Electoral Authoritarian Regimes. Evidence from Russia's Presidential Election Campaigns of 2000 and 2008 | ISBN 978-3-8382-1013-1

165 *Yulia Krasheninnikova* | Informal Healthcare in Contemporary Russia. Sociographic Essays on the Post-Soviet Infrastructure for Alternative Healing Practices | ISBN 978-3-8382-0970-8

166 *Peter Kaiser* | Das Schachbrett der Macht. Die Handlungsspielräume eines sowjetischen Funktionärs unter Stalin am Beispiel des Generalsekretärs des Komsomol Aleksandr Kosarev (1929-1938) | Mit einem Vorwort von Dietmar Neutatz | ISBN 978-3-8382-1052-0

167 *Oksana Kim* | The Effects and Implications of Kazakhstan's Adoption of International Financial Reporting Standards. A Resource Dependence Perspective | With a foreword by Svetlana Vlady | ISBN 978-3-8382-0987-6

168 Anna Sanina | Patriotic Education in Contemporary Russia. Sociological Studies in the Making of the Post-Soviet Citizen | With a foreword by Anna Oldfield | ISBN 978-3-8382-0993-7

169 Rudolf Wolters | Spezialist in Sibirien Faksimile der 1933 erschienenen ersten Ausgabe | Mit einem Vorwort von Dmitrij Chmelnizki | ISBN 978-3-8382-0515-1

170 Michal Vít, Magdalena M. Baran (Eds.) | Transregional versus National Perspectives on Contemporary Central European History. Studies on the Building of Nation-States and Their Cooperation in the 20th and 21st Century | With a foreword by Petr Vágner | ISBN 978-3-8382-1015-5

171 Philip Gamaghelyan | Conflict Resolution Beyond the International Relations Paradigm. Evolving Designs as a Transformative Practice in Nagorno-Karabakh and Syria | With a foreword by Susan Allen | ISBN 978-3-8382-1057-5

172 Maria Shagina | Joining a Prestigious Club. Cooperation with Europarties and Its Impact on Party Development in Georgia, Moldova, and Ukraine 2004–2015 | With a foreword by Kataryna Wolczuk | ISBN 978-3-8382-1084-1

173 Alexandra Cotofana, James M. Nyce (Eds.) | Religion and Magic in Socialist and Post-Socialist Contexts II. Baltic, Eastern European, and Post-USSR Case Studies | With a foreword by Anita Stasulane | ISBN 978-3-8382-0990-6

174 Barbara Kunz | Kind Words, Cruise Missiles, and Everything in Between. The Use of Power Resources in U.S. Policies towards Poland, Ukraine, and Belarus 1989–2008 | With a foreword by William Hill | ISBN 978-3-8382-1065-0

175 Eduard Klein | Bildungskorruption in Russland und der Ukraine. Eine komparative Analyse der Performanz staatlicher Antikorruptionsmaßnahmen im Hochschulsektor am Beispiel universitärer Aufnahmeprüfungen | Mit einem Vorwort von Heiko Pleines | ISBN 978-3-8382-0995-1

176 Markus Soldner | Politischer Kapitalismus im postsowjetischen Russland. Die politische, wirtschaftliche und mediale Transformation in den 1990er Jahren | Mit einem Vorwort von Wolfgang Ismayr | ISBN 978-3-8382-1222-7

177 Anton Oleinik | Building Ukraine from Within. A Sociological, Institutional, and Economic Analysis of a Nation-State in the Making | ISBN 978-3-8382-1150-3

178 Peter Rollberg, Marlene Laruelle (Eds.) | Mass Media in the Post-Soviet World. Market Forces, State Actors, and Political Manipulation in the Informational Environment after Communism | ISBN 978-3-8382-1116-9

179 Mikhail Minakov | Development and Dystopia Studies in Post-Soviet Ukraine and Eastern Europe | With a foreword by Alexander Etkind | ISBN 978-3-8382-1112-1

180 Aijan Sharshenova | The European Union's Democracy Promotion in Central Asia A Study of Political Interests, Influence, and Development in Kazakhstan and Kyrgyzstan in 2007–2013 | With a foreword by Gordon Crawford | ISBN 978-3-8382-1151-0

181 Andrey Makarychev, Alexandra Yatsyk (Eds.) | Boris Nemtsov and Russian Politics. Power and Resistance | With a foreword by Zhanna Nemtsova | ISBN 978-3-8382-1122-0

182 Sophie Falsini | The Euromaidan's Effect on Civil Society. Why and How Ukrainian Social Capital Increased after the Revolution of Dignity | With a foreword by Susann Worschech | ISBN 978-3-8382-1131-2

183 Andreas Umland (Ed.) | Ukraine's Decentralization. Challenges and Implications of the Local Governance Reform after the Euromaidan Revolution | ISBN 978-3-8382-1162-6

184 Leonid Luks | A Fateful Triangle. Essays on Contemporary Russian, German and Polish History | ISBN 978-3-8382-1143-5

185 John B. Dunlop | The February 2015 Assassination of Boris Nemtsov and the Flawed Trial of his Alleged Killers. An Exploration of Russia's "Crime of the 21st Century" | ISBN 978-3-8382-1188-7

186 Vasile Rotaru | Russia, the EU, and the Eastern Partnership. Building Bridges or Digging Trenches? | ISBN 978-3-8382-1134-3

187 Marina Lebedeva | Russian Studies of International Relations. From the Soviet Past to the Post-Cold-War Present | With a foreword by Andrei P. Tsygankov | ISBN 978-3-8382-0851-0

188 Tomasz Stępniewski, George Soroka (Eds.) | Ukraine after Maidan. Revisiting Domestic and Regional Security | ISBN 978-3-8382-1075-9

189 Petar Cholakov | Ethnic Entrepreneurs Unmasked. Political Institutions and Ethnic Conflicts in Contemporary Bulgaria | ISBN 978-3-8382-1189-3

190 A. Salem, G. Hazeldine, D. Morgan (Eds.) | Higher Education in Post-Communist States. Comparative and Sociological Perspectives | ISBN 978-3-8382-1183-1

191 Igor Torbakov | After Empire. Nationalist Imagination and Symbolic Politics in Russia and Eurasia in the Twentieth and Twenty-First Century | With a foreword by Serhii Plokhy | ISBN 978-3-8382-1217-2

192　*Aleksandr Burakovskiy* | Jewish-Ukrainian Relations in Late and Post-Soviet Ukraine. Articles, Lectures and Essays from 1986 to 2016 | ISBN 978-3-8382-1210-4

193　*Natalia Shapovalova, Olga Burlyuk (Eds.)* | Civil Society in Post-Euromaidan Ukraine. From Revolution to Consolidation | With a foreword by Richard Youngs | ISBN 978-3-8382-1216-6

194　*Franz Preissler* | Positionsverteidigung, Imperialismus oder Irredentismus? Russland und die „Russischsprachigen", 1991–2015 | ISBN 978-3-8382-1262-3

195　*Marian Madeła* | Der Reformprozess in der Ukraine 2014-2017. Eine Fallstudie zur Reform der öffentlichen Verwaltung | Mit einem Vorwort von Martin Malek | ISBN 978-3-8382-1266-1

196　*Anke Giesen* | „Wie kann denn der Sieger ein Verbrecher sein?" Eine diskursanalytische Untersuchung der russlandweiten Debatte über Konzept und Verstaatlichungsprozess der Lagergedenkstätte „Perm'-36" im Ural | ISBN 978-3-8382-1284-5

197　*Alla Leukavets* | The Integration Policies of Belarus and Ukraine vis-à-vis the EU and Russia. A Comparative Case Study Through the Lenses of a Two-Level Games Approach | ISBN 978-3-8382-1247-0

198　*Oksana Kim* | The Development and Challenges of Russian Corporate Governance I. The Roles and Functions of Boards of Directors | With a foreword by Sheila M. Puffer | ISBN 978-3-8382-1287-6

199　*Thomas D. Grant* | International Law and the Post-Soviet Space I. Essays on Chechnya and the Baltic States | With a foreword by Stephen M. Schwebel | ISBN 978-3-8382-1279-1

200　*Thomas D. Grant* | International Law and the Post-Soviet Space II. Essays on Ukraine, Intervention, and Non-Proliferation | With a foreword by Stephen M. Schwebel | ISBN 978-3-8382-1280-7

201　*Slavomir Michalek, Michal Stefansky* | The Age of Fear. The Cold War and Its Influence on Czechoslovakia 1945–1968 | ISBN 978-3-8382-1285-2

202　*Iulia-Sabina Joja* | Romania's Strategic Culture 1990–2014. Continuity and Change in a Post-Communist Country's Evolution of National Interests and Security Policies | With a foreword by Heiko Biehl | ISBN 978-3-8382-1286-9

203　*Andrei Rogatchevski, Yngvar B. Steinholt, Arve Hansen, David-Emil Wickström* | War of Songs. Popular Music and Recent Russia-Ukraine Relations | With a foreword by Artemy Troitsky | ISBN 978-3-8382-1173-2

204　*Maria Lipman (Ed.)* | Russian Voices on Post-Crimea Russia. An Almanac of Counterpoint Essays from 2015–2018 | ISBN 978-3-8382-1251-7

205　*Ksenia Maksimovtsova* | Language Conflicts in Contemporary Estonia, Latvia, and Ukraine. A Comparative Exploration of Discourses in Post-Soviet Russian-Language Digital Media | With a foreword by Ammon Cheskin | ISBN 978-3-8382-1282-1 *ibidem*.eu